Mark W. Elliott

The Song of Songs and Christology in the Early Church 381–451

WIPF & STOCK · Eugene, Oregon

MARK W. ELLIOTT, born 1965; 1987 graduated from Oxford University (St. John's College) with honours in Jurisprudence; 1990 joint honours in Old Testament and New Testament from Aberdeen Universtiy; 1997 PhD from Cambridge University; 1994–96 Assistant Director of The Whitefield Institute, Oxford; 1998–1999 temporary lecturer in theology, Nottingham University; since 1999 lecturer in Christian Studies at Liverpool Hope University College.

Wipf and Stock Publishers
199 W 8th Ave, Suite 3
Eugene, OR 97401

The Song of Songs and Christology in the Early Church, 381 - 451
By Elliott, Mark W
Copyright©2000 Mohr Siebeck
ISBN 13: 978-1-61097-154-6
Publication date 5/1/2011
Previously published by Mohr Siebeck, 2000

"This edition reprinted 2011 by Wipf and Stock through special arrangement with J.C.B. Mohr (Paul Siebeck).
Copyright J.C.B. Mohr (Paul Siebeck) 2000".

To my parents

Foreword

This work is a slightly modified version of a doctoral thesis passed by the University of Cambridge in 1997: The Song Of Songs And Christology In The Early Church, With Special Reference To The Period 381–451. It was written under the careful supervision of Dr. Lionel R. Wickham. Additional guidance came from Drs. Nicholas de Lange, Caroline Bammel, and William Horbury. A short time in Paris spent learning from Prof. Marguerite Harl and Dr. Alain LeBoulluec was also invaluable. The quality of library resources in Cambridge and Oxford should be gratefully acknowledged, not least that of Tyndale House, Cambridge. The help of Rev. Drs. David Marshall, Andrew Goddard and David Instone Brewer was much appreciated at the later stages of preparing the thesis

Sources of financial assistance also should be mentioned. I am grateful to the Dr. Williams' Trust Fund, Fitzwilliam College, Cambridge, the Divinity Faculty of the University of Cambridge, the E. Drummond Trust and the Honeyman Gillespie Scholarships, as well as the Whitefield Institute, Oxford and Tyndale House, Cambridge.

I am thankful to Prof. Dr. Christoph Markschies for his readiness to include this work in this series, and for his comments, advice and encouragement. I would also like to acknowledge the support and interest of colleagues at Nottingham University and at Liverpool Hope University College over the last two years.

Lastly I would like to dedicate this book with gratitude to my parents, Ian and Ann Elliott for all the ways in which, through them, something of love human and divine has been demonstrated to me.

Mark W. Elliott   Liverpool, April 2000.

Table of Contents

Foreword V

1. Introduction 1

   1.1 Figures and Images 1
   1.2 The Song of Songs: early influences on its interpretation 3
   1.3 Exegetical Styles 5
   1.4 Setting the scene 10
   1.5 The beginnings of Christological deliberation 11
   1.6 The Christological interpretation of the Song 11
   1.7 The task ahead 13

*2. Establishing the Context of the Commentators
on the Song of Songs* 15

   2.1   Hippolytus 15
   2.2   Origen (Greek) 15
   2.3   Methodius 18
   2.4   Dionysius of Alexandria 18
   2.5   "Athanasius" 18
   2.6   Apollinarius 20
   2.7   Didymus 20
   2.8   Philo of Carpasia 21
   2.9   Jerome 22
   2.10 Pacianus 22
   2.11 Ambrose 23
   2.12 Gregory of Elvira 23
   2.13 Gregory of Nyssa 24
   2.14 Epiphanius of Salamis 29
   2.15 Pseudo-Theophilus of Alexandria 30
   2.16 Rufinus and his translation of Origen's Commentary
        on the Song of Songs (= Rufinus-Origen) 31
   2.17 Augustine 34
   2.18 Theodoret 34
   2.19 Nilus of Ancyra 35
   2.20 Cyril of Alexandria 39
   2.21 Pseudo-Athanasius: Synopsis Scripturae 39

2.22	Apponius	40
2.23	Conclusion	50

3. The Groom 51

3.1	The way the Song relates to the Incarnation. Cant 1:2	51
3.2	Myrrh and the Groom's divine spirit. Cant 1:3-4	53
3.3	The distillation of myrrh as fragrance and the availability of the mind of Christ. Cant 1:12-14; 2:13	57
3.4	Mutual belonging. Cant 1:7, 10; 2:6, 16; 3:3-4	63
3.5	The motif of "leaping" and the Incarnation as the Word's descent and ascent. Cant 2:8	76
3.6	Coronation as the Word's triumphal passion. Cant 3:11	82
3.7	The Groom's descent. Cant 4:16-5:1	83
3.8	The Groom's "coming to the door" and manifestation. Cant 5:2-6	85
3.9	"The body of God"? The Groom's body and the Word's potencies. Cant 5:10-16	93
3.10	The Cosmic Groom transcendent. Cant 6:9f and beyond	105
3.11	The Cosmic Groom and nature imagery. Cant 8:14 et al	115
3.12	Conclusion	118

4. The Bride 120

4.1	The Essence of the Human Christ. Cant 1:3	121
4.2	The Bride as a prepared Church-humanity. Cant 1:5-7	125
4.3	The identity of the purified Bride ascending. Cant 3:6 (and its doublet, 8:5)	132
4.4	The "bed" image. Cant 3:7f (with reference to Cant1:16)	134
4.5	The Bride as walled garden and spring. Cant 4:12	137
4.6	The Bride as the imitator of the Groom. Cant 5:2 and 5:12,14	138
4.7	The Bride's chosenness as new Jerusalem. Cant 6:4	140
4.8	The Bride as the perfect human one. Cant 6:8-10	142
4.9	Conclusion	156

5. Conclusion 159

5.1	Factors militating against a Christology inspired by the Song's imagery	159
5.1.1	The limits of imagic theology	159
5.1.2	"No" to mutuality in Christ	161
5.2	The abiding message: love and loves	165

Bibliography of Primary Works: Texts and Translations 168
Bibliography of Secondary Works 173
Scripture Index 197
Name Index 200
Subject Index 204

Chapter 1

Introduction

1.1 Figures and Images

The figures of Bride and Groom, together with the details of action, vision and dialogue contained in the mysterious Song have lent themselves to the consideration of how the Word of God and the believer's soul relate to each other, or how the Church, as Christ's body, is loved by and loves her 'Head' who is the exalted Christ. Since Herder and then Renan,[1] the increasing prevalence of interest in the physically sexual eroticism of the Song as part of the plain historico-grammatical sense has made these erstwhile popular understandings vulnerable. However, in an age where the rational 'plain grammatical and historical sense' of Scripture is no longer as privileged as it was, and where for many people there is more to our apparently most physical actions than may at first appear (a feeling sharply expressed in terms of a belief in a 'divine power' as the ground of being or mystery of the world), it is not surprising to see some treating the Song as doing more than praising marriage and/or love expressed in physical pleasure.

One way to justify the religious reading of the Song of Songs is the way proposed by Eric Gill, that:

> ...all art properly so-called is religious, because all art properly so-called is an affirmation of absolute values.... . The poet cannot be accused of the bestial naturalism of the purveyor of ecclesiastical symbols. To say *venter ejus eburneus, distinctus sapphiris* (v.14) is not photographic, though to say *inter ubera mea commorabitur* (i.12) is not obscure. To say that the Song of Solomon is a naked poem is not to say it is naturalistic. It is heraldic rather than naturalistic, and as in all good heraldry there is no obscurity about its symbolism. The symbol is not obtained by using words in any but their strictly natural senses, but by the intention of the poet.[2]

However, to claim such was the mind of the author of the Song seems to beg the question.

---

[1] Herder, *"Lieder der Liebe"* (in *Werke* III) insisted on the purity of the passion: see Rowley (1965), 217, n 6; Renan (1860), 478; see also Pelletier (1989), 417.

[2] Gill (1921), 2; 5-6.

In any case how could a moving picture of human love point say something about divine love? As (Pseudo)-Dionysius observed, one cannot remake God in our own image: "Between God and his creatures, there is no similarity by reason of something held in common but by imitation; whence we say the creature resembles God but not the inverse"[3] Whereas the love between the Father and the Son is totally beyond representation as an *Ur/Hinter-bild*, its *Abbild*, the love between Christ and Church (Paul had allowed as much if 1 Corinthians 11:1-4 is spliced with that of Ephesians 5:22ff) *can be* represented in a *Bild* of human love.[4] Yet the reference of the symbolism in the Song was, for the writers looked at in this study, the 'divine-human love' in the Incarnation, a sort of hybrid.

According to Dionysius: "theological tradition has a dual aspect, the ineffable and mysterious on the one hand, the open and more evident on the other. The one resorts to symbolism and involves initiation. The other is philosophic and employs the method of demonstration."[5] Doctrine feels like negative, mystical theology, while symbolic, imagic theology seems like 'positive, revelatory'. The genre of poetry (also found in the prophets) is a source for such positive, image-based theology. As P. Ricoeur has insisted, one can be moved by poetic metaphors at level of depth. Ricoeur argues, basing himself on Aristotle's treatment of metaphor in *Poetics* and *Rhetoric*, that this trope aims to persuade as it describes.[6] The Song is not narrative, but possibly something that, in the reciting, shines light further down into the human condition than stories can. One question which exercised the early church was: how much faith should theology put in such metaphors? The problem with metaphor is that certain ones resonate with some situations better than others, so that none of them can be seen as universally or diachronically efficacious in their communicative power. The purpose of metaphor as Aristotle saw it was not to confuse nor even elaborate a thought, but was one of clarification; behind it God as simple accommodates himself to the perverse, fragmented, and difficult thought-processes of humans.[7] But the patristic or perhaps simply Platonic standard was to think of imagery in

---

[3] Cited by Thomas, *Commentary on Book One of the Sentences: Distinctio* XXXV, qu.1, art.4; cf. Ricoeur (1978), 274, 360. Cf. Gill (1921): "In an irreligious age, on the contrary, divine things will be made symbols of human things, and that humanity was created in the image of God will be forgotten, or remembered only as a jest." (5-6)

[4] Cf. Frank (1975).

[5] Rorem (1993), 224: Letter 9:1105D: τὸ διττὴν εἶναι τὴν τῶν θεολογων παράδοσιν, τὴν μὲν ἀπόρρητον καὶ μυστικήν, τὴν δὲ ἐμφανῆ καὶ γνωριμωτέραν καὶ τὴν μεν συμβολικὴν καὶ τελεστικήν, τὴν δὲ φιλόσοφον καὶ ἀποδεικτικήν.

[6] Ricoeur (1978), 12f.

[7] See his introduction to *Ars Rhetorica*; 1354a1-3. Vickers (1988), 300, comments: "the rationale of rhetorical figures as the crystallization of real-life emotional states." Cf. also Ricoeur (1978), 43: "Lively expression is that which expresses existence as alive."

Scripture as merely presenting things like spiritual realities in all their difficulty.[8] The complexity may relate to the diversity of creation, especially humans, so that even if the biblical message comes from God, its accomodation to the subtleties of conscious and subconscious minds means any simplicity is soon lost.

Marcia Falk has claimed that because the Song, perhaps more than any other biblical text, is composed from a string of metaphors, there is a *prima facie* case for reading it as an allegory, by which she means an extended metaphor.[9] This is precisely what the fathers did, projecting higher the reference of the Song's own metaphors or similes. The Song characteristically draws from the world of nature and applies to the world of humans (physical, lovely qualities). Moralising exegesis of the Song moves from these aesthetic 'givens' to speak of virtues and right emotions. Allegorising goes yet a step further and by-passes the human to refer the natural world to the spiritual world which is itself a re-ordered paradise. Allegory gets humans away from seeing any tropology as merely about themselves or that which reflects themselves; just as the Song itself sets a human love affair in the context of nature, order, disorder, covenant and spontaneity. Both the Song and its allegorical interpretation are holistic.

1.2 The Song of Songs: early influences on its interpretation

There is almost no evidence of Christians reading the Song, or at least paying it the honour of citation as Scripture, until the beginning of the third century. There are, however, a few places in the NT where a case could be made for a Messianic if not properly "Christological" interpretation. While most of the claims that the Song is the source of other verses in the Johannine corpus are fanciful,[10] Jesus's promise that streams of living water would come out of anyone who believes in him *according to the Scriptures* (John 7:38) clearly refers to something more precise than a *locus communis*. Cant 4:12 in the Hebrew certainly has גל (spring), even if the Greek renders κῆπος, as if reading גן (garden). Daniélou avers that in Hippolytus, Tertullian, Cyprian, Irenaeus, Aphrahat and Ephraim, but *not* Origen, the fountain is understood to be Jesus; he then pointed to Ezek 47 as the primary text associated. Yet Ezek 47 lacks, while Cant 4:15 (in the same passage, a few verses later) has, the phrase ὕδατος ζῶντος. Also, the case for Rev 3:16's being dependent on Cant 5:2 has been skilfully supported by M. Cambe.[11]

---

[8] So Augustine *De Doctrina Christiana* II, 6,7-8; CCL 32, p. 35.
[9] Falk (1982), 82ff.
[10] E.g., Hengel (1994)'s claim for 2 Jn 1 no less so than Feuillet (1984)'s for Rev 12.
[11] Cambe (1962)

For many Jewish commentators the Song was related to God's self-revelation in his deeds. For them it was a song recounting God's leading and instructing of Israel (R. Akiva) or even the manifesting of his very self at the Red Sea (R. Eliezer). It seems increasingly clear to scholarship that the proto-kabbalistic *Shiur Qomah*, based around the description of the Groom's body in Cant 5, has a long pedigree as a form of mysticism which claims or aims at the vision of God's own form if not face. This is quite a different movement from Qumranic mysticism which tends to present itself as oriented towards preparation of a community for holy warfare at the Messiah's coming. The radical orientation of *Shiur Qomah* (or its antecedents) was redirected in so far as it affected mainstream Palestinian Judaism; first by R. Akiva and then by R. Johanan.[12] Contrary to Barthélemy's surmisings, there is just no hard evidence that the canonical status of the Song was established before and without any recourse to a spiritualising explanation. Even if the LXX translation, whose date is probably late, is fairly literal in its renderings, there are more small glosses than is sometimes made out. Nor was there in Judaism a strict canonical principle as far as the *ketubim* were concerned before the Common Era; thus the Song could be seen by some as sacred and by others as profane, depending on one's estimation of Solomon.[13] The spiritualising approach confirmed by Akiba was extended into a new translation by Aquila, as can be seen from Field's *Hexapla Origenis* on, e.g., Cant 6:12; 8:5.[14] A specifically messianic interpretation was side-lined, only to find later approval in the Targumists. Perhaps it is not such a surprise that the Christian writer who makes the greatest overtly Christian 'Christological' use of the Song is Apponius who manages to blend the Origenian and Hippolytan ways of reading the Song. However, as we shall see, Christian opinion was united in seeing Christ as the form of God whose appearance is predicted and described in the verses of the Song.

The Song, like its heroine (Cant 3:6), appeared out of the wilderness of a general neglect which continued in conservative situations. It is not purely coincidental that it was regarded as canonical and cited as Scripture in areas where the unity of Christ was emphasised. Origen is clearly the central player in that not only did he give the Song a worldwide audience where before it had been the preserve of Palestinian and Jewish-minded Christians — it was

---

[12] For early Jewish interpretations, see Urbach (1971); Kimmelman (1980); Manns (1990). In the Targum, the story unfolds throughout the course of the Song, from the early verses where Moses is the one whose soul is the bride to God the bridegroom, through to the last verses which speak of the Messianic age when the Shekinah will rest on Jerusalem.

[13] See Hanig (1993).

[14] LXX: ἔθετό με ἅρματα Ἀμιναδάβ;   Ἀ: ἅρματα λαοῦ ἐκουσιαζομένου ἄρχοντος.

LXX: ἐκεῖ ὠδίνησέν σε;   Ἀ: ἐκεῖ διεφθέρη.

in Melito's 'Palestinian' canon long before any other[15] and was championed by one from that area, Hippolytus. Consequently the similarity of ideas of a heavenly Groom and a heavenly bridal chamber to those Gnostic fables and systems could not have been missed — especially among those Syriac churches who made sure that God as a Groom was to be thought of as present on earth in performing these mysteries (in baptism[16], eucharist), and not far removed in another corner of reality to which we have remote access. By way of reaction, an insistence on letting God be God and (wo)man be (wo)man prevented the Song from being taken seriously in a spiritual sense. However, those who made room for it in their theology believed that Christ was somehow a unity of God and humanity in the heavenly realities before or as well as the person who appeared on earth.

1.3 Exegetical Styles

The realisation that metaphor easily extends into something which needs to be taken as pointing to another reality in a forward then upward motion (e.g. to the Church and the final Kingdom of Heaven) is peculiarly Christian. The approach to the Song is grounded in the sure belief that there is something about human courtship which overlaps the divine-human engagement.[17]

It has become increasingly difficult to hold to any easy classification of hermeneutical styles in the Church of Late Antiquity. The comfortable bifurcation into 'Alexandrian' and 'Antiochene' is still used and reinforced by notions that one is 'Platonic', the other 'Aristotelian', but it has for a long time been under attack.[18] C. Schäublin has shown how keen Theodore of Mopsuestia was to see much of the packaging and expression of the ideas and events of the Old Testament as rhetoric which was attributable not to God, but to the prophet himself, who often was not speaking from the kind of direct experience which the apostles would have, but who was trying his hardest to get the point across.[19] Thus Old Testament *texts* are susceptible to a sort of 'rhetorical analysis' and therefore the Song of Songs can be best classified as

---

[15] See Melito of Sardis (1979), 66: Fragment 4.

[16] So, Hesychius of Jerusalem; cf. SC 187, 264-5; also, Cyril of Jerusalem *Bapt. Cat.* 3.

[17] See Kittay (1987), 275f about the "common boundary" of "perception" in Plato's use of the sunshine as a metaphor for the Good. That metaphorical language is usually more than "mere metaphor", see Soskice (1985), Ch 6.

[18] Cf. B. Studer in "Die patristische Exegese, eine Aktualisierung der Heiligen Schrift" (paper read at XII International Patristics Conference) following M Simonetti (1985), 355: "Man sah ein, dass die beiden genannten Schulen um 400 einander viel näher standen, als dies zuvor behauptet worden ist."

[19] Jerome subscribed to a more nuanced but close view which explains, to some extent, his sense for sense theory of translation.

a table song. Schäublin's account is slightly at odds with Theodore's own version, insofar as this is found in the proceedings of his condemnation.[20] The heretic there would seem to rule out any table song as not belonging to a canonical genre, for there needs to be some moral or typological value. (One might compare Eustathius of Antioch, who made sure that the text of 1 Samuel 28 affirmed that the deluded woman saw an illusion of Samuel, not that Samuel was brought up from the dead: the lesson is a moral one, that one should not consult the dead, not an insight into biblical cosmology.) Theodore argued that so-called allegory was actually just a Hebraic love of metaphor. Moreover these metaphors were in fact similes, only the presence of the preposition ὡς in the LXX was often missing due to a lack of an equivalent preposition in the Hebrew *Vorlage*.[21] Yet Schäublin recognises that Theodore, at least up to that point, was atypical of the majority of so-called "Antiochenes", in that the other leading representatives, notably Diodore and Theodoret, had views which respected the possibility of texts *in their wording* having some hidden meaning which pointed forward to the gospel, which were in fact divinely inspired, i.e., prophetic.

Other reasons counting against making too fixed a categorisation include the lack of uniformity among those apparently of the 'Alexandrian' persuasion. For example what debt did Cyril have to Origen and Didymus? Not very much it would seem.[22] He shared their interest in Scripture's semantic triplicity, with importance added to the moral outworking by the hearer; yet the Origenian tradition conceived of this more mystically, while Cyril saw particular historical realities as containing, not pointing to, the truth. For Origen (and for his disciples), words as symbols mattered. The context of the immediate text or of the Bible as a whole yielded priority to a love of contrasting 'paired' terms, such as ἀγάπη (*caritas*) and ἐρῶς (*amor*),[23] thus manifesting his unfamiliarity with the notion of biblical poetry's sympathetic parallelism. Origen viewed the ensuing tension or *diaphora* of meaning as an occasion to show how the reconciliation of such contradictions had to be found at a higher level of sense. The LXX did not

---

[20] *ACO* IV, 1, 68-70.

[21] Cf. Rompay *Introduction*, xxxix ff to *Théodore: Psaumes* (1982). The Hebrew Scriptures were mostly intended to tell Christians what they should *not* do.

[22] Cyril does not seem to have followed Didymus; e.g., there is no mention of ἀναγώγη in Cyril: cf. Abel (1941), 164; Kerrigan (1952), 443.

[23] Cf. the contrast of ἀγαπάω and φιλέω. "Die methodische Herkunft dieser Begriffsunterscheidungen weist jedoch in eine pagane Richtung": Neuschäfer (1987), 142. The process of semantic differentiation between synonyms in which both terms get pulled towards the sense of respective homonyms was very popular with Origen.

1. Introduction

provide a divine language but did contain some inspired forms and pictures so that the Word and his Spirit could be said to speak in and through it.[24]

Origen may have taught the Cappadocians to deprecate literal exegesis, especially when it concerned the Trinity,[25] but such concerns were also evident in Marcellus and Athanasius, albeit in a modified form. For the latter, according to Sieben, *skopos* meant that which the Spirit points us to behind the texts, particularly what refers to the pre-existent Logos and what to the incarnate Son. In Scripture we have *paradeigmata*, which are not the divine realities themselves;[26] yet they are not simply human conceptions (*epinoiai*). The "fountain" paradigm, i.e., where the Bible speaks of the Father as source and the Son as the river, connoting the ideas of both continuity and distinction can be found in Jer 2:19, Bar 3:10-12 and Ps 65:9.

Athanasius in turn sponsored Didymus as teacher of the catechetical school in Alexandria, probably as late as the mid-360s.[27] Any association with Origen seems to have become disadvantageous only at the time of the Origenist controversy. Before then Didymus had promoted the earlier Alexandrian interpreter's heritage to, *inter alios*, Jerome, Rufinus and Evagrius. The two epithets *oculum habens sponsae de Cantico canticorum* (Jerome) and *divina luce fulgentem Didymum* (Rufinus), which both play on the faculty of sight, contrast with Epiphanius' naming of the lay teacher as a heretic in the line of Origen's errors,[28] but not for his method or skill in exegesis at large. The moderate nature of Didymus' approach can be further appreciated from W. Bienert's conclusion that *Allegoria* and *Anagoge* are not interchangeable, *pace* Doutreleau.[29] According to Bienert's analysis, allegory (for Didymus anyway) was often the projection of OT the text's meaning into

---

[24] Neuschäfer (1987), 143, and 403, n. 60: "Obwohl Origenes durch die Wahrnehmung typischer Wortbildungen der LXX die Spracheigentümlichkeit der LXX klar erkannte — dies lag durch seine textkritische Vergleichsarbeit ohnedies nahe, sind seine Darlegungen zu dieser Frage noch nicht so entwickelt wie bei den späteren Antiochenern." Cf. Schäublin (1974), 127ff.

[25] For example, the regular use of ἐν with the Holy Spirit in the gospels should not (according to Basil, against Eunomius) be taken to imply his subordination. See Pelikan (1981).

[26] Cf. *Ep. Serap*.1.20: In Lebon's translation (1947), 119: "... la divine Écriture nous a donné aussi des exemples tels que par eux ... il soit possible à ce sujet de parler d'une manière quelque peu simple."

[27] Thus within Athanasius' lifetime and after the disruptions of the early 360s.

[28] Epiphanius, *haer.* 64 (GCS 31, 403ff); for Epiphanius' *Bildungsfeindlichkeit* (and consequently his iconoclasm!) see Schneemelcher (1962): 925f.

[29] Bienert (1972), 107, on *ZaT* 145,24f: "im ersten Fall das Wort 'Babylonier' als Bild versteht, als Chiffre für Grausamkeit und Unterdrückung; im zweiten Fall (140,19) kennzeichnet er die Stellung der 'allegorisch' verstandenen Babylonier im Heilsplan Gotes als dämonische Mächte".

the area of New Testament theology; *anagoge* goes one step further. This seems hardly different from Diodore's or Theodoret's *theoria*.

From this it can be seen that it was almost always the exegesis of the Old Testament that was the acceptable field for spiritualising exegesis. Origen's understanding of John's Gospel as allegory probably went beyond the pale for many. Yet even Origen was aware of the possibility of harm to hearers, and refused to imitate a readiness, common since Aristotle, to *critique* any sacred text.[30] It may be that the question was answered in practice according to one's audience. In the case of the nascent monastic movement, some Egyptian and Asian monks (e.g., the Tall Brothers, Olympias' convent) favoured some allegory, others (e.g., the Nitrians, Bethlehemites) did not. Nevertheless it is more than the dictates of academic fashion which demand that interpretation be seen as a task of *aggiornamento*, especially in the context of liturgy. Edification, not doctrinal edifices, was requested through clarification of the more obscure passages, leaving plain ones to the work of paraphrase. Without rhetorical flourishes the hard-pressed Ambrose tailored his exegesis to the preaching of the gospel. The Bible led to Christ who revealed the Father in the fullness of the Holy Spirit in the hearer.[31]

However, as recent studies have made clear, allegory arises out of a sense that the Scriptural text must mean something. It seems likely that there was a 'turn to experience', a subjectivising of truth, around the half-way stage of the fourth century, in line with philosophical developments and the ascetic movement.[32] It is also noticeable that, unlike Didymus,[33] Evagrius makes little mention of doctrinal issues. Although the Song was hardly used by the Desert Fathers, while the dialogical praying of the Psalms *was* standard, this may be accounted for by the simple fact that the Scriptures were not in such a physical form as to be readily taken into the wilderness. So theological education does not seem to have been a priority for eremitic monasticism,

---

[30] According to Neuschäfer (1987), pp. 79-81, ΕΠΟΠΤΕΙΑ is found in Plato, but is especially prominent in Stoics; (Sextus Empiricus *Adv Math* 7,16; cf. Augustine *De civitate Dei* VIII, 4 Diog. Laert. 7,39). As for the Platonists, see A tius *plac.1 prooem*, 2 for ΦΥΣΙΚΗ, ΕΘΙΚΗ, ΛΟΓΙΚΗ Jerome (Ep. 30,1) has *logicam* as the highest and then, later (in Ep. 121,10,25), *theologiam*. It seems that Aristotle and his scheme — ΠΟΙΗΤΙΚΗ, ΠΡΑΚΤΙΚΗ, ΘΕΩΡΕΤΙΚΗ (MET 6,1:1025-6) was ignored (cf. H. Dörrie, 1974.) After all Aristotle's own text hardly lent itself to allegorical interpretation. In other words the "intellectual" understanding by Origen of the highest level (and not stages of advancement) reveals a strong Stoic influence, and thus an eschewing of any 'Aristotelian' way of reading.

[31] Cf. Studer's conclusion in "Die patristische Exegese, eine Aktualisierung der Heiligen Schrift."

[32] Cf. Burton-Christie (1991), 22, writing about the Desert Fathers as influenced by Neoplatonism: "the hermeneutical key to Plotinus' interpretation... a radical interiorization of Plato's world of forms."

[33] See, for Didymus, Bienert (1972), 123-26.

while the Psalter's popularity was due not only to its 'memorisability' through widespread liturgical use (although perhaps also owing to its having a greater affinity with the warfare of the desert than the lyrical scenes of the Song. Perhaps the atmosphere of the Song seemed too eudaemonistic to be able to correspond to even the best of God-given experience of this life, let alone to austere or Evagrian 'intellectual' monasticism, and so was left alone. Then again its appeal to the passions, even in the context of sublimation, may have appeared unhelpful. Even in the Macarian homilies, replete as they are with affective mysticism, the Song is used sparingly.[34]

At the extreme end of this process was a view of Old Testament Scripture (along with the liturgy) as a stock of symbols. This can be seen to some extent in Pseudo-Dionysius the Areopagite.[35] Talking of God from a source which is largely non-philosophical was, as Pépin has claimed, a Stoic-style therapeutic operation of correct reading which would transport people back to their original pure state. However for the majority, the recognition of Porphyry's criticisms of Christian allegorising by Augustine[36] (perhaps significant for Augustine and others' neglecting the Song as a source of theology) are a sign that, in the early fifth century Church, the idea of a salvation by texts would have been played down. Whereas Origen, in reliance on Philo, but with more of a paedagogic intent, had tried to build a Christian philosophy on the Old Testament, for the North African, while meaning was indeed hidden in places, the story and message of Scripture was largely clear and allegory need be resorted to only in those rare cases. It would therefore only be a slight exaggeration to speak of a depreciation in the value of the Old Testament mysteries.

---

[34] This seems to be included as a concession to the idea of the soul's being "wounded" by divine *eros*, along with 'the five senses' as another borrowing from Origen. The figures of bride and groom are there, but they seem based on NT texts; e.g., Makarios/Symeon, *Reden und Briefe* II, 110,12ff. G. Bunge's work (e.g.) should make one careful of seeing Evagrius' relation to Macarius in dialectical terms.

[35] Ps-Dionysius, *Ep.* 9; (1991), 194. Cf. Pépin (1987), 209.

[36] In *De Civ. Dei* X,11; Dombart-Kalb, 420f; see also *De Doctrina Christiana* III which counsels against resorting to allegory too quickly: see esp., 13. For both thinkers the lower soul needs purifying and instruction from the *mind*, rather than entertaining by pictures. But for Augustine the stakes seemed higher (cf. *De civ. Dei* X,9). Thus his polemic against the *physiologi*: "Ipsas physiologias cum considero, quibus docti et acuti homines has res humanas conantur vertere in res divinas, nihil video nisi ad temporalia terrenaque opera naturamque corpoream vel etiamsi invisibilem, tamen mutabilem potuisse revocari; quod nullo modo est verus Deus."

1.4 Setting the scene

It is a commonplace that one's hermeneutic reflects one's world. A sketch of that world must be modest in compass. Suffice to say, the latter part of the fourth and the earlier part of the fifth centuries saw a continued and possibly intensified sense of the importance of the sacramental; heavenly things could be grasped but not naturally or directly. However, there was also a process of Christianisation through demolition and building, law (cf. Theodosius' edicts), and (as coined by M. Foucault) 'totalising discourse',[37] although one wonders how far outlying regions were affected by such propaganda. The Church was conceived of as already perfect 'by definition' (e.g., in Epiphanius *Ancoratus* 118, and Chromatius, *Sermon* 10[38]) as a model for the State to learn from. By this time the definitive answer to the Arian threat had been given and largely received in the definition of the action of God as proceeding out from his essence. Rhetoric, under the influence of the Second Sophistic, was restrained and appropriate to the content, as Gregory of Nyssa showed in his denunciation of Eunomius as bombastic and "Aristotelian". Long, difficult journeys were normal; there seems to have been almost a dialectical relationship between the public careers and the monastic preference of many of our commentators. Particular controversies and local issues must have left their mark on the various men, but a growing sense of freedom from institutionalised heresy after Theodosius I and a rooting out of heresy which now seemed multiform and indigenously rooted, e.g., Priscillianism, Arianism, Donatism, Pelagianism and Photinianism (in the West), Origenism, Messalianism, Sabellianism and Nestorianism (in the East).[39] The lack of cultural as well as political cohesion is best attested to by the repeated efforts of Julian, the Theodosii, and, later, Zeno and Justinian (to give but some examples) to supply it.

In these circumstances a theology which could catch the unpredictable popular imagination while remaining true to the New Testament and the formulae of the fathers must have seemed desirable. Evidence of such a theology would be found in liturgy, poetry and hymns of the period, but also simply in the homilies of the commentators, the genre of which was rarely "pure scholarship".

---

[37] Cf. the thesis of Averil Cameron (1994), and, less ambitiously, McMullen (1984).

[38] *Sermo X*; CCL 9a, 22: "Nupta dicitur (Ecclesia), quia per Spiritum sanctum Christo coniuncta est; virgo, quia innupta et incorrupta manet a peccato."

[39] Even the so-called "Eutychianism", proscribed at Chalcedon, could be seen as essentially a "two-natures" heresy. According to this school, the human nature existed already in Mary and contributed to his 'overall' person through its mingling with the Word.

1.5 The beginnings of Christological deliberation

The period (381-451) which saw greatest activity in the production of commentaries on the Song was also that in which Christology moved, from being a side-issue in the controversies regarding the constitution of the Christian God for all eternity, to becoming a subject which attracted treatises in its own right. Whatever the controversial area of doctrine, Christology was always in the near background with the question of 'who/what is He?' and 'who/what then is the one(s) he saves?'[40] This is not the place to delineate the anatomy of the Christological question of that era. Suffice to say, it was not yet a doctrine sealed off from others, but was self-consciously related to ecclesiology and spirituality as well as to the doctrine of God. Thus doctrines of soteriology, anthropology, ecclesiology and Christology were fluid, one example being the Marcellian identification of Christ's humanity as the one humanity for the many in the Church, and the way this was picked up by the following generation of exegetes.[41]

1.6 The Christological interpretation of the Song

Although the Song of Songs has played a central role in the history of Christian spirituality[42], it cannot be said ever to have made a great contribution to the official doctrine of Christology. Thus, partly from a pan-human awareness, there has developed a firm sense that the Redeemer God has a positive purpose for all his creatures, and so in one sense the Song can be taken "cosmologically", witnessing to a joyful covenant between God and the universe, not least our natural world. Or it can be taken as a universal charter of God's undying love towards all human beings, and thus about the joining of Word and representative humanity in the Incarnation.

Given that the Christian faith holds Christ to be central in redeeming both cosmos and human beings, can the Song be applied to his Person? While the NT gives no real evidence of understanding the divinity and humanity, as related in a way that is analogous to the male-female love relationship, it is equally hard to find *any* proof texts for the details of the hypostatic union, or on the 'psychology' of Christ. However, if love can be seen as the quality

---

[40] See, above all, the careful work of A. de Halleux (1976); (1994).

[41] See Hübner (1974), 210: "Die Universalität des alle Menschen umfassenden Heils scheint bei Gregor in einer besimmten Auffassung von der Einheit der Menschennatur begründet zu sein, die sich in einer Identifizierung von Menschheit und Menschheit Christi als Leib Christi und Kirche ausdrückt."

[42] See McGinn (1991).

which 'binds' the inner-Trinitarian relations, how much more so the Christological union, as love for the other rather than for the same. Even within a orthodox tradition not much given to Christological speculation, there is the sentiment expressed by Augustine that the human being Jesus Christ is closer to the divine Jesus Christ than the Son of God is to the Father.[43] Augustine's eye is on the point he is making about the distinction of persons *within the Trinity*, and represents the very opposite of the idea that *in Christ* two persons co-existed: just as body and soul in us make one *tu*, so there is only one *Christus* from *Verbum, anima et caro*. Nevertheless Augustine does make an analogy between *homo* and *filius*, and elsewhere he can write of Christ's speaking *ex persona hominis*, speaks of Christ's two wills in the *Enarrationes in Psalmos*,[44] and uses the analogy of the 'two becoming one' from Genesis 2.[45]

The *totus Christus* type of hermeneutic which Augustine, following Tyconius, was developing into a Christological principle *could have* developed into a Christology modelled around the figure of a Bride-Groom, "one flesh" relationship. In any case, the *mimesis* of the imagery of the Song is suited to the Christology since it provides a series of icons/similes which actually have a surreal — that is defined as the juxtaposition of natural and supernatural — quality. This does not mean that such interpretations are *kitsch*, since that which is being described is not the *physical* but the *moral* qualities of Christ; in the moral life of the Saviour, divine and human meet. To have avoided the Incarnation in their accounts of the Song's meaning for spirituality would have been Gnostic, and it is to the credit of most of the fathers examined that the meeting of divine and human in Christ was a controlling hermeneutic on their readings of the Song, even if their interpretations do not appear primarily Christological.

---

[43] *De Trinitate* I, 10: 21; CCL 50, 57: "Quapropter cum filius sit et *deus* et *homo*, alia substantia *deus,* alia *homo,* homo potius in filio quam filius in patre; sicut caro animae meae alia substantia est ad animam meam quamvis in uno homine quam anima alterius hominis ad animam meam."

[44] We should recognise the extent to which Augustine was conscious of Leporius' heresy which itself was so much a reaction against *commixtio*-type Christologies as to state that God did not really become man. Augustine did not consider Christ's human nature as perfect from the outset: "ostendit hominis quamdam privatam voluntatem, in qua suam figuravit et nostram, quia caput nostrum est." (*Enarr. in Ps.* 32,II/1:2: CCL 38, p249) However any human moral agency before God came from the Church "within him", which he in turn straightened out and transfigured in himself (*ibid.*).

[45] *Enchir.* 36 (*PL* 40,250); cf. van Bavel (1954), 41-44.

1.7 The task ahead

The temporal parameters of the study mean that Origen is met primarily in those whom he inspired to translate him or attempt to imitate him. Although the earlier attempts of Hippolytus and Methodius marked out paths for interpretation, it is only with the reappraisal of the Alexandrian's comprehensive commentary that the Song is declared to be "Christo-soteriological" in the sense that verses are held to refer to the Word incarnate as a unified Person who continues to approach and draw souls after him. At the other end of the period, the Song's imagery was finally dispensed with in favour of more precise means of theological expression during the time of the Christological controversies up to "Chalcedon". The trail of Canticles-interpretation seems to have run into the sand even before 451, after which, on the evidence available, commentary writing in general was quiescent compared with our period.[46] The genre seems to require less heady and fractious times to flourish than the mid-Fifth Century could offer. One could proceed by examining verses by verse, but if these are the records of homilies, it is more faithful to the spirit to analyse the dominant images, thus treating groupings of verses. These preachers believed in a *skopos*, or perhaps the *res* more than the *verba*. The old truism of the rule of faith looming larger than the canon of Scripture applies. Accordingly, they were less interested in the details of the Song than in the central nuptial relationship (even though a lot of the detail is used to provide moral teaching) and less concerned with that than with the Groom and Bride as "individuals". There just is not a full nuptial mutuality. Nor, as we shall see, did the Song drive Christology in its successive formulations, although perhaps its influence on this doctrine, through being given a Christological hermeneutic in places, was rather more subtle. The Groom is clearly the Word in his incarnate state, seeking out, attracting and making himself available to humanity, while the Bride is that humanity, attracted, gathered in, and rejoicing. This study looks more at texts than at their authors. And yet this does not mean it ignores the author, only that it does not become so historicist that nothing can be said unless it can be related to their lives. Especially in large works (and more so where they avoid much reference to this world or are even anonymous, as with Apponius), the text as it might have been read, not information about its origins, is at the centre of the discussion.

---

[46] See Grillmeier (1987), 87f.

Chapter 2

Establishing the context of the commentators on the Song

This chapter attempts to clarify the background of the comments on the texts to be examined in the next two chapters. This background means the lives, times and other pertinent works of these writers. This outline will deal with each author in chronological order. Hippolytus, Origen and Methodius lie outside the time period (381-451), but are considered in terms of their being *read* during it.

2.1 Hippolytus

The Georgian text edited by Garitte provides the fullest and most reliable account of what Hippolytus thought of the Song.[1] The Armenian text is quite different and seems, in many places, to include additions which reflect a fifth century period. This shows how highly Hippolytus was regarded in fifth century Armenian circles. The Greek paraphrase presented by Richard is interesting for its 'Apollinarian' interpolations.[2] The exegete is agreed by most to be more akin to the writer of *Contra Noetum,* given the imagery commonly used.[3] Whether the same Hippolytus ended up in Rome to write the *Elenchos* is a hard question, which should probably be answered negatively.

2.2 Origen (Greek)

Origen's mature work on the Song, the Commentary, remains extant in the shape of a full Latin translation by Rufinus of four out of the ten books written, and two homilies in Jerome's translation.[4] As for the Greek originals of these, only a fragment of the Commentary has been preserved in the

---

[1] CPG 1871; Garitte (1965).
[2] Richard (1964).
[3] See Frickel (1989); Nautin (1992); Simonetti (1989), (1996).
[4] Respectively listed as CPG 1433 and 1432.

Cappadocian *Philocalia*.[5] This, a preface, laments the problem of not knowing who is the πρόσωπον speaking — which is the chief cause of the opacity of Scripture.[6] It is noteworthy that here Origen seems to associate the Song with "prophetic writings", i.e., those which predict the Incarnation.[7] The Commentary and Homilies will be mentioned further below.[8]

Jerome attests that Origen produced "youthful work" on the Song.[9] M.N. Esper has plausibly argued that what Jerome was referring to as early *scholia* were what have previously appeared to be paraphrastic excerpts extant in the Procopian *catena*.[10] Baehrens' attempt to harmonise the Rufinian Latin version with the Procopian fragments in the *GCS* edition showed that the latter certainly do not correspond to this more mature and larger undertaking which shall be considered below. Any suspicion that what we have in Migne is based on a poor manuscript tradition is a separate question from that of the possible shaping given to the work by Procopius of Gaza (465-530) himself. M.A. Barbara has promised a more reliable edition.[11] Yet in her more recent article she affirms that although the British mss (*Bod Misc gr 36* and its 'parent' *Cantab. Trin Coll* O154) are reliable in reproducing Gregory of Nyssa and Theodoret and therefore should be trusted for Origen, *Paris* 153 and *Paris* 154, are still better witnesses to the Procopian tradition, since they rely on the later (S. XI) *Epitome* of Procopius.[12] Even so Barbara discounts them in favour of the *Codex Barb.* which she believes to be independent of the Procopian tradition. However, her edition is still awaited. The British manuscripts which manage to preserve at least something of the original work of Procopius and are in published form cannot, given the inchoate state of research, either be overlooked or given undue respect.

---

[5] The editors of SC 375, pp. 10-17 note that the second piece from Origen on Cant in the Philocalia (27,13) corresponds fairly well to Rufinus' rendering. It does not appear that stylistic comparison has been made between the preface and the "Procopian" fragments.

[6] *Philocalia* VII; Robinson (1893), p. 51, 7-9: ἥτις καὶ αἰτία ἐστὶν οὐχ ἡ τυχοῦσα μὴ διακρινομένη τῆς ἀσαφείας τῶν λεγομένων. ἔστι δὲ καὶ αὕτη συνήθεια τῆς γραφῆς, τὸ ταχέως μεταπηδᾶν ἀπὸ τοῦ περί τινων λόγου εἰς τὸν περὶ ἑτέρων. καὶ τοῦτο ἀσαφῶς ποιεῖν καὶ ὑποσυγκεχυμένως μάλιστα τοὺς προφήτας.

[7] Ibid., p. 50f: Περὶ τοῦ ἰδιώματος τῶν προσώπων τῆς θείας γραφῆς. ἐκ τοῦ εἰς τὸ ᾆσμα μικροῦ τόμου, ὃν ἐν τῇ νεότητι ἔγραψεν.

[8] Sections 9 and 15.

[9] *Ep.* 33,4; CSEL 54, p. 256 speaks of two books written on the Song during Origen's youth.

[10] Esper (1979), 155, n. 5: "Es liegt der Schluß nahe, daß sie aus Origenes' Excerpta zum Canticum stammen....hat er Excerpta, d.h.σχόλια verfaßt, z.B. zum Buch Exodus, zu den Psalmen. Excerpta zum Canticum führt Hieronymus nicht an, doch meint er damit wohl, was er mit 'alios tomos II, quos super (insuper Ritschl) in adulescentia scripsit'...bezeichnet."

[11] Barbara (1992).

[12] Barbara (1993).

2. Establishing the Context of the Commentators on the Song

On the part played by Procopius, J. Irmscher states: "In P.'s name we have two commentaries on the Song of Songs, one authentic, the other a fragment of the *catena* of the three Fathers, based on Nilus, Gregory of Nyssa and Maximus Confessor."[13] This attribution of the first work to Procopius, based on H.-G. Beck's view,[14] surely over-estimates his contribution. For, as W. Aly attests, paraphrasing Procopius' *ipsissima verba*, the work of Procopius (at least on the Octateuch) was to excerpt and select the comments of other writers: "Daraus ergeben sich zwei verschiedene Phasen des Werkes, einmal die Materialsammlung, bestehend aus wörtlichen Perikopen aus den exzerpierten Schriften mit Anführung der Quellen, dann ein fortlaufender Kommentar ohne die Namen und unter Ausscheidung der zahlreichen Doubletten...das erstere ἐκλογαί, das zweite ἐπιτομαὶ ἐκλογῶν."[15] So, to call what we have preserved in Migne (at PG 87,2,1545-1754) "echte Prokopius Katena" in contradistinction to "Ps[eudo]-Prokopius" at PG 87,2,1755-1780 (the "three fathers"), lacks foundation.[16] Both work at degrees of approximation. M. Harl has also championed a position of scepticism with regard to the value of the Procopian *catena* as witnesses to Origen, with special reference to the Alexandrian on Ps 118.[17] Likewise R. Heine has reached somewhat negative conclusions in the case of fragments of Origen's John Comentary.[18] Nevertheless, while bearing these arguments in mind, the reception of Origen in the early fifth century rather than a bold reconstruction of the pure Origen of the 220s is of greater interest to this study. Given that Procopius was compiling in the earliest years of the sixth century, he is not separated from the chosen time-period by too large a gap.

It is perhaps no coincidence that, if the chronology established by Nautin and Trigg is correct, [19] Origen was simultaneously engaged in his 'Hexaplaric' edition of the text of the Song; its presentation was governed by his hermeneutic of 'knowing the speaker, object, addressee'. Origen in the Hexaplaric edition of the Song applies different rules from those applied by Proclus to the *Timaeus* and the *Parmenides*; this may be because, as would be the case in a tragedy, in the dialogues the speaker and adressee is clear.[20]

Thus Origen seems to be treating oracular discourse as if it were a philosophical or dramatic text. [21] Turning to the great codices of the Hexaplaric texts, *Alexandrinus* simply offers the identification of the speaker

---

[13] Irmscher (1992), 713.
[14] Beck (1977), 413-15.
[15] Aly (1957), 270.
[16] See Beck (1977), 415.
[17] Harl (1972a).
[18] Heine (1986).
[19] Nautin (1977); Trigg (1983).
[20] Cf. I. Hadot (1987).
[21] For the significance of the Chaldean Oracles, see P. Hadot (1987).

as "bride" or "groom" (perhaps where it is not entirely clear) for Cant 1:2,3,5; 2:10,17; 3:6; 4:16; 5:3; 6:3,9; 8:5; however, *Sinaiticus* contains markings of the *dramatis personae*. The "young women" in the Song are represented as a chorus, e.g., at 5:9: πυνθάνονται τῆς νύμφης. Two of the marginal comments are explicitly 'Christianising': Cant 1:7 is glossed with πρὸς τὸν νυμφίον Χριστόν and at 5:1(4:16) there is ἡ νύμφη αἰτεῖται τὸν πατέρα. In the *catena*, the latter verse (Cant 4:16c: καταβήτω ἀδελφιδός μου εἰς κῆπον αὐτοῦ) has no commentary on it, but only this marginal summary, which implies that the marginal note was commentary enough. Origen's debt to the Old Testament and Judaism is less apparent in these *scholia* than in the fuller, later Commentary.

2.3 Methodius

Methodius ventured to comment on the Song as relating to the Incarnation by means of the speech of his character Procilla in his *Symposium* VII; otherwise the Song was interpreted as an exhortation to sexual continence.[22]

2.4 Dionysius of Alexandria

The fragment preserved by Feltoe[23] is considered inauthentic by W. Bienert.[24] However, even on his debatable assumption that Dionysius was *anti*-Origenian,[25] there is nothing within the fragment, which mentions Adam and Eve that is particularly pro-Origenian. There is no mention of "garments of skins" put on, but only of the apparel, lost at the Fall, which awaits the soul.

2.5 'Athanasius'

Photius is the sole witness to any comments by Athanasius on Ecclesiastes and the Song.[26] In the assuredly Athanasian texts the Song's few appearances relate to the attitude of nuptial submission of a monk to Christ.[27]

---

[22] CPG 1818; in *Methodius Werke GCS* 27, (1917); SC 95 (1963).

[23] CPG 1585; Feltoe, 228f.

[24] Bienert (1978), 54f, who follows what Procopius reports to be Dionysius' opinion on Gen 3:21 (PG 87,221B).

[25] Ct. the summary of Williams (1995), 414.

[26] Photius Cod. 139, in Henry (1960), 108, refers to these ὑπόμνημα.

[27] The Syriac-preserved *Sermo de Virginitate* (CPG 2145).

An Athanasian passage of dubious authenticity interprets Cant 4:16 as referring to the Lord coming from the south to deliver his body which had lain for three days (he, the Word, having presumably left it) in the tomb to the north (of Jerusalem; cf. Hab 3:3; Ps 47:3).[28] The bride figure calls on the Saviour as Spirit to "blow" or come from south to north; then with Jesus' entrance (presumably to the disciples as in Jn 20: 22) "the garden breathed out and emitted sweet smells". "The garden" is the risen Jesus, and is not just breathed through but does the exhaling: Τότε λοιπὸν, εἰσελθόντος τοῦ Ἰησοῦ, ἔπνευσεν ὁ κῆπος, καὶ ἔρρευσαν τὰ ἀρώματα.[29] For, "our fragrance is the immortality of the body which he put on." This deification happened through the ἀνάπαυσις of the Word, his resting on humanity:[30] "when was the body able (nb. *aorist*) to put on immortality if not through the 'rest' of the Word?"[31]

Given these themes, Richard's suggestion that this is Marcellus, or his school, is hardly compelling.[32] Marcellus had referred Ps 44:1 to the Incarnation;[33] yet, for Marcellus, Jesus is very much identified now as the divine Logos who came down and took flesh; this "flesh" is defined as the man who is the instrument in the soteriological process and who stays passive for as long as he was joined to the Logos.[34] There is little personal interplay between what God does and what the creature does. Marcellus held that the Saviour could not have two natures together for more than a temporary arrangement, a 'marriage of convenience'. However, in this homily God and human souls are held to be already related through the image in creation, and so the flesh assumed is a shining one. There is the emphasis on the body on the Cross healing our bodies and the Word going alone to Hades. Further

---

[28] CPG 2239: see E. Schwartz (1924), 6; (1925), 35, who associated it with the *Sermo Maior de Fide*; the whole section is reproduced in PG 27, 1348-61.

[29] PG 27, 1355AB.

[30] Cf. Lampe (1961), 115 (E.3.a.)

[31] PG 27,1356BC: Ἀρώματα δὲ ἡμῶν ἡ ἀφθαρσία τοῦ σώματος, ἣν ἐνεδύσατο. Διὰ τοῦτο γὰρ καὶ ὁ Παῦλος ἔλεγεν Δεῖ τὸ φθαρτὸν τοῦτο ἐνδύσασθαι ἀφθαρσίαν, καὶ τὸ θνητὸν τοῦτο ἐνδύσασθαι ἀθανασίαν. [1 Cor 15:53] Πότε δὲ ἐνεδύσατο τὸ σῶμα τὴν ἀφθαρσίαν εἰ μὴ διὰ τῆς ἀναπαύσεως τοῦ Λόγου; ἀμέλει γε ὅ τε ἀνέστη ὁ Σωτὴρ, καὶ ἦλθον αἱ γυναῖκες ἅψασθαι αὐτοῦ, ἔλεγεν αὐταῖς Μή μου ἅπτεσθε..

[32] Richard (1949), 129, on the basis of alleged similarities to the *Sermo Maior de Fide* (CPG 2803) and to the *Contra Theopaschitas* (CPG 2805) which contains Christology "du type Verbe-chair", affirming the unity of hypostasis in God.

[33] *Apud* Euseb. Caes., *Contra Marc.* fr. 129; GCS 58, 215, 15-19: Ἰησοῦς Χριστὸς... κατελθὼν δια τὴν ἡμετεράν σωτηρίαν καὶ ἐκ τῆς παρθένου Μαρίας γεννηθεὶς τὸν ἄνθρωπον ἔλαβεν.

[34] Cf. fr. 117, *ibid.*, p. 210,29-33. Acts 3:21 is interpreted thus: "περὶ τοῦ ἀνθρώπου τούτου...καὶ αὗται (*viz*, The Acts) ὥσπερ ὅρον τινὰ καὶ προθεσμίαν ὁρίζουσαι ἐν ᾧπερ προσήκει τὴν κατὰ ἄνθρωπον οἰκονομίαν ἡνῶσθαι τῷ λόγῳ οὕτω λέγουσιν."

there is the identification of the divinity as the one separated from the flesh (i.e., body and soul in conjunction) who leaves the soul with the body before He comes back to reclaim *for perpetuity* that which he had laid down: this is no association for the *interim* only. (The writer, like Apollinarius, regarded Christ's death not as the separation of soul from body, but of mind, or Word, from soul and body.) This is the kind of thing *attacked* in the Marcellian *Contra Apollinarium*, where the anthropology of mankind in general and of Christ in particular was contested.[35] As A. Le Boulluec puts it, Marcellus' Christology was weak in that: "elle est dépourvue en outre d'une réflexion approfondie sur la relation entre l'individu homme-Christ et la collectivité homme-Eglise."[36] In the Athanasian fragments on the Song collected in Migne, however, the theology of a comment on Cant 5:1cd [37] is quite different.

2.6 Apollinarius

There are two printed sources for Apollinarius on the Song: first, thirteen short *scholia* in Procopius' *catena* on the Song[38] and second, three from the Procopian *catena* on the Psalms.[39] Most pay attention to the figure of Jesus and particularly the Cross.

2.7 Didymus

Didymus's comments can be found principally in the Procopian *catena* on the Psalms[40] and in his commentary on the Psalms discovered at Toura.[41] A. Gesché has shown how pivotal were both the phrase ὁ κυριακὸς ἄνθρωπος

---

[35] Cf. Winling (1988): Apollinarius was also accused of understanding the flesh as 'heavenly' because of its inseparability from the Word, and therefore as 'within' the Trinity; yet his accusers, while preferring a sober view of the soul as the rational animator of the body, by definition belonging to a humble, never so exalted state, nevertheless held that the Logos never left the soul and body but stayed with them both in their separate states. The soul descends to Hades, albeit as a veil for the Word; whereas for Apollinarius the soul and body must stay together while the divinity alone does the rescuing — to return as The Spirit. Winling concludes that "les deux traités insistent sur la pleine humanité du Christ et adoptent le schéma logos-anthropos... CA2 [*Contra Apollinarium*] met en lumière la volonté humaine du Christ en montrant comment elle s'harmonise avec la volonté divine" (p. 109).
[36] Le Boulluec (1985), 378.
[37] PG 27, 1353D-55A.
[38] CPG 3684; PG 87:1548-1749.
[39] CPG 3681; see Mühlenberg (1975-77-78).
[40] CPG 2551; see Mühlenberg, ibid.
[41] CPG 2550; Gronewald (1968-70).

— rare among other fathers, and a Christology in which Christ's sufferings were redemptive — rare outside Origen.[42] The significant convergence between the exegesis contained in the *Catenae* and the Toura-collection is "l'analyse de l'âme humaine de Jésus ou...la préexistence des âmes." Also, such attention to the soul of Christ is distinctive in that it did not derive from Athanasius but was carried on by the predominantly Evagrian form of Origenist Christology. Didymus probably commented on the Psalms before 386 when Jerome asked him to do the same on Zechariah.[43] M.-J. Rondeau has connected Didymus and the Apollinarian Pseudo-Athanasius as believing in two types of soul in Christ:[44] the *monogenes* and the *psyche*. The former (identical with the Apollinarian νοῦς) stays united to the Logos at all time. The latter unites and thus facilitates the divinisation of all believers. There are also similarities of exegetical style which supports a picture of Didymus and Apollinarius as co-heirs of Origen.[45]

2.8 Philo of Carpasia

Ordained bishop by Epiphanius,[46] according to Jerome,[47] Philo was already "of blesssed memory" by 394. E. Prinzivalli[48] regards him as conservative by temperament, while J. Dechow affirms: "Epiphanius considered his episcopal jurisdiction so extensive that he allowed his colleagues, Philo of Carpasia and Theopropus to ordain priests in distant parts of the diocese."[49] This close tie of loyalty is asserted in Epiphanius/Jerome. The reflection of some of Epiphanius' influence suggests a dating of Philo's full commentary on the Song to be no earlier than the mid-380s.

Philo's commentary exists in two forms: first, the Greek in the edition of M.A. Giacomelli, published in PG 40: 27-162, which is based on the Procopian *catenae*,[50] and second, the Latin, a translation by Epiphanius Scholasticus commissioned by Cassiodorus in the 520s at Vivarium, which has been produced in a critical edition by A. Ceresa-Gastaldo.[51] In the introduction the editor makes a good case for regarding the Latin version as

---

[42] Gesché (1962), 412f. Cf. Grillmeier (1977).

[43] Ibid., 415. Cf. Bienert (1972), 25.

[44] Rondeau (1985), 269, adducing *Ps Cat* 21,21 and Mühlenberg (1975), I, 231,2-7.

[45] Cf. Riedmatten (1952).

[46] Polybius Rhinocurorum, *Vita S. Epiphanii*, II, 49, as mentioned by Giacomelli in his introduction to PG 40:27-162.

[47] Ep. 51.2.2; CSEL 54, 398.

[48] Prinzivalli (1992), 683.

[49] See Dechow (1990), 50.

[50] There is also the Ps-Eusebian catena (published first by J. Meursius (1617) which gives some of the important readings.

[51] Philo of Carpasia (Ceresa-Gastaldo) (1979).

witness to a *Vorlage* which is more original than that which the extant Greek *catena*-based manuscripts provide.[52] One critic is less sure of this on the grounds of the loose style of translation in the early monastic world;[53] and yet she admits both that the citations are literally faithful to the LXX and that the *lemmata* are drawn from Jerome's pre-Vulgate 'hexapla-emended' (yet not too far from the literal LXX) revison from which clumsy Semitisms still protrude.[54]

2.9 Jerome

Jerome's interest in the Song started with his translation of Origen's two homilies on the Song, commissioned by Damasus in 383. Having made a revised Latin translation on the basis of the Greek Hexapla, he translated from the Hebrew text in 394 and incorporated the rubrics already suggested by Origen.[55] These had the effect of making the text itself appear to speak about God, thus relieving it from any suspicion of profanity. Immediately after the work on the homilies he communicated their spiritual message to Eustochium[56] and around the time of the Vulgate version he confronted Jovinian's literalist approach to the Song.[57]

2.10 Pacianus

Bishop of Barcelona (who died between 379 and 393), his comments on the Song come in the third letter to Simpronianus, a Novatian. The recent edition by C. Granado mentions a work called *Cervus* which is interested in the issue of bestial representation, opposing the festal practice of dressing up in animal skins.[58] In his dispute with the Novatians Pacianus used the Song imagery to stress that the Church was peaceful and non-elitist.[59]

---

[52] Thus what we have in Migne (Giacomelli) is paraphrastic; Ceresa-Gastaldo's note, at Philo (1979), p. 234, undermines Giacomelli's contention that the Latin was translated from a 'second edition', now lost.

[53] Sagot (1981a).

[54] Ibid., 364-70.

[55] See Schulz-Flügel (1992), 21.

[56] Kelly (1975), 100-103.

[57] Ibid., 182f.

[58] Granado (1995), 42.

[59] Ibid., 256: "...ecclesiam Dei columbam non felle amaram, non unguium laceatione violentiam, parvulis quoque plumis exigiuisque candentem. Scimus etiam puteum aquae vivae fontemque signatum nulla haeretici gurgitis labe sordere, hortumque conclusum plenum oleribus magnis pariter et parvis, vilibus atque pretiosis."

2.11 Ambrose

Ambrose's comments are found scattered throughout several works, but cover almost every verse of the Song, to the extent of enabling William of St. Thierry to make one commentary out of the discrete comments.[60]

While in the early *De virginibus* (377), the Song is used in exhortations to chastity, after the doctrinal works of the *De fide* (379-80) and the *De incarnatione* (382) the later period witnesses a change to a more theological understanding, from the *Expositio Psalmis 118* (384) and the *Apologia David altera*[61] through the *De Isaac vel anima*,[62] (dated variously as 386 [Courcelle], 391 [Dassmann],[63] or between these dates [Sagot][64]), onwards up to the late *Expositio Psalmis 45* (394). These works saw Ambrose come to appreciate an interpretation of the Song which focussed on the relationship of souls to the Word within them (microcosmically) and above them (cosmically), as they ascended, morally and mystically to heaven. Indeed Ambrose so often seems so aloof or other-worldly that his particular circumstances appear of no obvious relevance to his writing.[65] Nor is there any great sense of development within his theology or hermeneutics, even if we admit there is a lot more theology than did the old orthodoxy of scholarship.[66]

2.12 Gregory of Elvira

Stalwart bishop against Arianism and the Montanist-like Priscillianism, Gregory approved the principle of *triplicem significantiam* in OT exegesis.[67] M. Simonetti has observed that the form of 'Arianism' he opposed was a homoian theology, as approved of at Rimini (359) — that the Son is a slightly

---

[60] See PL 15, 1851-1962.

[61] M. Roques (1996) has recently argued convincingly for receiving this text as authentically Ambrosian; he shows (424) that its paragraph 38 was the basis for some of the *Expositio in Lucam*, which, as the most recent study attests, was compiled from sermons delivered between 386 and 390: Graumann (1994), 'Einleitung'.

[62] Singled out for mention by Cassiodorus in his list of writers on the Song.

[63] So, Dassmann (1978), 374; Courcelle (1968), 122-32.

[64] Sagot (1981b), 13, provides a compromise by suggesting that there might well have been a re-editing which would have allowed Ambrose access to Jerome's Hexaplaric revision of the text (387).

[65] A point well made by McLynn (1994), 336f.

[66] See Dassmann (1978). A revising, more positive intellectual portrait is painted by Markschies (1994) and Graumann (1994).

[67] *Tract. Origenis* 5,1; CCL 69, 34.

lesser (because visible) form of the greater invisible God.⁶⁸ Against this heresy Gregory argued, in the *De fide* (360s), that Father and Son are one, not because they are identical, but because they are equal. The Son's nature did not change but was hidden because it was 'unseeable' by humans. As for the dating of the Commentary on the Song, he seems to have had some knowledge of Jerome's translation (383) of Origen's two homilies, but not of Rufinus' work (c.410). Yet why that should mean that any second edition by Gregory's own hand, which Schulz-Flügel argues for, has to be dated as late as the first few years of the Fifth Century, as she demands, is unclear.⁶⁹ The CCL edition will provide the text for examination,⁷⁰ but as supplemented by Schulz-Flügel's edition.

2.13 Gregory of Nyssa

Apart from a handful of brief mentions, the Song does not appear in works prior to the Fifteen Homilies, as if Gregory had been saving up his comments for that task or more likely had lately come to realise the significance of the book.⁷¹ H. Langerbeck's edition (*GNO* VI) rightly highlights the Syriac translation's pre-eminence as a textual witness.⁷²

In attempting to fix the occasion of these homilies, Daniélou wrote: "On imagine difficilement que ces Homélies d'inspiration mystique aient été données à Nysse. Les sermons donnés par Grégoire dans sa ville épiscopale ont un tout autre ton. Ils concernent avant tout des problèmes moraux."⁷³ G. May, while at odds with J. Daniélou's precise reconstruction of the dating and setting of Gregory's Fifteen Homilies, nevertheless agrees that it must have been in the early 390s.⁷⁴ May argues convincingly that this would be sufficient time for Olympias, the dedicatee of the sermons, having been been given leave by the Emperor Theodosius to abandon her life of preparation for courtly marriage, to have built up in Constantinople her spiritual community ("...also frühestens 391"), the fledgling colony of spiritual men and women

---

⁶⁸ Simonetti (1975a), 14f.
⁶⁹ Schulz-Flügel (1994), 43-51.
⁷⁰ CPL 546; CCL 69:169-210.
⁷¹ The modern critical edition used is that by H. Langerbeck edited under the auspices of W. Jaeger, *Gregorii Nysseni Opera* VI, W. Jaeger (ed.), Leiden, Brill, 1960; referred to henceforth as "GNO VI".
⁷² Not withstanding the criticisms by Dünzl (1993), 5.
⁷³ Daniélou (1966c), 168.
⁷⁴ May (1966), 130, n149 and 131, with reference to GNO VI, 222, suggests that Gregory saw monastic asceticism as an experiment to test what kind of Christian existence was possible partly in response to evidence of slackness of morals among bishops: cf. GNO VI, 398, 7-17.

2. Establishing the Context of the Commentators on the Song

whom Gregory addresses in the Homilies.[75] May admits that Gregory addressed Letters 6, 18 and 21 to a community of monks and nuns at Nyssa and, as J.B. Cahill observes,[76] Gregory would not have neglected his pastoral duties at home in order to preach during Lent to Olympias' community. Although the sermons were possibly inspired by recent travels, notably to Palestine, they would have been delivered at home. However, in favour of supposing that Gregory maintained a public ministry, the most solid piece of information about Gregory in the 390s is that he was last seen alive in public at the 394 Synod of Constantinople[77] and in the conciliar record was ranked in sixth place of importance in the list of delegates, after the Metropolitans and before Amphilochus.[78] May has convincingly argued, contrary to the received image of Gregory as a mystic-writer who withdrew from the public domain into which he had been shunted in the late 370s by Basil's death, that Gregory continued to exert influence on *Kirchenpolitik* and the Emperor himself until as late as 394.[79]

In the event it is probably because of Gregory's untimely death that we have commentary only up to Cant 6:9. Cahill's opinion, that Gregory wrote the preface with only the half-way point reached when he was not sure of living much longer,[80] portrays only half the picture. Gregory reports the concern of an old man who is too busy; he is concerned not only with the amount of time available to him, but also with the lack of peace in his time. In the biblical text the half-way point is at Cant 5:2: if Gregory meant this, it points to his having only just written the first ten homilies. It would appear that these were first published with the preface and the remaining five came later. F. Dünzl[81] argues well that there was a collective audience to whom the addresses were given — thus their homily 'form', although they were redacted by a team for wider dissemination and sent on to Olympias.

Gregory intended the upbuilding of a community not a literary masterpiece: "if we are thought to compare our effort to that of Origen's exhaustive copiousness on this book, let no one accuse us with the apostle's saying that 'Each one will receive his own reward according to his own work'. But my literary work which I composed is not for display."[82] Gregory,

---

[75] May (1971), 64f.
[76] Cahill (1981), esp. 449, n. 2.
[77] According to Mansi iii, 851-2; see PG 119, 821C.
[78] May (1966), 132.
[79] Ibid., 123; see also 130f.
[80] GNO VI, 13, 18-21: εἰ δὲ παράσχοι καὶ ζωῆς χρόνον ὁ τῆς ζωῆς ἡμῶν ταμίας θεὸς καὶ εἰρηνικὴν εὐκαιρίαν, καὶ τοῖς λειπομένοις ἴσως ἐπιδραμούμεθα· νῦν γὰρ ἡμῖν μέχρι τοῦ ἡμίσεος προῆλθεν ὁ λόγος καὶ ἡ θεωρία.
[81] Dünzl (1993), 9f; 17-23.
[82] GNO VI, 13, 3-8: εἰ δὲ τοῦ Ὠριγένους φιλοπόνως περὶ τὸ βιβλίον τοῦτο σπουδάσαντος καὶ ἡμεῖς γραφῇ παραδοῦναι τὸν πόνον ἡμῶν προεθυμήθημεν, ἐγκαλείτω μηδεὶς πρὸς τὸ θεῖον τοῦ ἀποστόλου λόγιον βλέπων, ὅς φησιν ὅτι

with just a touch of impatience, replied that anything which produces spiritual results is not to be regarded as an unusual method of exposition.[83]

The slightly earlier companion piece *De Vita Moysis* includes no defence of allegory but assumes spiritual *theoria* as a good to be appreciated. R. Heine suggests that Gregory's opponents were from the Antiochene school of Diodore,[84] for example Theodore, and understands them as those referred to at the start of the Prologue[85] where Gregory mentions τίσι τῶν ἐκκλησιαστικῶν. They "uphold the literal sense of Scripture and do not concede (συντίθενται) anything in it to be speaking enigmatically with deeper meanings for our benefit. I think it is a priority to answer those who reproach us about these things". Heine translates the above Greek phrase as "certain clerics", although it could just as well mean "certain orthodox".[86] Yet Heine's argument confines itself to literary "correspondences" for lack of any historical evidence of confrontation, adducing as evidence (e.g.) Theodore's literal approach to the Song.[87] However, Diodore was not opposed to the term allegory as such,[88] while Theodore did not gain the

---

Ἕκαστος τὸν ἴδιον μισθὸν λήψεται κατὰ τὸν ἴδιον κόπον. ἐμοὶ δὲ οὐ πρὸς τὸ ἐπίδειξίν ἐστι συντεταγμένος ὁ λόγος. It is possible here that Gregory makes a wry allusion to Origen's doctrine of *post mortem* judgement.

[83] *Prologus* (GNO VI, 5, 6-9): ὧν τὴν διὰ τῆς ἀναγωγῆς θεωρίαν εἴτε τροπολογίαν εἴτε ἀλληγορίαν εἴτε τι ἄλλο τις ὀνομάζειν ἐθέλοι, οὐδὲν περὶ τοῦ ὀνόματος διοισόμεθα, μόνον εἰ τῶν ἐπωφελῶν ἔχοιτο νοημάτων· (GNO VI, 5,19-6,5) ἀλλὰ νῦν μὲν ἀλλάσσειν φησὶ τὴν φωνήν, μέλλων μετάγειν τὴν ἱστορίαν εἰς ἔνδειξιν τῆς περὶ τῶν διαθηκῶν οἰκονομίας, εἶτα μνησθεὶς τῶν δύο τοῦ Ἀβραὰμ τέκνων, τῶν ἔκ τε τῆς παιδίσκης καὶ τῆς ἐλευθέρας αὐτῷ γεγονότων, ἀλληγορίαν ὀνομάζει τὴν περὶ αὐτῶν θεωρίαν, πάλιν δὲ πράγματά τινα διηγησάμενος τῆς ἱστορίας φησὶν ὅτι Τυπικῶς μὲν συνέβαινεν ἐκείνοις, ἐγράφη δὲ πρὸς νουθεσίαν ἡμῶν. For the idea that just as the Incarnation involved the *philanthropia* of the created revealing the creaturely — where there was spiritual enlightenment — so too the words of Scripture are not to be taken at face value, cf. *Contra Eunom.* III, 4,53; GNO II, 154.

[84] Heine (1984), 366f.

[85] GNO VI, 4,10-13.

[86] See Lampe (1961), 433.

[87] Heine (1984), 366-68, referring to Swete (ed.) I, 73; but cf. I, 79: "*allegoriam* vocans illam comparationem quae ex dudum factis negotiis comparari poterat illis quae ad praesens sunt." The main difference between Theodore and Gregory was that for the former any biblical passage without value when read literally should not be counted as Scripture. The key issue was just what *sursum Hierusalem* meant: Theodore demythologises it to mean our state of indwelling Christ (83): "ad comparationem ergo huius illam nominavit *quae sursum est Hierusalem*; conversationem nostram illam quam in caelis habemus hoc modo indicans, eo quod illo commorabimur simul cum Christo degentes."

[88] For Diodore, Paul used the word ἀλληγορία to show that whenever it was to be thought of it should be understood as meaning θεωρία. See *Prologus* in Olivier (ed.), (1980), 7: ...οὐ κωλυόμεθα σεμνῶς ἐπιθεωρεῖν καὶ εἰς ἀναγωγὴν ὑψηλοτέραν ἀποφέρειν τὰ νοήματα. This, neither rejecting history (as Greeks) nor *theoria* (as Jews) is

seniority to criticise colleagues by episcopal pronouncement before 392. One surmises either that the attack on allegorising was not something Gregory was defending himself against, or that he was being maligned by a more major figure, perhaps a sponsor of Theodore.[89] Chrysostom confined himself to insisting on the *akolouthia* of events and to explaining that *allegoria* simply means 'proclamation'.[90]

However the senior statesman Epiphanius had recently written: "We are required to take these numbers thoughtfully according to the 'uplift' of the 'insight' (θεωρία), not overstepping, not talking of vain matters, but measuring the words in truth through the true scriptures with true insights (θεωρίαις)."[91] In 392-3, whilst preaching in Jerusalem, Epiphanius had turned his anti-heretical activities towards Origenist tendencies in the East. The collection of latter-day heresies in the *Panarion* suggests Epiphanius viewed Apollinarianism, Origenism and even Messalianism[92] as sharing a common Trinitarian flaw. He had dedicated his *De gemmis* (hyperbaric in its literalism) to Diodore of Tarsus,[93] quite probably around 392, and may have given Jerome a copy when they met in Bethlehem in 394. Flavian owed a lot to the Cappadocians who had defended his cause in the Antiochene schism after his master Meletius' death, against the Western Nicenes on the one side and Epiphanius on the other.[94] However, by the 390s the Antiochenes had made peace with Epiphanius (indeed perhaps the latter had realised by then the unsuitability of Paulinus and his tainting with tritheism). Gregory's doctrinal sympathies were not always predictable: the whole tenor of the *Antirrheticus* (*GNO* III.1) shows that, whatever earlier hesitations, by the time of his Song Commentary Gregory was opposed to the idea of any loss of divine-human distinction; the "drop of wine in the ocean" was not noticeable

---

very similar to Gregory's opinion, that *theoria* is all about finding a lasting spiritual sense in the Old Testament.

[89] See, e.g., Devreesse (1949), XVI.

[90] *In Epist ad Galat Comm.* 72: τῆς τῶν πραγμάτων ἀκολουθίας"...(73f): Καταχρηστικῶς τὸν τύπον ἀλληγορίαν ἐκάλεσεν. Ὁ δὲ λέγει, τοῦτό ἐστιν · ἡ μὲν ἱστορία αὕτη · οὐ τοῦτο δὲ μόνον παραδηλοῖ, ὅπερ φαίνεται, ἀλλὰ καὶ ἄλλα τινὰ ἀναγορεύει · διὸ καὶ ἀλληγορία κέκληται. Τί δὲ ἀνηγόρευσεν ; Οὐδὲν ἕτερον, ἢ τὰ παρόντα πάντα.

[91] Epiphanius *De fide* 3; GCS 37, 499, 6-10: ὧν τοὺς ἀριθμοὺς εἰς νοῦν λαμβάνοντες κατὰ τὴν ἀναγωγὴν τῆς θεωρίας ἐπεργάσασθαι ἐν τῳ τόπῳ ἀναγκαζόμεθα διὰ τὸ μὴ ὑπερβαίνειν, οὐ ψυχρολογοῦντες, ἀλλ' ἐν ἀληθείᾳ λόγους διὰ τῶν ἀληθινῶν γραφῶν ταῖς ἀληθιναῖς θεωρίαις ἀντεξετάζοντες. I see no reason why this supplement to the *Panarion* could not have been penned by Epiphanius.

[92] See *Pan* 80, 1, 4; GCS 37, 485.

[93] So, F. Foggini's introduction to the *De Gemmis* at PG 43, 305-20. Bardenhewer alone among the Patrologies prefers Diodore of Tyre, bishop from 381, according to the *DCB*.

[94] On the Antiochene schism and the Council of Constantinople (381), see Dechow (1990), esp. 77ff; Simonetti (1975a), esp. 446-53. Also, Spoerl (1993).

in its effect until after Christ was/will be glorified, and not during his earthly life.[95] Gregory's love of metaphor in theology could have meant he continued to be suspect as a maverick.

Statements such as "the Spirit bubbling in us erotically"[96] in Gregory's First Homily on the Song, were, as Daniélou observed, much more 'Messalian' than 'Evagrian'. Although, as Daniélou admits, there are no actual references to the sect as such by name,[97] his description of the ideal cenobitic community in the "Hypotypose" (i.e., *De Instituto Christiano*) may have both inspired and been dependent on the Messalian community for its details. As late as 393 Gregory wrote to Flavian to complain that Helladius had snubbed him for painting a profile of an ideal candidate that looked very Messalian during the elections to the see of Nicodemia.[98] Gregory's admiration for Macarius is clear as he remodelled and 'corrected'[99] much of the latter's "Great Letter". J. Gaith concludes: "La réduction de tout dynamisme à l'amour nous livre l'aspect le plus profond et le plus original de la conception grégorienne de la liberté."[100] One might compare with Gregory's Homilies those of Ps-Macarius which contain citations of and allusions to verses from the Song, especially Cant 2:5.[101] The idea of *epektasis*, the insatiety of joy, was first in Macarius then in Gregory.[102] God is known through his energies, according to Gregory[103] and these energies relate to the Holy Spirit as breathed out by the soul of Christ after his resurrection — as favoured by Messalians.[104] "For the Spirit is the life of the soul, and on this account the Lord came, in order to give his Spirit to the soul on this earth."[105] Messalian anthropology was unorthodox.[106] Fasting and baptism were only efficacious for the body; the soul needed direct heavenly aid of the Spirit (as controlling mind) rather than moral effort. The Spirit is thus granted much power, as an invited guest.

---

[95] See Stead (1994), 207f: "even so his (Gregory) language seems extravagant"; also, e.g., D. Balás (1985).
[96] GNO VI, 27, 13: μόνῳ τῷ πνεύματι ζέειν ἐρωτικῶς
[97] Daniélou (1966c), 132.
[98] Ep. XVIII. See Staats (1994), 607-13, esp. 609; also Staats (1982), 241f.
[99] Parmentier (1977), 299; Stewart (1991), 79.
[100] Gaith (1953), 200.
[101] Logos NA, 6-8: Berthold (1973), II, 135-137;...ἔρωτι πνεύματος οὐρανίου τετρωμένη, καὶ πόθον ἔμπυρον διὰ τῆς χάριτος ἀεὶ ἐν ἑαυτῇ ἀνακινεῖ πρὸς τὸν οὐράνιον νυμφίον. . (136,25f)
[102] See Berthold (1973), 136,16ff.
[103] Cf. Louth (1981), 91, with reference to the 6th Homily on the Beatitudes, 1269A.
[104] Cf. Guillaumont (1980), 1080f.
[105] Cf. Hom 30,6; GA Maloney's translation: (1992), 192.
[106] So, Guillaumont (1980).

Gregory also wrote *Ad Ablabium quod non sint tres dii* when old ("ἡμῶν τῶν γερόντων"),[107] to counter allegations of tritheism, or subordinationism according to a divine hierarchy, with the Spirit more an effluent of divine substance than God in the highest.[108] Gregory believed the Spirit was a divine *hypostasis* but it is not clear to what extent he thought he was a person in as full a way as Son and Father, quite probably because His mode of origin was uncertain. When commenting on the Song Gregory is not only old, he is perhaps approaching the borderlands of orthodoxy.

2.14 Epiphanius of Salamis

Epiphanius's two chief works, the *Ancoratus* and the *Panarion*, are to be found in *GCS* 25, 31 and 37.[109] All were edited by K. Holl early this century; however the second and third volumes have been revised by J. Dummer.[110] According to scholarly consensus,[111] Epiphanius wrote the former in 374 and the latter in a three-year stretch from 374-77.

Epiphanius ends his *Panarion* with an attack on the Messalian heresy. According to R. Staats,[112] the Church around the Mediterranaean appears to have become acquainted with Messalianism only in the last decade of the fourth century. Whereas the Theodosian promulgation against sects of 381 does not mention them, they are condemned by the Council of Side, which Staats wants to date nearly seventeen years later than its received[113] dating of 383. "Die Spätdatierung von Side (vor 400) ist wegen der obengenannten, relativ wohlwollenden Bewertung messalianischer Phänomene bei namhaften Kirchenvätern noch in 80er Jahren wahrscheinlicher als die Frühdatierung (nach 383)."[114] It would therefore seem that Epiphanius's opposition to the Messalians would have crystallized in its written form at least a decade after 377 (the received *terminus ante quem*), around the time "the Origenist controversy" was brewing.

The *Suntomos* (commonly known as the *De Fide*)[115] which follows smoothly and seamlessly on from the last words of the eightieth and last

---

[107] Bardenhewer (1923), 202.

[108] Cf. Staats (1979), 251: "An Basilius, Makarius-Symeon und besonders an Gregor von Nyssa war uns deutlich geworden, daß charismatische und asketische Gruppen prämessalianischen Typus durchaus die Konzilereignisse mit beeinflußt haben könnten."

[109] CPG 3745.

[110] For the necessity of this revision, in part due to Holl's over-fondness for conjectural emendation, and the reaction of e.g., H. Lietzmann against this, see: Dummer (1987).

[111] See, e.g., Altaner (1960), 281-84.

[112] Staats (1994), 607-13

[113] See Mansi (1758-98), iii, 651f, following Photius.

[114] Staats (1994), 609.

[115] GCS 37, 496-526.

chapter of the *Panarion* proper is noteworthy for three things. (1) According to J. Dummer, the text of the *De Fide* is marked by *lacunae* at crucial points.[116] (2) He seems to be using terminology and numerology beloved of certain heretics, notably the Valentinians (read: "Apollinarians") against them, with all the inconsistency and apparent *non sequitur*s typical of an *ad hominem* style. Both the above features make the argument difficult to follow. (3) If any one piece of Scripture dominates this "coda" to Epiphanius's major work, and hence has a shaping influence on the whole *Panarion*, it is the small cluster of verses following Cant 6:8. While it would be over-speculative to hold that this became a key text in a debate,[117] Epiphanius found his echo in Philastrius, the contemporary of Ambrose, through whom Augustine took over Epiphanius' list of eighty heresies.[118]

2.15 Pseudo-Theophilus of Alexandria

A short excerpt of a comment on the Song appears in PG 87, 1629B. This is, however, even shorter than that in the Meursius edition of the Eusebius-Polychronius-Psellus *catena*, which is in turn based on *Bodleian. Misc.* 36, as reprinted in PG 6, 1604.[119] However, R.M. Grant has contested the genuineness of the excerpt and attributes it all — except for the last sentence which is by Gregory of Nyssa whose name is clearly given to the next excerpt a few lines on (PG 87, 1630C) — to Philo of Carpasia. Grant claims that there has been a scribal misreading of "Philo" as "Theophilus". Comparing Philo on Cant 3:6 (PG 40, 83BC) and the excerpt, there is undoubtedly a resemblance of ideas and a common explanation of the "litter" as the saints in whom Christ rests, but the wording is not particularly close. M. Richard commented that the confusing (or perhaps baroque) manner of interpreting φορεῖον as now the body of Christ, now love, now God-bearing souls, is either to be explained by the text's being of composite authorship, or by its being of a late fourth century origin, possibly by the Alexandrian Theophilus.[120] "On serait presque tenté de ne retenir comme vraiment authentiques que les deux phrases citées par Procope. Si l'on conserve tout le texte édité par Meursius, il faut plutôt l'attribuer à Théophile d'Alexandrie; car cette exégèse compliquée se comprend mieux sous la plume d'un auteur

---

[116] Dummer (1987), 121.

[117] Even if we follow Holl (1928, 95-98) and assume that the Ἀνακεφαλαίωσις (*De fide*) is not by Epiphanius, it was there to be used by Augustine in 428.

[118] Philastrius, *Diversarum Hereseon Liber*, CSEL 38, 123f: "...putant eum mulierum et iuvenarum atque concubinarum numerum edixisse...ignorantes quod haec rationabilia sunt et intellectibilia ab eodem nuntiata...".

[119] Richard (1938), 396: "La chaîne de Procope n'en cite qu'une partie".

[120] Ibid., 396f.

du IVe siècle. À notre avis la question reste ouverte." In support of Richard's choice of Theophilus of *Alexandria*, there is the consideration that apart from one small example of exegesis preserved by Jerome in *Ep.* 121, there are *no* other signs of the *Antiochene* Theophilus' writings being preserved in *catenas*. (In fact, *CPG* shows that apart from this and the fragment under discussion, only *Ad Autolycum* is attributed to the Antiochene bishop.[121]) In addition Origen seems presupposed and there is the similarity to the other *catena* fragments bearing the name of the Alexandrian Theophilus given by Richard.[122]

2.16 Rufinus and his translation of Origen's Commentary on the Song of Songs

The first half of the original was written during the period spent in Athens between 244 and 246; it saw Origen at a turning point between adding to his speculative daring the elements of pragmatic spirituality of the Commentary on Matthew and the offensive-taking apologetics of the *Contra Celsum*.[123] At the time of writing Origen was fresh from a series of homilies on historical books of the OT — as confirmed in *Prol* 4, 2;[124] thus it may then be valid for Crouzel in the *Sources Chrétiennes* edition to interpret the content of the text in the light of the use other LXX texts by Origen.

The edition is that of Baehrens (*Origenes Werke* VIII). Rufinus' translation of this commentary was his last piece of work; death's interruption is an adequate explanation of why it proceeds only to Cant 2:15. What we have before us bears the stamp of Rufinus; yet it is a moot point as to how much he has changed the tenor of Origen's thought. According to a consensus of opinion, Rufinus took an increasing amount of liberty with the Greek of his master. Although of course this does not mean that his witness to the *ipsissima vox* of Origen is less valuable than what is provided by others more antagonistic towards him; if anything Rufinus adopts a middle way.[125] However, it was still Rufinus' own way.[126] B. Studer argues convincingly that, in the statement: "*Post haec omnia, quae sunt, a deo facta esse, et nihil*

---

[121] CPG I, p. 53f.

[122] The first fragment, [Richard, (1938), 389] has: Οὐ γὰρ εὐλογία κατὰ Ὠριγένην ἐστὶν ἡ τῶν σωμάτων ποίησις, ἀλλὰ κατάρα πλανωμέναις ψυχαῖς (Barb. gr. 569; Vat. gr. 747).

[123] Le Boulluec (1985), 460.

[124] Baehrens (1925), p. 80,1ff; see also, SC 376, p. 757f.

[125] Sfameni Gasparro (1987); Winkelmann (1970).

[126] Cf., e.g., the generous use of "Trinitas" even where we can be sure the Greek only had ὁ Θεός. Also, N. Pace (1990). So, B. Studer (1972), 405: "Mehr als einmal steht vor und nach dem Gebrauch von Trinitas einfach Deus."

esse quod factum non sit praeter naturam patris et filii et spiritus sancti..." (*De Principiis* 4,8,8), Rufinus added the last five words.[127] Thus it is possible to imagine that Rufinus has toned down more speculative elements in favour of the emphasis on spirituality: there is a tendency to psychologise that which would have been cosmological in Origen. It seems, overall, that the translator was not ashamed of Origen when it came to 'lesser' issues. Origen's writings could be accused of heresy (and these were the things Rufinus would omit, regarding them as interpolations) only when dealing with the subject of the Trinity.[128] It was part of Rufinus' apologetic to insist that those who esteemed Origen were actually anti-Arian.[129]

E. Clark notices these two points (Origen's Alexandria as the fount for cosmic theology and strong Trinitarianism) as features of the 390s 'Origenism' but omits to connect them. The fight against Arianism and the resistance of corporeal images (both of which detracted from the Son's deity) were connected, especially in Egypt (a location of which Rufinus had first hand knowledge). According to the *Epistle to Melania* 6, bodies and souls will be raised to the level of νόες. As one of Rufinus and Melania's circle, Evagrius also wrote that Christ is the only one who has the One in him and alone knows the One essentially;[130] ordinary human beings had lost that image in the process of enfleshment.[131] What Christ did was to bring saving knowledge to the corporeal nature and thus within reach of the human νοῦς who has then to seek it by contemplation of the Trinity as revealed by Christ. Rufinus was more balanced than Evagrius in his Origenism, and he chose works to translate which would console; he also theorized that his work should be free enough to change content as well as to cut (as interpolation) and add (as paraphrasis). We have in the Latin version of this commentary a

---

[127] Studer (1972), 408.

[128] Cf. Clark (1992), 14-16. There is continuity between what Rufinus translated at II, 5 (Baehrens, p. 146): "Sed et iuxta quorundam quaestiones utrum [sc. anima] facta an omnino a nullo sit facta; et, si facta sit, quomodo facta sit, utrum, ut putant aliqui, in semine corporali etiam ipsius substantia continetur et origo eius pariter cum origine corporis traducitur, an perfecta extrinsecus veniens parato iam et formato intra viscera muliebria corpore induitur" and at (*Apologia ad Anastasium* 27; CCL 20, 6:10-13): "Alii factas iam olim, id est, tunc cum omnia Deus creavit ex nihilo, nunc eas iudicio suo disponset nasci in corpore. Hoc sentit et Origenes et nonnulli alii Graecorum", followed by the conclusion to the effect that 'all I know for sure is what the Church has clearly handed down', i.e.:"Deum esse et animarum et corporum conditorem."(18-19).

[129] Cf. *Apolog. ad Anast.* 2; CCL 20,25: "Quamvis igitur fides nostra persecutionis haereticorum tempore, cum in sancta Alexandrina ecclesia degeremus...et nunc si qui est, qui vel tempatare fidem nostram cupit vel audire vel discere, sciat quod de Trinitate ita credimus...Nec inter Patrem et Filium et Spiritum Sanctum sit prorsus ulla diversitas, nisi quod ille Pater est et hic Filius et ille Spiritus Sanctus."

[130] Cf. Keph. Gnos. III, 2&3 (the S1, original text); also Guillaumont (1962), 245.

[131] Cf. Clark (1992), 92-95; 100f.

moderating of speculative elements — a method previously adopted in the *De Principiis* translation — even to the extent of writing "some say" before the opinion that the *exinanivit* of Phil 2:6f applies to *that* soul.[132] As concerns *De Principiis* III, J. Rist has observed we have here examples of cosmology switched to morality, and philosophy changed into rhetoric.[133] The Romans commentary comes via Rufinus and shows signs of fence-sitting similar to that of *De Principiis* on teaching concerning the pre-cosmic fall of souls.[134] Unfortunately, in the case of the Canticles Commentary we do not have much of the Greek text preserved (the one exception is *Philocalia* 27,13) which might give us an indication of the extent to which Rufinus was free with it. In the passage which refers to the figure of the Sun in Cant 1:6 there are two examples of significant changes by Rufinus in addition to his omission of Origen's detail that the slave-labour of the Israelites in Egypt was done "in the valleys". First, where the Greek has: "Pharaoh, having a ruling principle which was not pure of mud, wanted the Hebrews to work mud", the Latin has simply: "And indeed his heart was muddy and miry in accordance with the things he thought about".[135] However, four lines later, Rufinus gives his own explanation, without parallel in the Greek text: "The Sun of Righteousness hardened Pharaoh's heart, in which there were muddy thoughts, for reason of the qualities of his motions." The Greek simply has, "in the same way he was hardened by God's rays visiting Israel." It would appear that Rufinus has understood what is said about the divine activity as meaning a judgment on the motions of the evil human heart, carried out by the person of Christ. There is no place for a cosmic dualism and the devil's work to which Origen himself would have attributed more responsibility. The phrase *motuum suorum qualitatibus* may reflect (as the opposite of *apatheia*) Evagrian thinking. Similarly, whereas the Greek at the end of the excerpt mentions that

---

[132] See, especially, *De Princ.* 4,4,4 at Koetschau (GCS 22), p. 354, 19ff: "De qua anima, quoniam totam in se sapientiam dei et veritatem vitamque receperat...Quis enim alius hic intellegendus est Christus, qui 'in deo absconditus' dicitur et postea 'appariturus', nisi ille, qui 'oleo laetitiae' unctus refertur, id est substantialiter deo repletus, in quo nunc 'absconditus' dicitur? Propterea enim et omnibus credentibus ad exemplum Christus exponitur, quia sicut ille semper et antequam 'sciret' omnino 'malum' sed 'elegit bonum'...Quidam autem volunt de ipsa anima dictum videri, cum primum de Maria corpus adsumit, etiam illud, quod apostolus dicit: 'Qui cum in forma dei esset...'"

[133] Rist (1975).

[134] See Hammond Bammel (1985), 52.

[135] Baehrens, p. 128: βούλεται καὶ τοὺς Ἑβραίους πηλοποιεῖν τὸ ἡγεμονικὸν ἔχων οὐ καθαρὸν πηλοῦ, ὅπερ ὡς πηλὸς ὑπὸ ἡλίου σκληρύνεται, οὕτως ὑπὸ τῶν αὐγῶν τοῦ Θεοῦ ἐπισκοπουσῶν τὸν Ἰσραὴλ ἐσκληρύνθη. // Et erat utique cor eius secundum ea quae cogitabat, luteum et limosum. Et sicut materiam luti sol iste visibilis stringit et indurat, ita 'sol iustitiae' his iisdem radiis, quibus illuminabat populum Istrahel 'Pharaonis cor', cui inerant luteae cogitationes, pro ipsis motuum suorum qualitatibus 'indurabat'."

"God did not heed the groan of those those who called out not from their works, but from the muddy and earthly deeds." Rufinus merely has: "God did not heed their groan, since he does not heed the groan of those who do not shout from their works."[136] It is as if Rufinus deliberately failed to adopt the distinction between spiritual and earthly works, perhaps lest his readership be discouraged from pursuing any works. So, unless the *Philocalia* compilers have themselves done some heavy editing of the piece from the Greek commentary, here is evidence that Rufinus as in other places accommodated Origen's theological exegesis of the Song to the tastes of his own audiences.

T. Heither makes the insightful judgement, based on her own and others' studies of Rufinus' translation method: "Vor allem die philosophische Terminologie des Origenes wird durch Rufin umgeformt...er mag das Werk des Origenes auf die Hälfte reduzieren, man weiß aber nicht, nach welchen Gesichtspunkten Rufin diese Kürzung vornahm... ."[137] As C. Bammel noted there is a simple moral thrust, and this may well be related to the fact that the Groom is presented supremely as the virtuous God-Man. Rufinus has demythologised in order to instruct.

2.17 Augustine

Augustine cites the Song about 175 times, which is not a great deal when one takes into account that there are 45,000 scriptural citations in his work as a whole.[138] The Donatist controversy provided the occasion for Augustine to interpret some of the Song's verses ecclesiologically.

2.18 Theodoret

This full commentary, temperate in its theology and showing signs of monastic influence, was likely the first he wrote, probably before the Nestorian controversy.[139] J.-N. Guinot's judgement challenges the shared preference of Richard and Bardy[140] for a post-Ephesus (431) dating. They

---

[136] Baehrens p. 129, 31-33: οὐκ εἰσακούων στεναγμοῦ τῶν οὐκ ἀπὸ ἔργων βοώντων πρὸς αὐτόν, ἀλλ' ἀπὸ πηλοῦ καὶ τῶν γηίνων πράξεων. // "'Exaudivit Dominus gemitum ipsorum', cum utique non exaudiat eorum gemitum, qui non 'ex operibus suis' clamant ad Dominum."

[137] Heither (1990), 17f.

[138] See Bonnadière (1955), 225.

[139] CPG 6203; PG 81,27-214; see Guinot (1985).

[140] See Richard (1935), 105: "Pas plus dans le commentaire du Cantique des Cantiques, le premier en date de la série, ... on ne saurait trouver la moindre trace de nestorianisme, ni même de ces formules un peu archa ques dans lesquelles la nature humaine du Christ est

had supposed that Theodoret was nothing other than a radical Antiochene during the 420s, ready to polemicize at the slightest opportunity; so it had to be written after he was "tamed". Such an *idée fixe* may explain why Garnier, in his prologue to the edition in Migne, went so far as to doubt the attribution of the commentary to Theodoret. Bardy showed however that it is attested to be Theodoret's work by as early a witness as Pelagius II,[141] even if the young Theodoret surprises the informed reader with an exclusively tropological interpretation.

In discussing the appropriate mode of interpretation, Theodoret lists a number of Fathers who took his book to be spiritual; in the list he includes Diodore and John Chrysostom "and those after (or with) them".[142] The Song was just an extended example of the kind of figurative writing found throughout the Old Testament.[143] He claims their approval despite the apparent absolute dearth of commentary on the Song by any other Antiochene.

Schäublin's thesis, that Theodoret and Theodore were representatives of two diverging streams from Diodore as their common source, should be restricted to their methods of exegesis and not extended wholesale to their respective theologies.[144] It is not certain that Theodore (d. 428) wrote his attack on the Song *before* Theodoret's commentary.

2.19 Nilus of Ancyra

Discovering what Nilus had to say about the Song is troublesome.[145] The chief problems are: (1) the question of who this writer was and which other works can be attributed to him so as to provide a context for our understanding of this work, (2) the complicated state of the Song of Songs *catenae* manuscript tradition, as well as the often elliptical nature of the comments on the Song attributed to Nilus.

As for Nilus' identity, K. Heussi wanted to preserve Nilus as a good Constantinopolitan whose memory was cherished by medieval Byzantine monasteries. He could not therefore be confused with the author-protagonist

---

désignée par une expression concrète et qui abondent dans les premiers écrits de l'évêque de Cyr." Bardy (1946): "L'evêque de Cyr rédigea l'explication du Cantique à la demande d' un certain Jean, que l'on identifie parfois à Jean d'Antioche (429-441), mais qui est plus probablement Jean de Germanicie (431-459)."

[141] In *Epist.* v, 20 (PL 72, 736).

[142] PG 81, 32C: καὶ οἱ μετ' ἐκείνους [cod. ἐκείνων].

[143] Ἔδει δὲ αὐτοὺς συνιδεῖν, ὅτι καὶ ἐν τῇ Παλαιᾷ πολλὰ τροπικῶς ἡ θεία λέγει Γραφή (PG 81, 33A).

[144] Schäublin (1974).

[145] CPG 6703.

of the *Account of the Raid on the monks of Sinai*, who was probably Anastasius of Sinai.[146] Heussi dismissed the witness of Nicephorus, the tenth-century historian, that Nilus left Ancyra for Egypt, as a romantic Byzantine (re)construction. However he opined that Georgios Monachos' information that Nilus was a disciple of Chrysostom was reliable.[147] Thus Nilus was based in Asia and was a contemporary (according to Georgios) of Proclus, Palladius, Mark the Hermit (Mark has been shown by Grillmeier[148] to have been an Origenist who flourished in the earlier part of the Fifth Century) and Isidore. This would place Nilus in the period just prior to the Council of Ephesus (431). This accords with other things which Nicephorus says about him on which Heussi had no reason to doubt him. This includes the information that Theodoret joined this group of monks a little later.[149] Heussi's conclusion, that there was one 'Asian' Nilus, who was responsible for the majority of the corpus which is under that name, and some other unknown person, to whom could be allotted the authorship of *Peristeria* (ascetical advice) and the *Account of the Raid* (*Narratio* or *Narrationes*), became almost a given of scholarship.[150]

However, a challenge appeared in the 1967 dissertation by H. Ringshausen who tried to demonstrate that all the major works of the Nilan corpus, *Peristeria* and the *Narrationes* included, were by the one Nilus, born in Ancyra but writing in Egypt. Thus Nilus' works are, along with the Commentary on the Song, *Peristeria*, *Narrationes* (Διηγήματα), *Sermo in Luc 22,36*, *De voluntaria paupertate* and *Epistularum Libri IV*. Ringshausen attributes what distinguishes each one to their respective genres. He speaks positively about the high "Berührungsquantität" and "Berührungsintensität" between the Commentary and the *Peristeria* (a coincidence every five columns),[151] and while that with the *Narrationes* is much less (every 13 columns), this he excuses on the grounds that "Märtyrerromane" and biblical Commentary are as far apart generically as is possible.[152] Likewise he is sanguine that the same author was responsible for the letters. He concedes that the Nilus-attributed *De Oratione* might have been by Evagrius, discounting Heussi's main witness, Georgios, as "äußeren Zeugen", who could only have known about Nilus's Antiochene 'juvenile' period before he became a writer.[153] Ringshausen wanted to put *Peristeria*, the Commentary,

---

[146] See Heussi (1920), 149.
[147] Ibid., 30.
[148] Grillmeier (1980).
[149] PG 146, 1249-52; Heussi (1920), 22.
[150] See Altaner, Quaesten, and Bardenhewer who all would detach *Peristeria* (CPG 6047) and the *Narratio* (CPG 6044) from the figure of Nilus of Ancyra.
[151] Ringshausen (1967), 23.
[152] Ibid., 26.
[153] Ibid., 59 & 64.

the Sinaitic *Narrationes* and *De voluntaria paupertate* together as the work of this Sinaitic Nilus. The spurious *De oratione* and *De monastica exercitatione* would then be from Evagrius or his 'school'. J. Gribomont, whose preference would be to preserve the integrity of all the work attributed to our author, comments: "...he (Ringshausen) may be right, at least in part. This would (still) leave us with two authors both called Nilus."

Now it is apparent that the content of the exegesis of Cant 7:4 is similar in *Peristeria* to that of the Commentary on Cant 6:9ff (as edited by S. Luca) without it being so close as to suggest copying of one from the other.[154] From this it would appear that the *Canticles Commentary* is a little more developed; it too contains the idea of the impregnability of the Christian mind to foreign ideas, but put in terms of the nature imagery which the Song supplies. In which case we would have an Egyptian author of the *Canticles Commentary* and *Peristeria*, and an Antiochene author of *De monastica exercitatione* (Λόγος Ἀσκητίκος).[155] This last work has great similarities with the offering of Chrysostom on the same subject, *Adversus oppugnatores vitae monasticae*,[156] which in turn, according to Guérard, is sufficiently Evagrian to raise a suspicion that Evagrius, not Chrysostom was its true author. In a mixed reference to Cant 2:2 and Mt 6:28f, the writer compares the perfect soul to the lily of the valley which is without anxiety.[157] Moreover, in the Λόγος Ἀσκητίκος there is the motif of doves and turtle-doves.[158] Yet on inspection the concerns do remind one as much of Chrysostom as of Evagrius. It is basically 'ethical' in tone with much OT citation and is rarely

---

[154] Cf., as Luca (1982), 382 notes, the similarity of the exegesis: in *Peris.* (PG 79, 961AB): Τράχηλός σου ὡς πύργος ἐλεφάντινος. Ποτὲ μὲν τὸ διανεστηκὸς τῆς ἀρετῆς, καὶ διεγηγερμένον τοῦ βίου, ποτὲ δὲ τὸ ταπεινὸν τοῦ φρονήματος, ποτὲ δὲ δηλῶν τὸ ἀνεπίβατον οἰήσεως λογισμοῖς. Οὔτε γὰρ ἐλεφαντίνῳ πύργῳ προσβῆναί τι ἢ προσέρθαι, μὴ ἔχον ἀντιλαβεῖν, δύναται, ἀπολισθαῖνον ἅμα τῷ πλησιάσαι διὰ τὴν λειότητα.

[155] CPG 6046.

[156] CPG 4307; PG 47: 319-86. See Guérard (1982), 348f. Also, F. Conca (1982) concludes (225) that the love of metaphors pervades even the letters (which he wants to take as genuine): "... Nilo poteva forse trovare un modello molto vicino proprio nelle opere di Giovanni Crisostomo." But see, *per contra*, Alan Cameron (1976).

[157] PG 79, 800D: Τελείας ψυχῆς ἐστι τὸ ἀμέριμνον, ἀσεβοῦς δὲ τὸ ταῖς φροντίσι κατατρίβεσθαι. Περὶ μὲν γὰρ τελείας ψυχῆς εἴρηται, ὅτι κρίνον ἐστὶν ἐν μέσῳ ἀκανθῶν.

[158] PG 79, 745D: Καλὸν οὖν, ἀγαπητοί, καλὸν, πάλιν εἰς τὴν ἀρχαίαν ἀναβῆναι μακαριότητα, καὶ τῆς τῶν παλαιῶν ἐπιδράξασθαι πολιτείας. Ἔστι γὰρ πᾶσιν εὔκολος, ὡς νομίζω, θελήσασι, κἂν δὲ τις προσῇ πόνος, οὐκ ἄκαρπος ἔσται, ἱκανὸν ἔχων παραμύθιον τὴν τῶν προωδευκότων εὔκλειαν.... . Φύγωμεν τὰς ἐν πόλεσι καὶ κώμαις διαγωγάς, ἵνα οἱ ἐν πόλεσι καὶ κώμαις τρέχωσι πρὸς ἡμᾶς· ἐρημίας μεταδιώξωμεν, ἵνα ἐπισπασώμεθα τοὺς νῦν ἡμᾶς φεύγοντας, εἰ φίλον ὅλως τοῦτό τισι. Καὶ γὰρ περὶ τινων ἐν ἐπαίνῳ γέγραπται, ὅτι... ἐγένοντο ὡς περιστεραὶ μελετητικαί.

speculative. The world-view contains the idea that the life of Christ itself was a shadow of the present post-resurrection fulness.[159] The theme of Christ as the one 'overseer'[160] is one of the themes repeated fairly often, with the corollary that monks can relax in his care and should simply follow his ascetic way. The point is that all these works display such a family resemblance that their differences could be best explained as owing to the one Nilus' development from an orthodox spirituality to a more Evagrian convictions. There may also have been some sympathy for Apollinarius.[161]

In conclusion, as to Nilus' identity, we do well to follow M.-G. Guérard's sober assessment that there was one Nilus, based in Galatia, who belonged to a group of Evagrian spiritualists, a friend of Albianos and Chrysostom (who coincidentally sheltered Egyptian monks). Socrates mentions that Leontius the leader of the Ancyrene community was involved in deposing Chrysostom; this suggests that Nilus belonged to an 'opposition' party in Galatian monasticism.[162] His works all come from the pen of one author whose style developed (with Ringshausen) but who was resident in Galatia (*pace* Ringshausen). Yet, as to dating, he wrote his commentary, not in the closing years of the 390s as Guérard thinks[163] basing this dating on two factors — a knowledge of Gregory of Nyssa's 'individualising' of Origen's Christ-Church hermeneutic, which must be considered a weak piece of evidence, and the allusion to the "inhumation *Ad Sanctos*": "...il ne la reprend pas son compte (τινὲς...εἶπον) et la signale encore comme quelque chose d'exceptionnel. Ce détail nous place toujours à la fin du IVe s., puisqu' une telle pratique est devenue courante pendant le Ve s.."[164] Rather, as Ringshausen points out, "the Account" reports events which themselves must have happened sometime between 380 and 400.[165] The tenth-century *Synaxarium Ecclesiae Constantinopolitaniae* mentions that Nilus "... connut les tribulations du Sinai et de composer des oeuvres ascétiques".[166] This suggests two phases in his life, the second phase being a quieter exile in Asia, and pushes the Song Commentary, stylistically the next most developed, towards the 420s. It is debatable that Nilus's Commentary on the Song is the nearest thing we have to an Evagrian commentary on that book, *pace* Guérard. She suggests that

---

[159] E.g., PG 79, 760A: μετὰ δὲ τὸν σταυρὸν φανερὸς πᾶσι γέγονεν ἐν τῷ οἰκείῳ καιρῷ διὰ τοῦ ξύλου ἀναδειχθείς.

[160] In PG 79, 764A, 773CD, 790CD.

[161] Nilus, *Ep. 1 /257 ad Diocletianum*: τὸν Ἀπολλινάρριον ἐν βίῳ σώφρονι τε καὶ σεμνῷ κατὰ γεγηρακότα τίμιον τε τῷ λόγῳ καὶ ὑπὸ τῶν Ἀρειομανιτῶν καιρῷ δεδιωγμένον: source: Lietzmann (1904), 66, Anm. 1.

[162] Socrates, *HE* VI, 18 (PG 67, 717B).

[163] Guérard (1994), 47.

[164] Ibid., 24.

[165] Ringshausen (1967), 46f.

[166] Guérard (1994), 17.

Nilus intended to complete the trilogy which Evagrius had embarked on with commentaries on Proverbs and Ecclesiastes.[167] However it is far from certain from the relevant passage in the *Historia Lausiaca* that Evagrius was much interested in writing commentaries.[168]

2.20 Cyril of Alexandria

Cyril's comments on the Song are preserved in the fragments which can be culled from the Procopian *catena*. These were edited by Mai in *Patrologia Graeca* 69.[169] In general Cyril's commentaries on the OT come from an early period in his life.

Cyril's hermeneutical approach to the Old Testament is typified by his seeing the book of Hosea as presenting a type of the relationship between Christ and the soul. Cyril went so far as to call Christ a μεσίτης, meaning one who belonged to two spheres of existence and in his one person put God and humanity, into communication with each other. This term can be found in Cyril's *Dialogues on the Trinity*[170] where he argues (through his two 'interlocutors') that it does not apply to the substance of the Son but rather to the obedience of Christ. Cyril thus avoids any implication that by becoming a μεσίτης, the Son had to lose some of the fullness of his divinity.[171] Thus we find an early Cyril of a more Origenian hue than his later emphases would lead us to expect.

2.21 Pseudo-Athanasius: Synopsis Scripturae

Since the work as a whole betrays Chrysostom and Epiphanius as sources, the date must be well into the fifth century.[172] The summaries of the biblical books are fairly brief until it reaches the Wisdom books where they expand to become mini-commentaries, explaining these difficult Scriptures as a whole, and illuminating certain especially hard verses. Klostermann concluded that the text is basically a stitching together of an Athanasian with a

---

[167] Ibid., 43. On the matter of style, see von Balthasar (1939).

[168] See Palladius, *Historia Lausiaca*, c.86 (PG 34, 1194B): Συντάττει οὖν οὗτος τρία βιβλία, Ἱερα, Μοναχὸν, Ἀντιρρητικὸν.

[169] CPG 5205 (4).

[170] See Dialogue 1; SC 231, p. 168, 34-37: Ὅταν οὖν λέγεται μεσίτης, οὐχ ὁριστικὸν τῆς οὐσίας τοῦ Μονογενοῦς οἰηθείη τις ἂν εἶναι τοὔνομα · πολλοῦ γε καὶ δεῖ · περιτρέψειε δ' ἂν μᾶλλον αὐτὸ εἰς ὑπακοὴν τοῦ Χριστοῦ.

[171] See ibid., p. 414.

[172] CPG 2249; PG 28, 349-357. See Klostermann (1895), 109-112. Zahn (1890) too has provided good arguments for dating this work as mid fifth-century.

Chrysostomian synopsis by an anonymous author.[173] He finds evidence for this in the fact that the text speaks neither of περιοχή nor of ἀνακεφαλαίωσις, but of both. They must be therefore post-Chrysostom but no later than the sixth-century edition of the canon by Antiochus of Sabas.[174]

While the synopsis on Ruth is very much cast in the form of an abridged version of the story, the synopsis on the Song is quite different; compared with that on Job, which hardly fills half a column of Migne, or on Isaiah, which takes even less space, it and the other Solomonic books receive disproportionate attention. The interest in these appears to be related not so much to Solomon himself (for Sirach receives full treatment) but a high estimation of biblical wisdom as a genre (Job excluded). Thus the Song has been privileged with a relatively extensive interpretation. By comparison with the florid style of the Psalms *catena* found in PG 27 (649-1344) under the name of Athanasius but attributed to Hesychius, the text in the *Synopsis* is a more rigorous piece of exegesis, making it 'Antiochene' in exegesis, 'Alexandrian' in theology. [175]

2.22 Apponius

Apponius' commentary is in twelve homilies which make up just over 310 pages of *Corpus Christianorum Latinorum* 19.[176] There are several mooring points which should help to locate this writer about whom posterity, including the very manuscript tradition of his commentary, is silent. The opening lines of the commentary give little else away apart from the author's name[177] and the allusion that his dedicatee, the "Armenian presbyter" is somehow like the biblical Daniel. It could be that Apponius meant an Armenian Daniel, perhaps even the one who, at the Persian king's instruction, helped in the first stage of devising the Armenian alphabet.

---

[173] See Klostermann, ibid..

[174] See Zahn (1890); especially 305-312.

[175] Cf. Bardenhewer (1923), 352, re. the connection between the Synopses attributed to Athanasius and Chrysostom: "Allerdings müssen diese beiden Synopsen in Verbindung miteinander erforscht werden. Die handschriftlichen Texte zeugen von gegenseitigen Entlehnungen."

[176] CPL 194.

[177] According to the *OLD* 148, *Aponus* is the name of a warm spring near Padua: "Aponus terris ubi fumifer exit" (Lucan *Phars* 7.19.3); "Apono gaudens populus" (Silvius Italicus 12.218); "fontes Aponus rudes puellis" Martial 6.42.4 Suet. *Tib.* 14.3.

The use of a text very near to the Vulgate in his citations, and his assertion early on that he has used the *exempla Hebraeorum*,[178] establish a case that the commentary must have been written after Jerome's translation would have reached him. To some extent the length of time would depend on his whereabouts in the Empire, although proximity to a cosmopolitan centre such as Aquilieia may have been more advantageous than a location in the Middle East,[179] especially as Jerome wrote with his eye on a Western "market". H.-J. Frede assumes that Apponius must come after Epiphanius Scholasticus,[180] since the latter's translation of Philo of Carpasia's commentary used Jerome's translation of the Hexaplaric text of the Song.[181] Yet it is more likely that Scholasticus was being faithful to Philo. How could he have given *lemmata* which excluded readings which were the basis for exegetical points in the commentary? In citations from other books the Vulgate is not favoured above *Itala*-style readings, although Vregille and Neyrand have observed the clear preference for Jerome's Psalter.[182] Thus P.M. Bogaert's cautious assessment is to be commended: "...on ne peut qu'être surpris du degré de contamination observé dans une traduction faite en 398. Je ne vois d'explication qui s'impose."[183]

J. Witte's thesis for dating Apponius in the first decade of the fifth century rested on, first, the fact of the absence of the name of any heretic more recent than Bonosus, and second, the apparent ignorance of Pelagius or Nestorius. The methodological weakness of the second string of this argument has contributed to doubts voiced at so early a *terminus ante quem*. Suspicion was voiced in 1987 by J.-P. Bouhot's review of the *CCL* edition;[184] he held that the reason Pelagius was not mentioned was more likely to have been because his error was not a Christological one, rather than because Apponius had never heard of Pelagius. This smoothes the way for his conclusion[185] that the Commentary reflects the times of meditative tranquillity of the post-Gregorian world, rather than the troubled early fifth century. However, the

---

[178] König (1992), 5, makes a good case that it is the Vulgate to which "exemplaria Hebraeorum" refers. Cf., at VIII, 96-98 (CCL 19, p. 183): "De quo rore clamat Esaias propheta: Ros, ait, qui abs te est, sanitas est illis; et secundum hebraea exemplaria: Quia ros lucis, ros tuus."

[179] Cf. Duval (1973b) on African influences on North-East Italy mediated by "les orientaux".

[180] Frede (1991), 192.

[181] Ibid., 445.

[182] For these details, see CCL 19, LXXVII ff.

[183] Bogaert (1988), 238f.

[184] Bouhot (1987).

[185] A view pioneered as early as the *Patrologia Latina Supplementum* edition of the commentary (1958) and shared by König, Stubenrauch and now Studer.

first string of Witte's argument is persuasive,[186] since Photinus is given the special treatment one would only devote to a heretic who is perceived as a still present threat.[187] Furthermore, although *Arrii* and *Montani* are categorised, there is no mention of *Photiniani* or *Bonosiani* to suggest Apponius was writing in a period suffering the after-effects of these latter-day heretics.[188] Both Arius and Montanus are named in the list of heretics at II, 206-8: "...*per Basilidem, Valentinum, Fotinum, Apollinarem, Macedonium, Eunomium, Montanum, Catafrigam, Manicheum, Arrium...* ."[189]

Photinus and Bonosus were both fervently opposed by Ambrose. It is Ambrose's preoccupation with Bonosus during an episode in his later ministry that is a yet more precise point of contact with Apponius, given the localised influence of the bishop of Nairsus which means that only those in Gaul over a short period would have found him worth denouncing.[190] The significant dates for the Bonosian affair are 391 (when the Capua Council referred the matter to the Macedonian and Thessalonian bishops under whose jurisdiction Bonosus stood) and 414 (when Innocent I condemned his teaching and ordered a tightening of discipline against Bonosian clerics). Zeiller found that Gennadius (in *De vir Ill 75*) reports that according to Paul of Pannonia, the Bonosians re-emerged in the form of Jovinian's heresy. Both heretics held that Christ's birth was not so extraordinary that anything virginal was required of Mary, but Paul is merely interested in Jovinian as an *exemplum* and neither he nor Gennadius makes any historical connection with Bonosus or the Bonosians. After 420 there is really a silence regarding Bonosians, except for Justinian's instructions to the bishops of Aquae in *Novella* XI.[191] In the case of the Photinians,[192] the fear was of a heresy from Pannonia practically indistinguishable from Arianism in that it refused full divinity to Christ, even if its roots were modalist. Zeiller explains how the Pannonian Arians made common cause with the Photinians against the homoousians at Antioch (341) and Sirmium (351). M. Simonetti paraphrases Hilary's observations: being humbled did not prove that the Son was ever inferior to the Father; and Christ suffered in his human soul; against Arians

---

[186] *In Cant Expositio* II, 263-4; CCL 19, 46: "ubi Fotinus vel Bonosus primi sunt, multitudinem, et non unum redemptorem totius mundi."

[187] XII, 171-4; CCL 19, 273: "sicut insanus Fotinus — ut in alio libello dictum est — non metuit dicere tantos effici christos vel salvatores, quanti reperti fuerint sermone suo et vitae exemplo convertisse impios ab errore, dum unus et solus ab uno Verbo sit adsumptus redemptor Christus et totius mundi salvator..."; also: IX,314-6; CCL 19, 225.

[188] Ibid., II, 275: CCL 19, 47.

[189] CCL 19, p. 44.

[190] See Zeiller (1918), 261: "Photin allait plus loin que son maître [Marcellus], en diminuant plus que lui l'élément divin dans la personne du Christ."

[191] Zeiller (1918), 350.

[192] Truzzi (1985), 127.

who saw him as having heavenly flesh.[193] But this fits with a move towards a climate in which Photinianism, which thought of God "materially", could have flourished: "il corpo di Cristo, pur habitatus et instructus dal Logos, inteso come mera virtus di Dio, era dotato di un'anima umana".[194]

So, although it might for other reasons seem attractive to view the names of Photinus and Bonosus as standing, in Apponius' text, for local outbreaks of the heresies associated with their names long after their lifetimes, this case does require special pleading.

Another method of anchoring Apponius is by applying the criteria of *Wirkungsgeschichte* and *Überlieferungsgeschichte*. Thus Crociani has tried to see the first six books as a bridge between primitive Syrian baptismal theology and the Hiberno-Carolingian prototype for medieval *Hoheliedfrömmigkeit* which is already there in the second six books which complete the good work in the ethos of the "tradition Vosgienne" of mysticism. However, early medieval Irish fondness for the work and its wide circulation amongst Hibernian monks do not prove its early medieval Irish authorship, while many of the baptismal images are shared by Ambrose, as demonstrated by Wenger and Pelletier. Wenger's comparison of the baptismal homilies of Chrysostom and Ambrose reveals more similarities than differences,[195] while, according to A.-M. Pelletier,[196] those of Cyril of Jerusalem show even more affinity with Ambrose, especially in their frequent use of the Song of Songs. The careful work of Vregille and Neyrand suggests that those in the Vosges region had only ever seen the half-commentary owing to some accident or suppression, due to the over-speculative nature of the second six of the twelve Homilies.[197] The witness of the two main traditions which often agree with each other against the 'Vosgeienne' tradition,[198] and which contain the full complement of twelve books, is preferable. The commentary need not be separated on grounds of the content of its two halves: Crociani qualifies his own thesis by providing evidence of continuity between I-VI and VII-IX, 238.[199]

---

[193] Cf. Hilary, *De Trin*. 10.

[194] Simonetti (1975a), 195. Cf. Hübner's analysis (1989), 163-75, based on Philastrius *De haer* 93.

[195] Wenger, introduction in John Chrysostom (1970).

[196] Pelletier (1989), 157-64.

[197] CCL 19, xv: "A l'origine de cette famille {sc. the Vosgiennes mss of Murbach, Lautenbach, Luxeuil} il y aurait eu un archétype en 2 volumes, dont le second se serait perdu." The Murbach ms (=épinal 78) is not such a good text as to warrant some claim to a pre-Caroloingian antiquity.

[198] See ibid., liv-lvi.

[199] Crociani (1990), 77: "...la prima sezione del testo nellla seconda parte dell *Explanatio* ripete molte parti dei primi sei libri o letteralmente o per allusione... ." Also, n. 20: "Per quanto riguarda i testi che si ripetono rispetto alla prima parte si veda sopratutto il libro VIII."

The hard fact that Cassiodorus' list of Commentaries does not mention one by Apponius has persuaded H. König of a *terminus* of 550.[200] "Sicher hat er aber nicht, wie bisher angenommen, zu Beginn des 5. Jahrhunderts, sondern eher in der 2. Hälfte des 6. Jahrhunderts gewirkt."[201] Cassiodorus mentions the Latin versions of Origen's homilies (Jerome) and commentary (Rufinus), and Epiphanius Scholasticus' translation of Epiphanius of Cyprus' (as he thought) succinct commentary. With these words he appears to be saying that he has made a compilation of writers on the Song, with the relevant excerpt from Ambrose's *De Isaac* included as a highlight.[202] What he is *not* doing is giving an exhaustive list of Latin commentaries. Would he really have been unaware of Gregory of Elvira? However the *argumentum ex silentio* applies just as much to what is deduced from Cassiodorus' omission of Apponius — that he must therefore be post-Cassiodorus, as it does to the opinion König opposes — that because Apponius omits to mention Pelagius he must have preceded him.

Yet more vague criteria are proposed in the form of "ethos" and "atmosphere". Studer has sensed the atmosphere of a Western institutional monasticism by then up and running (with reference to the work of K.S. Frank) and Gribomont detected an aura of confidence fitting the world of Gregory the Great.[203] In Apponius there is found an expression of Roman Christian ideology similar to the edicts of Theodosius II and the works of Prosper of Aquitaine (so, Frank[204]). Frank also overvalues, on the basis of a few obscure lines, the significance of Rome and papal ecclesiology as tied to the *vicarius Dei* concept of abbots. This hinges on the equally overstated thesis of B. Jaspert that Apponius extended the monastic theory of ordering into the wider church and political sphere.[205] According to König, he came just after Cassiodorus: "...er gelegentlich Begriffe in dem besonderen und eher seltenen Sinne verwendet, wie dies Cassiodor tut,"[206] listing as some examples uses of (1)*pervasor*, (2)*magister*, (3)*meritum*, (4)*schema*, (5)*consors regni*. However, to take just the last of these, at I, 174 (p. 9) the phrase is used on its own; even if there is an allusion here to Esther 16:13, it shows that Jerome himself felt sufficiently comfortable with the phrase to use it to translate (τὴν ἄμεμπτον) τῆς βασιλείας κοινωνόν (Εσθηρ) — it is

---

[200] König (1991), 129-36.
[201] Ibid.,129.
[202] *Institutes*, I, 5,4; Mynors (1937), p. 24: "quapropter praedicti libri diligentissimos expositores sub uno codice comprehendi, ut simul omnes legentibus offerantur qui tractores unius voluminis extiterunt. unde etiam et sanctus Ambrosius in libro tertio Patriarcharum, ubi de persona Isaac loquitur, multa salubriter luculenterque disseruit."
[203] See his review (1987), 636-39.
[204] Frank (1985b).
[205] Jaspert (1974).
[206] König (1991), p. 101, n.9.

not a sixth century coinage. Furthermore, studies of Cassiodorus' style in his Psalm exegesis and a reading of his comments *en passant* on the Song reveal he inherited an Augustinian type of vision of the Christ-Church union[207] which is quite foreign to Apponius' understanding. R. Schlieben describes Cassiodorus' inheritance: "(f)reilich fühlt sich Cassiodor niemandem geistig so verpflichtet wie Augustin, dem 'doctissimus pater'... . Der zeitgenössische Formalismus (Aristotelismus) der Christologie findet bei Cassiodor seine Entsprechung in der Exegese. Damit ist die von Augustin geforderte Synthese von christlicher und weltlicher Bildung vollzogen."[208]

Vregille and Neyrand observed the verbal similarities between the work of Ps-Pelagius and Apponius' *Expositio*. Studer and König have countered by arguing that the similarities are confined to the Prologues which in any case are based on a standard form. Yet Studer does say that there are remarkable similarities between the Prologue to the *De Induratione* and the *Expositio*. Studer also concedes that if matters of content were admissible, then Apponius fondness for the baptism-penance-martyrdom triad would suggest a dating in the Pelagian period. However, that the Pelagian period lasted a very long time in some areas where "Pelagianism" was not seen as particularly heterodox.[209]

The author may have been no less semi-Pelagian than Leo when it came to questions of grace and free will, but was he as Chalcedonian in his Christology? König thinks so and, criticising Grillmeier, cites as evidence the notion that the assumption of the perfect soul by the Word is, for Apponius, what a more orthodox contemporary would have described as "the assumption of humanity". The soul is understood by him as a sort of representative of humanity.[210] Apponius belongs to the pre-Chalcedonian world; even Leo (before 451) did not really believe in a hypostatic union where the One Person of the Son made unity of the natures possible, but rather in a one person that was the result of the coming together of the two natures.[211] Studer summarizes Leo's 'Augustinian' concept of unity in Christ, *pace* H. Arens: "Die eine Person, zu der sich die beiden Naturen vereinen, wird vielmehr als das Resultat dieser Einigung hingestellt. Gewiss wird die Menschwerdung allein dem Sohn Gottes zugeschrieben. Doch dies geschieht noch nicht im Sinne des späteren *Unus ex Trinitate passus est*. Es wird noch

---

[207] See Simon (1960), 24-41.

[208] Schlieben (1979), 238, 241.

[209] Despite (e.g.) Studer's attempts to convince that by 430 the *catholica* was Augustinian. Vregille and Neyrand in Apponius (1997) have made a good case for dating Apponius as early as c. 420.

[210] König (1991), p. 68f, n. 30: "[Grillmeier] übersieht aber, daß Apponius 'anima', 'caro' und 'homo' als Bezeichnungen für die Menschheit, die Menschennatur Christi verwendet, je nachdem, wie es der Hoheliedtext ihm geboten erscheinen."

[211] Studer (1985).

einige Zeit dauern, bis man in der Annahme der menschlichen Natur durch den Sohn Gottes die persönliche Konstituierung des Menschen Jesu sehen wird."[212] A full-blooded Chalcedonian understanding would take some time to filter through. In which case the commentary is more likely to have been written before the latter part of the fifth century.

Apponius shares terminological preferences with the Chalcedonian Leo. Here are four examples: (1) *substantia* rather than *essentia* for God's being, (2) *coaeterna*, (3) a Chalcedonian style 'double *aliud*' and (4) *novo ordine*. Yet these all can be explained as due to their shared inheritance of the Augustinian tradition and, in any case, their beliefs were quite different in substance. Unlike Leo, Apponius believed in Christ's freedom from personal sin only, not from original sin. This is admitted by König,[213] (although she then goes on to account for the dissimilarity in phrasing as owing to Apponius' originality).[214] Moreover, he saw the Virgin Birth only as pointing to the miracle rather than being itself the miracle which produced the new order. König further admits:

> Apponius sieht also in Empfängnis und Geburt aus der Jungfrau nicht so sehr die neue Zeugungsordnung begründet, als daß er dieses Geschehen als das bedeutsame Zeichen betrachtet für eine neue, die alte Unordnung aufhebende Ordnung zwischen Gott und Mensch, die vor Zeiten im Vorauswissen Gottes ihren Ursprung hat und in der gottmenschlichen Einung verwirklicht wird. Damit zeigt Apponius, indem er die Sündlosigkeit der Seele Christi betont, einen deutlichen Unterschied zur Auffassung Leos... .[215]

If Apponius sees the new bond between God and Man as established primarily in the eternal "pre"-science of God, he also views the locus of sin as the personal will which is thus also the place of salvation. Yet this sinlessness is only realised by the grace of the Word in coming near and preserving the soul of Christ. The Word is thus still the agent of salvation. Leo prefers to see the Saviour's humanity as sinless through Mary's virginity breaking the chain of sin.[216]

König asserts that Apponius goes beyond Leo to a more full-blown Chalcedonianism. First, "(j)edenfalls spiegeln seine Aussagen den Stand der Christologie, den auch das Lehrschreiben Leos wiedergibt, ja sie gehen zumindest an einer Stelle (V,10), wo die Definition von Chalcedon anklingt, darüber hinaus",[217] and she cites: "*Sine causa igitur laborem impendit*

---

[212] Ibid., 487.
[213] At p. 83*f, on IX, 23 (CCL 19, 224) and XII, 51 (224).
[214] Ibid.,pp. 85*-89*.
[215] König (1991), 84*.
[216] See ibid., 83*f.
[217] V,10; CCL 19, p. 84f: see also König (1991), 79*.

quaerendo, qui aequalem hominibus absque peccato et coaeternum Patri (non fuerit) utraque natura (confessus)." Yet when compared with 'Chalcedon' — "...*consubstantialem Patri secundum deitatem et consubstantialem nobis eundem secundum humanitatem, 'per omnia nobis similem absque peccato'*" — the differences are striking. The use of *coaeternus* in Trinitarian discourse was a feature of Westerners like Jerome and Hilary, who felt discomfort in the presence of *consubstantialis*. The only words shared by the formulae are *Patri* and *absque peccato*. Second, *manente materia* is employed, according to König,[218] eight times in the commentary; at IX, 257 the words *natura* and *materia* are used in parallel, but since the latter is the more common, less technical usage, a conclusion that Apponius was Chalcedonian should be avoided. A closer parallel is offered by Zeno of Verona: "*Descendit quippe gladius pius* (=Word of God) *in viscera peccatoris et uno eodemque ictu, incolumni corporis manente materia, interficit hominem veterem, creat novum,....*"[219]

Despite König's stimulating and fresh arguments, Apponius hardly appears representative of an era of theological reflection which presupposed Chalcedon. Thus, while Leo is typically "late" Augustinian, Apponius' debt to Augustine, if any, is to that early form of thinking as we find it tantalisingly expressed as Catholic or Ambrosian doctrine in *Confessiones* VII, 19.[220] Alypius had thought that Christ's saving perfection was due to a perfect though mutable soul, and Augustine admits of his own equal but opposite error as close to Photinianism.

Origen rather than a mature Augustine seems to have been Apponius' mentor on several issues throughout the commentary. For both Apponius and Origen, it is sin rather than "the law" which has to be overcome by the baptised Christian.[221] The synergism of human soul and Spiritual power is also shared.[222] The Origenian notion of Christ the Groom going out through

---

[218] Ibid., 20f, n. 30.

[219] Zeno *Tractatus* 2.10.2; CCL 22, p. 182.

[220] CCL 27, 109: "Quia itaque vera scripta sunt, totum hominem in Christo agnoscebam, non corpus tantum hominis aut cum corpore sine mente animum, sed ipsum hominem, non persona veritatis, sed magna quadam naturae humanae excellentia et perfectione sapientiae praeferri, ceteris arbitrabar.... . Sed postea haereticorum Apollinaristarum hunc errorem esse cognoscens.... . Ego autem aliquanto posterius didicisse me fateor, in eo quod verbum factum est, quomodo catholica veritas a Photini falsitate dirimatur."

[221] Cf. Molina (1983), 311: "Esta singular exégesis es posibilé gracias a la introducción del tema del pecado-como habia hecho Origenes y la interpretación del verbo como predicado del pecado y no del velo o del Antiguo Testamento como hacen las otras interpretaciones."

[222] For example, IX, 53-58; CCL 19, p. 257: "Egressus est namque ad agrum gentium supradictum per adventum Spiritus sancti, qui igne virtutis suae, per apostolorum splendorem, et noctem ignorantiae, in agnitione veritatis, in matutinam lucem converteret, et

the Spirit to woo the Gentile souls also features strongly in Apponius' Book XI. There is one eye on theodicy and another on freedom of human will, which, as W. Geerlings has explained,[223] are typically Origenist concerns. There is also a North-Italian and possibly pro-Origenist correspondence to Apponius in the end of century figure of Chromatius[224] who wrote in a treatise (re. Cant 2:1): "It is not that the Lord is the flower of humanity; rather he prophesied here that he would take on the flower of human flesh."[225] Chromatius died in 408 after sheltering Rufinus; after Theodosius death he had also tried to reinstate Chrysostom by writing a letter which that John thanked him for.[226] Truzzi observes:

> il vero pericolo da combattere, per Cromatio, era quello di Fotino e che l'errore cui opporsi con maggiore energeia era la negazione della divinità piuttosto che dell'umanità di Cristo. Per questo il nome di Fotino ricorre in vari luoghi dell'opera cromaziana, piú attenta però alle afermazioni cristologiche che alle tesi trinitarie elaborate da quell'eretico.[227]

In Zeno of Verona too, as in Apponius, the Stoic-Christian, Latin inheritance is fully present in the idea of the *hegemonikon* lost at the Fall but restored in baptism as the new man put on, with plenty of nuptial associations.

Even the early Augustinian "assumption of the likeness of the flesh of sin" was already emphasised by Ambrose. Thus what can be called 'early Augustinian' Christology can be thought of as largely Ambrosian. Apponius, in the cast of his Christology, is more like the early Augustine or (even more so) Ambrose in respect of any elements which 'corrected' his Origenism, or stood in dialectical relationship with it. There is also a resemblance to the ideas of Ambrose on the Incarnation, as well as the way he connects

---

spinas turpium cogitationum comessationumque de praedicto agro abstergeret. Per haec utique egreditur ad agrum, gentium conversationem... ."

[223] See Geerlings (1981).

[224] Cf., e.g., Chromatius *Tractatus* 32, CCL 9A, p. 353 :"Unde non immerito ipse Dominus ut et principem se omnium sanctorum ostenderet et florem se suscepturum carnis humanae monstraret, eodem vocabulo nuncupare dignatus est, dicendo per Salomonem: Ego flos campi... ."

[225] Also cf. the heresiological concern, e.g., ibid., p. 50 (*Sermo* XI, 4, 98): "Unde aliquanti haeretici qui Christum hominem solummodo confitentur, denegata eius divinitate, ut Fotinus, pedes quidem tenent, sed caput non habent, quia caput fidei amiserunt."

[226] See Truzzi (1985), 49. In 403 Chromatius was one of the three to whom Chrysostom appealed. See Duval (1973), 175.

[227] Truzzi (1985), 122: "Zeno vede la terza e definitiva tappa della storia della salvezza nelle nozze di Cristo con la chiesa, dalla quale nasce il nuovo popolo dei cristiani provenienti dal paganesimo", i.e., in humankind's three-stage march from paganism through Judaism to Christianity.

Christology with the Christian life through the place given to the *sensus moralis*.[228]

Apponius can be seen to stand in a line of the Western exegetical tradition that used the Apocalypse to work out the relationship of the Jews to the Antichrist. One thinks of the interpretation of the Apocalypse by Victorinus of Petovium, a martyr in 304, the "forerunner of Latin biblical exegesis" with a "predilection for Origenian-allegorical exegesis".[229] Jerome mentions a commentary by Victorinus on the Song of Songs, now lost.[230] It is thus quite possible that Apponius too had access to it; especially if, like him, Latin was not Victorinus' first language and his patrimony was relatively Eastern (Pannonia). The extant Apocalypse commentary [231] is noted for its Origen-inspired modification of mainstream materialist millenarianism (i.e., the use of Irenaeus, Hilary, Gregory of Elvira) in its belief that spiritual as well as material goods are to be enjoyed.[232] The specific motif that only the lost tribes qualify for the eternal kingdom is not shared by Apponius,[233] but the general *topos* is similar. The people of God or the Church remains the "bride" with some differences of detail such as her becoming identified as "the people", a term previously used (in I-VI) for the Jews. As for the alleged marked differences in Books IX-XII, the Roman Church's becoming the *plebs fidelis* can be interpreted as the development through the Song (properly interpreted) of *Heilsgeschichte* up to the author's time.

Apponius thus reflects a mixture of third and fourth century influences, most of these North Italian, but with some eastern leavening. Whether one sees a Pelagian, or a form of naïve semi-Pelagianism *avant la lettre*, or even a tacit, prudent Pelagianism is a question which is very hard to answer from the internal evidence of the text of the commentary. However, that is all we have at our disposal.

---

[228] See e.g., *Expositio* V, 80; CCL 19, p. 105.

[229] C. Curti (1992), 867.

[230] *Vir ill* 74; PL 23, 683.

[231] *CSEL* 49, 152.

[232] See Daniélou (1977), 363.

[233] Bardenhewer, II, 656, sketches the picture painted by Victorinus: "Endlich erscheint Christus bzw. Gott mit den verlorenen Stämmen der Juden, welche jenseits Persiens in glücklicher Verborgenheit gelebt haben; sie überwinden den zweiten Antichrist, nehmen Besitz von der heiligen Stadt und begründen ein neues Weltreich von ungeahnter Herrlichkeit. Außer jenen Stämmen der Juden sind die nunmehr aus den Gräbern erstehenden Gerechten zur Teilnahme an diesem Reiche berufen."

2.23 Conclusion

There was a variety of genres; from the full commentary, such as those by Philo of Carpasia, Nilus, Theodoret, and Apponius, to homilies and *scholia* (Origen through Jerome and Procopius, respectively) or running commentary on parts of the Song which were purposively on their way to full treatments (Hippolytus, the two Gregories, Rufinus-Origen), or accidentally so (Ambrose) down to the passing reference to the Song as a means of illustrating a point argued on the basis of New Testament texts or dogma (the rest). The principal concern, wherever the Groom gets mentioned, was with Christology. Almost all these writings show some awareness of the Christological debates of their period, even if the concern was often more to do with a Christology which reinforced their ecclesiologies than with a science of the Incarnation, strictly understood. Their Christology seems closely connected to the social, ecclesiological and spiritual issues of their lives and times, to the extent that it was perfectly natural for them that their ecclesiological and spiritual readings of the Song should very quickly lead to Christological interpretations.

Chapter 3

The Groom

Some verses in the Song focus on the figure of the Groom. These inspired most early Christian writers to speak of the Word as that Groom, the agent or person in Christ who continues to play the initiating role towards souls, drawing them into following him. The Christ-Church connection, so often associated with the Song, was seen by many not so much as a static domestic relationship as a covenant whose fulfilment needed seeking until the end-times consummation. However the reality of the fulfilment, namely some sort of God-Human union, had already been achieved in Jesus. The subject of this chapter is how the Word relates to humanity: this means his self-presentation in Christ as a groom holding out love to an ideal bride. Set out in all his magnificence, he is depicted as the initiator of salvation, the Spirit-provider, the holder of a tension of two extremes, the buffer between God and Humanity, the perfecter of salvation-history, the condescending one, the one with beautiful virtues, the cosmic ruler who reflects in himself the harmony of creation.

It is this rather than the desire to imitate a *nous*-like Christ which motivated the ascetic interest in the Song. The epiphany of the Word was what made spirituality possible, since only the One who is fully divine can also draw and raise the soul up towards union and is the One with whom the hungry soul longs for spiritual union.[1]

3.1 The way the Song relates to the Incarnation

Cant 1:2
Φιλησάτω με ἀπὸ φιλημάτων στόματος αὐτοῦ, ὅτι ἀγαθοὶ μαστοί σου ὑπὲρ οἶνον.

It is a notably Jewish practice to focus on the first line of a book of Scripture as particularly inspired. Christian commentators were happy to use the

---

[1] Here I take issue with the tendency of Clark (1992) to assume that spirituality c. 400 was of an Evagrian type of Origenism with its emphasis on the *nous* and associated "isochristic" beliefs.

boldness of the request in Cant 1:2 as the occasion for establishing that these kisses, and ergo the contents of the Song as a whole, are holy. The word used is (as at Cant 8:1) not the προσκύνησις of reverence but the more intimate Φιλήματα.² This is no kiss from worshipper to worshipped but signifies something which *she* hopes to receive *from him* in his coming to the world.

The contrast between two exegetes of this verse is instructive. For Theodoret, spiritual development presupposes the close following of the human Christ as described in the gospels; hence in his commentary he supplies a Christology, however sketchy.³ Love and its benefits come directly from the divinity; the place of protection from evil is found in Christ's humanity. The employment of the verb συνάπτω alludes to the prioritising of Christ over the family.⁴ So the relationship between believing soul and the Word is not described in terms which suggest 'consummation'; he has already (on Cant 1:1) explained that for the purposes of the commentary this is merely a "union of mouths" (presumably the firstfruits of full copulation), and such an image is to be understood as spiritual communion.⁵ The full union with the Word — and even then, only *synapheia* — will be for the coming age when she will be incorporated into the humanity of Christ. This reflects the Antiochene hermeneutic, that much prophecy is still to be fulfilled.

However, in Ps-Athanasius, *Synopsis Scripturae Sacrae*, the *synapheia*-union is only "to come" in the sense of the expectations of the Israelite prophets; from the commentator's viewpoint it has already arrived. He describes the four *dramatis personae* and some of the resulting permutations: "The whole book is full of conversations of the old (*sc.* people) with the Word, and of the whole human race with the Word, and of the Church from the nations with him, and of the Word again with her and with the human race."⁶ Thus the statements which are of a "looking-forward" nature should

---

² The liturgical *Proskynesis*, according to the so-called *Edict of Milan* in 313, was interpreted as one of reverence towards Christ the εἰκὼν θεοῦ, but not of worship (*latreia*) which was due to the invisible God alone: Chifar (1993), 12-15.

³ PG 81, 88D: Ἐν τῇ τούτου σκιᾷ λέγει ἡ νύμφη ἐπιθυμῆσαι καθίσαι, καὶ τοῦτο πεποιηκέναι (i.e., eat the fruit)...Βούλεται γὰρ φυγεῖν τὰς τῆς κακίας ἀκτῖνας συγκαίειν ἐπισταμένας, ἵνα μὴ πάλιν γένηται μέλαινα· σκιὰ δὲ τοῦ νυμφίου τὰ νῦν ἐν ἐσόπτρῳ καὶ αἰνίγματι… . For a similar sentiment, cf. PG 81, 108A on Cant 2:14.

⁴ PG 81, 89CD: Τάξατε τοίνυν ἐπ᾽ ἐμὲ ἀγάπην, ἵνα τῷ νυμφίῳ μου συναφθῶ, καὶ τοῦτον καὶ πατρὸς, καὶ μητρὸς, καὶ τῶν ἄλλων προτιμήσω.

⁵ PG 81, 57AB: Φίλημα δὲ νοοῦμεν οὐ στομάτων συνάφειαν, ἀλλ᾽ εὐσεβοῦς ψυχῆς καὶ θείου λόγου κοινωνίαν.

⁶ PG 28, 352D-353A: Ἔστι δὲ ὅλον τὸ βιβλίον τοῦτο διαλόγων πλῆρες τοῦ παλαιοῦ (Supple., λαοῦ) πρὸς τὸν Λόγον, καὶ καθόλου τοῦ ἀνθρωπίνου γένους πρὸς τὸν Λόγον, καὶ τῆς ἐξ ἐθνῶν Ἐκκλησίας πρὸς αὐτὸν, καὶ τοῦ Λόγου πάλιν πρὸς αὐτὴν καὶ πρὸς τὸ ἀνθρώπινον γένος.

be put in the mouths of "the former people", e.g., Cant 1:1. This time "mouths" are in the service of divine-human dialogues in preparation for the union that will be the Incarnation.

Pseudo-Athanasius emphasises the Incarnation as the fulfilment; Theodoret would see that as only the means to consummation. Yet for all the differences, the two exegetes are united in naming the Groom as the Word who achieves his goals through his assumed flesh.

3.2 Myrrh and the Groom's divine Spirit

Cant 1:3-4

1·3 καὶ ὀσμὴ μύρων σου ὑπὲρ πάντα τὰ ἀρώματα, μύρον
    ἐκκενωθὲν ὄνομά σου. διὰ τοῦτο νεάνιδες ἠγάπησάν σε,
1·4 εἵλκυσάν σε, ὀπίσω σου εἰς ὀσμὴν μύρων σου δραμοῦμεν.

The presence of God himself as an active protagonist in the Song of Songs appears quite explicitly in many of the commentaries. As God the Word he can be both the one who was and will be corporeally manifest to the creaturely Bride and yet also the one who communes with her from heaven. However, he does not bypass the Incarnation, but rather draws her to him through it, by evocation of it as a real spiritual presence. This objectification is what Hippolytus takes "the Groom's fragrance" to mean, which in turn P. Meloni has seen as of great significance in the history of soteriology, the proof-text for the doctrine being Cant 1:3. The Groom is the Word of God, to whom Hippolytus does not assign a separate *hypostasis*,[7] yet who is accorded a name (meaning here, a nature) which in turn is likened to a fragrance, as an obvious reference to the Spirit before and after the earthly life of Christ.[8]

According to Ambrose, the outpouring of fragrance is the presupposition of the desire of human flesh (ie the body of the baptised, not the whole of humanity) to rush to be joined in spirit to Christ.[9] Such a comment on Cant 1:3b, can only be called 'functionalist'. The Incarnation served to impart a spirit of virtue, in keeping with Ambrose's opening remarks in this work, where he says there is as much *moralia* as *mystica* in the Song.[10] It is

---

[7] See Zani (1984), 107-54.

[8] *De Cantico* II, 8; Garitte I, 38; Translation: II, 27: "*nomen eius* infusum est (litt.suppositum est) in ventrem, et creavit novum hominem genitum; depositum est super aquas, et aquas purificavit; effusum est inter gentiles, et gentiles congregavit."

[9] *In Ps 118*, 1,5; CSEL 62, p. 8: "unguentum exinanitum nomen tuum, hoc est: totus immundus impuritatibus diversorum facinorum faetebat hic mundus; nunc spirat ubique suavitas pudicitiae, unguentum fidei, flos integritatis. et a moralibus venit ad mystica dicens: *introduxit me rex in cubiculum*... ."

[10] Ibid., 1,3; p. 6.

interesting that in the *De Isaac*, on the other hand, Ambrose appears to have skipped Cant 1:3b in his discussion of the early verses of the Song; it is possible that Ambrose felt the relationship between Word and Spirit to be a weak point in his theology. In this identification of the Word with spirit-nature, Ambrose, like Hippolytus, avoids the Trinitarian question and focuses on the Groom in his operation as Spirit who provides spirit.

In the *De Isaac*, Ambrose considers that at Cant 1:3 the text moves from "moral things" to mystical ones, suggesting, with a subtle sexual image, that doctrine (like a kiss) is simple, introductory, and that it is Christian experience which causes or should cause profound thought.[11] A similar idea is found at *In Ps 118*, 6,33, where it speaks of the body of Christ as a store of spiritual grace for the 'martyr'.[12] Again, there is a debt to Hippolytus, which has been clearly illustrated by Meloni.[13] Only once, and then in the early *De virginibus*, was Cant 1:3 used in relation to inner-Trinitarian relationship and creation; most of the time Ambrose follows the Hippolytan line that while the inner workings of the Incarnation are an impenetrable mystery, it enabled divinity, which is primarily spirit, to spread among men by the breaking of the container. The humanity of Jesus is a mere vessel. Not naturally incorruptible, it is made so by the divinity which adjoins it; and it is mortal, unlike the Spirit who is the one who unites Father and Son in being. Until the point of Christ's death the divinity, as Word, is rather anonymous. It is the Holy Spirit as fragrance who is released to fill the emptiness of those lacking divine life, inviting them to partake of the divine Christ as food.[14] Ambrose implies that the "Spirit", unlike Christ, has no created, perceptible side. The Spirit in the Ambrosian treatise *De spiritu sancto* is in no sense a divinised *anima* of the human Christ, but is the same divine power as "the Name" who is the uncreated Spirit.[15] For here Ambrose is aiming to assert his heavenly origin by calling him "spirit". As he writes: *Nemo enim est qui copulam vel animae et spiritus, vel Christi et Ecclesiae non beatam putet.*[16] There is a

---

[11] *De Isaac* 3,9; CSEL 32/1, p. 648, 20-23: "adspirat enim in verbo odor gratiae et remissio peccatorum, quae in totum diffusa mundum omnia tamquam exinanito replevit unguento, quia per universos gravis concluvies detersa vitiorum est."

[12] CSEL 62, p. 125, 17-19: "In tegimento enim corporis Christi, quo redemptus est a peccato, munimentum gratiae spiritalis invenit, ut salutaria sibi et sentiat et loquatur."

[13] Meloni 1975, 223-27.

[14] Ibid., 265 and Ambrose, *De Spiritu Sancto*, I, 96. Cf. *In Ps 118*, 5,9; *CSEL* 62, p. 86f: "Christus ergo adfixus ad lignum, sicut malum pendens in arbore, bonum odorem mundanae fundebat redemptionis, quia peccati gravis detersit faetorem et unguentum potus vitalis effudit. tamquam malum, inquit, in lignis silvae, ita consobrinus meus in medio filiorum,... sed non solum odor, verum etiam cibus suavis in malo est; ergo cibus suavis est Christus."

[15] *De Spiritu Sancto*, II, 9, 95; CSEL 79, p. 124.

[16] *In Ps 118*, 36 (alluding to Cant 8:9); CSEL 62, p. 506.

close relationship between Christ incarnate and the soul's needed driving-force, the *spiritus* or *animus*.[17]

The kind of economic modalism implied by Hippolytus' loose association of Word and Spirit which reappears in Ambrose's imagery can be seen as theologically 'alternative' rather than 'primitive'. Since W. Bauer and more recently G. Lampe and H. Drijvers, the acceptability of a Christology which is different in degree from the indwelling of believers by the Spirit has been championed: it obviates certain metaphysical obstacles.[18] However Meloni goes too far in his claims that this 'fragrance-wafting' is the dominant motif even in Hippolytus, let alone in the rest of the early Christian soteriological tradition. He asserts that Gregory of Nyssa has a scheme whereby the attempt to restore a triunity of nature, humanity and church, is sparked into life by the significant content of verses like Cant 1:3 about the divine outpouring of aromatic divine "virtù".[19] "In questa visione il discorso prevalentemente orientato sull'anima da forma concreto al discorso sulla Chiesa-umanità, offrendo agli uomini una guida alla realizzazione sulla terra dell'esperienza trinitaria..."[20]; the metaphysical is turned into experiential theology and the commentary is bi-partite: "Nella prima [parte] offre sopratutto l'interpretazione dell'anima (ed anche della natura umana), nella seconda, dalla VII omelia in poi, sopratutto della Chiesa."[21] In any case, Meloni contends, as with the Hippolytan traditon of interpretation, the Incarnation is mere presupposition which is soon left behind as the Song and the Commentary's courses develop in their parallel ἀκολουθία.[22]

Meloni links this with Gregory's careful use of this verse with reference to Trinitarian relationships in *Contra Eunomium*:[23] the Son was the radiance of his glory before his earthly birth in that he contained the essence of the Father in another form, making the unseen God 'knowable' to humans, by his traces in the world. He compares this with Eusebius' earlier cavalier interpretation in which the "perfume" image reinforced his emanationist view of the Logos as icon.[24] As he admits, Eusebius' problem was to interpret this verse in the light of O.T. theophanies and play down the Incarnation; yet although the

---

[17] *Apologia David altera* 8,9,43; CSEL 32/2, p. 388: "viget autem animus, quando etiam flos videtur in terris. quis iste flos boni odoris nisi ille qui dixit: *ego flos campi et lilium convallium*."

[18] Cf. also, Baillie (1955); Drijvers (1984); Lampe (1977).

[19] Meloni (1975), 185ff.

[20] Ibid., 186.

[21] Ibid., 187.

[22] Moreschini in his introduction to Gregory of Nyssa (1988) contends that some homilies focus on the Church and others on the soul, these being distinct if related subjects for Gregory.

[23] GNO II, 202, 5-20.

[24] See Meloni (1975), 178-81; *Dem Evang* IV,16, 194AD; for Eusebius the Logos himself was the mediator who took the place of a soul in Christ. Cf. Lorenz (1983).

Incarnation is key for Gregory in the sense of being foundational, the maturing soul learns about God from the traces in the natural order.[25] The Incarnation remains the exegetical key, for it opened up a new possibility for God-human relating; but essentially it remains a mystery, only to be studied in its soteriological effects. The fragrances are virtues; the name being myrrh means that God's nature cannot be grasped but his power can be felt by meditating on his names so that God is known through love. *Pace* Meloni, Gregory skilfully avoids speaking of any one "fragrance" in the naive way of Ambrose;[26] the principle of unity resides in the Word.

Gregory's advance on Ambrose's spirit-mysticism can be related to his debt to the type of Stoicism in Origen. For Origen the world is imprinted with Logos already, so that Cant 1:3 which refers to another divine agent with ubiquitous properties, must mean the Spirit whose gift is soteriological. Yet for Origen in Procopius and in the translation by Rufinus the *kenosis* is not about leaving behind but sharing out the divine "Spirit" so that souls benefit and have a less mighty Saviour to take hold of. In the 'Procopian' comment on Cant 1:3 this was equated with the mind of Christ in which believing souls share.[27] Rufinus betrays his interpolation by the addition of *sanctum* to *Spiritum*.[28] Thus the idea of the fulness which is emptied as that of the Spirit is Origen's own reading of Phil 2:6 in the light of Cant 1:3. But by "Spirit" he would have meant the earthly presence of the Word made available to all/many souls, not just the perfect one. The point is that, according to Origen, after a pre-existent betrothal, a consummation has already taken place in the earthly life and resurrection of Jesus between the Word and the νοῦς of Christ. The Word thus appropriates that mind, so that as *spiritus* it (the mind) becomes divine, or rather has an openness to God it never had before. The progress of individual souls and the Church as a whole presupposes that the soul of Christ has got something to offer them, namely the means of seeing and understanding this revelation, but also of putting it into practice. The

---

[25] Meloni (1975), 193: "...così come possiamo conoscere tutte le altre realtà del mondo divino solo attraverso le orme di esse presenti nell'universo.....Gregorio è pienamente cosciente dell'importanza dell'incarnazione come momento centrale dell'incontro fra anima e Dio, ma il piano teologico del suo discorso lo porta a rimandare alle omelie successive la riflessione su di essa."

[26] GNO VI, 36,15-39,1.

[27] PG 17, 253: ῎Ηγουν ἀδύνατον τὴν ἀξιέραστον λέγει ψυχὴν ἢ ᾽Εκκλησίαν ἢ τὸ ἡγεμονικὸν τοῦ Χριστοῦ · εἰς ὅ Παῦλος εἰσελθὼν ἔφη · ῾Ημεῖς δὲ νοῦν Χριστοῦ ἔχομεν, ἵνα ἰδῶμεν τὰ ὑπὸ Θεοῦ χαρισθέντα ἡμῖν. Cf. Baehrens p. 107,19 - p. 108,2: the reference to the quasi-Gnostic "fullness" which Origen demythologised and located within Christ: *Exinanivit* autem *de plenitudine* sine dubio, in qua erat... . Nisi enim *exinanisset unguentum*, hoc est plenitudinem divini Spiritus, et *humiliasset se usque ad formam servi*, capere eum nullus in illa deitatis *plenitudine* potuisset, nisi sola fortasse sponsa pro eo... ."

[28] Cf. Baehrens, p. 100,6; p. 101,6.

Spirit thus proceeds from the Word Incarnate who is the central agent in wooing and winning souls.

3.3 The Distillation of myrrh as fragrance and the availability of "the mind of Christ"

Cant 1:12-14; 2:13.

1·12 Ἕως οὗ ὁ βασιλεὺς ἐν ἀνακλίσει αὐτοῦ, νάρδος μου ἔδωκεν ὀσμὴν αὐτοῦ.
1·13 ἀπόδεσμος τῆς στακτῆς ἀδελφιδός μου ἐμοί,
ἀνὰ μέσον τῶν μαστῶν μου αὐλισθήσεται·
1·14 βότρυς τῆς κύπρου ἀδελφιδός μου ἐμοὶ
ἐν ἀμπελῶσιν Εγγαδδι.
2·13 ἡ συκῆ ἐξήνεγκεν ὀλύνθους αὐτῆς
αἱ ἄμπελοι κυπρίζουσιν, ἔδωκαν ὀσμήν.

This image is used to speak of the invisible being contained in and distributed by the visible; in other words a picture of the Word in the Incarnation.

The alternative nature of Ambrose's 'functional' Christology is demonstrated in cross-section in his comments on Cant 1:14 ("My kinsman is a shoot of the cypress among the vineyards of Engaddi"):

> He was crushed although He was the Word made man; and He became poor, although He was rich, that we might be enriched by His want. He was powerful, and offered himself to be despised, as when Herod rejected and mocked Him; He was moving the earth, and He hung on a cross; He covered the sky with shadows and crucified the world, and He was crucified. He bent his head and the Word went out, he was emptied out and refilled everything; God came down, Man went up. The Word was made flesh that flesh might claim for itself the throne of the Word on the right hand of God; He was wounded and the perfume flowed. The beetle was heard and God was recognised.[29]

It is noteworthy that all the verbs connected with humiliation in the above passage are in the perfect tense, and those with the Word's eternal existence

---

[29] In Ps 118, 8; CSEL 62, p. 45: "Nam et constrictus erat, verbum cum esset homo factus: et pauper factus est, cum dives esset; ut nos illius inopia ditaremur potens erat, et despiciendum se praebuit, ita ut Herodes sperneret eum et inluderet ei terram movebat, et haerebat in ligno caelum obducebat tenebris, mundum crucifigebat, et crucifixus erat inclinabat caput, et exibat verbum exinanitus erat, et replebat omnia. descendit deus, ascendit homo, verbum caro factum est, ut caro sibi verbi solium in dei dextera vindicaret, vulnus erat et fluebat unguentum, scarabeus audiebatur, et deus agnoscebatur." The last phrase, an echo of Hab 2:19, sees the impenitent's shout on the Cross as the dark side of *the* saving history. On the theme of 'suffering and glory' in Ambrose's treatment of Paul, see Angstenberger (1997).

as well as those with the effects of his ministry among mankind are in the imperfect. This two level scheme in which Christ visibly suffers but invisibly acts is in keeping with Ambrose's heavily Platonised Song of Songs-inspired spirituality.

Where the kinsman (*fraternus*) is compared to a "binding of (myrrh) drops" (Cant 1:12), this gives us a hint that for Rufinus/Origen the divine power in Christ's body was like a human soul contained in a human body yet one which is identified as that which by its likeness to the divinity ties it to the humanity. This "indicates the mystery of his bodily nativity; for in the way a body is the binding and tie of the soul, by such a tie is the drop of divine power (*virtutis*) and sweetness contained."[30] Also, the more literalistic, *Vetus Latina* translation of the LXX given by Rufinus (*Alligamentum guttae fraternus meus mihi*) is quite different from that by Jerome in Hom II,3: *Fasciculus stillae fratruelis* (Vulg, *dilectus*) *meus mihi*, as also is Rufinus/Origen's understanding of the synagogue as the sister of the 'gathered' Church. While *fraternus* suggests the similarity of nature, that both Groom and Bride are of intelligible nature, the Old Latin translation also allows wordplay on the idea of Christ's power. The myrrh itself signifies the divine purity within Christ[31] and this unaffected beauty of Christ (in scent or appearance) is to be imitated.[32] The smallness of the drop is no hindrance to the gathering up of Jacob or even all the nations, which are after all just a drop themselves; the myrrh comes out from the teachings of the Word of God.[33] In this passage the Word's becoming incarnate is understood as "tying"— an earthing and pledging for perpetuity of divine power and wisdom, now available to all souls.

Explaining Cant 1:12a, Nilus writes that, whereas most people see God only in miracles, the perfect soul alone can realise that the divine can also suffer, albeit only in the sense of his power being dormant.[34] Yet that is

---

[30] Baehrens p. 169,2-5: "...corporeae nativitatis eius indicat sacramentum; videtur enim quodammodo 'alligamentum' esse et vinculum quoddam animae corpus, quo 'alligamento gutta' in Christo divinae virtutis ac suavitatis adstringitur."

[31] Baehrens, p. 169, 9-12: "Denique et lex mundum dicit 'esse omne vas', quod alligatum est, 'immundum' vero, 'quod solutum fuerit et non ligatum' (Nu 19:15). Cuius rei haec profecto figura erat quod Christus, in quo numquam fuit ulla immunditia peccati, 'alligamentum guttae' dicitur."

[32] Baehrens, p. 179, 8ff; "Possumus... florem fieri Verbum Dei et initia bonorum operum docere."

[33] Baehrens, p. 170, 6-9: "A 'vestimentis' ergo Verbi Dei, quae est doctrina sapientiae, 'myrrha' procedit, mortis dumtaxat indicium(iudicum ?) pro humano genere susceptae. 'Gutta', ut supra diximus, 'exanita divinitatis forma, servilis formae' suscepta dignatio."

[34] SC 403, 200, 25 – 202, 30: Καὶ γὰρ ἐν τῷ θανάτῳ τὸ βασιλικὸν εἶχε κράτος, ἀμερίμνος ὑπνώσας καὶ τῆς ἀναστάσεως τὴν ἐξουσίαν κεκτημένος ἀνεμπόδιστον. Ὅθεν καὶ ἐπιφέρει· τίς ἐγειρεῖ αὐτόν; ἀντὶ τοῦ οὐδείς, ἀλλ'

exactly what the saving message of the Incarnation is about; like a sachet of myrrh he rests between the breasts of the bride in a condescension, a self-entrusting to humanity, which goes as far as infant vulnerability in the mother's care.³⁵ Beautifully and allusively he writes that like an apple the flavour of divinity is sent out via the body/skin — in the actions of divinity, in the life of the κυριακὸς ἄνθρωπος. The virtues of Christ protect her and allow her to come close; in this sense the soul or actions of Christ act as a screen, so that only the smell but not the brilliance of the divinity reaches her in her sensitivity.³⁶

A cloak which is his humanity during the Incarnation is described as infused with and effusing an invisible effect. The Syriac Peshitta of Cant 1:3 is helpful because it was a translation made not long after the period under examination. It has the theologically charged ܪܝܚ, whose cognate which would commonly be predicated of God's nature in the Old Testament, and the spiritually-informed rendering: "virgins" (root: ܥܠܝܡ.)

In the Antiochene tradition, influenced by the Syriac, the metaphor of "the cloak" is the leading representation of Christ's humanity. Separable from the ascended Word, its role was to cover and pick up humanity until the eschaton. In the interim period, there is time for spiritual sanctification by God the Holy Spirit. In fact, the Groom-Word's divinity is evidenced by his ability to impart the divine Spirit; this is seen in post-Constantinopolitan (381) comments such as Theodoret's. For the Antiochene, the point is that the cloak of humanity is "perfumed" with divinity which has seeped through it, from inside outwards. As with Origen the nard (Word) itself is said to be found lodging between each of the Church members' breasts, i.e. within their ἡγεμονίκον.³⁷ Yet while Origen on this verse (Cant 1:13) asserted that the nard/divinity is found resting in believers' hearts in a similar if lesser way to

---

αὐτὸς ἑαυτόν · τὸ δὲ οὐδείς καθ' ὑπεξαίρεσιν τοῦ πατρὸς εἴρηται. Also, see ibid., 204.

³⁵ Ibid., 206, 41-44: Τὸ δὲ ἀνάμεσον τῶν μαστῶν αὐτὸν τῆς νύμφης αὐλίζεσθαι τὴν ἕως τῆς νηπιότητος συγκατάβασιν δηλοῖ καὶ τὴν τῶν ἀνθρωπίνων παθῶν πείνης καὶ δίψης, ὕπνου τε καὶ κόπου σωματικοῦ ἀνάληψιν.

³⁶ Ibid., 250, 13-28: Ἔπειθ' ὅτι τὸ μῆλον τῷ δέρματι ἐμπεριεχομένην φυλάττον τὴν εὐωδίαν καὶ ἐπὶ τὸ ἔξω ταύτην διαδίδωσιν ἐγκρεμαμένην... . Οὕτω δὲ καὶ ἡ θεότης ἐπεκρύπτετο μὲν τῷ σώματι, ἀλλ' ὅμως τὴν ἐνέργειαν διεδίδου καὶ ἐπὶ τὰ ἔξω τοῦ φαινομένου ἐνδιήτατο τῷ σαρκίῳ καὶ περιεφοίτα τὸν ναὸν διὰ τῶν σημείων, πάντας τῆς εὐεργεσίας ἀντιλαμβάνεσθαι παρασκευάζουσα. Σκιὰ δὲ αὐτοῦ ἐστιν ἐν ᾗ καὶ ἐπεθύμησεν καὶ ἐκάθισεν ἡ νύμφη, ἐπειδὴ μᾶλλον ὡς ἐπὶ τὸ πλεῖστον ἐκ τῶν φύλλων ἡ σκιὰ γίνεσθαι πέφυκε τῷ συνηρεφεῖ τῆς τῶν πετάλων ἑνώσεως τὴν ἡλιακὴν ἀκτῖνα ἀποτειχίζουσα, ὅσα κατὰ φύσιν τῆς ἀνθρωπότητος ἐπετέλει ὁ κυριακὸς ἄνθρωπος ἐσθίων καὶ πίνων... .

³⁷ Theodoret, PG 81,81C: *Ἀναμέσον τῶν μαστῶν μου αὐλισθήσεται.* Τουτέστιν ἐν τῷ ἡγεμονικῷ τῆς ψυχῆς μου, ὃ τῇ καρδίᾳ ἐπαναπαύεται μεταξὺ τῶν μαστῶν διακειμένη.

its residence in Christ's unique soul, [38] Theodoret makes nothing of this comparison. As with Marcellus the proximity of Word and raw humanity was only a temporary expedient; it is supremely 'Antiochene' to speak of the Word as above the confinement of location.

For Rufinus-Origen, it is the free will of Christ, understood as the moral freedom to do good, which marks his ability to undergo human temptations.[39] The effect of grace is to restore the original possibility of free choice; guided this time by the angels who did not fall, the churches and the souls will be trained to become *capaces Dei*.[40] Nevertheless the moral fruits of spiritual maturity come from Christ himself, for he is the vine, while the Father is the gardener.[41] It is the Christ of the gospels who also, by his pioneering stature as the vine and the one who breaks through, makes possible the new Word-soul relationship and thus also for the exegete a further level of interpretation — that which points to the future consummation, when and only when there will be intercourse with God who for now remains as heavenly Father, even Logos, transcendent. The Groom here is depicted as dressed in his outward aspect, as a human being created and passionate for others.

For Apponius, the Spirit seems to be that which operates between heaven and earth. Just as Ambrosiaster maintained: "If you think this power is not Christ there will be two powers and two sons of God; but what about the Scripture 'the only-begotten Son of God'?... the power of God which worked embodied in the world is one and the same, who is called power and Son of God?",[42] so too Apponius' lack of awareness of the Spirit's nature suggests he is not too far from the near binitarianism such as found in M. Victorinus. Coming against Photinus whom he calls "*Fotinus Judaizans*",[43] Ambrosiaster shows the inadequacy of attempting obedience without the recognition of the

---

[38] See Baehrens, p. 169, 1-5: "'Alligamentum guttae fraternus meus mihi', corporeae nativitatis eius indicat sacramentum" and p. 170.

[39] Baehrens p. 227, 6-12: "Et non sine causa puto quod non dixerit: odorem 'dederunt', sed 'odorem suum', ut ostenderet inesse unicuique animae vim possibilitatis et arbitrii libertatem, qua possit agere omne quod bonum est. Sed quia hoc naturae bonum praevaricationis occasione deceptum vel ad ignaviam vel ad nequitiam fuerat inflexum, ubi per gratiam reparatur et per doctrinam Verbi Dei restituitur, 'odorem reddit' illum sine dubio, quem primitus conditor Deus inoleverat, sed peccati culpa subtraxerat."

[40] Baehrens, p. 227, 13-17: "Possunt autem et 'vites' vel 'vineae' intelligi virtutes caelestes et angelicae, quae hominibus largiuntur 'odorem suum', id est doctrinae et institutionis bonum, quo instruunt et imbuunt animas, donec ad perfectionem veniant et incipiant capaces fieri Dei."

[41] See Baehrens, p. 225.

[42] Ambrosiaster, CSEL 50, p. 153, 20-26 (41, 3) writes: "Aut si putas virtutem hanc non esse Christum, duae erunt virtutes et duo filii dei; et ubi est illud quod legitur: unigenitus filius dei... virtutem dei, quae operata est corporata in mundo, ipsam unam esse, quae et dei virtus dicatur et filius."

[43] Ibid., (79,1), p. 473f.

3. The Groom

source of Christ's power. For Apponius this is developed in an 'Augustinian' conception of the unity of the three persons in operation and the principle of the Spirit as the guarantor of the internal moral unity. B. Stubenrauch contends: "Er verstand die Einwohnung des Heiligen Geistes in die Seele Jesu als die theologische Ermöglichung ihrer innigsten Einheit mit dem Wort Gottes und damit der menschlichen *sarx*."[44] However, to claim to trace an Origenist idea of the Holy Spirit as necesssary mediator between Word and flesh in the soul is a misinterpretation of Origen as much as it is of Apponius. If Origen ever took Ps 44:8 to mean a sort of soldering by the Spirit of divinity and humanity to make "the Christ", he did not express so much in the passage adduced by Stubenrauch.[45] It simply means that the Word-soul unity became confirmed by the Spirit and thus became the Anointed One/Messiah/Christ: — all that Origen says is that "the soul with the Word" became Messiah/Christ. Nor is it fair to conclude, as Stubenrauch does,[46] that in this commentary the man assumed is depicted, in being made *imperator* by God the Holy Spirit at the Jordan, as one who undergoes a change from being a mere man to heavenly king.[47] It is interesting that Stubenrauch's citation[48] omits from the middle of the sentence the underlined words, omitting to see that the Spirit makes him from being already the head of the Church to become chief of all. A sudden elevation, at the Jordan, into a proper union was the very thing *Photinus*, not Apponius seemed to stand for. The relevant text speaks of the Spirit's benediction's crowning Christ's head so abundantly that the Church also has her head crowned. The lines are in the setting — at the start of the Seventh Book (on Cant 4:2) — of the soul looking for this favour from God; each soul is taught that it must go through Christ humiliated.[49] Where the soul is prepared to give its will to obedience by descent to baptism it replays Christ's life. There are five ways to get 'crowned' — belief in God when he is calling, baptism (of course),

---

[44] Stubenrauch (1991), 79-88, esp., 87.

[45] Origen, *De Principiis* II, 6, 4: "Dilectionis igitur merito unguitur oleo laetitiae, id est anima cum verbo Dei Christus efficitur. 'Ungi' namque 'oleo laetitiae' non aliud intellegitur quam spiritu sancto repleri; ibid., 85f: "Der Heilige Geist gilt ihm als Prinzip der Liebesverbindung zwischen der menschlichen Seele Jesu und dem Logos Gottes, zugleich aber als die vom Vater herkommende Gabe des Gottesmenschen an seine Gläubigen", and Anm. 55.

[46] Ibid., 91ff.

[47] VII, 5, 68ff; CCL 19, p. 157: "...ita et haec benedictio Spiritus sancti de capite Patre omnipotente super Christum porrecta, qui est Ecclesiae caput, verum imperatorem adsumptum hominem fecit, cui omnis lingua confiteatur et omne flectatur genu."

[48] Ibid., 87; CCL 19, p. 157.

[49] VII, 57; CCL 19, p. 156: "Benedictio est ergo credentis in Christo animae corona"; VII, 77; CCL 19, p. 157: "Ubi ergo vocata venerit anima ad Christum, fit quaedam placidissima commutatio; dat videlicet oboedientiae voluntatem descendens ad Iordanis lavacrum."

anathematising the devil, self-joining to the body of Christ and the appropriation of Christ's blood. In other words the passage is more soteriological, more concerned to appreciate how the Church benefits; Christ *qua* Head of the Church is recognised by anointing *because the Word has made the soul he wears perfect*, rather than because there descended on Jesus something which 'increased' his person, a heresy common to Gnostics and Ebionites. In Origenian thinking, when the union of the divinity to the humanity in Christ is read as two 'before' becoming one 'after', that is *unus spiritus*, it is not surprising that from the point of view others, phenomenologically speaking, he is seen as the one person of the Word who expressed himself in the common spirit-mind he shared with his humanity. He is composite in origin but integral in his incarnate state.

On Cant 2:14 ("show me your appearance") Philo of Carpasia observes:

> Wanting to show himself to her, he put on a body like a cloud and hid himself in it, that to his own bride he might show himself on account of the way of virtue, through perseverance and innocence, handing on to her the example of the life of piety... . Therefore he showed her his appearance, born through the God-bearer, Mary.[50]

The revelation of God then is not a glorious, overpowering one of the divine substance, but of the divine appearance — one filtered through the life of the perfect man. The Word-Church union is prepared for on the Cross in the way that a groom prepares a bed for his bride. This can be demonstrated in what he says about "the bed of Solomon" (Cant 3:6):

> Before he took the Church he said: 'The Son of Man has nowhere to rest his head'. But when he took her she then became the bed of Solomon, that is of the Peacemaker who made peace both in heaven and on the earth... .[51]

---

[50] PG 40, 72CD: Ταύτῃ δὲ βουλόμενος ἐπιδεῖξαι ἑαυτὸν, νεφέλης δίκην ἠμφιάσατο τὸ σῶμα, καὶ ἑαυτὸν ἔκρυψεν αὐτῷ, ἵνα τῇ ἰδίᾳ νύμφῃ δείξῃ ἑαυτὸν διὰ τὸν τρόπον τῆς ἀρετῆς, διὰ τῆς ὑπομονῆς καὶ τῆς ἀκακίας, τὸν τύπον αὐτῇ παραδιδοὺς τοῦ τῆς εὐσεβείας πολιτεύματος... . Ἔδειξεν οὖν αὐτῇ τὴν ὄψιν αὐτοῦ, κυηθεὶς διὰ τῆς Θεοτόκου Μαρίας. The Latin version shows no variation in content; cf. Courcelle (1948), 367. Ceresa-Gastaldo in his edition of Philo of Carpasia (1979), 229 notes that the Latin Commentary on this half-verse was cited in a letter from Adrian I to Charlemagne in 791, which shows the Western Church took 'Philo' seriously.

[51] PG 40, 80CD: Πρὶν γὰρ λάβῃ τὴν Ἐκκλησίαν, ἔλεγεν «Ὁ Υἱὸς τοῦ ἀνθρώπου οὐκ ἔχει ποῦ τὴν κεφαλὴν κλίνῃ» ὅτε δὲ ταύτην ἔλαβεν, τὸ λοιπὸν κλίνη γίνεται τοῦ Σαλομών, τουτέστι τοῦ εἰρηνοποιοῦ, τοῦ εἰρηνεύσαντος τά τε ἐν οὐρανῷ, τά τε ἐπὶ τῆς γῆς. The Latin version is almost identical in content. Cf. Cosmas Indicopleustes (1973), p. 295 on Cant 1:4: Τοῦ δὲ ἐπουρανίου βασιλέως τὸ ταμιεῖον, δῆλον ὅτι τὸ σῶμα ὃ ἑαυτῷ ᾠκοδόμησεν οἶκον,* ἔπειτα δὲ καὶ ἡ τῶν οὐρανῶν βασιλεία.   *also allusion to Prov 9:1.

The last phrase, with its echo of Col 1:20, is a clear reference to the Cross. The point is that the union occurred at the death of Christ. Thus Christ's humanity, at its lowest situation, is the location at which the Word-Groom meets the Church-Bride.

Ambrose offers a wholly different interpretation of this passage. The soul is directed in prayer to leave earth behind and become involved in heaven; again clearly Neoplatonic. There is no thought here of a 'perfect' soul, only of the 'faithful' one or ones.[52] He employs imagery from Cant 3:9 ("the bed/litter of Solomon") and gives it a wholly baptismal slant in which the 'bed' in which Jesus lay (and our souls are condemned to lie) is that body. It represents death, which does not mean the termination of the soul, but is the slumber of self-mortification from which Christ has risen and the place where our souls may rise with Him.[53] "Christus" has become the bed; unlike Origen (Rufinus) whose glorified humanity of Christ is almost fused with the heavenly Word but works to protect as veil and attract as being in the median zone of the spiritually sensible realm. According to K. Baus, the themes of Christ-worship, Jesus-intimacy and Bride-mysticism compose an outworking of Origen's spiritual theology mixed with the popular cult of the martyrs; it is not that Ambrose had Arianism in his sights.[54] This conclusion seems a bit tired, trading, as it does, on the false dichotomy of 'heavy duty' dogma and 'spiritual writing'. Certainly, Ambrose tried to fulfil two functions in all his writings but he managed neither convincingly. (*De Isaac* and *De fide* are equally theologically impressionistic and, for pastoral usefulness, surely too abstract.)

3.4 Mutual belonging

Cant 1:7, 11; 2:6, 16; 3:3-4

1·7 ποῦ ποιμαίνεις, ποῦ κοιτάζεις ἐν μεσημβρίᾳ.
1·11 ὁμοιώματα χρυσίου ποιήσομέν σοι μετὰ στιγμάτων τοῦ ἀργυρίου.
2·6 εὐώνυμος αὐτοῦ ὑπὸ τὴν κεφαλήν μου,
καὶ ἡ δεξιὰ αὐτοῦ περιλήμψεταί με.
2·16 Ἀδελφιδός μου ἐμοί, κἀγὼ αὐτῷ,

---

[52] Cf. PL 15,1871 A = *In Ps 118*, 4,18; CSEL 62, p. 77f.

[53] PL 15, 1899 C = De Isaac 44-45; CSEL 32, p. 668, 14-17 and p. 669,14-18: "Videntes itaque eam filiae Hierusalem Christo inhaerentem et adhuc ascendentem cum eo—dignatur enim quaerentibus frequenter occurrere et condescendere, ut eos elevet—dicunt: 'quae est haec, quae ascendit a deserto?'... Hae igitur filiae Hierusalem sponsam ascendentem... agnoscentes quoque Salomonis illius esse pacifici sponsam, etiam comitatu sedulo persequuntur usque ad lectum Salomonis, eo quod ei vera in Christo requies debeatur. Lectus enim sanctorum Christus est, in quo universorum fessa saecularibus proeliis corda requiescunt."

[54] Baus (1954), 24.

3·3 εὕροσάν με οἱ τηροῦντες οἱ κυκλοῦντες ἐν τῇ πόλει
Μὴ ὃν ἠγάπησεν ἡ ψυχή μου εἴδετε;
3·4 ὡς μικρὸν ὅτε παρῆλθον ἀπ' αὐτῶν,
ἕως οὗ εὗρον ὃν ἠγάπησεν ἡ ψυχή μου·
ἐκράτησα αὐτὸν καὶ οὐκ ἀφήσω αὐτόν,
ἕως οὗ εἰσήγαγον αὐτὸν εἰς οἶκον μητρός μου
καὶ εἰς ταμίειον τῆς συλλαβούσης με.

In the Latin West, "Son" was Gregory of Elvira's preferred term for the second Person of the Trinity (rather than "the Word" which may have seemed too vulnerable to Arian loading). However, while Gregory always avoids *Verbum* or *Sermo*, after the second book the subject is nearly always plain "Christus" and not "Filius"(which may coincide with the fact that Books III-V appear to have been unredacted).[55] Therefore, when in Books I and II (e.g., I, 4; I, 6; II, 28) "Christus" is followed by "filius Dei", this appears like the amendment of one who wanted to be orthodox in his phraseology, while leaving just what is meant by the phrase open: Gregory thought of the Groom as the incarnate Son.

For Simonetti,[56] Gregory was not a *homoousian* in the radical sense: "...Gregorio ha interpretato l'unità di sostanza fra il padre e il figlio come l'unità che collega fra loro gli esseri appartenenti ad uno stesso genere." *Verbum, sapientia, spiritus* — these were regarded as names in accordance with the function the Son took on in the economy of creation; "the Son" seems alone in being more than just a term for a function. The omnipotent Son who needs no *kenosis* to accommodate the flesh is understood as "on view" in the Song. For in the mixing of the divine and the human in the Incarnation the former is always the stronger influence, as one might suppose from an understanding of divinity as immutable. Regarding Cant 1:7 ("where do you rest *in meridiano*?"), implying refuge in Egypt, [57] Gregory writes:

> Inasmuch as there is a remainder of a spiritual sense, we take *meridianum* to be the very body of Christ because *meridianum* is near to the extremity, not at the extremity — i.e., because it has been undertaken towards the end of the age it is called meridianum 'spiritually'; secondly, because as in the meridian region, although the air is temperate, nevertheless heat oppresses more than cold. [58]

---

[55] See Schulz-Flügel (1994), 41ff.
[56] Simonetti (1975a), 16.
[57] Cf. II, 6, 38 & 45; CCL 69, p. 181: "Quando eum Herodes quaerebat occidere" if one is interested in the plain historical sense, "...sed hoc iuxta simplicem historiam dici potest."
[58] II, 6, 45-56; CCL 69, p. 181: "...caeterum quantum ad spiritalem sensum pertinet, meridianum ipsum Christi corpus accipimus, primum quod meridianum prope finem est, non in fine; sic et prope finem saeculi salvator induit corpus; deinde quod in meridiana parte quamquam sit temperatus aer, tamen plus illic aestus quam frigus incumbit; sic {etiam} in

So although in the Incarnation the natures of God and Man are mixed (and the sexual metaphor was surely suggested by the text's use of *cubas*), nevertheless spiritual energy is more efficacious than fleshly weakness. Interestingly, where one would expect, in opposition to "*calor spiritalis*," "*carnalis frigiditas*" the text has "*carnalis fragilitas*". Since there appear to be no textual difficulties recorded by the apparatus in the *CCL* edition, nor by Schulz-Flügel, it would seem that "*fragilitas*" is what Gregory did write, "*calor*" meaning heat as energy, the opposite of "*fragilitas*."[59] In any case, the sense is that holy energy cancels out sin's torpor, allowing human beings to be sinless yet while remaining creatures; and hence there is a tempering of God and Man in the same flesh although the end-result is activity, energy, a pleasant climate because of the infinity of the divine input. The same idea is expressed at II, 278-84 under the metaphor of the smith's working of gold and silver; ''gold'' is the work of the Holy Spirit who fashioned the perfect humanity: "silver" shows the splendid holiness of his ordinary humanity. "For the Holy Spirit joined with pure and complete human nature makes the image of gold with garnishings of silver";[60] the basic idea, as here, is that the silver, still human, plays a reflective and thus responsive role.[61]

According to Ambrose, Christ is the one who is a "brother to me" (Cant. 2:16); this means that he is pre-figured by Levi, whose name means "assumed for me", "my own" (*adsumptus mihi/ipse meus*) and two other permutations. But the first means he was "assumed for me" while the second means "God's ('my own')", since his priestly function works two ways. Although this text is a digression from the discussion of Ps 118:57, and does not explicitly mention Christ or Cant, both are so ingrained in his mind that the Christologically-interpreted "formula of mutual belonging", as Robert[62] called it, dominates his understanding of Christ's two-way mediation. In *In Ps 118*, 8,4 Ambrose writes in a way that suggests the Groom is to be understood as a human being, a priestly one.[63] Dassmann associates the

---

carne Christi licet sit permixta dei et hominis substantia et quasi meridiani climatis temperamentum *spiritalis gratia* {om} praestet {praestat}, tamen plus calor spiritalis quam carnalis fragilitas operatur; et proinde dei et hominis in eadem ut dixi carne temperamentum est, <et> quod prope saeculi finem susceptum est, meridianum spiritaliter nuncupatur."

[59] Indeed "frigidus" can mean "weakness/death" — cf. *OLD*, 736,7,8.

[60] In Cant II, 278-84; CCL 69, p 190: "Quod vero adiecit: *similitudinem auri faciemus tibi cum distinctionibus argenti*, aurum cum dicit, sancti spiritus fulgorem ostendit... . Spiritus ergo sanctus cum pura et integra carne coniunctus similitudinem auri facit cum distinctionibus argenti." For the meaning of 'distinctionibus' cf. Pliny, *N.H.* 28, 3, 3, s.13.

[61] As for the connotations of the first person plural understood in Cant 1:11, cf. *Vulgate* Gen. 1:26: "Faciamus hominem ad imaginem et similitudinem nostram".

[62] See Robert et al. (1963).

[63] CSEL 62, p. 150, 14-17, then 28-p. 151,3: "*Dilectus meus mihi et ego illi; in medio uberum meorum commorabitur...* Levi enim, ut habet interpretatio, significat 'ipse mihi adsumptus', significat et 'ipse meus', significat et tantum 'adsumptus', significat et

"*Jesusfrömmigkeit*" of Ambrose's writings as something that was developed by his "*Hoheliedexegese*" (under Origen's influence). Christ is one who is not really humbled by humility, but who rejoices in lifting up our load.[64] However it is strictly *Hoheliedexegese* with one eye on the doctrine of Christ's person. A double *homoousion* is not stated explicitly; he is not "mine" until "I deserve this possession" and he is only God's in the sense of possession, not kinship.

Apponius in the same vein, but more explicitly, highlights the human aspect of the Groom. By *frater* it means someone who is *homoiousios* with the sister-bride. This is properly the soul of Christ, the humanity which he adopts and sanctifies. As in the Syriac tradition she is a bride who is worn by her Groom but who also melts to become one with him but still provides an external mode of operation (*unus in ea*) which relates the Saviour to other human beings and becomes the new "spiritual body", a sort of mode of being for them. Yet, even in a comment on *her* feelings, the Groom takes the limelight — her will is for him while his "turning" is understood as becoming a man so as to be able to redeem. [65]

Theodoret was already occupied by Christology when he wrote his commentary on the Song. J.-N. Guinot is also overly cautious in considering that there is only one comment where divinity is discussed (on Cant 3:3-4).[66] There is indeed an unusual feature in that "she" is Christ's own humanity who wraps around the divine Word. However, while in Christ's lifetime the Word

---

'adsumptus mihi ipse'. idem et mihi Levi et deo est, quomodo idem et mihi sacerdos et deo est... Adsumptus mihi vel adsumptus a me, non potest hoc sine divina esse gratia. Sicut enim possessio non potest mea esse nisi emero eam, sic non potest esse Levi nisi fuerit adsumptus a Domino. cum enim adsumptus fuerit, recte dicitur, "ipse meus."

[64] Dassmann (1978), 376: "Die humilitas Christi wird der Schnittpunkt der Beziehungen zwischen Gott und Mensch. Sie macht Christus zum mediator Dei et hominum (*In psalmum 118*,18,32)...."

[65] *Expos in Cant* XI, 1-16: CCL 19, p. 256:"*Ego dilecto meo, et ad me conversio eius*. Haec vox illius animae intellegitur quam filiae, reginae et concubinae admirando collaudant. Quae dilecto suo, Verbo Dei, ita totum sui amoris adfectum totamque suam obtulit voluntatem, ut nec in cogitationibus alterius cuiuspiam rei dilectionem admitteret sed indivisibiliter semper inhaereret ei. Pro quo munere, ad eam conversio eius facta per incarnationis collegium comprobatur, ita ut Verbum caro fieret, de quo nunc ait: Et ad me conversio eius, et unus in ea Dei Filius praedicatur. In quo mysterio praesentis versiculi vaticinium completum cognoscitur. Ego dilecto meo: quid, nisi sanctam voluntatem? Et ad me conversio eius: et quae conversio, nisi pro immensa bonitate et facturae redemptione Deus homo fieri dignaretur, quatenus iustitiae tramitem tenens caro victa, aliquando vinceret hostem et homo redimeret hominem verumdatum propria voluntate, de quo dixit propheta: *Frater non redimet, redimet homo?*"

[66] Guinot (1985), 258, who later (1992), 458, asserts that Theodoret presents "une union mystique dont l'épaisseur charnelle même s'il agit d'une chair sanctifiée et glorieuse, est pratiquement absente". This overlooks much of the force of Theodoret's use of the Song's imagery.

was on the inside, from the Ascension onwards He is on the outside of that humanity, acting protectively like a cloak for her.[67] Of course this is as much inspired by Neoplatonic axioms that the divine cannot be circumscribed, as it is by Syrian baptismal imagery.[68] The clothing with light is the assurance meant for souls in this life (what one might call the subjective reality of transfiguration) and originates with Platonizing exegesis as represented by Gregory of Nazianzus on such narratives as the Transfiguration.[69] The believer grows into Christ's form, not his substance.[70]

On the occasion of this commentary Theodoret is more concerned with questions of embodiment, spirituality and the resurrection in which the soteriological necessity is a raising of Christ's humanity by his divinity, so that in Christ the one is passive and receives the benefits of the work of the Other. Thus Guinot goes too far in claiming that Theodoret shows an "Antiochene" predisposition towards highlighting Christ's human nature. It is simply, rather, that Theodoret has already implied at the outset that the Groom who saves is the creator Word of God, with the typical Antiochene guard against Arianism — that the Groom's humanity was one of us, and so as the patient was totally passive.[71]

In his interpretation of the Song Theodoret must have been aware that if too much were made of separate parties of divinity and humanity the caricature of Antiochene Christology as involving δύο πρόσωπα would receive justification. Theodoret would have accepted Nemesius' attack on the Eunomians[72] — that they saw the union of Word and body κατὰ τὰς ἑκατέρου δυνάμεις, which was somewhat synergistic. Thus, in Theodoret's thinking, "nard" and "oils" can all be explained as issuing through a divinised humanity who has no more independent personality than a multi-coloured robe.

---

[67] See PG 81, 52CD: τὸν ποιητήν, καὶ πλάστην, καὶ δημιουργὸν, καὶ Κύριον, καὶ Θεὸν, καὶ Δεσπότην, καὶ ἀεὶ ὡσαύτως ἔχοντα, τὸ πήλινον τοῦτο ζῷον, καὶ παθητὸν, καὶ φθαρτὸν... .

[68] Cf. Bou Mansour (1988), 235: Ephraim "gets past apophaticism" by using symbols in which the relation of the visible to the invisble is simply what the Incarnation [to put on body = lbes galyuta (SdDN 45,24)] is all about. Thus the semi-corporeal metaphor for divinity: 'fire' went into the womb and came out clothed.

[69] Gregory Nazianzen, Or. 32.18. Cf. McGuckin (1986), 111, who mentions also Or.40 ('De baptismo') as connecting illumination as well as eschatological 'metamorphosis' with this sacrament.

[70] PG 81, 76C: Ὃς μετασχηματίσει τὸ σῶμα τῆς ταπεινώσεως ἡμῶν εἰς τὸ γενέσθαι αὐτὸ σύμμορφον τῷ σώματι τῆς δόξης αὐτοῦ.

[71] PG 81, 81AB: εἰκότως αὐτὸν ἀδελφιδοῦν ἡ νύμφη καλεῖ, ὡς τῆς ἀδελφῆς αὐτῆς υἱὸν γενόμενον κατὰ τὸ ἀνθρώπινον. A few lines later he highlights Aquila and Symmachus' variant of "myrrh" (σμύρνας for στακτῆς) to reinforce the idea that the humanity's raison d'être was to suffer death.

[72] Nemesius De natura hominis; Morani (ed.) (1987), p. 43.

As is well-known the Origenian tradition posited the soul of Christ as the buffer between divine and human in Christ. In the commentary on the Song the lovers' trysting-places (rock, tree) are interpreted as the soul which is the shade for the glory. In Rufinus/Origen the cover of the rock signifies the teaching and faith of Christ. That is: the ongoing effect of the soul is the revealed knowledge and the right response to that. It provides cover from the scorching temptations for souls; he is the rock on which the incendiary devil has no influence. Christ is thus described, in terms provided by Ps 17 and Ps 39, as a stepping stone as well as a veil to see at least the glory of God.[73] In other words his soul acts as a meeting place for the divine Groom and humanity.

Rufinus presents a relationship of "the Word encased in a special man" to the Church. As for Crouzel's view of Origen's Christology[74] — that Origen thought of the Word-Son being necessarily contained within the human soul — Rufinus perhaps has played this theme down, not so much because it was obvious or inadequate, but because it might provoke controversy concerning adoptionism and 'pre-existence'. In any case, the 'perfect soul', as an extraterrestrial reality, a 'universal' did not fit the edifying task of presenting the message in the down-to-earth terms of love. Furthermore, the text of the Commentary reveals that the soul, compared to inanimate objects in the Song, is in no way an essential part of the Groom himself: that is reserved for the Word.

As for the question, "who was the agent in redemption?", A. LeBoulluec has claimed that *even* within *Peri Archôn*, it is not always the soul of Christ; sometimes it is the Word, and so the teaching is ambiguous and inconsistent.[75] It may have been this confusion which led Theophilus to accuse Origen of teaching 'two saviours'. Yet, in the relevant sections of *De Principiis*, according to Rufinus' translation, it is only clearly 'the Word' who is meant when Phil 2:7 is alluded to; it is said (*DP* II, 6,1) and implied (IV, 4,5) that the Son of God himself is meant where the Scripture says the one who descended was "in very nature God". It is better to rest with what is said in *DP* II, 6,3 and 6 — that by a a rapprochement of the iron in the fire towards 'fire' itself, the two are identifiable with the one person, the Word, as

---

[73] For all these attributes of Christ, see Baehrens, p. 230, 14-15 and p. 231, 5-7: "... sed petram vult ei esse velamen, id est firma et solida Christi dogmata."... "apud David petra haec quasi fundamentum et crepido quaedam est animae, per quam pergit ad Deum, et apud Solomonem velamen est animae ad mystica sapientiae secreta tendentis..."

[74] E.g., Crouzel (1989), 110.

[75] Le Boulluec (1987). See especially 228ff, for discussion of Theophilus' opposition; e.g., his citation of and reaction to a piece, apparently omitted by Rufinus of *PArch* IV, 4,4, as preserved in *Eranistes*, Flor. II, 58: Ettlinger (ed.), p. 171f, which indicated that the union between the Word and the Soul of Christ was the same as that between the Father and the Son.

agent of salvation; *Contra Celsum* IV, 18 teaches that the Word became the *deus absconditus* behind the human soul, and so the make-up of Christ is conceived of after a linear model: Word-human soul-physical appearance. But the person is the Word to which the soul and ultimately body are assimilated through their own inclination. In the *Commentary on the Song of Songs* which treats the Groom as one *persona*, there is no question of two agents of salvation. Rufinus promotes the scheme wherein the Incarnate Word is Saviour via and by means of the Man Jesus, with the Word as totally permeating the humanity as far as the soul but not so far as the body; there is a lack of emphasis on Christ's physical sufferings or his miracles. He is one who offers change and salvation through an affective life lived wisely. So the Groom's soul-humanity, although not, strictly speaking, his person (*contra* Crouzel), is that which, having been specially made, screens the divinity, pioneers salvation and gathers in other souls — to make available his benefits by access to a salvific relationship with the Groom who is the Word. What is offered is cast in 'masculine' imagery of "rock" and "shelter", and human souls are expected to enter into that protection from Satanic attack and God's blinding light.

In the Third Book of the Rufinus-translated Commentary, on Cant 1:16, it is more that Christ's body is the bed where God and humans meet. "The Word" is distinguished from Christ as belonging to a higher level of faith; the latter belongs to the inferior 'earthly' foundation of the 'economy' which the former presupposes. We have already observed that the Christ-Church and Word-Soul schemas are so often treated separately.

> But these ones who only believed in the Groom, but were not able to see the extent of the beauty of the Word of God, say: 'We saw and he did not have looks or fairness, but was bad-looking and lacking before the sons of men' (Is 52:3f).[76]

The believing soul may come close to the Word because Jesus, (as the 'person' of the Groom) made his body to be their meeting place:

> Think, of course, if it may also be possible for that body which Jesus assumed to be called 'bed' shared between him and the Bride [ie the created wisdom, his soul], since through it [the bed] the Church seems to have been joined to Christ and to be able to take a share of the Word of God, according to which he is said to be "Mediator of God and men" and according to what the Apostle says, that in him we have 'access through faith in the hope of the glory of God'. [77]

---

[76] Baehrens, p. 175, 8-11: "Hi vero, qui tantummodo credunt sponso, non tamen perspicere potuerunt, in Verbo Dei quanta sit pulchritudo, dicunt: *et vidimus, et non habebat speciem neque decorem, sed species eius indecora et deficiens prae filiis hominum.*"

[77] Baehrens, p. 176, 18-24: "Considera sane, ne forte possit etiam illud corpus, quod assumpsit Iesus, commune ei cum sponsa *cubile* nominari, quoniam quidem per ipsum videtur ecclesia Christo esse sociata et participium Verbi Dei capere potuisse secundum quod

Notice that, speaking precisely, it is Jesus (who is the Wisdom *persona* whom the Word was protologically united with) who assumes the body like one more layer, and thus enables the Word to commune with the Church-Bride. The opinion[78] is not necessarily 'semi-Pelagian', although Rufinus shared with Cassian the inheritance of Evagrian spirituality and its emphasis on participating in the perfect mind of Christ's love for God.[79] According to what we find later, only "lovers" are eligible for salvation; it is not that their souls made a choice for God before they were born but that they have followed the example given by Christ's acting in the image of God.[80]

The vision is hierarchical with steps between Word-perfect soul-humanity-other souls; yet the Word's presence reaches down through all of the others. Perhaps unfortunately, the Cistercian development of this hermeneutical disjunction into an ontological one, separating the icon of the humanity from the Word and presenting it as the limit to contemplatives ultimately meant that the humanity of Christ would become the person, with his divinity reduced to "spiritual wisdom" which the spiritual receive as they love that form.[81]

Concerning the motif of the Groom's "shadow", H. Crouzel observes that the second half of Cant 2:3 which deals with the *umbra* of the "apple-tree" as "the protection of the Son of God" in which the Church longs to sit, with allusion to Ps 90 (91):1 LXX.[82] Crouzel explains that by employing *virtus Altissimi* in Lk 1:35 Rufinus-Origen understands that: "...la Puissance du Très-Haut, c'est-à-dire le Fils, dont Puissance est 'une dénomination', 'un aspect', met sur Marie son ombre, son âme humaine, unie au Verbe dès la préexistence." Also: "C'est donc le Verbe, Puissance de Dieu, qui met en Marie son 'ombre', son âme, pour qu'elle prenne chair en elle."[83] Crouzel

---

et *mediator Dei et hominum* dicitur et secundum quod Apostolus dicit quoniam in ipso *habemus accessum per fidem in spe gloriae Dei.*"

[78] Baehrens, p. 169, 9-12: "Denique et lex mundum dicit *esse omne vas*, quod alligatum est, *immundum* vero, *quod solutum fuerit et non ligatum*' (Nu 19,15). Cuius rei haec profecto figura erat quod Christus, in quo numquam fuit ulla immunditia peccati, *alligamentum guttae* dicitur." The beauty of Christ (in scent or appearance) is to be imitated; cf. p. 179, 8ff: "Possumus...florem fieri Verbum Dei et initia bonorum operum docere."

[79] *Pace* Brésard-Crouzel, in Origen (1991), p. 520f.

[80] Baehrens, p. 189. As Harl (1987b) has shown, choices made by souls in the heavenly realms are only parallel to, or simultaneous with, human choices on earth and do not pre-exist or cause them.

[81] See McGinn (1994), 193-224.

[82] Crouzel et al., (1993), 531, n. 2. Rufinus (Baehrens, p. 181): "Igitur *in huius meli umbra concupiscit* sponsa *residere*, vel ecclesia, ut diximus, in protectione filii Dei". The LXX of the psalm has: ἐν βοηθείᾳ τοῦ ὑψίστου, ἐν σκέπῃ τοῦ Θεοῦ τοῦ οὐρανοῦ; the VL of the Psalter has: "in protectione Altissimi".

[83] See Crouzel (1981), 74, n. 57.

admits all this is said "elliptiquement". It may well be that, as *virtus Altissimi* in Ps 90:1 is interpreted as *virtus filii Dei*, so too in Lk 1:35 the shadow of the power of the most-high is taken by Rufinus-Origen to be the worldly or economic manifestation of the Eternal Son's protectiveness; thus the shadow is actually defined as equivalent to the *life* (*vita* doing service for ψυχή) or, as subjectively appropriated, *faith* in his Incarnation (cf Lam 4:20)[84]; Crouzel notes that the Lamentations verse is a major text for Origen's Christology [85] and that the shadow of Christ there is referred to his human soul, his humanity, under which we live, protected, in this world: "L'ombre du Christ désigne son âme humaine, son humanité, sous laquelle nous vivons en ce monde-ci. Pour nous, hommes terrestres, elle est en quelque sorte, après le Verbe, Image de Dieu, une seconde image intermédiaire, par laquelle nous parvient la participation à l'image de Dieu et qui sert de modèle immédiat à notre imitation."[86] This shadow is presumably a facet of the Bridegroom's protection. Crouzel then hints at a position he develops more fully elsewhere,[87] that this soul mediates between the Logos which remains in the Godhead at all times and the rest of human souls.

What Crouzel emphasises is the Commentary's fondness for the human Jesus as the model soul who exercises virtues and communicates what human beings can know of the divine Logos. "Ce n'est pas la divinité; c'est l'âme parfaite assumée par le Verbe qui est proposée en modèle; c'est l'humanité du Christ qui est médiatrice entre le Verbe et les hommes."[88] However, Crouzel elsewhere holds it to be a key tenet of Origen and Origenist theology, represented in the Commentary, that this soul was pre-existently joined to the Word from creation and that such a hybrid figure is the Husband in the Song, the Groom of the pre-existent Church: "Le Christ-homme existe donc dès la préexistence, bien avant l'Incarnation. Il est l'Epoux de l'Eglise de la préexistence, formée de l'ensemble des créatures raisonnables."[89]

---

[84] Baehrens, p. 183, 13-p.184, 1: "Sed hunc ardorem* tenuiter quidem legis umbra propellit, *Christi* vero *umbra*, in qua nunc *in gentibus vivimus*, id est incarnationis eius fides, avertit penitus et exstinguit...quamvis etiam eius umbrae tempus in fine saeculi compleatur..." (*= the heat of temptation).

[85] Baehrens, p. 182, 1ff: "Ait Hieremias in Lamentationibus: *Spiritus vultus nostri Christus Dominus comprehensus est in corruptionibus nostris*, cui diximus: *in umbra eius vivemus in gentibus*. Vides ergo, quomodo Spiritu sancto propheta permotus vitam de umbra Christi praeberi gentibus dicit; et quomodo non vitam nobis praebeat umbra eius, cum et in conceptu corporis ipsius ad Mariam dicatur: *Spiritus sanctus veniet super te, et virtus altissimi obumbrabit tibi*? Si ergo obumbratio fuit altissimi in conceptu corporis eius, merito umbra eius vitam gentibus dabit." Daniélou (1966), 76-95, saw this as exegesis with a rich ancestry in the *testimonia*.

[86] SC 376, p. 530, n. 1.

[87] Eg, Crouzel (1981), 78; also 1989, 109-110

[88] Origen (1991), p. 389.

[89] Crouzel (1981), 73.

I have spelled out Crouzel's case in order to give it a fair hearing. However attractive it may be, the more conventional understanding is that the Groom in our commentary is the Logos and one who latterly became joined to a lowly humanity; thus, M. Harl: "L'union célébrée ensuite par l'épithalame pourra prendre chez certains exégètes le sens de l'union entre le Verbe divin et l'humanité, entre le Verbe et la 'chair', lors de l'Incarnation. Lorsque cette idée sera exprimée plus nettement, peut-être se rattachera-t-elle, au commentaire d'Origène."[90] While her identification of the Word as the masculine player in the Canticles Commentary is sound — so much that, *contra* Grillmeier and implicitly, Crouzel,[91] Origen did not see Christ's human soul as the personality —, nevertheless I think Harl errs in suggesting that the theme of the Incarnation itself is only latent. In fact a theme which is stressed continually is that of the love of the soul/Church for the Word and the communication given by the latter to the former. "Bearing the image of the inner man — not the earthly, but the heavenly" is achieved by contemplating and adoring the Word which is gained through envisaging the beauty of things created in him.[92] The *iaculo electo* is the Word's messenger who speaks to the world of men and in whom is focussed the beauty of the natural order. The "chosen arrow" points to a perception of sublimity sent by the Word through *his* beauty in creation. The Word himself became our 'neighbour' and thus rescued us not on the grounds of image but because the distance had been bridged.[93] The idea is that in the love for God and neighbour as taught in the parable of the good Samaritan, the latter is founded on a love for one who is God and Man. In Origen's Christology, the distance between the Logos and '*logikoi*' is analogous to that between Father and Son/Word.[94] It seems however that (at least) Rufinus preferred to stress what bridged these two distances, the 'consubstantiality' of love, rather than the

---

[90] E.g. Harl (1987a), 254.

[91] Grillmeier (1975), 147: "Origen could ultimately be on the way to a metaphysical interpretation of the unity of Christ by means of the concept of person... For the soul of Christ was conceived as a centre of activity."

[92] See Prologue; Baehrens, p. 62, 8-11. Baehrens, p. 67, 7-16: "Amore autem et cupidine caelesti agitur anima, cum perspecta pulchritudine et decore Verbi Dei speciem eius adamaverit... . Igitur si quis potuerit capaci mente conicere et considerare horum omnium quae in ipso creata sunt, decus et speciem, ipsa rerum venustate percussus et splendoris magnificentia ceu *iaculo*, ut ait propheta, *electo* terebratus salutare ab ipso vulnus accipiet et beato igne amoris eius ardebit."

[93] Baehrens, p. 70, 25-32: "Etenim natura omnes nobis invicem proximi sumus; operibus vero caritatis fit proximus ille, qui potest benefacere ei, qui non potest. Unde et Salvator noster factus est proximus nobis nec 'pertransivit' nos, cum *semineces* ex *latronum vulneribus* iaceremus. Igitur sciendum est Dei caritatem semper ad Deum tendere, a quo et originem ducit, et ad proximum respicere, cum quo participium gerit, utpote similiter creatum in incorruptione."

[94] Daniélou (1948), 249-69.

3. The Groom

distinctions. In this it may have been, as H.-J. Vogt has argued, that over-philosophical discourse confused or bored him.[95]

In understanding what it meant for the Son of God to become the Son of Man, *propter nos* was so much a *Leitmotiv* for Augustine that in his Psalms exposition Christ's sufferings are really the Church suffering.[96] The Church has a "caractère théandrique"[97]. But in what sense? Christ may be the Church as well as the Son of God but that does not entail a *communicatio idiomatum* such that the Church is Christ; the *totus Christus* schema is merely an imprecise way of stressing the totality of Christ. As P. Borgomeo himself admits, following R. Desjardins,[98] the *sponsus-sponsa* metaphor is used to describe not the intimacy but rather the distance between the two parties as the "Head" awaits the arrival of the "Body".

The soul sees Christ's form as the provisional picture of God. Augustine, in Platonist mode, holds that the fully real is not the visible, as he explains Cant 1:10 (*Similitudines auri faciemus tibi cum distinctionibus argenti quoadusque rex in recubitu suo est*) in *De Trinitate* I, 8.[99] The arguments of the Donatists about the geography of the visible Church had foundered on the corollary that the Groom would have to be placed somewhere, which was blasphemy. Unsurprisingly, in the later Augustine's writings such Scriptures must have reference to the invisible Christ (and his invisible Church).

The priority of invisible grace over visible works in Cyril of Alexandria is apparent in his comment, supposedly on Cant 2:6 ("His left hand under my head and his right embraces me"), that the Word draws and shoots the believing soul from his bow, sending her towards that blessed destiny.[100] This is a metaphor which Cyril manufactured from biblical material.[101] There is

---

[95] Vogt (1987).

[96] Cf. Borgomeo (1972), 229: "En effet, le Christ-homme qui est tête de l'Eglise n'existe réellement que dans l'union hypostatique dans laquelle Dieu et l'homme sont un." (*Enarr in Ps* 30,2,s.2,1; CCL 38, 202): "...ut omnino dubitari non posset Christum esse caput et corpus, sponsum et sponsam, Filium Dei et ecclesiam, Filium Dei factum filium hominis propter nos, ut filios hominum faceret filius Dei."

[97] Borgomeo (1972), 235.

[98] Desjardins (1966).

[99] CCL 50, p. 49, 70ff: "...id est ut necessaria non sit dispensatio similitudinum per angelicos principatus et potestates et virtutes. Ex quarum persona non inconvenienter intelligitur dici in cantico canticorum ad sponsam: *Similitudines auri faciemus tibi cum distinctionibus argenti quoadusque rex in recubitu suo est*; id est quoadusque Christus in secreto suo est, quia vita nostra abscondita est cum Christo in deo (Col 3:4)... ."

[100] PG 69, 1281D: Δείκνυσι τοίνυν, ὅτι ὁ αὐτὸς καὶ νυμφίος καὶ τοξότης ἡμῶν ἐστι, νύμφη τε καὶ βέλος ἡ κεκαθαρμένη ψυχή · ὡς βέλος οὖν πρὸς τὸν ἀγαθὸν εὐθύνει σκοπόν. Ὡς νύμφην εἰς κοινωνίαν ἀναλαμβάνει τῆς ἀφθάρτου ἀϊδιότητος, μῆκος βίου καὶ ἔτη ζωῆς, διὰ τῆς δεξιᾶς χαριζόμενος.

[101] Cf. Wickham (1981a), 44f: "Cyril often said that the union of God and man in Christ was impenetrably mysterious and that it was very hard indeed to find the right words in

also less than in other commentators on the same theme the sense that the soul has a long journey to get to God: the distance between Creator and humankind has simply been bridged by "the embrace" — surely that of the Incarnation.[102] Cyril develops this (the Τάχα δὲ does not introduce an alternative, rather a speculative advance along the same line) by saying that it is the deeds of Christ's soul which embraced humanity even while the deeds of his body sustained it. It seems very likely that Cyril was qualifying any synergist claim that God was in Christ only like a helping right hand.[103]

So the foundation and the perpetual focus of any spiritual response is to be the economy of God in Christ.[104] For Cyril, Nicaea had not expressed the mode of union in Christ because it was inexpressible. He lacks the precision of a Theodotus or a Severus. Yet the most unlikely biblical images are harnessed, often to maintain that Christ's divinity and humanity had to be respected as complete and perfect:

> Perhaps therefore the hands are a symbol of actions. The actions of the left hand signify the body, those of the right hand the things of the soul. Those being 'right' have obtained the better portion as they embrace the bodily necessities. For as the hand which embraces is above and has that which it embraces within its clasp, so too those actions set apart in view of the life to come bind tightly around every irrational movement of the body, guarding the life firm and secure; nor is anything able to effectively conspire against the soul which is embraced by the Groom.[105]

---

which to pin down even the features of its mode, never mind explain it... . Yet where metaphysics runs dry, imagination is an ever-flowing stream."

[102] PG 69,1284B: δεῖ γὰρ τὰ τοῦ παρόντος βίου κἂν πολὺ νομίζηται χρηστὰ καὶ περίβλεπτα, ὑποτετάχθαι τῇ κεφαλῇ τῆς τελείας ψυχῆς, μόνην τὴν ἀναγκαίαν χρείαν παρέχοντα τῷ σώματι, ὡς τὸ προσκεφάλαιον τῇ κεφαλῇ. Τὰ δὲ τοῦ μέλλοντος αἰῶνος, ἐπειδὴ θεῖα ὄντα ἐπάνω τῆς ἀνθρωπίνης ἐφέστηκε φύσεως, διὰ τῆς περιλήψεως τὸ ὑπερέχον ᾐνίξατο.

[103] The connection between Theodore and *Odes of Solomon* 8:6 is made by Drijvers (1985), 104, with reference to Norris (1963), 191-207 and 221ff. The "indwelling" Christology means the opposite of reciprocity, allowing the human only the freedom to be perfectly human.

[104] According to Wickham (1984).

[105] PG 69,1284 BC: Τάχα δὲ, ἐπειδήπερ αἱ χεῖρες πράξεων εἰσι σύμβολον. αἱ δὲ τῆς ἀριστερᾶς χειρὸς πράξεις τὰ τοῦ σώματος σημαίνουσιν, αἱ δὲ τῆς δεξιᾶς, τὰ τῆς ψυχῆς · δεξιὰ ὄντα τὸν ἀμείνω κλῆρον εἴληχε, περιέχονται τὰς σωματικὰς ἀνάγκας. Ὡς γὰρ ἡ περιλαμβάνουσα χεὶρ καὶ ἐπάνω ἐστὶ καὶ ἐντὸς ἀγκάλην ἔχει τὸ περιληφθὲν, οὕτως αἱ πρὸς τὸν σκοπὸν τῆς μελλούσης ζωῆς ἀποτεταγμέναι πράξεις, πᾶν κίνημα τοῦ σώματος ἄλογον περισφίγγουσαι, εὔτακτον καὶ συνδεδεμένην φυλάττουσι τὴν ζωήν· οὐδ' ἑνὸς ἐπιβουλεύειν δυναμένου τῇ περιληφθείσῃ ὑπὸ τοῦ νυμφίου ψυχῇ.

3. The Groom

The talk of the divinity as ruling the soul, or the life, fits with what Cyril says elsewhere of the inseparability of the natures.[106] As perfume gives the lily its liliness so does the Godhead "all but become corporeal". This intimates the closeness of the union, according to which Christ's body "effected things divine".[107]

It is certainly a tendency of the Alexandrian tradition to view the human soul in Jesus as an attribute of his body as 'ensouled'; yet where there is no risk of its rivalling the Word or being confused with it, it is the important faculty which receives power from the Word. Thus Cyril's legacy included ἐμψυχομένη ψυχῇ λογικῇ καὶ νοερᾷ (promoted by Constantinople 553, *Anathema* 9) which has all the signs of warding off Apollinarianism but little else that is positive about Christ's soul. As G. Jouassard demonstrated, Cyril spoke of the human soul of Christ only when using the soul-body analogy; it was not essential to his Christological scheme. P. Galtier too has shown that Cyril really only paid lip-service to the idea of a soul in Christ, merely avoiding Apollinarianism but without saying anything positive about the role of his soul in a way that left the door open for post-Chalcedonian monotheletism.[108]

Supreme value is ascribed to the Incarnation itself, where the "gold" of Cant 3:10 is held to signify the union.[109] The comparison with a section of Severus' *De Beata Maria*, which Mai proposed,[110] affords an insight into how the metaphorical language of gold, incense and other priestly accoutrements were used for Christological insight by a later writer in the same tradition. Yet it is hard to be sure that Severus was much influenced by the associations provided by the Song in particular; in the sermon the gold is that of the ark of the covenant as distinct from the wood which he suggests is an inadequate (possibly Nestorian) analogy as it does not allow for the divinity to influence

---

[106] E.g., *Scholion* no. 10: Schwartz, *ACO* I, 5, p. 190: "In cantico canticorum ipse nobis introductus est dicens dominus noster Iesus Christus: *ego flos campi, [et] lilium convallium.* quemadmodum ergo tamen unum ex utroque intelligitur lilium, corrumpetur tamen ratio ipsius unius rei discessu (in subiecto enim corpore odor est), ita etiam de Christo intellegimus divinitatis naturam, quae suam excellentissimam maiestatem, ut oderem suavissimum, mundo dispergat, tamquam in subiecto esse corpore humanitatis et id quod incorporale est per naturam, per adunationem dispensatoriam, paene dicam, fatum fuisse corporale, propterea quod voluit sese cognosci per corpus. in eo enim divina signa operatus est. igitur id quod incorporale est, tamquam in suo corpore intellegatur, quemadmodum etiam odor in flore subiecto; lilium tamen iam et odor nominatur et flos."

[107] See translation by Wickham (1981a), 51, n. 11; cf. also *Dialogues on the Trinity* 6 (PG 75, 593) and *In Io* 11, 2 (Pusey 2, 639).

[108] Jouassard (1957); Galtier (1952).

[109] PG 69, 1288AB: Ἡ πνευματικὴ δὲ συνάφεια νοείσθω χρυσίον, ἡ τιμία καὶ θεία. Καὶ τὴν κατὰ τὴν ἔρημον γὰρ κιβωτὸν ἔσωθεν καὶ ἔξωθεν, χρυσίον ὑπήλειφεν εἰς ἐμφάνειαν τῆς θείας ἐνώσεως.

[110] At p. 215 of his own translation from the Syriac (*Spicilegium Romanum* t. X.)

the humanity. Cyril had already commented on the unity of the gold and the wood in the ark — in *Scholion* 11.[111] So, for Cyril, the Groom is very much the Word who is not tied to, but rather directs his human 'vehicle'.

3.5 The motif of "leaping" and the Incarnation as the Word's descent and ascent

Cant 2:8, 10b

2·8 Φωνὴ ἀδελφιδοῦ μου· ἰδοὺ οὗτος ἥκει πηδῶν ἐπὶ τὰ ὄρη διαλλόμενος ἐπὶ τοὺς βουνούς.
2·10b Ἀνάστα ἐλθέ, ἡ πλησίον μου, καλή μου, περιστερά μου...

G. Chappuzeau opines that, according to the preface to Hippolytus' commentary, the revelation is of how the Father wants the Church to be ordered; it is this theme that "...besingt der Geist in der mannigfaltigen Ökonomie der Bilder."[112] She rightly observes that Hippolytus' definition of "economy" is wider than the common Second Century one: "Es handelt sich um alles das, was zum Heil des Menschen getan wird... . Sie ist keine Erklärung der trinitarischen Lehre."[113] Practical, pastoral, the Word is only described in his effects, and there is scant interest in speculation. For example, in relation to Cant 2:8:

> What, I ask, is the meaning of 'leaping'? It leapt down from the sky into the womb of a virgin; it leapt out of the holy belly upon the tree. It leapt from the tree into the underworld, it leapt up again from there in this human flesh to the earth. O new resurrection ! From there it leapt from the earth to heaven; he is sitting at the right hand of the Father, and from there he will leap down on to the earth to pay back the exchange of retribution.[114]

Hippolytus is simply painting salvation history from the OT to his present age with broad strokes provided by the Song. P. Meloni sees Hippolytus basing the commentary on a structure of the seven leaps ("sette salti") which the Bridegroom takes, after Cant 2:8. According to the system Meloni detects seven stages of the course which the Word takes in order to lead men back to

---

[111] *ACO* I, 5; p. 190; cf. Wickham's comment (1981a), 46f: "... fixed though the gold is, the ark is a symbol precisely because it moves."
[112] Chappuzeau (1976), 83.
[113] Ibid., Anm. 14.
[114] XXI, 2; Garitte, p. 40: "Quidnam est saliendi verbum? Desiluit de caelo in vulvam virginis; insiluit de ventre sancto super lignum; saluit de ligno in infernum; sursum saluit inde in humana hac carne ad terram. O nova resurrectio! Deinde insiluit a terra ad caelum; hic sedens a dextera Patris, et deinde desiliet in terram, ut commutationem retributionis rependat."

the Father : "1. Il Verbo è nel Padre. 2. Il Verbo è emesso dal cuore e dalla bocca del Padre. 3. Il Verbo opera la creazione insieme col Padre. 4. Il Verbo agisce nel mondo attraverso la parola dei profeti. 5. Il Verbo si fa carne. 6. Il Cristo effonde la sua divinità dalla sua carne umana consumata sulla croce. 7. Il Cristo risorto diffonde la vita nella Chiesa."[115] The Song reveals the Trinity's relationship with mankind, and the Spirit who leads Jesus and constitutes his divinity is also the life in the Church. The Spirit may be the instrument of salvation, and the Word the agent, but neither are stated to be divine in the way the Father is. Such would have been too close to the position of Noetus. However it is safe to say that Hippolytus is not especially interested in 'metaphysical' questions, and even the neat soteriological system that Meloni detects is only for Cant 2:8ff.

In Ambrose the range of the Groom's activity has been expanded: he is more at home in heavenly reaches than in the holy land. Behind the moral lesson of our need to follow adopt his soul's dispositions lis the metaphysical truth that the Son is "the young stag" to whom, like any son, is attached the force of the paternal nature (*quasi filius, cui paternae inoleverit vis naturae*) The word *inolesco* was used tropologically of implanting ideas like seeds.[116] Thus, even when in the flesh, or "surrounded by its chains", Jesus, the Lord, was not really prisoner.[117] The reference in the last sentence is to Christ's universal origins as a human being, on the principle that the free Word is not tied to any one people that he had to assume.[118]

The idea that the history of salvation operates in two distinct stages is thus reflected in Ambrose. This means that the love relationship between Christ and the Church (in all its mutuality — it is not simply Christ's love for the Church) is something realised between Jesus and his Jewish witnesses in the Incarnation, and is over by time of Jesus's Ascension; whereas that between the Word and the soul is something which begins with the New Testament and is projected from the Christ-Church relationship into the realms between

---

[115] Meloni (1977), 100; 120. Meloni's attempt (1989) to find a prototype as far back as Ignatius for this "anointing" motif is strained. For in Ignatius, *Eph 17,1*, despite Meloni's claims: "La vita immortale del Cristo risorto serà comunicata a tutta l'umanità" (59), it is simply ἀφθαρσία that he pours out - there is no mention of "spirit" or "soul" (*vita/psyche*).

[116] See *OLD*, 917.

[117] *In Ps 118*, 6, 23; CSEL 62, p. 119f: "...*exsurge, veni, proxima mea*, hoc est: surge a mortuis, exsurge a vinculis quibus circumdata tenebaris. *exsurge*, quia ego resurrexi tibi, solve vinculum iniquitatis, quia ego iam solui tibi. *veni*, quia iam retia soluta sunt. virgo peperit, puer natus ex virgine est, nihil debet muliebri hereditati, quasi filius mulieris non tenetur."

[118] Cf., e.g., *In Ps 43*, 35ff; also: Dassmann (1978), 376. Ct. especially, the local Jewish "ecclesia" as Christ's humanity in Philo of Carpasia.

heaven and earth.[119] Ambrose here gives notice of his desire to go (with Origen) beyond Hippolytus's interpretation how the disciples (Church) have been, figuratively, leapt upon, and to transfer the primary reference of the Song beyond the Incarnation to its aftermath in the souls' "rising up" (Cant 2:11).

A good example of exegesis in theological service appeared in the late 370s when he attacked 'literalistic' Arianism as the *incubus* of Gothic destabilization.[120] Ambrose insisted that there is no hierarchy in the Father-Son relationship, but that they dwell side-by-side in single divine substance. This was for Ambrose the "categoria cardine della riflessione sul mistero divino."[121] It was not that he misunderstood τρεῖς ὑποστάσεις as meaning "three gods" and so qualified or glossed this by the preferred πρόσωπα,[122] but that even the more moderate idea of there being three πρόσωπα, characters or personalities within God was still anathema; the Son and Spirit were distinct and divine only because they were aspects of the one God in meta-historical (thus avoiding modalism) manifestation. Thus for all Ambrose's supposed closeness to the Cappadocians he remained ultimately 'Western', for he accepted τρία πρόσωπα like τρεῖς ὑποστάσεις as meaning God in three aspects; the fact that in Aquileia's symbol the two phrases are side by side untranslated perhaps confirms suspicions that Ambrose misunderstood both. So nothing can be said about Him in human language terms; rather, He is known, impressionistically, through Scripture's images. He was interested in the reality of God among real people, both his flock and the patriarchs. This does not mean that Western versions were any less theology or Christology, but rather that they focussed on Christ more from the moral angle, on matters of will and receptivity to grace.[123] Ambrose's reaction was to consider the Son as of equal standing and will as the Father (moving away from the dominant Western position under the influence of Neoplatonism[124]) the consideration of the force of the Trinitarian analogy led him to consider the Spirit as the power of God, not vice-versa.

---

[119] *In Ps 118*, 6, 8; CSEL 62,112: "Diximus de Christo et ecclesia; dicamus de anima et verbo. Anima iusti sponsa est verbi. Haec si desideret, si cupiat, si oret et oret adsidue et oret sine ulla disceptatione et tota intendat in verbo: subito vocem sibi videtur eius audire quem non videt et intimo sensu odorem divinitatis eius agnoscit... ."

[120] Cf. Paredi (1985), 145-166, esp. 156, concerning *De Fide* III-IV (380): "L'arianesimo peccava spesso di letteralismo esagerato nell' interpretazione della Bibbia. 'È lo Spirito che vivifica' insiste il vescovo."

[121] Cf. Alzati (1993), 61ff: *substantia* never had the sense which ὑπόστασις had for the Greek church.

[122] *Contra* Simonetti (1975b), 549f.

[123] Herrmann (1958), 198: "Die Synode ist das Werk des Ambrosius... . Der Sohn habe einen unbeseelten Leib angenommen und in der Passion mitgelitten."

[124] Ibid., 217f.

3. The Groom

Yet the price was a low-grade conception of humanity which acted as the Word's buffer against passion and was empowered by the Spirit in order to let the Spirit out. In both early and late Ambrose the humanity of Christ is little other than a sacrament — a created if special thing[125] — which points beyond itself to a cosmic realisation of a new standing of God the Word to the human soul. The fate of Christ's own soul is of little interest, and Ambrose presents the notion of a soul-God nuptial union which presupposes but by-passes the Incarnation.

A focus on the interplay of the Word and the believing soul is also evident in the treatment of Cant 2:9-10 by Rufinus-Origen; yet this comes only after spending time on the second level of interpretation which involves Christ and the Church, and thus has Christology at its heart. Christ calls the Church out of the house of the OT so that she might make spiritual progress,[126] but before he can summon her he has to go through the lattice of temptation so that she is able as invited to come out through the gap he has made. The beneficiary of Christ's passing through and breaking the lattice-snare is the soul, but it is the escape route of the humanised Christ who has no original sin which she has to follow out.[127]

When, famously at Cant 2:9 the Groom is likened to a stag peering through the lattice, Rufinus-Origen show how the "deer" and "gazelle" are seen to refer to Christ. As the former, he has killed the serpent.[128] Yet this identification is made only as the last thought after describing how progressing souls are like deer with reference to verses in Scripture mentioning deer, with the intended effect that Christ is presented as the last and *perfect* example of all these.[129] The chance to stress the voluntary

---

[125] *In Ps 118*, 5,9; CSEL 62, p. 86f: "Christus ergo adfixus ad lignum, sicut malum pendens in arbore, bonum odorem mundanae fundebat redemptionis, quia peccati gravis detersit faetorem et unguentum potus vitalis effudit. *tamquam malum*, inquit, *in lignis silvae, ita consobrinus meus in medio filiorum*, eo quod super prophetas et apostolos intima corda hominum verborum suavitate mulcebat. sed non solum odor, verum etiam cibus suavis in malo est; ergo cibus suavis est Christus."

[126] Baehrens, pp. 220, 27-221,12.

[127] Baehrens, p. 222, 19-26: "Venit ergo ad ista *retia*, sed involvi in iis solus ipse non potuit; quin immo diruptus iis et contritis dat ecclesiae suae fiduciam, ut audeat iam calcare *laqueos* et transire *per retia* et cum omni alacritate dicere:*anima nostra sicut passer erepta est de laqueo venantium; laqueus contritus est, et nos liberati sumus.* (Ps 123:7 LXX) Quis autem *contrivit laqueum* nisi ille, qui solus in eo teneri non potuit? Quamvis enim et in morte fuerit, sed voluntarie et non, ut nos, necessitate peccati. Solus enim est, qui fuit *inter mortuos liber* (Ps 86:6 LXX)."

[128] A patristic commonplace, but *contra* Domagalski (1994) and Simon (1951) it is more likely that *Physiologus* drew on Origen for the content of the Christological interpretation rather than vice-versa.

[129] Baehrens, p. 213,25 - p. 214,2: "*Cervus* quoque *amicitiarum* quis alius videbitur nisi ille, qui perimit *serpentem* illum, qui *seduxerat Evam* et alloquii sui flatibus peccati in eam venena diffundens omnem posteritatis eius subolem contagio praevaricationis infecerat, (et)

humiliation of Christ is not missed; he was, to speak more specifically, like the diminutive fawn of deer because he was born as a tiny boy.[130] But his 'deerness' is taken from those from whom he has descended *secundum carnem*; his fleshly stock was made perfect by the voice of the Lord.[131] However the translation *perfectos* indicates a following of Symmachus (πληθύνοντος).[132] As for being like a gazelle, this is different and relates to the Word as the inner essence of Christ who alone sees or (rather) knows God — the qualification, probably added by Rufinus, of 'knows' is to stress that God remains invisible while he is known to one only.[133] The idea in our passage[134] is that from within the inwards of Christ there is provided an antidote (the Spirit) to spiritual blindness for others as well as himself, to enable them to 'see' him as well as he can 'see' God.[135] "And he said to his disciples: 'He who has seen me has seen the Father.' We should not be so silly as to think that [this means that] he who saw Jesus according to the flesh also saw the Father."[136] The point is not that the Scribes and Pharisees knew who Jesus was but not the Father; they did not even know Jesus.[137] As it says a few lines later, of all those who saw him only those who knew that he was the 'Word of God' and 'the Son of God' really saw him. Christ's humanity

---

venit *solvere inimicitias in carne sua*, quas inter Deum et hominem noxius mediator effecerat?" The deer specification comes from Prov 5:19 whose 'literal' sense concerns the 'wife of your youth', who in the LXX is called ἔλαφος φιλίας.

[130] Baehrens, p. 214, 6-11: "Quod si etiam hoc requirendum est, cur non *cervo*, ut in aliis, sed *hinnulo cervorum* comparatur, illud adverte quod, *cum in forma Dei esset, filius datus est nobis et puer natus est nobis, cuius potestas super humerum eius*. Ideo ergo *hinnulus cervorum* est, quia parvulus *puer natus est*."

[131] Ibid., p. 214, 11-15: "Et forte possunt *cervi* accipi sancti quique, ut Abraham et Isaac et Iacob et David et Solomon et omnes ex quorum semine *Christus secundum carnem* desendit. Quos *cervos vox Domini perfectos fecit* (Ps 28:9 LXX) et ipsorum est *hinnulus* iste, qui ex ipsis secundum carnem *natus est puer*." The psalm reference is: φωνὴ κυρίου καταρτιζομένου ἐλάφους; cf. Jerome, *iuxta Hebraeos*: "Vox Domini obstricans cervis"; Vulg: "Vox Domini praeparantis cervos".

[132] See Field, *Origenis Hexapla*, II, 129.

[133] Cf. *P Arch* I, 1,8. Koetschau, p. 26, 2-4: "Aliud est videre, aliud cognoscere: videri et videre corporum res est, cognosci et cognoscere intellectualis naturae est."

[134] Baehrens, p. 215, 10f: "Visus, quo Deus videtur, non est corporis, sed mentis et spiritus".

[135] Baehrens, p. 215, 4ff: "Asserunt namque hi, quibus medicinae peritia est, inesse huic animali intra viscera humorem quendam, qui caliginem depellat oculorum et obtunsiores quosque visus exacuat. Merito igitur *capreae* vel *damulae* Christus comparatur, quia non solum ipse *videt patrem*, sed et videri ab his facit quorum visus ipse curaverit."

[136] Baehrens, p. 215, 15-18: "Et ideo dicebat ad discipulos quia: '*qui me vidit, vidit et patrem*'. Et utique non ita inepti erimus, ut putemus quod qui secundum corpus Iesum vidit, viderit etiam patrem (Jn 14:9)".

[137] Baehrens, p. 215, 18-21.

operates as a screen for the soul to know the light without being blinded.[138] But it is the Word who is the light who can be known, intimately, like a Groom.

In Origen's two homilies which were translated by Jerome, both Groom and Bride are called "lilies", for both display the function of emitting fragrance.[139] In the Groom's case, he became like that to stand in for the tree of life (*pro ligno vitae*), thus renewing paradise. The *kenosis* is described in terms of a small piece of the Logos coming to earth. The metaphor is borrowed from the interpretation of Dan 2:34.[140] The one descended was no less than the Word. When dealing with the Song himself, Jerome likewise prefers a *Christusmystik*,[141] urging himself and Eustochium to expect the return of the corporeal Christ in the geographically defined Holy Land. Mary becomes the paradigm of such expectation, as distinct from her exalted function in the Ambrosian *Logosmystik*.[142] The presupposition is that Christ has shed something of his sanctifying power on the sacred sites which the Queen of the South came to visit "prophetically".[143]

---

[138] Baehrens, p. 215, 26 - p. 216, 1: "ita et cum plures essent, qui eum videbant, nullus *vidisse* eum dicitur, nisi qui agnovit quod *Verbum Dei* et *filius Dei* est; in quo simul utique *agnosci* et *videri* dicitur pater." The notion of the soul and "warmth" as a lesser form of light is also found in Plotinus, *Enneads* VI, 7,22.

[139] Baehrens, p. 49, 24 - p. 50, 7: "Post haec sponsus loquitur: '*ego flos campi et lilium convallium*'. Propter me, qui in *valle* eram, descendit in *valle* et in *valle* veniens fit *lilium vallium* pro *ligno vitae*, quod plantatum est in paradiso Dei, et totius *campi*, id est totius mundi et universae terrae, *flos* factus est. Quid enim sic potest esse *flos* mundi ut vocabulum Christi? '*Unguentum effusum nomen eius*'; aliter id ipsum dicitur: '*ego flos campi et lilium convallium*', et haec quidem de semet ipso. Deinde sponsam laudans ait: '*ut lilium in medio spinarum, sic proxima mea in medio filiarum*'."

[140] Baehrens, p. 45, 3-11: "Et sicuti secundum alium sensum *lapis erat praecisus e monte sine manibus* nostri in carne Salvatoris adventus — neque enim totus *mons* fuit, qui descendit ad terras nec poterat humana fragilitas totius montis magnitudinem capere, *sed lapis ex monte, lapis offensionis, petra scandali* descendit in mundum —, sic secundum alium intellectum *stilla* nuncupatur. Oportebat quippe, ut, quia *omnes gentes in stillam situlae reputatae sunt*, [Is 40:15] is qui pro omnium salute factus est omnia, etiam *stilla* ad eas fieret liberandas. Quid enim pro nostra salute non factus est?"

[141] Especially in a remarkable passage: *Ep.* 22 *Ad Eustochium*, 25-26: *CSEL* 54, pp. 178-82.

[142] Cf. Simon (1951), 165-82, with reference to *Adv Jovinianum* I, 30-31; PL 23, 154.

[143] Hennings (1991), 51f, n.10, claims that Jerome in *Ep.* 121, 10 (CSEL 56, p. 3) read שב (Cant 7:1) as seva to make the connection with the Queen of Sheba. For "holy places" see Kelly (1975), 393. "tu regina appellanda es Saba, in cuius mortali corpore non regnat peccatum et quae ad dominum tota mente conversa audies ab eo: *convertere, convertere, Sunamitis*."

3.6 Coronation as the Word's triumphal passion

Cant 3:11

ἐξέλθατε καὶ ἴδετε
ἐν τῷ βασιλεῖ Σαλωμων
ἐν τῷ στεφάνῳ, ᾧ ἐστεφάνωσεν αὐτὸν ἡ μήτηρ αὐτοῦ
ἐν ἡμέρᾳ νυμφεύσεως αὐτοῦ
καὶ ἐν ἡμέρᾳ εὐφροσύνης καρδίας αὐτοῦ.

Two points can be made from Philo of Carpasia's commentary.[144] First, the Greek text of Philo refers "his coronation" to his *triduum spatium*, the Latin to his day of hanging on the Cross. Second, while both Greek and Latin agree that his "mother" was the synagogue and that the coronation and betrothal are contemporaneous (on the Cross), a comparison of the two underlined clauses (below) shows a difference of approach. In the Greek, it is Christ who is the subject of the second sentence and is said to have originated from the Jews; according to the Latin, it is his mother who was Jewish. When Philo moves on to talk of the *spiritual* mother, although Welserheimb takes Philo to be saying that the Bride is secure in the arms of the mother Wisdom, awaiting her wedding day,[145] the truth is that for Philo, "'the mother of the bride' is Wisdom, 'the kinsman' is Our Lord Jesus Christ, in whom he carried the man, in whom wisdom was also present, that is the eternal Word was poured in." The Word, all-competent is thus the mother as well as the Groom (the divine Son), so that that she enjoys him within her mother's house.[146]

---

[144] PG 40, 88A: ἐν τῷ στεφάνῳ ᾧ ἐστεφάνωσεν αὐτὸν ἡ μήτηρ αὐτοῦ, ὅτε τὸν ἀκάνθινον στέφανον ἐπέθηκεν αὐτοῦ τῇ κεφαλῇ ἡ τῶν Ἰουδαίων Συναγωγή. Μητέρα δὲ τῆς σαρκὸς αὐτοῦ ταύτην καλεῖ ἐπειδὴ τὸ κατὰ σάρκα ἐξ Ἰουδαίων ἀνέτειλεν. Ἡμέραι δὲ νυμφεύσεως αὐτου αἱ τρεῖς εἰσι τοῦ πάθους. — Philo (Ceresa-Gastaldo) (1979), p. 122: "quando enim crucifixerunt eum coronam de spinis super caput eius posuerunt. Mater autem carnis eius est synagoga quae secundum carnem ex Iudaeis est; videte quando eum coronavit mater eius: in diebus — inquit — desponsationis eius, hoc est in diebus passionis; tunc enim sanctam hanc desponsabat ecclesiam quando in cruce pendebat...."

[145] Welserheimb (1948), 439.

[146] PG 40, 137C, is as follows: Μήτηρ τῆς νύμφης ἡ σοφία, ἀδελφιδὸς δὲ ταύτης ὁ Κύριος ἡμῶν Ἰησοῦς Χριστός, ἐν ᾧ ἐφόρεσεν ἀνθρώπῳ [leg. ἄνθρωπον], ὃν καὶ παροῦσα ἡ σοφία, τουτέστιν ὁ πρὸ αἰώνων Λόγος, ἐν αὐτῷ συνεκεράσατο. In Latin (p. 184): "Mater autem sponsae sapientia est, fratruelis vero dominus Iesus incarnatus et factus perfectus homo, qui est ante saecula deus verbum."

3. The Groom

3.7 The Groom's descent

Cant 4:16-5:1

4·16 Ἐξεγέρθητι, Βορρᾶ, καὶ ἔρχου, νότε, διάπνευσον κῆπόν μου, καὶ ῥευσάτωσαν ἀρώματά μου.
καταβήτω ἀδελφιδός μου εἰς κῆπον αὐτοῦ
καὶ φαγέτω καρπὸν ἀκροδρύων αὐτοῦ.
5·1 Εἰσῆλθον εἰς κῆπόν μου, ἀδελφή μου νύμφη,
ἐτρύγησα σμύρναν μου μετὰ ἀρωμάτων μου,
ἔφαγον ἄρτον μου μετὰ μέλιτός μου,
ἔπιον οἶνόν μου μετὰ γάλακτός μου·
φάγετε, πλησίοι, καὶ πίετε καὶ μεθύσθητε, ἀδελφοί.

It is not without significance that the (Pseudo) Athanasian, Apollinarian and Didymian fragments and occasional comments on the Song should centre so much on Chapter Five. These three writers were each concerned with to what extent Christ's body was the expression of the Word's nature. The fragmentary nature of the comments makes it difficult to tell how much the Song inspired ideas of the nature of Christ's descent.

There is detailed 'Athanasian' exegesis of only two verses (Cant 4:16 and 5:1), which suggests the work is a homily. These lines are referred to the instructive model of the blessed disciples after Christ's crucifixion as presented in John 20:19ff, with the message that spirituality has the resurrection as its centre. At the crucifixion sin fell down because Christ at that point descended to search for and seize the devil in Hades; that it was a hidden work — this the Jews do not understand. [147]

In the Ps-Athanasian fragments there is a passage which interprets Cant 4:16 as referring to the Lord coming from the south to deliver his body which had lain for three days in the tomb in the north; this has been examined in the course of attributing it to an "Apollinarian" writer (see Ch.1). This is a typically Origen-like theme which suggests an ontological change to the humanity through its union with the Word. He, the Word, calls her "sister and bride" to help the reader realise that this is not a carnal relationship ("of the shameful flesh"); he calls her "bride" on account of the Word who is betrothed to the soul; but when he calls her "sister" it is on account of the

---

[147] PG 27, 1353C: Οὗτος γὰρ κρεμάμενος ἐπὶ ξύλου, αὐτός ἐστιν ἡ σωτηρία ἡμῶν· ἡ γὰρ τούτο σταύρωσις κάθαρσις ἁμαρτιῶν ἦν. Καὶ ἦν θέαμα μέγα τότε γιγνόμενον, ὅτι, τοῦ σώματος σταυρουμένου, ἡ ἁμαρτία ἔπιπτεν. Εἰ μὴ γὰρ ἦν οὗτος ἐσταυρωμένος ἄχρι τοῦ νᾶν, εἴλομεν τοὺς μώλωπας καὶ τὰς ἀσθενείας τῷ σώματι... . Τοῦ γὰρ σώματος κινουμένου ἐν τῷ σταυρῷ, ὁ Λόγος ἐσκύλεσε τὸν ᾅδην. Then the disciples say the words of Cant 4:16: Ἐξεγέρθητι, Βορρᾶ, καὶ ἔρχου, νότε, διάπνευσον κῆπόν μου, καὶ ῥευσάτωσαν ἀρώματα μου.

flesh which he bore.[148] However it should be understood that, as the one soul, she asks selflessly that he come a second time to take up the whole world.[149] In this sermon God and human souls are held to be already related through the image in creation, and the flesh assumed is a shining one: this has an Apollinarian tenor. There is the emphasis on the healing of our bodies by the body on the Cross, and on the Word's going alone to Hades. The mind (νοῦς)-like One separated himself from the flesh (i.e., body and soul in conjunction) but came back to reclaim what he had laid down.

According to one fragment from Apollinarius, while the same Word-Groom is everywhere at all other times through his "energies", and especially among the saints, the "symbols" of the Song almost directly reveal the Saviour "living on earth"; but these symbols also "pose the riddle", as Cant 5:17 (LXX 6:1)[150] reminds Apollinarius, as to the time of the Saviour's suffering, wounding and "stripping of his cloak". The Cross is the key point in history and, implicitly, the place where the Word took off the flesh in order to put it back on, now completely free from "passions".[151] The notion of kinship with God is noticeable throughout and gets explained elsewhere by Apollinarius as something realised through the coming of the Logos Saviour as the νοῦς ἔνσαρκος. This allows all humanity to be placed with the Godhead by participation.[152] 'Sabellius' is really Marcellus of Ancyra, attacked for his 'dynamic' concept of the expansion of the Monad into the Triad and back again, with the man born of Mary the image of the invisible God. This became popularised by "Sabellians"(notably Photinus) who took Christ to be a man energised by God rather than being or even including a divine hypostasis, since the Father and Son were considered so much to be 'one'.

It is useful to compare here Apollinarius' comments on the Song culled from the Procopian Catena on the Psalms. The *monogenes* (Rondeau has shown how Didymus and Apollinarius both like this term) is depicted as one

---

[148] PG 27, 1357CD: ὧδε δὲ καὶ ἀδελφὴν καὶ νύμφην αὐτὴν ὀνομάζει, ἵνα δείξῃ, ὅτι οὐκ ἔστιν ὁ θάλαμος ἐπᾳδομένος σαρκός. Ὅταν μὲν γὰρ ὀνομάζει αὐτὴν νύμφην, διὰ τὸν Λόγον, τὸν μνηστευθέντα τὴν ψυχήν... Ὅταν δὲ καὶ ἀδελφὴν αὐτὴν ὀνομάζει, διὰ τὴν σάρκα ἣν ἐφόρεσε.

[149] PG 27, 1357D: Ὅτε μὲν γὰρ παρεκάλει αὐτὸν ἡ μακαρία αὕτη ψυχή... ὅταν μὲν γὰρ ἀκούσῃ ψυχήν, μὴ μίαν ψυχὴν ὑπολάμβανε, ἀλλ' ὅλον τὸν κόσμον.

[150] Cant 6:1: Ποῦ ἀπῆλθεν ὁ ἀδελφιδός σου, ἡ καλὴ ἐν γυναιξίν; ποῦ ἀπέβλεψεν ὁ ἀδελφιδός σου; καὶ ζητήσομεν αὐτὸν μετὰ σοῦ.

[151] PG 87, 1704D: Πανταχῇ μὲν πάρεστιν ὁ Νυμφίος Λόγος· πρὸς δὲ τὸ ἐπιτήδειον ποιεῖται τὰς ἐνεργείας, ὡς ἐν τῷ Ἰσραὴλ πρότερον, καὶ νῦν ἐν τῇ Ἐκκλησίᾳ τὸ ὅλον τοῦ Σωτῆρος ἡ παρουσία, ἐξαιρέτως δὲ ἐν τοῖς ἁγίοις· ἐνταῦθα τοίνυν διὰ τῶν συμβόλων δείκνυσιν αὐτὸν διατρίβοντα· τὸν καιρὸν αἰνιξαμένη καθ' ὃν ἔφη πατάσσεσθαι, καὶ τραυματίζεσθαι, καὶ τὴν περιβολὴν ἀφαιρεῖσθαι.

[152] See Hübner (1989); argument summarized in Hübner (1987).

who came down to his garden (with Canticles imagery employed), having loved the righteousness which from his presence grew out of faith (presumably the OT saints, inspired by epiphanies of the Word), gave himself to the Father's will, to become man and be anointed with the Holy Spirit.[153] Unlike Didymus however the condescending *monogenes* is clearly not a pre-existent soul but is the Word.

3.8 The Groom's "coming to the door" and manifestation

Cant 5:2-6

5·2 φωνὴ ἀδελφιδοῦ μου, κρούει ἐπὶ τὴν θύραν
"Ἄνοιξόν μοι, ἀδελφή μου, ἡ πλησίον μου,
περιστερά μου, τελεία μου,
ὅτι ἡ κεφαλή μου ἐπλήσθη δρόσου
καὶ οἱ βόστρυχοί μου ψεκάδων νυκτός."
5·3 Ἐξεδυσάμην τὸν χιτῶνά μου, πῶς ἐνδύσωμαι αὐτόν;
ἐνιψάμην τοὺς πόδας μου, πῶς μολυνῶ αὐτούς;
5·4 ἀδελφιδός μου ἀπέστειλεν χεῖρα αὐτοῦ ἀπὸ τῆς ὀπῆς,
καὶ ἡ κοιλία μου ἐθροήθη ἐπ' αὐτόν.
5·5 ἀνέστην ἐγὼ ἀνοῖξαι τῷ ἀδελφιδῷ μου,
χεῖρές μου ἔσταξαν σμύρναν,
δάκτυλοί μου σμύρναν πλήρη
ἐπὶ χεῖρας τοῦ κλείθρου.
5·6 ἤνοιξα ἐγὼ τῷ ἀδελφιδῷ μου,
ἀδελφιδός μου παρῆλθεν·

From Gregory of Nyssa's interpretation, it should be noticed that the verses which are referred to the Incarnation speak of the Groom's actions in terms of their effects. The visit of the Word to earth is seen as a foundational but past event. The body of the Groom is obviously the Church and the Cappadocian takes great delight in honouring it, before maintaining that the perfect monastic soul is even more praiseworthy. The Word himself is absent, in heaven, with the sense of his presence mediated, almost prosaically, through the practice of virtue. The visit of the Word to this earth has made the difference in his sanctifying it with common grace. The influence of Aristotle in Gregory's modification of Platonism on the simultaneous origins of the soul and body in *De anima et resurrectione*, and Gregory's preference for

---

[153] Mühlenberg, I, 338 (on Ps 44:8): Εἰ δὲ εἴη πρὸς τὸν μονογενῆ υἱὸν τοῦ θεοῦ ταῦτα, ὁ υἱὸς τοῦ θεοῦ μισήσας τὴν πρὸ τῆς ἐπιδημίας αὐτοῦ πολιτευομένην ἀνομίαν, ἀγαπήσας δὲ τὴν ἐκ τῆς παρουσίας αὐτοῦ φυομένην ἐκ πίστεως δικαιοσύνην ἐπιδέδωκεν ἑαυτὸν εὐδοκίᾳ πατρικῇ ἄνθρωπος γενέσθαι καὶ χρισθῆναι ἐλαίῳ ἀγαλλιάσεως τουτέστιν τῷ ἁγίῳ πνεύματι.

hiding his philosophical traces in a way his contemporary Nemesius did not, means that Gregory operated with a split image with action at two realms, the heavenly and the earthly.

For that reason Gregory's mysticism is actually quite down-to-earth. C.W. MacLeod concluded in agreement with Völker's thesis: "...in so far as Gregory conceives of a consummation, it is God-likeness, not union or vision." MacLeod contended that Gregory is referring, not to a spiritual experience of search in response to what there is revealed of God's goodness, but rather to the process of moral sanctification.[154] This is through looking at his energies' imprints on the Church. But this account of Gregory's spirituality as 'ethical spirituality', a sober drunkenness in which the senses are numbed,[155] is not the view of many. Thus, the position taken by H. Urs v. Balthasar is quite different. For him, Gregory believes that God is revealed as He is whenever one has faith that He is.[156] It is a case of this knowledge (or secure faith) "that He is" allowing a sense of His presence to burst out.[157] According to Gregory, although he insists that God cannot be known as 'being', that does not mean God is beyond being or that he is inaccessible in that being. There is no reality beyond God as He is, as the statement of his opposition to Eunomius never tired of insisting — that which is not inexistent we call being and we do not say being is inexistent.[158] Actually, according to Balthasar, God is, for Gregory, perfectly accessible to those who trust that He exists. This claim is buttressed by a short sentence from *Homily* XI, — "He gives the soul a sense of presence,"[159] — something which is not knowledge of an object but rather an apprehension of a subjective reality.

---

[154] MacLeod (1971), 363.

[155] Cf. Lewy (1929) who contrasts Philonic and Gregorian "ecstasy".

[156] Balthasar (1988), xx-xxiii.

[157] Balthasar (1988), xxi: "Mais ce résidu négatif se révèle comme étant éminemment positif: de l'impuissance d'attribuer le 'ceci' et 'cela', c'est-à-dire le non-être des choses Dieu, surgit l' être lui-même... . Il faut trouver l'être présent dans l'essence, sans toutefois le confonde avec elle ou l'exprimer par elle." — *Contra Eunomium* 12, 1040C (=GNO I, 338, 30 - 339, 3.)

[158] See *Contra Eunomium* 12, 1040C (= GNO I, 338, 30 - 339,3): ὡς γὰρ ὁ μὴ ἐγεννήθη ἀγέννητον λέγεται καὶ ὃ μὴ φθείρεται ἄφθαρτον, οὕτως καὶ τὸ μὴ ἀνύπαρκτον οὐσίαν κατονομάζομεν, καὶ τὸ ἔμπαλιν ὡς τὸ γεννητὸν οὐκ ἀγέννητον λέγομεν καὶ τὸ φθαρτὸν οὐκ ἄφθαρτον ὀνομάζομεν, οὕτω καὶ τὴν οὐσίαν ἀνύπαρκτον εἶναι οὐ λέγομεν.

[159] GNO VI, 324,10-12: ἀλλ' αἴσθησιν μέν τινα δίδωσι τῇ ψυχῇ τῆς παρουσίας, ἐκφεύγει δὲ τὴν ἐναργῆ κατανόησιν τῷ ἀοράτῳ τῆς φύσεως ἐγκρυπτόμενος.; 13-15· ἅπτεται τῆς θύρας ὁ λόγος. θύραν δὲ νοοῦμεν τὴν στοχαστικὴν τῶν ἀρρήτων διάνοιαν, δι' ἧς εἰσοικίζεται τὸ ζητούμενον. The Macarian influence on Gregory means that πληροφορία (which Gregory renders as παρρησία) is equivalent to δύναμις it is an affective phenomenon involving *aesthesis*; cf. Stewart (1991), 117: "Codex

However, R. Leys argued that Balthasar was mistaken here, in that this passage about 'the Groom in the night' is merely a statement about humankind's experience of God as obscure, with the corollary that the darkness of God means he is only attainable by analogy of words in Scripture and the created order.[160] Leys holds what St. John of the Cross would understand as the 'dark night' intimacy to be reserved, in Gregory's thinking, for an experience *post mortem et resurrectionem*. Nevertheless, this is much more a qualification of Balthasar's position than a rebuttal of it. Balthasar goes on in the third part of the book (*'Philosophie de l'Amour'*) to describe the effects of the Incarnation in the believer's present life as the first stage of the Trinitarian working in the eucharist towards that soul's divinisation in the monad,[161] when there will be a knowledge of God qualitatively (but not structurally) different from the poor glimmer which we have down here.[162] The Incarnation is not a source of new knowledge of God here and now, but it guarantees such in the end-time and reflects it in the form of a prescience rather than a preview.

Balthasar read 'the sense of his presence' as beginning in this life in which the Saviour was himself incarnate and intensifying as we are drawn towards heaven. Both Balthasar and Leys believed that 'the sense of his presence' was not thought of as contained within the Incarnation; for the latter the Groom is in no sense 'God Incarnate' in Gregory's interpretation. So in the commentary in Homily XI on Cant 5:3 Balthasar sees the 'sense' as the *effect* of the Incarnation and Leys[163] takes it to be simply about the experience of the 'common soul' as she is assimilated to God by the working of the divine *energeiai*. However, the reference is clearly to Christ coming down to lead the way out of 'the clay' and his becoming 'the rock', or solid ground; the

---

Sinaiticus adds to the *Song of Songs* 5:2 the notation. 'The bride hears (αἴσθεται)the bridegroom knocking on the door'; the LXX uses this verb to render Heb. *da'at*".

[160] Leys (1951), 36: "La comparaison ne porte pas sur le caractère immédiat de la présence (c'est le cas pour l'époux, ce ne l'est pas pour Dieu) mais sur son obscurité (ce qui est le cas pour les deux)."

[161] Balthasar(1988), 146: "C'est l'instant de la résurrection qu'elle saisit sa proie et l'enlève dans une dimension inconnue...dans la lumière [l'homme assumé] devient lumière, dans l'incorruptible, incorruptible, dans l'invisible, invisible, dans le Christ, Christ, dans le Seigneur, Seigneur." See *Contra Eunomium* V (706AC-708CD = GNO II, 130-132) and *Adversus Apollinarem* II (1168A-1221C = GNO III/1, 161-200) and concludes with reference to *In Cant* I, 1009D (= GNO VI, 333f).

[162] Balthasar (1988), 149: "Elle semble [n. 7: Remarquer en effet le ἴσως, 'peut-être'—*In Cant* XI, 1001D] aussi promettre une connaissance de Dieu qualitativement (ne pas structurellement) différente de cette pauvre lueur que nous possèdons ici-bas... ."

[163] Ibid, 45, n.1.

energeiai are mediated through him as incarnate; 'the entrance of sanctification is the confession, the sanctification is the Lord.'[164]

Thus Gregory as a good Neoplatonist could not accept any mediating agent in our knowledge of God that was not God himself, and this applied even to a mediating *nous* in Christ.[165] Rather than *epinoiai* which accommodated the various levels of creaturely comprehension, Gregory understands God's self-communication in terms of *energeiai*, issuing from the heavenly *dunamis* located through the incarnate Christ on earth. He appears to have been cautious about the *Tendenz* which he found in part of the 'Syriac' tradition of regarding divine and created as interchangeable, as easily inter-substituted as words and names themselves. The only place where God and man are mutually identifiable was in the sacred person of Christ.

J. Daniélou and M. Canévet consider the 'sense of his presence' passage[166] and surrounding material differently, but also inadequately. The latter writer supports the former in thinking that Gregory understands a sort of 'real presence' of divinity as made possible by the Incarnation; however this is 'real' in the sense that it is not limited to subjective experience and comes as an aural/mental suggestion.[167] This mere αἴσθησις τῆς παρουσίας comes when the bride is wrapped in divine night and inaugurates revealed knowledge, a sort of voice whose content is that it is impossible to know the nature of God. The phrase is thus a motto of negative theology. In other words, there is a fully adequate compensation for the modest returns contemplation offers; that, when all is said and done, most concepts for speaking about God are to be avoided by the mature, but may be needed as guides while yet in the spiritual foothills, and that in the ascent the blind effort of trying to speculate gets one to the right place where God can take over. That 'potential' compensation or consolation is the doubtlessly reassuring presence (albeit in no sense a demonstrably present fact) of God as The Word. Unlike 'the Neoplatonists', Gregory soberly maintains that the

---

[164] GNO VI, 331,16 - 332, 8: πέτραν δὲ νοοῦμεν τὸν κύριον ὅς ἐστι φῶς καὶ ἀλήθεια... . δι' ὧν ἡ πνευματικὴ ὁδὸς διαπλακοῦται...ἡ γὰρ ὁμολογία..εἴσοδος γίνεται τοῦ ἁγιασμοῦ ἐπὶ τὴν οὕτω παρεσκευασμένην ψυχήν. ἁγιασμὸς δὲ ὁ κύριος. The Lord as light and truth means the Johannine Jesus; he is also the way of transcendence.

[165] Balthasar (1988), 145; also *Introduction*, xx: "Personnalisé par Origène, qui l'identifia au Logos, le Nous avait gardé dans la métaphysique chrétienne une place intermédiaire entre le Père (Βύθος) et l'âme. Mais une fois la transcendance absolue de l'essence divine reconnue, cette place devenait intenable. Augustine essayera de la maintenir, non sans frôler la contradiction."

[166] GNO VI, 324:10: see above.

[167] Canévet (1972), 445: "La présence de Dieu dont il est question et que Grégoire oppose une manifestation visible...n'est une allusion ni au fait de l'Incarnation, ni l'événement de la Résurrection.".

3. The Groom

soul remains conscious of the One to whom it is joined, whereas for Plotinus that perception is lost by ontological absorption. Seeing God in the sense of knowing what he is not is now possible for those prepared to travel.

In this frankly sceptical account of Gregory's spirituality it would seem that Canévet and Daniélou have related what is certainly the case for Gregory's *Life of Moses*, but their version carries less conviction when used to analyse the text in the 11th *Homily on The Song*. After all, the setting of Cant 5:2-5 is a domestic one with a garden outside, not a desert terrain with 'mountains' as immediate obstacles. In other words there might be some input of joy for immediate experience. So when Canévet writes that the presence of God is an allusion neither to the fact of the Incarnation, nor to the event of the Resurrection, but rather to the phenomenon of spiritual ascension,[168] she has missed the motif of *descensus*, with the house representing human life.[169] The hand coming in through the door-hole symbolises the dwelling of the Word, "the creator of all things (τὴν πάντων τῶν ὄντων ποιητικήν), in the meanness and good-for-nothingness of human life, to perfect it by the partaking of our nature"— effecting a much more radical intrusion, with the garden as the location where the Word starts to relate to human existence.[170] Since, in terms of eternity, the truth (i.e., The Word) stands outside of human nature (the house) it/He gives the believer four keys — four names to be understood allegorically to open the door of the sensible.[171] The keys are left in the mind for the soul to decide whether to turn or not. We could add to this the consideration that after verse 5 of Cant 5 the Groom disappears altogether and only then is the search on. It is interesting that although Gregory included verses 6 and 7 in his citation at the start of *Hom* XI, he decides to leave discussion of them for *Hom* XII, perhaps indicating an awareness of a significant division in the unfolding (or *akolouthia*) of the Song's message.

---

[168] Ibid., 448. Cf. D. Turner (1995)'s assessment of medieval mysticism as a description of philosophical grasp of the limits of presence and meaning, in language as in prayer.

[169] GNO VI, 338, 2-4: οἶμαι γὰρ οἶκον νοεῖσθαι τῆς νύμφης πᾶσαν τὴν ἀνθρωπίνην ζωήν..... .

[170] GNO VI, 338, 5-6: ἐνδημήσασαν πρὸς τὸ βραχύ τε καὶ οὐτιδανὸν τοῦ ἀνθρωπίνου βίου ἑαυτὴν συστεῖλαι διὰ τοῦ μετασχεῖν τῆς φύσεως ἡμῶν.

[171] GNO VI, 324, 15- 325, 4: ἔξω τοίνυν ἑστῶσα τῆς φύσεως ἡμῶν ἡ ἀλήθεια διὰ τῆς ἐκ μέρους γνώσεως, καθώς φησιν ὁ ἀπόστολος, ἐν ὑπονοίαις τισὶ καὶ αἰνίγμασι θυροκρουστεῖ τὴν διάνοιαν Ἄνοιξον λέγουσα καὶ μετὰ τῆς προτροπῆς ὑποτιθεμένη τὸν τρόπον, ὅπως ἀνοιγῆναι προσήκει τὴν θύραν, οἷόν τινας κλεῖς ὀρέγουσα τὰ καλὰ ταῦτα ὀνόματα, δι'ὧν τὸ κεκλεισμένον ἀνοίγεται· κλεῖδες γὰρ εἰσιν ἄντικρυς αἱ τῶν ὀνομάτων τούτων ἐμφάσεις αἱ τὰ κρυπτὰ διανοίγουσαι· ἀδελφή καὶ πλησίον καὶ περιστερὰ καὶ τελεία. εἰ γὰρ βούλει σοι, φησίν, ἀνοιγῆναι τὴν θύραν καὶ ἐπαρθῆναι τῆς ψυχῆς σου τὰς πύλας... .

Canévet (in her book) finds that Gregory's prevalent method aimed at the reconciliation of various examples of dialectic throughout Scripture, with the God-Man paradox being merely one of them. After the Incarnation there remains a lot to be understood about faith and the illumination it brings to the question of knowledge. Thus, for her, given that Gregory sees the Song as developing in profundity,[172] with the text mirroring the spiritual life, Cant 5:2-7 is simply too far into the Song to be dealing with the Incarnation. Thus only the early homilies (II-V) are dominated by a reflection on the role of the Incarnation as the foundation of a mode of existence for humanity, a sort of 'merely' ethical example.[173] So, according to this view, already in these early chapters the Incarnation counts only as a presupposition, perhaps the ἐθική stage of spiritual development, and the corollary is that the later chapters build on this solution of the opposition between created and uncreated which comes about through the downwards movement of the Incarnation and the upward movement of faith/love.

The reluctance to see this Cappadocian's understanding of the Song as having the union of natures in Christ at its heart can also be seen pointedly in Daniélou's mature contribution.[174] He spots a reference to the human soul as operating as a μεθόριος ('frontier') between two realities (intelligible/sensible) but continues: "c'est le seul cas où Grégoire emploie μεθόριος pour désigner la dualité des natures dans l'homme."[175] As he puts it, this way of uniting spirit to body/matter could not mean for a Christian, as it might have done for Posidonius, that there is here a mixture of opposites and we are like 'no-man's land' in the war between them. In fact, Daniélou continues, Gregory may actually be saying that man's free will has the choice in him to be the one or the other, as he describes such potentialities available to man in a Philonic way. The opposites are not really part of humanity's make-up except metaphorically; to be human is to be somehow other than literally μεθόριος between two realms.[176] However Daniélou avoids passages in Gregory where he clearly does, by analogy with Stoic physics, speak of some form of κρᾶσις. His one mention of it, in a footnote,[177] is to the effect that it is only used in the sense of the soul's internal cohesion, not to its relation with anything else. Yet the Cappadocian idea of 'mixture' was, when transposed *Christologically*, more akin to what modern chemistry understands by 'mixture' where the elements keep their electrons to

---

[172] See also Dünzl (1994), I, 62. Moreschini (Introduction to Gregory of Nyssa [1988]) sees no spiritual development through the homilies.

[173] Canévet (1983), 277.

[174] Daniélou (1970).

[175] Daniélou (1970), 119.

[176] Ibid, 120f.

[177] At ibid., 53.

themselves in opposition to 'compound'. The notion of παράθεσις in cases such as 'the mixture of peas and beans', which might be respectably Platonic,[178] but betrays a hopelessly materialistic way of looking at both 'the divinity' and 'the humanity'. The Apollinarian nuance of κρᾶσις (approximating to σύγχυσις) was what was condemned in 451. Now, while Gregory's thinking is far from Apollinarian, he did understand unfallen Adam as μεθόριος and consequently Christ who renovates Adam as μεθόριος. *Fallen* humanity had slipped too far under the half-way line. Christ carries in him a pure νοῦς by virtue of the power of the Logos keeping it above the line through associating with it. So, although Gregory was wary of the concept of a 'natural' κρᾶσις in his anthropology,[179] it should not be surprising to find his account of the 'supernatural' Christological bond a somewhat closer form of union.

Rather than consign Gregory to a Procrustean bed of 'Christological agnosticism', one should note that Homilies XI-XIV are devoted to the person of the Groom. Finally there is Homily XV in which the Bride holds centre stage. Yet in some ways this is a bit of an anti-climax after the first four mentioned homilies which return to the subject matter of Homily V but treat it more fully. The content is simply the story of the woman who after her beloved's nocturnal call is more concerned for her luxury than his comfort, is consequently too late to let him in and has to go to find him. She is still perfumed and excited but, possibly because of this, is all the more likely to be apprehended by hostile men enjoying the enforcement of the public morality to the letter. This differs dramatically from the rather wandering, purposeless and fruitless search of Cant 3:1ff.[180]

The crucial discussion around Cant 5:3 leads to the strange conclusion that since she cannot see the Groom in his totality (just 'his hand'), therefore she does not see him. This necessitates an explanation:

> To make it clearer I will give an example: just as if someone be near that spring, which the scripture said came up from the earth in the beginning (Gen 2:6) such being the fulness as ever circled the face of the earth, the one having come near the spring would wonder at that unceasing water... (for how can anyone see what is hidden in the bowels of the earth?...). Thus the one looking at the divine and infinite beauty, since something always being discovered is newer and stranger than the rest already seen, wonders at that which shows forth forever... .[181]

---

[178] I am indebted to Prof G.C. Stead for this clarification. See further Stead (1994), 208f.

[179] Cf. Nemesius, *De Nat hom.* 2; Morani (1987), 37.

[180] Did Gregory share in Messalian anti-sacramentalism? Cf. Guillaumont (1980), 1432. Ephrem also thinks of body in soul, soul in human spirit, and human spirit in Holy Spirit— as a reaction against the theology of the *Odes of Solomon* which would fuse these last two.

[181] GNO VI, 321, 5-20: ὡς δ'ἂν σαφέστερον ἡμῖν τὸ νόημα γένοιτο, εἰκόνα τινὰ δι' ὑποδείγματος προσθήσω τῷ λόγῳ· ὥσπερ γὰρ εἴ τις πλησίον ἐκείνης γένοιτο τῆς πηγῆς, ἣν ἀναβαίνειν εἶπεν ἐκ τῆς γῆς κατ' ἀρχὰς ἡ γραφὴ

This is a pleasing image, but the point of water is that, as with the Incarnation, what is seen is essentially the same as what is hidden. The idea is that God as such cannot be so local as to be ever totally visible in creation, but in revelation there is truly something eternal which is fully set forth. Another watery image, the "dew of the night"(Cant 5:2) signifies the divine darkness from which the meditating soul receives some drops. There *has* been some revelation of God, that is, with respect to his economy, but no more with respect to him 'in himself' is promised. Gregory develops the spirituality of the soul with regard to the God who has revealed himself by insisting that she must look towards the νοῦς which believers and the incarnate Word share, and not to the body and the bodily understanding, as her 'veil' is removed by angels. So Gregory seems intent to spare his readers eventual disppointment; 'face to face' will not at any time, at any place, mean just that.

Gregory concludes that he who longs to see God may see the one he desires through following him always, while the *theoria* of his face is the unceasing journey towards him through the 'behind going' (*literally*, following) of the Word. The knowledge of God's divinity is reserved for the Trinity:

> How does she describe to them what she seeks? How to paint in speech the character of the longed for?... Since there is the created and uncreated of Christ (we say the uncreated to be his eternity and before ages and creator of all things that are, but created in accordance with the economy for our sakes in the body of our lowliness... We say uncreated to be the Logos in the beginning, ... but created to have become flesh and dwelled among us, of whose enfleshed being the glory was revealed, in that God was shown in the flesh while still the only begotten God...indeed the appearing was man but the Glory known was through him the Only Begotten with the Father...) the one uncreated and before ages and eternal remaining completely ungraspable and unrevealable in nature, while the other was able to be revealed to us through the flesh and to come to knowledge... .[182]

τοσαύτην οὖσαν τὸ πλῆθος ὡς ἅπαν τῆς γῆς ἐπικλύζειν τὸ πρόσωπον, θαυμάσει μὲν ὁ τῇ πηγῇ πλησιάσας τὸ ἄπειρον ὕδωρ... (πῶς γὰρ ἂν ἴδοι τὸ ἔτι τοῖς κόλποις τῆς γῆς ἐγκρυπτόμενον;...), οὕτως ὁ πρὸς τὸ θεῖον ἐκεῖνο καὶ ἀόριστον κάλλος βλέπων, ἐπειδὴ τὸ πάντοτε εὑρισκόμενον καινότερόν τε καὶ παραδοξότερον πάντως παρὰ τὸ ἤδη κατειλημμένον ὁρᾶται, θαυμάζει μὲν τὸ ἀεὶ προφαινόμενον,... .

[182] GNO VI, 380, 13-20: πῶς ὑπογράφει αὐταῖς τὸ ζητούμενον; πῶς ζωγραφεῖ τῷ λόγῳ τοῦ ποθουμένου τὸν χαρακτῆρα...ἐπειδὴ γὰρ τοῦ Χριστοῦ τὸ μὲν κτιστόν ἐστι τὸ δὲ ἄκτιστον (λέγομεν δὲ ἄκτιστον μὲν εἶναι αὐτοῦ τὸ ἀΐδιόν τε καὶ προαιώνιον καὶ ποιητικὸν πάντων τῶν ὄντων, κτιστὸν δὲ τὸ κατὰ τὴν ὑπὲρ ἡμῶν οἰκονομίαν συσχηματισθὲν τῷ σώματι τῆς ταπεινώσεως ἡμῶν. ...(381,1) ἄκτιστον λέγομεν τὸν ἐν ἀρχῇ ὄντα λόγον...κτιστὸν δὲ τὸν σάρκα γενόμενον καὶ ἐν ἡμῖν σκηνώσαντα, οὗ καὶ σαρκωθέντος ἡ ἐμφαινομένη δόξα δηλοῖ, ὅτι Θεὸς ἐφανερώθη ἐν σαρκί, θεὸς δὲ πάντως ὁ μονογενής, ὁ ἐν τοῖς κόλποις ὢν τοῦ πατρός...τοίνυν τὸ μὲν ἄκτιστον αὐτοῦ καὶ προαιώνιον καὶ ἀΐδιον ἄληπτον

3. The Groom

Having protected the Word's reputation from any imputation of 'graspability' (love is about hope not consummation), Gregory makes it clear that the Groom is as good as God himself. But this Groom is the one who became incarnate and:

> ...when he had once, through the firstfruits, sprinkled for himself the bitter nature of the flesh, which he assumed through the chaste virgin, forever co-sanctifying the common leaven of the nature by the firstfruits through those joined to him according to the communion of the mystery feeding his own body, the church, and mutually holding together the growing members in the common body through faith in him — causing them to be fit to be eyes and mouth and hands... .[183]

So Gregory does identify the members with the Word who controls them to the extent that he sees them as part of the one person. Every soul can find God through his Church, because his body is not simply the Church, but part of Christ.

3. 9 "The body of God"? The Groom's body and the Word's potencies

Cant 5:10-16

5·10 Ἀδελφιδός μου λευκὸς καὶ πυρρός,
ἐκλελοχισμένος ἀπὸ μυριάδων·
5·11 κεφαλὴ αὐτοῦ χρυσίον καὶ φαζ,
βόστρυχοι αὐτοῦ ἐλάται, μέλανες ὡς κόραξ,
5·12 ὀφθαλμοὶ αὐτοῦ ὡς περιστεραὶ ἐπὶ πληρώματα ὑδάτων
λελουσμέναι ἐν γάλακτι
καθήμεναι ἐπὶ πληρώματα ὑδάτων,
5·13 σιαγόνες αὐτοῦ ὡς φιάλαι τοῦ ἀρώματος φύουσαι μυρεψικά,
χείλη αὐτοῦ κρίνα στάζοντα σμύρναν πλήρη,
5·14 χεῖρες αὐτοῦ τορευταὶ χρυσαῖ πεπληρωμέναι θαρσις,
κοιλία αὐτοῦ πυξίον ἐλεφάντινον ἐπὶ λίθου σαπφείρου,
5·15 κνῆμαι αὐτοῦ στῦλοι μαρμάρινοι
τεθεμελιωμένοι ἐπὶ βάσεις χρυσᾶς,
εἶδος αὐτοῦ ὡς Λίβανος, ἐκλεκτὸς ὡς κέδροι,
5·16 φάρυγξ αὐτοῦ γλυκασμοὶ καὶ ὅλος ἐπιθυμία·
οὗτος ἀδελφιδός μου,
καὶ οὗτος πλησίον μου, θυγατέρες Ιερουσαλημ.

μένει καθ'ὅλου πάσῃ φύσει καὶ ἀνεκφώνητον, τὸ δὲ διὰ σαρκὸς ἡμῖν φανερωθὲν δύναται ποσῶς καὶ εἰς γνῶσιν ἐλθεῖν.

[183] GNO VI, 381, 19 - 382, 5: ὃς ἐπειδὴ ἅπαξ πρὸς ἑαυτὸν διὰ τῆς ἀπαρχῆς ἐπεσπάσατο τὴν ἐπίκηρον τῆς σαρκὸς φύσιν, ἣν διὰ τῆς ἀφθόρου παρθενίας ἀνέλαβεν, ἀεὶ τῇ ἀπαρχῇ συναγιάζει τὸ κοινὸν τῆς φύσεως φύραμα διὰ τῶν ἑνουμένων αὐτῷ κατὰ τὴν κοινωνίαν τοῦ μυστηρίου τρέφων τὸ ἑαυτοῦ σῶμα, τὴν ἐκκλησίαν... .

The exegetical fragments by Didymus found at Toura reveal how the Groom of the Song was identified with the Word of God. There Cant 5:9f is cited in support of the idea that the divinity woos the believer into desiring 'the Groom'. The paraphrase of Cant 5:10 "My kinsman is white and [lacuna], he is not one. He is man and God", is delivered in the context of how "our Lord and Saviour" is 'wisdom', 'truth', 'light', 'righteousness' and even 'desire'.[184] This suggests, *pace* A. Gesché, that it means his appearance is always to be seen in terms of combinations. Gesché[185] maintains that here the Saviour is conceived of as ἀσύνθετος since the passage refers to Christ's twoness as that of two *prosopa*.[186] Jesus having 'two *prosopa*' simply means he can be seen by some as only human and others as human and God; what matters is seeing him as God, in fact as God's unseen *prosopon*. Didymus here is not being 'Antiochene' *avant la lettre*, even though in another passage,

At another point Didymus employs the phrase αὐτὸς ὁ κεκραμένος ἐξ ἀμφοτέρων.[187] Even here, Gesché concludes that this means a close arrangement but not that the Word took over the flesh completely and that in neither passage, while the author does not think of two individualities in Christ, yet (and vaguely, as befits one writing in the fourth century) there were, for him, somehow two independent realities. However, the author throughout shows scant allegiance to the idea that the 'life' of the body pre-existed the body: the soul is special, even μονογενής and ἄτρεπτος, because it is so close to God the Word as to share his qualities, his titles.[188] (The ultimate goal is a monistic union of all souls with God.) Didymus' debt to Origen's Christology is apparent, but so is his own development of that tradition: the Groom has a side to him which is not an *alter ego, but* which is in some way to be viewed by human souls as 'feminine', welcoming, and closer to their weak humanity.[189]

This did not mean for Gregory of Nyssa, any more than for Didymus, that, in the Incarnation, the created nature prevented God's coming closer to

---

[184] Gronewald, III, 151; p. 112,23-25: δυὸ πρόσωπα εἶχεν Ἰησοῦς, ἀνθρώπου καὶ θεοῦ. ὅσοι κατὰ σαρκὰ αὐτὸν γιγνώσκουσιν, ἐν τῇ φ[αν]ερώσει τοῦ προσώπου αὐτὸ[υ] λαμβάνουσιν.

[185] Gesché (1962), 316-20.

[186] Gronewald III, 151, 23; p. 112-114: δυό πρόσωπα εἶχεν Ἰησοῦς, ἀνθρώπου καὶ θεοῦ. ὅσοι κατὰ σάρκα αὐτὸν γιγνώσκουσιν ἐν τῇ φ[αν]ερώσει τοῦ προσώπου αὐτὸ[υ] λαμβάνουσιν, ὅσοι δὲ ἀποστάντες ἀπὸ τοῦ κατὰ σάρκα αὐτὸν εἰδέναι...οὗτοι κατεκρύβησαν ἐν ἀποκρύφῳ τοῦ προσώπου τοῦ θεοῦ.

[187] Gronewald I, 11, 27f; p. 46: αὐτὸς ὁ κεκραμένος ἐξ ἀμφοτέρων γίνεται παράκλητος (1Jn 2:1); Gesché (1962), 310f.

[188] Cf. Gronewald III, 153, 30-31; p. 124: ὁ λόγος σὰρξ ἐγένετο. ἴδε τὸ ἔξω πρόσωπον.

[189] Cf. Bienert (1972), 135.

3. The Groom

humanity in any new way. The popular interpretation of Gregory, that he viewed the Incarnation but as a parable, setting up a mystery only to be clarified by experience in the Church, rests on a view of Gregory as more 'Antiochene' (the assumed flesh in no way 'fitted' for the Word) than he was. Just as his anthropology chose a middle way, so too his Christology.[190] This view is based on a passage such as the interpretation of Cant 5:10.[191] It is clear, *pace* K. Bjerre-Aspergen,[192] that Gregory thinks something of God did appear through the flesh; compare, e.g., what he says about miracles at *Oratio Catechetica* XI,2. On her view, God who is above all Νοῦς-like in his economy and who deigns to live in the soul effects something affective and profound: God cannot be known essentially but he can, in that way, be joined with.[193] Yet for Gregory this is not itself a reason for agnosticism about whether knowledge of God is available (i.e., that presence replaces *pensée*) since God has revealed himself as graspable and not *utterly* transcendent. The passage from movement through disordered movement, to ὁμοίωσις θεῷ, has as its goal a viewing of God, which though never close enough, eschatological/*post-mortem*, is nevertheless real. It is just as real as the celebrated late-Platonic, (or, in Christian terms) anti-Arian distance between creature and Uncreated.[194] The whole point of the Incarnation, as Dünzl has rightly paraphrased Gregory, was to overcome God's inaccessibility owing to his being pure light by his self-darkening in his Incarnation:

> Gottes prinzipielle Unfaßbarkeit wird durch seine 'Selbstverdunklung' soweit überwunden, daß der Mensch zur Gemeinschaft (*suzugia* etc.) mit dem Unfaßbaren befähigt wird; der Gegensatz zwischen der Unendlichkeit Gottes und den (begrenzten) Möglichkeiten des Menschen wird damit überbruckt.[195]

---

[190] Bjerre-Aspergen (1977), 49: "In seiner Schilderung betonte er dort den Unterschied zwischen der göttlichen und der menschlichen Natur Christi. Der Mensch könnte in der Inkarnation Christi Erkenntnis jenes Teils seiner Natur erreichen, der sich im Körper offenbart habe."

[191] GNO VI, 381, 10-16: ἐπειδὴ τοίνυν τὸ μὲν ἄκτιστον αὐτοῦ καὶ προαιώνιον καὶ ἀΐδιον ἄληπτον μένει καθ' ὅλου πάσῃ φύσει καὶ ἀνεκφώνητον, τὸ δὲ διὰ σαρκὸς ἡμῖν φανερωθὲν δύναται ποσῶς καὶ εἰς γνῶσιν ἐλθεῖν, τούτου χάριν πρὸς ταῦτα ἡ διδάσκαλος βλέπει καὶ περὶ τούτων ποιεῖται τὸν λόγον ὅσα δύναται γενέσθαι χωρητὰ τοῖς ἀκούουσιν.

[192] Bjerre-Aspergen (1977), 46f.

[193] See ibid., 50-52 on Hom II (GNO VI, 68) which she reinforces with *De beatitudinibus* (PG 44, 1273-77).

[194] Balás (1985), 177, comments: "Er hat bewußt eine spezifisch christliche Unterteilung alles Seienden in Ungeschaffenes und Geschaffenes auch metaphysisch begründet." recapitulating his own argument in Balás (1966). On this essentially "middle"-world of 'ideas', see Ivánka (1990).

[195] Dünzl (1993), 103. He claims the support of Mateo-Seco for his interpretation of this point.

Here Gregory picks up on Origen's idea of Christ's humanity as a shadow, but for Gregory it does not merely transmit something of the light's effect, allowing proximity to God without understanding, but rather makes that light itself accessible albeit in 'accommodated' form to our minds. The transfiguration is paradigmatic here.[196] Bjerre-Aspergen wants to show that the Incarnation does not reveal everything of God *because* the Church and sacraments provide further revelation, with which Dünzl concurs and adds that Gregory does not see the *Menschwerdung* as soteriologically exclusivist *because* he concludes the work with a monist universalistic vision: "...eine Theologie der Gottesbeziehung beinhalten (nicht: 'entwickeln')... ."[197] Unlike Dünzl she does not think Gregory saw the Incarnation as the answer, providing the ladder to God.

What does lead to God is the revelation of God in his effects in the Church as the new creation,[198] which are experienced as felt (internally) rather than seen (as in others' behaviour). Bjerre-Aspergen and Dünzl are of like mind, however, in understanding that, for Gregory, the body of Christ which reveals the rest of this 'all' is the Church.[199] God, like the Groom, does come near and go far away; there is a dialectical side to Gregory's thinking, for the Incarnation itself involves a going away and thus Gregory's theology is not totally 'positive'.[200] Yet it is *at least* positive.

It seems the vision which the ascending soul enjoys is the Word-Groom's body as the Church: this is clear from Gregory's commentary on Cant 5:10ff.[201] The beauty of the Groom, if not the Groom in himself, is here visible for the soul who looks the right way. There is thus no mysticism independent of the Incarnation which provides it with its cognitive content, even though the soul's ascent is not viewed as a participation in Christ's own

---

[196] See McGuckin (1986) on Gregory Nazianzen and the Transfiguration.

[197] Ibid., 396.

[198] Moreschini in Gregory of Nyssa (1988), 729, comments: "Nella stessa omelia (XIII), citato il *Ct* 5,10 — 'il mio Diletto è bianco e rosso'—, ricorda l'azione del Padre e dello Spirito, grazie alla quale Maria, Madre della Vita, concepisce e partorisce nella gioia. È così superata l'idea del parto doloroso dovuto al peccato originale."

[199] Dünzl (1993), 200: "Gregor zielt hier aber nicht darauf ab, durch die Inkarantion im engeren Sinn die Faßbarkeit des Unfaßbaren zu erklären, sondern dehnt die Vorstellung der Inkarnation auf die Kirche als den 'Leib' des 'Bräutigams' aus (der in Cant 5,10-16 beschrieben wird) [Vgl. dazu in Teil B Hom XIII zu Cant 5,10-16], um schließlich die eingangs erwähnte Parallele ziehen zu können: durch die Beschreibung des 'Bräutigams' wird nach dem apostolischen Wort (des Paulus: Röm 1,20) auch das Unsichtbare an ihm geschaut, indem es durch die Werke wahrgenommen wird, weil es durch die Einrichtung des kirchlichen Kosmos sichtbar wird." Why the Church on earth should reveal more to humans here, while those in paradise have less declared to them, Dünzl does not explain.

[200] Bjerre-Aspergen (1977), 103:"und dennoch dem Menschen ebenso nahe, wie ein Bräutigam seiner Braut in der physischen Vereinigung."

[201] GNO VI, 382, 2-7.

soul, as was the case in Origen. Yet the body is not simply the Church as human beings but a unity like a body which the Word is all the time building up: in other words, 'the body' seems to be much more than a 'mere metaphor'.

> [The description is]... rather of those things revealed according to the economy when he appeared on the earth and putting on human nature lived among men, through which things... even his invisible intelligibles were viewed by the creatures, appearing through the preparation of the ecclesiastical world.[202]

Having sounded like Origen in respect of the phrase "the ecclesiastical world"[203], Gregory explains:

> [Just as one looking at the sensible world recognises the wisdom appearing in the beauty of things]... so too the one looking on this new world of the creation "according to the Church" would see in it the all in all, who, coming into life through spatial and graspable things, leads knowledge by the hand to the infinite.[204]

The reference here is to the Word visible in his new creation, the Church. That suggests Gregory believed in a close association here and now, of the invisible's being wrapped up in the mass of believers, ubiquitous as far as the limits of the faithful. Yet it is not an aesthetic or visible revelation; the Groom is revealed to onlookers by the virtues of the souls, which are really his own virtues, as described in Cant 5:10ff.

But Ps-Athanasius, *Synopsis Sacrae Scripturae* sounds less sophisticated. That which the prophets were longing for was simply "the embodiment of the Word". After defining how this will (from the OT perspective) happen, they declare (Cant 8:2) their longing to take him into the "mother's house".

> For they asked him to take a body not from outside but from the womb of our birth, except not as we do from a man and woman; for from the Virgin alone, he took a body for himself, as Creator, except that it was from a human ; for Mary the Mother of God was the human. And these words are from the Word to those who had asked, as he now took the flesh from the Virgin: "I have come into my garden, my sister-

---

[202] GNO VI, 384, 16 - 385, 3: ἀλλὰ τῶν κατ' οἰκονομίαν φανερωθέντων, ὅτε ἐπὶ τῆς γῆς ὤφθη καὶ τοῖς ἀνθρώποις συνανεστράφη τὴν ἀνθρωπίνην ἐνδυσάμενος φύσιν, δι' ὧν...καὶ τὰ ἀόρατα αὐτοῦ τοῖς ποιήμασι νοούμενα καθορᾶται διὰ τῆς τοῦ ἐκκλησιαστικοῦ κόσμου κατασκευῆς φανερούμενα.

[203] κόσμος τῆς ἐκκλησίας. cf. Origen, *In Jn* I,4; p. 7, 29-34. Yet ct. Danielou's translation (1961a), 273: "The establishment of the Church is the re-creation of the world".

[204] GNO VI, 386, 4-9: οὕτω καὶ ὁ πρὸς τὸν καινὸν τοῦτον κόσμον τῆς κατὰ τὴν ἐκκλησίαν κτίσεως βλέπων ὁρᾷ ἐν αὐτῷ τὸν πάντα ἐν πᾶσιν ὄντα τε καὶ γινόμενον διὰ τῶν χωρητῶν τε καὶ καταλαμβανομένων ὑπὸ τῆς φύσεως ἡμῶν χειραγωγῶν τὴν γνῶσιν πρὸς τὸ ἀχώρητον.

bride. I have gathered my myrrh with my spices. I have eaten my bread with my honey, I have drunk my wine with my milk" (Cant 5:1). Going into his own garden, the creation, he took for himself a body from the Virgin and became man. His body was mortal but was united with the fragrance of the all-holy Word. And if, as man, he allowed his body to consume milk, nevertheless he also gave it a share of the wine of his perfection. And even as it consumed milk, so he worked the deeds of divinity in it.[205]

There is little of an ecclesiological aspect here. Rather, this rather crude-sounding idea of the Word making his humanity out of the Virgin masks what may be the careful deliberations by this Cyrillian disciple. It seems fairly close in some of its phrasing to the kind of Christology maintained by Diodochus of Photike[206] — one nature of the incarnate Word, with the human nature as the 'raw material' existing beforehand in Mary and thus having an earthly, not heavenly, origin and *physis*. What is particularly interesting, however, is the one-way communication or influence of the divinity on the humanity; the Word 'permits' the body to take physical sustenance. It would appear that there is nothing standing between the two natures whether a νοῦς or a ψυχή, but instead the ἐνέργειαι[207] of the Word 'go between', even from the earliest moments of infancy.

> Whoever departs from evil will also see the unchanging uniting of the Word to (πρός) the body. For when the Word's marriage to us took place through the uniting of the body, at that time he also wrought victory over death, on account of which he has filled all things with joy. Such are the meanings of the speeches in the Song of Songs; whoever takes these as a starting-point will be able from this very book to match like things to their like according to the sense.[208]

---

[205] PG 28, 353B-C: Οὐ γὰρ ἔξωθεν, ἀλλ' ἀφ' ἧς ἐγεννήθημεν μήτρας, ἀναλαβεῖν αὐτὸν ἠξίουν τὸ σῶμα, εἰ καὶ μὴ ὡς ἡμεῖς ἐξ ἀνδρὸς καὶ γυναικός. Ἐκ γὰρ μόνης Παρθένου, ὡς πλάστης, ἑαυτῷ ἔλαβε τὸ σῶμα, πλὴν ὅτι ἐξ ἀνθρώπου · ἄνθρωπος γὰρ ἡ Θεοτόκος Μαρία. Καὶ τοῦ Λόγου δὲ πρὸς τοὺς ἀξιώσαντας, ἀναλαμβάνοντος ἤδη τὴν σάρκα ἐκ τῆς Παρθένου, ταῦτα · *Εἰσῆλθον εἰς κῆπόν μου, ἀδελφή μου νύμφη, ἐτρύγησα σμύρναν μου μετὰ ἀρωμάτων μου, ἔφαγον ἄρτον μου μετὰ μέλιτός μου, ἔπιον οἶνόν μου μετὰ γάλακτός μου.* Εἰς γὰρ τὸν ἴδιον κῆπον εἰσελθών, τὴν κτίσιν, ἔλαβεν ἑαυτῷ ἐκ τῆς Παρθένου τὸ σῶμα, καὶ γέγονεν ἄνθρωπος. Θνητὸν μὲν ἦν τὸ σῶμα, ἀλλὰ μετὰ εὐωδίας τοῦ παναγίου Λόγου συνῆπτο· Καὶ εἰ γάλα, ὡς ἄνθρωπος, ἤφιει τὸ σῶμα φαγεῖν, ἀλλὰ μετεδίδου αὐτῷ καὶ οἴνου τῆς ἑαυτοῦ τελειότητος. Καὶ γὰρ ὥσπερ ἤσθιε γάλα οὕτως ἐν αὐτῷ τὰ τῆς θεότητος ἐποίει ἔργα.

[206] Cf. PG 65, 1145B-C; cited by Grillmeier (1987), 234.

[207] If the phrase ποίει ἔργα ἐν can be accepted as sharing the same concept as ἐνέργειαι.

[208] PG 28, 357AB: Ὁ γὰρ ἐξερχόμενος ἀπὸ τῆς κακίας ὄψεται καὶ τὴν τοῦ Λόγου πρὸς τὸ σῶμα ἄτρεπτον ἕνωσιν. Ὅτε γὰρ γέγονε νύμφευσις τοῦ Λόγου πρὸς ἡμᾶς διὰ τῆς τοῦ σώματος ἑνώσεως, τότε καὶ τὴν κατὰ τοῦ θανάτου νίκην πεποίηκε, δι' ἣν εὐφροσύνης πάντα πεπλήρωκε. Τοιαῦτα ἐν τῷ Ἄσματι τῶν

The use of πρὸς highlights the distance and perhaps the one-way dynamic flow between the Word and the body in what is described as a 'marriage' union as two distinct entities in the one person (observable by a new convert who contemplates the Church). He has made humanity immortal through an association in which there is neither sense of fusion nor of mutuality between the two parties: in other words, like a marital arrangement traditionally understood. In the Ps-Athanasian *Synopsis Scripturae* then, as with Cyril, the Song of Songs provides little inspiration for the idea of a human soul of Christ as a partner in dialogue with the incarnate Word; the Groom's person is wholly the Word. In all cases, with the possible exception of Apponius, that which is distinctly human has only a passive role. For in Origen, even where the Word is joined with the soul, such a close association being no problem, yet there is a clear separation of function and the function of the humanity or soul of Christ is to defend and shield, though not to save.

Ambrose's Groom is above all the ruling Son who rejoices in his followers imitating him. This is perhaps nowhere more apparent than when the male physical qualities of Cant 5:10ff are made to correspond to the ascended Valentinian's virtues in such a way that the deceased emperor is presented as a *post mortem vicarius Christi* ; or is he thus the perfect Solomon — the political Messiah whose *Nachleben* are the ethical virtues which he bequeathed to the Church and her Empire?

It seems clear that Ambrose saw the qualities of the male figure in Cant 5:10-16 as applying to the human souls called to love Christ. Valentinian and his sibling, the pre-deceased Gratian are marked with the brand of their lord and soldiers are designated with the name of their emperor.[209] In this funeral oration he recites the description of the Groom in Cant 5:10-16, without treating each verse individually until he reaches Cant 5:14, where he describes the sweetness of the words which came from the Emperor's mouth and regrets he was unable to be present to administer baptism — but in God's eyes the deed was as good as done.[210] He then proceeds, having spoken about his 'body' (the external life) to speak about his soul. Valentinian had made good progress towards God; Christ asks him to turn around just once to reassure those left on earth.[211] There is to be one turning back to the world,

---

ἀσμάτων τὰ τῶν διαλόγων ἐστίν · ἐξ ὧν ἀφορμήν τις λαβών, δύναται ἀπ' αὐτοῦ τοῦ βιβλίου τὰ ὅμοια τοῖς ὁμοίοις συνάπτειν κατὰ τὸν νοῦν.

[209] *De Obitu Valentiniani*, 58; *Bibliotheca Ambrosiana*, p. 196: "Valentinianus meus, iuvenis meus candidus et rubeus habens in se imaginem Christi — talibus enim prosequitur ecclesia in Canticis Christum; nec iniuriam putes: charactere domini inscribuntur et servuli et nomine imperatoris signantur milites. Denique et ipse dominus dicit: *Nolite tangere christos meos* (Ps 104:15)."

[210] Ibid, 65; p. 200.

[211] Ibid., 74; p. 204: "*Convertere, Solamitis, convertere, convertere et videbimus in te.* Convertere ad nos 'pacifica', ut gloriam tuam sororibus tuis monstres et incipiant se tuae

but the turning to heaven is finer. Thereafter he repeats the exegesis he gave of the images of feet, legs and belly as in *De Inst Virg* 14, 87 (bare feet indicate humility in the presence of the holy) and *Ep* 54. The tone is 'moral' and the hermeneutic key the (implicit) equating of Valentinian with the son of David. G.H. Kramer has argued that the Emperor was considered to be the Lord's Anointed,[212] a sort of Christ himself, in keeping with Ps 104:15. The Ambrosian concept of virtue was inherently militaristic in tenor, as fitting a belief that Christian Rome signified a return to the true Rome from which pagan Rome had deviated. Ambrose also bequeathed to Augustine a philosophy of *Heilsgeschichte* moving up the 'steps' of a series of ages (*aetates mundi*); there is also, in the lack of interest in the theme of resurrection, a tempering of eschatology more radical than Augustine's. Most significant is the mimetic notion whereby the Bride and Groom become interchangeable: the dominion of the earthly Emperor is a reflection of the Son's Universal Lordship which is greater because it is invisible. So he takes Cant 5:10-16 to be about the visible lover fixated on the invisible beloved Son which reflects a Neoplatonic notion of the quest of soul after intellect.

As befits an Antiochene, albeit a moderate one, Theodoret declares that the Word is the Groom who is in heaven, while the bride who is the soul has a long way to go to reach union. As Guinot notes, Theodoret is not in the habit of attributing the designation ὁ νυμφίος to the divine Word. Guinot's reason why there is much less said about the divine nature is, however, less convincing: "[cela]...s'explique aisément: au Ve s., les discussions théologiques portent moins sur la nature divine du Verbe (οὐσία) que sur la nature humaine assumée et sur l'union de ces deux natures dans le Christ".[213] I submit instead that it is the author's Antiochene (and Cappadocian) heritage which makes him interested in Christ qua τέλειος ἄνθρωπος. His own contribution is to add, inspired by desert Christianity, an account of the Word as like a male lover, even if he is not explicitly identified as such, since he is hidden and relates to souls indirectly. What is meant by 'perfect' hinges on the understanding of that which is complete being ethically supreme. Now, whereas Origen at *De Princ* 4.2.4 taught the tripartite nature of man so that the spirit-faculty was the locus of perfection over and above the soul-body nexus, more normative for the Fathers was a bipartite conception (cf. Irenaeus *Haer.* 5.6.1):and perfection meant a soul-body harmony. Origen's notion of

---

quietis et gratiae securitate solari. Semel tantum ad nos convertere, ut te videamus, et rursus convertere atque ad Hierusalem illam civitatem sanctorum tota intentione festina. Aut certe, quia ad animam piam Christus hoc dicit, iubet illam paulisper converti, ut nobis gloria eius appareat et requies futura cum sanctis, et postea praecipit eam ad illud supernum sanctorum festinare consortium."

[212] Kramer (1983), 243-249 (English summary).

[213] Guinot (1985), 258.

3. The Groom

the νοῦς as humanity's built-in perfection finds little trace here. Even where Theodoret or other Antiochenes adopted a tripartite anthropology it was only to resist the Apollinarian eschewing of νοῦς as essential for the human constitution; the rational ψυχή belonged in the body and had to work upwards rather than operating at a higher level.[214] The Groom is *both* he who underwent suffering and death in a human lifetime, (with the suggestion present in Theodoret's mind that this Groom's life was one of '*potest non peccare*'[215]) *and* he who is eternal and invisible. But when Theodoret refers to the Groom it is the incarnate One of whom he is thinking.

It seems then that Guinot has only told one side of the story when he concludes that for an Antiochene commentator the young Theodoret was swayed by Origenist influences so as to concentrate on a disembodied relationship of the Word and the individual soul. For Guinot, "...l'union de l'Epouse avec l'Epoux est présentée moins comme celle de l'humanité au Christ que comme l'union de l'âme au Verbe divin, une union mystique dont l'épaisseur charnelle, même s'il s'agit d'une chair sanctifiée et glorieuse, est pratiquement absente."[216] Indeed in passages examined and unexamined by Guinot there is quite an emphasis on the humanity of Christ as that which comes close (to those watching) in the Incarnation. It is his smallness or weakness which accounts for his ability to defeat evil.[217] It is through the humanity (an instrument but not an agent) that the Word reveals himself as Groom.

When commenting on the description of the Groom in Cant 5:10-16 Theodoret takes the opportunity to add to the Christological content of his commentary. There he makes it clear that the 'I', the driving agent in Christ was the Word alone[218] who let the passive humanity be abused: "It did not say 'I sprinkled' but 'my clothing, that is my body, was sprinkled by their conqueror' (viz., Satan)." The continuing presence of Isaianic allusions accords with Theodoret's insistence on the victorious unscathed progress of

---

[214] See Gahbauer (1984); Grillmeier (1977); Sagi-Bunic (1965); Montalverne (1948).

[215] PG 81, 45CD: Καὶ ἐν τῷ καιρῷ δὲ τοῦ πάθους, ἄγγελοι παρῆσαν τὸ ἀνθρώπινον ὑπερείδοντες.

[216] Guinot (1992), 458.

[217] PG 81, 97B: Νεβρῷ δὲ αὐτὸν ἐλάφου ἀπεικάζει· ἐπειδὴ οὐ μόνον ἄνθρωπος, ἀλλὰ καὶ Υἱὸς ἀνθρώπου προσαγορεύεται, καὶ οὐ μόνον λέων, ἀλλὰ καὶ σκύμνος λέοντος·....προτέτακται δὲ ἡ δορκὰς τῆς ἐλάφου, ὡς τύπον ἔχουσα διὰ τὴν ὀξυδορκίαν τῆς πίστεως... .

[218] PG 81, 156D: Θεὸς γὰρ ἀεὶ ἦν,...οὐδὲ τραπεὶς εἰς ἄνθρωπον, ἀλλ' ἀνθρωπείαν ἐνδυσάμενος φύσιν.....(157AB)· ...καὶ θαυμάζουσιν αὐτοῦ καὶ τὸ ἐν σώματι κάλλος, στολὴν αὐτοῦ τοῦτο προσαγορεύσαντες. Ὡραῖος γάρ ἐστι κάλλει παρὰ τοὺς υἱοὺς τῶν ἀνθρώπων, (Ps 44:4) ὡς ἄνθρωπος · τὸ γὰρ θεῖον αὐτοῦ κάλλος ἀσύγκριτον, ὡς ἀνέφικτον · .... (157C)· Καὶ προσεκτέον ἀκριβῶς, ὡς οὐ λέγει κατερράνθην ἐγώ, ἀλλὰ κατερράνθη τῷ κατανικήματι αὐτῶν τὰ ἱμάτιά μου, τουτέστι τὸ σῶμά μου· (Is 63:3).

the Word in his incarnation on earth; the body was marred but the divine beauty shone out nevertheless; not for him the idea of two separate *prosopa*, for the human nature is actually envisaged as an external vehicle for the bride to climb into, a representative in functional-soteriological terms. Theodoret emphasises that the divine nature is impassible while the body received suffering while he trod the demonic force within the nature[219]; almost casually it reports the "clothing"/body received "a few drops" of blood. The one who is then described as "white and red" (not pink) is the ἀπαρχή who is greater than every nature and was chosen from the myriad; it is his purity that is the acceptable offering.[220] The divine Word flows with the body but remains white when the body is red. Theodoret is describing one who is perfect because of the divine power within. A perusal of his *Eranistes* or indeed of his *Curatio* (written before Ephesus 431) suggests one of whom "le milieu intellectuel est imprégné des écrits de Plotin."[221] A.H. Armstrong remarked of Plotinus that his was: "...a mysticism in which the soul seeks to attain a union with the Absolute of which the best analogy is the union of lovers, not a mysticism in which the soul seeks to realise itself as the Absolute."[222] The importance of the humanity as the external form which the Word used is also standard in Antiochene Christology.

Nilus is marked by a similar understanding. When he says that while Adam died, Christ only experienced the "likeness of death"— which is a patent misreading of Rom 6:5 ("We have been engrafted with him in the likeness of his death") — this is because the person of Christ is the Word who cannot die. Guérard, comparing four other fathers, states that only Nilus does this.[223] In the same way for him "the form of a slave" is just a coating for the divinity. Christ laid down his body like a lamb with its wool (a kinder fate) and was the one who, having merely slept, was able to raise himself, although

---

[219] PG 81,157BC: Καὶ συνεπάτησα αὐτούς, φησὶν, ἐν τῷ θυμῷ μου, καὶ συνέθλασα αὐτοὺς ἐν τῇ ὀργῇ μου, τοὺς τῆς ἀνθρωπείας φύσεως πολεμίους δαίμονας, καὶ τῶν ἐκείνων στρατόν · Καὶ κατερράνθη τῷ κατανικήματι αὐτῶν τὰ ἱμάτιά μου · ἐν γὰρ τῷ νικᾶν καὶ καταλύειν αὐτῶν τὸ κράτος, ἔλαβόν τινας αἱμάτων ρανίδας ἐν τοῖς ἱματίοις · δηλοῖ δὲ τὸν τριήμερον θάνατον.

[220] PG 81,157C: ἀπαθὴς γὰρ ἡ θεία φύσις, τὸ δὲ σῶμα τὸ πάθος ἐδέξατο· σύροντος μὲν αὐτὸ (αὐτῷ) τοῦ ἑνωθέντος Θεοῦ Λόγου, πάθος δὲ ἐκεῖθεν οὐχ ἑλκύσαντος, ἐπειδὴ φύσει τὸ Θεῖον πάθους ὑπέρτερον. Διὰ τοῦτό φησιν ἡ νύμφη · Ἀδελφιδοῦς μου λευκὸς καὶ πυρρός, ἐκλελεγμένος ἀπὸ μυριάδων. Ἁπάσης γὰρ φύσεως κρείττων ἡ ἀπαρχή· Ἁμαρτίαν γὰρ οὐκ ἐποίησεν, οὐδὲ εὑρέθη δόλος ἐν τῷ στόματι αὐτοῦ . διὸ θυσία ἄμωμος ὑπὲρ παντὸς προσηνέχθη τοῦ γένους ·

[221] Canivet in Intro to SC 57 (*"Thérapeutique"*), 32. This was a work which like his *On Providence* (PG 83, 556-773) was set against the Greek treatises in praise of *paideia*, while doing them the honour of accurate citation.

[222] Armstrong (1967), 263.

[223] Guérard, in SC 403, 201, n.2.

in conjunction of operation with the Father. The one thus named is compared to the fawn on account of his ability to overcome evil with virtue.[224] But it is the responsibility of the soul gifted with 'vision' to let this vision be a calming icon for 'her' emotions[225] (in interpreting Cant 2:14). Nilus is not simply interested in defending the divinity of Christ; having assumed that the Word is the Groom, he goes on to inspect the impact on and through his humanity of divine power.[226]

While there is influence from Origen (e.g., the exegesis about the heart of the Groom) and Evagrius, the contribution of Marcellian theology should not be overlooked. To take, for example, the phrase, κυριακὸς ἄνθρωπος, which Jerome translated from Didymus as *homo dominicus*;[227] as Guérard notes, the term can also be found in Epiphanius and Gregory of Nyssa as well as in the Ps-Athanasian works by followers of Marcellus.[228] "Elle appartient à la querelle antiarienne comme expression de la double nature du Christ, permettant la distinction en lui de la divinité et de l'humanité, tout en évitant l'usage des substantifs abstraits",[229] so that its meaning would seem to vary with usage. According to Guérard, Nilus provides an answer to Arianism in the form of a concept of 'divinised humanity': "Ces lectures appartiennent en outre à une communauté dont la foi a été récemment ébranlée par les controverses de l'arianisme, c'est pourquoi la divinité de la nature humaine du Christ se trouve au centre du commentaire."[230] Yet Nilus does not mean by κυριακὸς ἄνθρωπος what Didymus meant. Nilus is more like Theodoret in seeing Christ's humanity as separate from the Word rather than the Didymian notion of a humanity divinised by contact with the Word. So Nilus, as an examination of his comments on Cant 5:10 reveals, is set on showing the Groom to be a man who is far from ordinary and perfect in virtue.[231]

---

[224] See SC 403, 282, 11ff.

[225] SC 403, 294, 20ff.

[226] *Pace* Guérard, ibid., 38f.

[227] See the latter's *De Spiritu Sancto* 230,1; also in Ps.-Didymus, *De Trinitate* III 70, 39-41.

[228] SC 403, 381: the lordly man, the one human stamped by the Lord (LXX: κύριος) as to become lordly. Cf. Maximus *Amb* (PG 91, 1048-9).

[229] Ibid., 61.

[230] Ibid., 61.

[231] Ogden ms, p. 83: τὰ γνωρίσματα... διὰ τῶν ἐπὶ σωτηρίαν φανερωθέντων ἡμῖν καὶ πᾶσαν τὴν ἐκκλησίαν ἐν σῶμα τοῦ νυμφίου ποιοῦσα. ἴδιον τε νοημα δι'ἑκάστου τῶν μελῶν ἐν τῇ ὑπογραφῇ τοῦ κάλλους ἐνδείκνυται δι' ὃν ὅλον ἐκ τῶν κατὰ μέρος θεωρουμένων τὸ τοῦ σώματος κάλλος συμπαρεικάζεται; ἐκ τοῦ σώματος τοίνυν καὶ τῆς κατηχήσεως ἄρχεται καθὰ καὶ ματθαῖος πεποίηκεν· ἵνα δὲ μὴ τῶν κατὰ σαρκά τις ἀκούσων γένεσιν πρὸς τὰ τῆς φύσεως κατα(ο?)λισθήσειε πάθη τῇ διανοίᾳ· τουτοῦ χάριν τὸν κοινωνήσαντα ἡμῖν σαρκὸς καὶ αἵματος λευκὸν μὲν εἶναι φησιν καὶ πυρὸν τουτοῦ σώματος δι' ἀμφοτέρων φύσιν αἰνιττιουμένη· οὐ μὴν ὁμοιότροπον αὐτῆς τὴν λοχην [??] τῷ

In Nilus then we see a hybrid Christology which is very sensitive to Scripture's imagery and more of a mystical tenor than one ruled by 'textbook' Christological formulae. The Groom is seen as the Incarnate One, although the Word usually plays his personality. The κυριακὸς ἄνθρωπος is already a completed reality in the Incarnation, *before* the resurrection.[232] Those looking on are next defined as either the angels who were κύκλῳ τοῦ κυριακοῦ ἀνθρώπου — meaning around Christ during the Incarnation — or as believing, ascetic souls, before the resurrection of Christ, in that perfect humanity, provided in the first place by Mary. The Word of God is constantly the protagonist in the voyage of conversion of the soul to the perfection achieved in resurrection (already by Christ, not yet by all others). Guérard is right to note that the Groom as the Word is always the centre of attention even when in the background. However Christology and not just 'Logology' (or Trinitarian theology) is indeed 'central'; which is why it is surprising that she denies that by the 390s (her date for the commentary) any theological issues had any real import: "Pourtant, à la fin du IVe et au début du Ve siècle, il n'est plus question à Ancyre que de monachisme."[233] Further, her insistence that Nilus deals in imagery rather than aims for strict doctrinal accuracy, should not obscure the fact that there are marked Christological allegiances which are suggestive of a date later than Guérard's preference. For example, in contrast to the Alexandrians, as Guérard herself notes, Nilus follows Gregory in arguing that it is the psyche as a whole which is called to participate in God, and not just the intellect, even though the latter plays the 'training' role.[234] Similarly, because of his 'modalist' associations, he can say that the Father is involved in Christ's being raised, but not that the Father alone raises him (the inclination of Origenian subordinationism).

Thus Guérard misinterprets when she writes that in the above-mentioned passage Nilus is keen to show the autonomy of Christ's power: "le Père a été exclu de la faculté de ressusciter du Fils, car toute activité du Père et du Fils est commune et telle qu'elle n'est pas séparée par la substance de leur caractère propre (τῇ ὑποστάσει τῆς ἰδιότητος), mais unie par la conjonction de leur nature (τῇ συναφείᾳ τῆς φύσεως). L'idée manque, pour le moins, de fermeté. Nil n'est pas très loin d'affirmer, à cause de τῆς ἰδιότητος une dualité d'hypostases. Mais 'hypostase' n'est pas au pluriel,

---

κοινῷ τόκῳ. ἔχειν γὰρ κατεξαίρετον τὸ μὴ ἐκ λε(υ)χος γεγενῆσθαι· τοῦτο γὰρ ἐκλελοχισμένος ἀπὸ μυριάδων.

[232] Cf. ibid., 340, on Cant 3:7f: *Καὶ τὸ κλίνη ἡμῶν σύσκιος ·γυμνάζοντες παρὰ τῆς νύμφης πρὸς τὸν νυμφίον ἐρημένον λέγομεν κλίνην εἶναι τὸ σῶμα τὸ κυριακόν, σύσκιον δὲ ἐπειδὴ συνεσκίαζε τῷ σώματι τὴν θεότητα καὶ ἔκρυπτε περιέλκον εἰς ἑαυτὸ τοὺς ὁρῶντας...* .

[233] Ibid., 21.
[234] Ibid., 86

et... l'auteur reste très prudent."[235] It is also unwise to conclude that, because the word φύσις is not used and that the unity of Christ is stressed, Nilus was negligent in his Christological expression. It is simply that the Word is the proactive partner, the Groom who allows his humanity to be seen as κυριακὸς ἄνθρωπος. The Logos is all that flesh could be and more (the significance of καθ' ὑπόστασιν). Any 'Origenian' idea of two *prosopa* seems as distasteful to Nilus as to all orthodox, such was the contemporary emphasis on the oneness of personality or hypostasis. What is most interesting for our study is that the formula καθ' ὑπόστασιν is first found unequivocally in Mark the Hermit.[236] Mark and Nilus at least may have belonged to a common circle; prayer to Jesus is a consequence of regarding the person of Jesus as the Word.

3. 10 The Cosmic Groom transcendent

Cant 6:9f and beyond

6·9 μία ἐστὶν περιστερά μου, τελεία μου,
μία ἐστὶν τῇ μητρὶ αὐτῆς,
ἐκλεκτή ἐστιν τῇ τεκούσῃ αὐτῆς.
εἴδοσαν αὐτὴν θυγατέρες καὶ μακαριοῦσιν αὐτήν,
βασίλισσαι καὶ παλλακαὶ καὶ αἰνέσουσιν αὐτήν.
6·10 Τίς αὕτη ἡ ἐκκύπτουσα ὡσεὶ ὄρθρος,
καλὴ ὡς σελήνη, ἐκλεκτὴ ὡς ὁ ἥλιος,
θάμβος ὡς τεταγμέναι;

Methodius' concern was to correct Platonic (and Origenian) cosmology partly by accounting for the mediation of Christ as not primarily ontological but moral; this parallels his understanding of Adam mediating between the good and evil in the cosmos, rather than between the intelligible and sensible.[237] Although this Adam-Christ figure functions for Methodius in a way which is very similar to what Plato attributed to *Eros* itself and although virginity seems to have been only truly possible through the possession of a divine nature,[238] nevertheless it is a moral, non-metaphysical, even de-mythologised account of the Song's message, putting it into terms concerning human purity.

---

[235] Ibid., 77.
[236] See Grillmeier (1979), 483, n. 35.
[237] *Symp* 67f: SC 95, p. 104: Ὁ δὲ ἄνθρωπος τουτῶν ὧν μεταξὺ ...Μεθόριος γὰρ τοῦ τῆς ζωῆς ξύλου καὶ τοῦ γνωστοῦ καλοῦ τε καὶ πονηροῦ τέθεις... .
[238] See H. Musurillo (1980), 1112, referring to *Symp* II, 2; III,8: "...ce mot est voisin de *partheia* [itself, according to Lampe (1961), 1033, a "fictitious word formed from παρθενία, and used to explain that παρθενία is almost divine"] ou 'conformité à la divinité' dont il diffère seulement par une lettre (*Symp* VIII,1)" (ibid, 1115). It is virginity which leads

In the Procopian fragments, already when commenting on Cant 2:4, Origen had explained that the believing soul is led into either the soul, the Church or the *hegemonikon* of Christ.[239] This place or position where the Word resides is called "loveable and inaccessible" (adopting the reading proposed by the PG 17 editor). Thus in Origen the Groom remains a long way off from human reality, sharing out his fragrance as an invitation to partake of *the* reality.[240] Most of the time the commentary describes the believing soul's ascent towards the Word; e.g., on Cant 5:6 ἀδελφιδός μου παρῆλθεν· ψυχή μου ἐξῆλθεν ἐν λόγῳ αὐτοῦ ("my kinsman came close; my soul went out at his word"): "The soul comes out and moves out of the body, having citizenship in heaven through the word of the Groom."[241]

Much more developed in cosmological orientation is Origen's description of the betrothal scene at Cant 6:8, where the bride is the λογικὸν ζῶον.[242] "The Groom is Word; the bride is rational creature; if soul contemplates and the Groom takes her as bride. But since this Groom is the Logos he does not 'commune' with one soul but with many and various, yet by royal and distinct honour, he may be said to be 'perfect dove'."[243] The Greek is not entirely clear but it seems that Origen takes the *Logos* himself to be called "perfect dove", and his numerical distance even from queens shows his transcendence, even if as *primus inter pares*. Nevertheless, on at least one occasion, there is further reference to the soul of Christ created yet joined to the Logos. In the comment on Cant 7:1 concerning the identity of the Shulammite, the soul who made peace by 'her' sacrifice on the Cross is the original and saving bride of the Word in the heavens.[244] The presence of

---

believers by the chariot of souls up towards heaven and the Father. A self-sacrificing *Partheneia* is perceived as the true force in the world — *Eros* was just an imposter.

[239] PG 17, 253CD: Εἰσήγαγέ (Εἰσήνεγκεν LXX) με ὁ βασιλεὺς εἰς τὸ ταμίειον αὐτοῦ. (Cant 1:4). Ἤγουν ἀδύνατον [frt l. ἄδυτον] τὴν ἀξιέραστον λέγει ψυχὴν ἢ Ἐκκλησίαν ἢ τὸ ἡγεμονικὸν τοῦ Χριστοῦ · εἰς ὁ Παῦλος εἰσελθὼν ἔφη · Ἡμεῖς δὲ νοῦν Χριστοῦ ἔχομεν, ἵνα ἴδωμεν τὰ ὑπὸ θεοῦ χαρισθέντα ἡμῖν.

[240] See *De Principiis* II, 6, alluding to Cant 1:3 as well as Ps 44 (LXX): 8.

[241] PG 17, 273 CD: ἐξέρχεται καὶ ἐκδημεῖ τοῦ σώματος ἡ ψυχὴ διὰ τὸν τοῦ νυμφίου λόγον ἔχουσα ἐν οὐρανῷ τὸ πολίτευμα .

[242] This 'Stoic' phrase is found in Justin, *dial.* 93.3 (PG 6, 697C): πλησίον δὲ ἀνθρώπου οὐδὲν ἄλλο ἐστὶν ἢ τὸ ὁμοιοπαθὲς καὶ λογικόν ζῶον. See Lampe (1961), 805.

[243] PG 17,277CD: λόγος ἐστὶν ὁ νυμφίος· λογικὸν ζῶον ἡ νύμφη. ἐὰν νοήσῃ ψυχὴ καὶ λαβῇ ὁ νυμφίος τὴν νύμφην ἀλλ᾽ ἐπεί ἐστιν ὁ λόγος οὗτος, οὐ μιᾷ ψυχῇ κοινωνῶν, ἀλλὰ πλείοσι καὶ διαφόροις, τιμῇ τινι βασιλικῇ καὶ διαφαινούσῃ, λεγέτω τελεία περιστερά.

[244] PG 17, 280CD: Ἀκύλας καὶ ἡ πέμπτη ἔκδωσις, τὸ Σουλαβίτις ἐξέδωκαν, εἰρηνεύουσα γάρ ἔστι δὲ ἡ νύμφη τοῦ λόγου ψυχή, ἡ τοῦ Χριστοῦ Ἐκκλησία, διὰ τὸν ποιήσαντα τὸ ἕν, καὶ τὸ μεσότοιχον τοῦ φραγμοῦ λύσαντα· ἐὰν δε ἡ Σουλαμίτις, ἡ ἐσκυλευμένη, κατὰ Σύμμαχον, λέγοι ἄν πρὸς αὐτὴν ὁ νυμφίος,

Hexaplaric readings is another sign that this is Origen's handiwork. The point is to show that, as E. von Ivánka has argued,[245] the Logos is *primus inter pares* and is the one who joins all and holds all together, according to the macrocosmic effect, as a sort of World-Soul figure.[246]

Any suspicion that these are merely later developments unparalleled in pre-Sixth Century sources can be allayed by a consideration of the place given to the Logos in the first (late third century) redaction of the Christian *Physiologus*.[247] If the Word is understood as joined to the man Jesus, yet also as the partner who contributes the personality of Christ,[248] then the attributes of the Logos are as good as the attributes of the Pantocrator who is the one raised and ascended glorious. It is the realisation of the full divinity of Christ rather than the 'Evagrian' desire to imitate his perfect νοῦς which motivated the ascetic person who took the Song as indicating the possibility of such a full union. The One who is fully universal Lord is the One who can pull us up to be on a par with heavenly creatures.[249]

Although the commentary does not reach Cant 6:8, within the Preface Rufinus-Origen is adamant that the Song should *not* be called "the Song*s* of Songs".[250] This preference for the singular is in itself a subtle allusion to the Platonic yet also biblical idea of 'oneness' or 'singularity', equivalent to perfection. It is possible that Origen sought to distance himself from a Neoplatonic belief that God and world could not mix; he solved this by a focus on the mysterious properties of God's love. 'Love' (as enfigured in the nuptial relationship) was less than identity of essences, yet its unifying qualities enabled much more than a moral union between parties of different substance. As Perfect Soul to Logos, so Son to Father; as God to World, so Christ to Church; the theological vision was one of *inclusion*. According to C. Osborne[251], in his Canticles Commentary, "Origen is working with a model of Platonic love very similar to that found in Plotinus", and in general one can thus see the shoots of monophysitism in Origen's Christology, in that the

---

Ὦ ἐσκυλευμένη καὶ ὑπὸ τῷ αἰχμαλωτίσαντί σε γεγενημένη, ἐπίστρεφε εἰς τὴν προτέραν εὐγένειαν.

[245] Ivánka (1990), 156f, argues that Origen did not conceive of Word and souls as ontologically necessarily different. Origen did think the biblical Fall necessitated a perfect saviour, but had fewer difficulties than other Christians in envisaging a *kat'ousian* union of Word and soul of Christ "pre-existently".

[246] It is surely no coincidence that, under Origen's influence, Maximus' scheme of the resolution of the *coincidentia oppositorum* would start with the man-woman tension; see *Ambigua* 41.

[247] Here I follow the judgements of Treu in her edition of Physiologus (1981) and Riedinger (1975).

[248] Cf. McGuckin (1994), 206, *contra* Grillmeier.

[249] *Contra* the dominant motif in Clark (1992).

[250] Baehrens, p. 87.

[251] Osborne (1992), 272.

Λόγος-νοῦς union in heaven in which they become 'one spirit', yet separable like two Λόγοι, could make a ψυχή with real human origins redundant.[252] Yet, in fact, as R. Williams observes, there was a telescoping of νοῦς and ψυχή, the latter as perfect gaining the status of the former through its unchangeable association with the Logos.[253]

The Son was one eternally oriented outwards in order to mediate; this may explain something of Origen's subordinationism, in that the Son has it in himself to unite with his creation, albeit only with its acme in any direct sense.[254] However the Father's love for the Son infected the soul of Christ so as to love the Logos;[255] it is the Father and the soul to whom *Philanthropia* properly belongs; the Word in that sense is more the object of *eros* and the place where the Father's love kindles human love for God; it is the soul who feels the pain of the Father's loss. Pietras adduces a key text (*Contra Celsum* IV,18) whose thrust is one of love's victory, which Chadwick translates: "what difficulty is there if the Word out of great love to mankind brings down a Saviour to the human race?"[256] Rational souls do not change their nature, especially when joined to the Word, so the descent out of *philanthropia* involves undergoing suffering but not change. However, any idea that the Logos, if not quite staying in heaven, at least keeps a respectable distance from suffering, as suggested by Pietras and Crouzel, goes against other texts by Origen, e.g., *In Jn VI*,42[257] which speaks of the soul suffering locally but the Logos universally, and *In Jn XX*, 19 (17)[258] where "Jordan" is explained as "*their* descent". Yet it is Crouzel's belief that it is not the Word but the soul of Christ who is the Groom of the Church, the "himmlische... Eros".[259] For Crouzel, the soul descended to Hades to destroy death and is thus "the ram" offered in place of Isaac the divine Son.[260] Yet the two are not really so

---

[252] See Görgemanns-Karpp (1976)'s thesis that Origen was at *De Princ* II, 6,3 in thrall to Clement's Christology, p. 793, Anm. 26; cf. Courth (1988), p. 103.

[253] Williams (1985).

[254] See Crouzel (1981), 65f: "Le Christ Médiateur et Sauveur. Il mérite des titres par son Incarnation, certes, par la rencontre en lui de la divinité parfaite avec une humanité complète, mais il les possède déjà en tant que Verbe par son divinité seule, orientée par sa mission de salut."

[255] As Pietras (1988) has shown.

[256] Chadwick, (1953), 196.

[257] Origen (1903), p. 151, 28-30: "Ἰορδάνην μέντοι γε νοητέον <τὸν> τοῦ θεοῦ λόγον τὸν γενόμενον σάρκα καὶ σκηνώσαντα ἐν ἡμῖν, Ἰησοῦν δὲ τὸν κληροδοτήσαντα ὃ ἀνείληφεν ἀνθρώπινον,... ." Pietras argues that the word λόγος actually means the account (presumably Phil 2:5-9) and thus translates the second half: "...perchè mai ciò dovrebbe essere un argomento contro il racconto che fa discendere il Salvatore a causa del grande amore verso gli uomini."

[258] Ibid., p. 351, 25ff.

[259] Cf. Dölger (1950), 273-75, who very much identifies "Christ" here as the Logos.

[260] Crouzel (1981), 75-77, following Alcain (1976).

distinct in Origen's account, which understands the soul of Christ as already part of the Groom who comes to love humans out of love for those formed in his image. Whatever went on 'pre-existently', Origen believed in only one agency in Christ during the Incarnation, as was understood in 543.[261]

Overall the Origenian vision is of the personage of the Groom not actually being, but *signifying* both earthly and heavenly realities simultaneously. Unlike Hippolytus the relationship of God and his people involves the mutuality of cycles of call and response, but a mutuality in time which tends towards a unity already gained in eternity. It makes theology 'interpersonal',[262] and as there developed the notion of the Song as a book about divine love, it was about God as Love supplying love for love of God — which had its foundation in that which was revealed between Word and soul 'in Christ', rather than according to any notion of inner-Trinitarian love. The bond is so tight that Origen does not speak of a perfect soul as having a separate identity after the union, on earth, which is the period the Song 'describes'. In his employment of the *hegemonikon* we have signs that Origen favours unity over duality because of the role played by Christ's humanity. To use A. Grillmeier's categorisation: "...der Logos hat in Christus ganz die Führung ergriffen... . Origenes konnte damit letztlich auf dem Wege zu einer metaphysischen Deutung der Einheit Christi aus dem Personbegriff sein. Denn im 'Leitprinzip' ist die eigentliche Personwürde des Menschen verankert, was schon an den modernen Personbegriff erinnert."[263] P. Meloni claims that Origen's intent was to stress the unity of the Logos and the pre-existent soul of Christ because they are of the same substance; however Origen is rather saying that only through uniting did they come to share the same substance.[264] Moreover, to say that this soul achieved by merit (*De Princ* II, 6, 4: "*Dilectionis igitur merito unguitur oleo laetitiae, id est anima cum verbo dei Christus efficitur.*") what the rest could only receive by gift, i.e., incorruptibility, did not mean that Origen was an adoptionist as Justinian misrepresented him. For Origen, the one who became "Christ" was a

---

[261] The causes of the Origenists and the Nestorians were pitted *against* each other during that period.

[262] Cf. Rondeau (1985), 50-52.

[263] Grillmeier (1979), 270f, on the exegesis of Ps 44:8 in *De Principiis* II, 6,2-5; esp. 6,3: "Et hac de causa per omnem scripturam tam divina natura hominis vocabulis appellatur, quam humana natura divinae nuncupationis insignibus decoratur. Magis enim de hoc quam de ullo alio dici potest quod scriptum est quia 'Erunt ambo in carne una, et iam non sunt duo, sed caro una' (Mt 19:5-6). Magis enim verbum dei cum anima 'in carne una' esse quam vir cum uxore putandus est. Sed et 'unus spiritus esse cum deo' cui magis convenit quam huic animae, quae se ita deo per dilectionem iunxit, ut 'cum eo unus spiritus' merito dicatur?"

[264] Meloni (1975), 134ff.

composite *anima cum verbo dei*.[265] The cloak of immortality for human bodies at the future resurrection is the same as that which the Logos once put on; they will share a common cloak of a perfect soul.[266] The soul of Christ is the "incorruptible" cloak for the heavenly banquet, just as the bride of Cant 6:8 is to be called "perfect dove".[267] For now though, what becomes available to the soul of the believer is only the provisional 'smell' of bodily immortality; *pace* Meloni, the fragrance is not the divinity itself, but its effects of virtue. The Song of Songs depicts the earthly outworking of the heavenly actions. Behind all the action, summoning it into being, stands the Word, the cosmic Groom.

Quoting from Book I, the editors[268] of the critical edition of Apponius conclude that, according to him, the Song's theme is the history of God's love for humanity and the Church as predicted by Solomon.[269] This perhaps fails to pay sufficient attention to the sentence which follows.[270] Apponius hints, by employing the motif *tecta*, that the Song is the reverse side of a tapestry which if turned over reveals the Incarnation in all its intrinsic clarity. However the economy of the Word is not limited, as it was for Hippolytus, to establishing the Church; rather there is a history of his dealings with the

---

[265] Görgemanns-Karpp (1976), 367, n.17: "Der Fehler steckt wohl im Anfang des Fragments. Das 'ein Mensch zu Christus wurde' dürfte eine irreführende Verkürzung des Satzes sein: Die Seele wurde, mit dem Wort Gottes vereint, zu Christus".

[266] *De Principiis* II, 3,2; GCS 115,10ff: "Haec ergo materia corporis, quae nunc corruptibilis est, *induet incorruptionem*, cum perfecta anima et dogmatibus incorruptionis instructa uti eo coeperit. Et nolo mireris si velut indumentum corporis perfectam animam dicimus, quae propter verbum dei et sapientiam eius nunc *incorruptio* nominatur; cum ipse utique qui est dominus et creator animae Christus Iesus indumentum sanctis esse dicatur, sicut apostolus dicit: '*Induite vos dominum Iesum Christum*'. Sicut ergo Christus indumentum est animae, ita intellegibili quadam ratione etiam anima indumentum esse dicitur corporis. Ornamentum enim eius est celans et contegens eius mortalem naturam. Tale est ergo quod dicitur: '*Necesse est corruptibile hoc induere incorruptionem*'. ut si diceret: necesse est naturam hanc corruptibilem corporis indumentum accipere incorruptionis, animam habentem in se incorruptionem, pro eo videlicet quod induta est Christum, qui est sapientia et verbum dei."

[267] At PG 17, 277CD.

[268] Vregille and Neyrand; CCL 19.

[269] *Expositio in Cant*, I, 48-50; CCL 19, p. 4: "quidquid ab initio mundi usque in finem in mysteriis egit acturusve erit Dei Sermo erga Ecclesiam... ."

[270] Ibid., 49-56: "...in figura et in aenigmatibus demonstratum. In quo Cantico omnia quae narrantur tecta mysteriis, in Verbi incarnatione revelata et completa docentur. ubi elisa erigitur humana progenies... regina et sponsa creatoris sui, Verbi Dei, Christi benignitate, effecta ostenditur." Thus the drawn-out events of the end-times are 'discovered' in the later verses of the Song but are held to be meaningful and universally salvific rather than terrifying and confusing because of what the Incarnation has revealed (which is made clear in Book IX.) Also, XI, 365ff: "Nunc vero a praesenti versiculo usque ad finem huius Cantici ea quae usque ad diem iudicii agenda sunt ostenduntur significari."

3. The Groom

whole human race. For the function of explaining the ancient mysteries of history and prophecy is attributed to the enfleshment of the Word, even with respect to things taking place after the Ascension. The Incarnation fulfils the potential of these enigmatic texts to signify the whole of the trans-historical reality while remaining itself the central part of that *res*.

Trinitarian relationships are merely alluded to in elliptical phrases.[271] He is one with the Father in the glory of resurrection, which implies that in his suffering he was not so since he was away from co-habiting in glory. At V, 529f there is an aside that hints people needed to be reminded of the Spirit's divinity.[272] The religion which has as its content the one God (presumably Judaism) is improved on by a grasp of revelation which believes in the victory of the Word which is in turn trumped by the *praxis* of meritorious living.[273]

Interpreting Cant 6:9f with the phrase "through her, with the threefold glory shining",[274] Apponius insists on the Incarnation as the revelation of the whole Trinity; the mention of the voice of the three being audible in the speech of the assumed man.[275] This indicates the close connection between "christologische(n) und trinitarianische(n) Aussagen" which are tied together, "…nicht nur und nicht vorrangig aus antihäretischem Interesse, sondern weil nur so die eine, unteilbare Offenbarung Gottes erfaßt werden kann." Apponius, like Augustine, holds that the person of Christ contains an invisible deity to be seen by the faith of the saved and a humanity alone for the eyes of the condemned.[276] With the soul of Christ as intermediary, "the souls to be redeemed might rejoice in the redeemer of their race, in whom is true flesh and true soul; and she [?] might awake the flesh by arising from the dead and at the same time gather the souls to judgement; and the true God might

---

[271] Cf. V, 181-83; CCL 19, p. 120: "Vidimus, inquit, gloriam eius: non illam passionis, ubi celatur divinitas, quam praedixerat Esaias futuram, sed illam resurrectionis, in qua unum cum Patre est."

[272] CCL 19, p. 132: "Aut non tibi videtur quasi mutato grabato Spiritum sanctum, qui Deus est… ."

[273] IX, 233-38; CCL 19, p. 223: "…tertius vero ordo est adulescentularum, quibus sola credulitas in unum Deum subvenit ad salutem: quae non sunt dignae adhuc sacrato numero copulari. Quae omnes licet habeant regem Verbum Patris, qui in principio erat apud Patrem, et semper in Patre Deus, tamen distat dignitas meritorum."

[274] König (1992), 179, n. 50, on IX, 24 (CCL 19, p. 224): "Per quam, trina gloria refulgente, ex carne caro visibilem iudicem uteretur. Per quam redimendae animae sui generis redemptorem gauderent, in quo vera caro et vera anima." The *lemma* is: *Sexaginta sunt reginae et octoginta concubinae, et adulescentularum non est numerus. una est columba mea, perfecta mea. Unica est matri suae, electa est genetrici suae. viderunt eam filiae et beatissimam praedicaverunt reginas et concubinae et laudaverunt eam* (CCL 19, p. 216).

[275] CCL 19, p. 235: "Quarum trium personarum de adsumpto homine vox sonare probatur."

[276] See König (1992), 180, n. 51.

present the immortal glory of his kingdom to those believing in him."[277] König observes that it is unclear who is the subject of the underlined verbs. It seems best to take it to be the Word of God with the soul as his agent, not as a distinct personality.

This does not imply that Christ's *Menschennatur* is deprecated.[278] In fact it is doubtful, both from the context and overall thrust of his commentary, that Apponius shared Hilary's concern to combat Arianism by demonstrating that it was not the Word who calls humans his brothers; it was obvious that such could be attributed to the human *anima* of Christ who is the Messianic equivalent of David. Now Apponius undoubtedly has *Christological* matters and Photinus, whose Christology is best labelled 'adoptionist', in his sights here; he will name him forty lines later as one who teaches "many saviours".[279] For Photinus Christ was simply a man who only came into being with his conception and began to become God from that point on. M. Simonetti helpfully explains that "Fotinus" taught that the Word created a man while essentially remaining in heaven; the man therefore had to be assumed in turn by the Spirit in order to fulfil his mission.[280] Soteriologically speaking, the divinity fled the Cross but not before enabling a soul so perfect that it could endure it and rise again by its own virtue.[281] The Word, the active Redeemer-subject, as judge is *visible* through the transparent soul-shining, glorious, and initiative-taking. The point is not, as König thinks, that in the soul as the humanity of Christ is God's means of veiling his divinity. Apponius thinks that God himself was revealed: "She displays one redeemer, the sole judge, the unique Son of God who is offered to/for the world". König summarises: "...die Seele Christi...kann so nicht nur den Gottessohn offenbaren, sondern auch den Vater, der den Sohn der Welt schenkt, und den Hl. Geist, der dieses Heilsgeschehen vorausweiß und verausverkündet...". Yet her wish to drive a distinction between nature and power in the text is less

---

[277] IX, 265-78; CCL 19, p. 224: "Per quam Sermo Dei Patris peccatum damnavit in carne,...ut hominem de eius manibus liberatum pristinae redderet libertati. Per quam trina gloria refulgente, ex carne caro visibilem iudicem uteretur. Per quam redimendae animae sui generis redemptorem gauderent, in quo vera caro et vera anima; et carnem, resurgendo a mortuis, suscitaret, simul et animas ad iudicium congregaret; et verus Deus immortalem sui regni gloriam in se credentibus condonaret. Haec est proculdubio una anima reginarum regina quam Dei Sermo adsumptam portasse probatur; per quam inferna concussit et clausis aperuit animabus et, reddito corpore, secum reduxit ab inferis resurgendo."

[278] *Pace* König (1992), 158, n.12; e.g. at IX, 95ff (CCL 19, p. 219): "Quae adhaerendo Verbo Dei concipiunt et pariunt reges. De quibus ipse rex adsumptus homo, ore David praedixit ad Patrem: *Narrabo nomen tuum fratribus meis*."

[279] For the theological roots of Photinus' heresy, cf. Riedmatten (1952), 87-119. "La théologie de Photin s'avère donc être un monarchianisme rigoureux joint à un adoptianisme non moins strict." (91).

[280] Simonetti (1975a), 136f.

[281] Riedmatten (1952), 118.

happy: "Apponius betont nicht, wie und daß die vollständige Gottnatur ganz in Christus eingeht, sondern er betont, wie und daß die Menschnatur durch die unauflösbare gottmenschliche Einung in Christus Anteil erhält an der Macht der Gottheit."[282] The Son's fire-like nature (*which is* his power) was communicated through her yet enduring 'metal'. The *cooperatio Trinitatis* means a communicating of nature to one special human soul so that that nature can be *seen by* its effects *in* some because the Son has so completely taken the soul into himself. A composite person (not a *tertium quid*[283]) is formed — Jesus the pilgrim (the theme of Book XII) who can mediate both ways by a *communicatio idiomatum* which is more than nominal, while the erotic imagery suggests Christological περιχώρησις. The soul plays the joining and the distinguishing role but cannot be understood as 'the person' spanning Word and flesh in the being of Christ.

That person who is the subject of the saving enterprise is the *Sermo divinus* in the Church who rewards their corresponding love by raising souls to heaven.[284] In heaven he continues to communicate and execute providence, yet, on earth, it seems that the soul of Christ is delegated special providence in the Church until 'she' hands over authority. König makes the observation that *Sermo* and *Verbum* are synonymous, but that the former is only used in the nominative,[285] and thus concludes: "Apponius dürfte sich also bei der Verwendung von *sermo Dei* und *Verbum Dei* an Rufins Übersetzung orientert haben." However it is not churlish to observe that *Sermo* is used for the one who resides in heaven but makes overriding forays into the world, while the *Verbum* is the one bound in a body via a soul and who was at times an object, thus finding himself mentioned in the accusative case. Likewise the change of gender in the subject of this comment on Cant 6:10 is simply due to Apponius' departure from the focus on the mechanics of the Incarnation and the soul of Christ towards the name "Jesus" as the name of the composite person who made salvation possible. He himself came to the garden of Israel which in effect was the vineyard-garden of Gethsemane where he was

---

[282] Ibid., 183, n. 56.

[283] *Expos in Cant* XII, 154-59; CCL 19, p. 272: "Nam, sicut omnis natus de carne non potest recusare corporis mortem quae per peccatum inducta est in mundum, ita et supradicta,[*viz.*,anima] unum effecta cum Verbo, manente materia, dividi non potest. Ideo et talem comparationem praesenti posuit loco, dicendo: *quia fortis ut mors dilectio, dura sicut inferus aemulatio.*"

[284] See CCL 19, p. 220f.

[285] Ibid, 5, n.3, except surely where the Bible text, e.g. of Jn 1:14 has *Verbum caro factum*: as at IX, 281; CCL 19, p. 224. Rufinus' translation of Origen (Cant. Comm.) does the same. Jerome, more sensitive to the fact that the referent as the divine Son is fixed and determines, rather than is determined by any variations *sermo* and *verbum* might supply, has no such scruples about using the two interchangeably.

persecuted and arrested.[286] She, the universal, can call the particular "my beloved". Jesus as the Groom was the *Verbum* in his incarnate state who embraces the soul of humanity within himself; everything that happened to the man Jesus happened to the Word, with the qualifier that the Godhead cannot suffer. For the power of deity which makes him one with the Father is emptied out, enabling a oneness with Man, since the weakness of humanity can grasp or receive him; thus he becomes mediator between both Father and Man.[287] This passage refers beyond the Incarnation itself to its effects on humans being able to connect with God through him, the universe-governing *Sermo*. Apponius writes a trans-historical commentary, in the sense of the Song's verses being linked to realities in, yet also beyond, world-history.[288] It is historical in that the focus is not on the *means* of the Incarnation *qua* metaphysical combination. Instead Apponius has moved on to consider the *modus operandi* in which the incarnate self-abasement of the Word brought him into contact with the hateful Jewish nation who had knowledge of him through the teaching of patriarchs and prophets.[289] The flesh allowed the Word to be revealed to human eyes — literal, not spiritual sight, such is the bounty of grace — and to experience and break death. Yet the Word's authority and realm means it is trans-historical. The eschatology is in no sense Apollinarian, for while the human soul's authority is to be surrendered, the Word's kingdom is eternal and uninterrupted.[290]

---

[286] IX, 422-426; CCL 19, p. 229: on the *lemma*: *Quae est ista quae egreditur quasi aura consurgens, pulchra ut luna, electa ut sol, terribilis ut acies ordinata*: "Quae excolentem spinosam mentem suam magnum agricolam blasphemiis egit in crucem, et deambulantem Dominum docendo, in hortum suum vel vineam, quae secundum prophetam Esaiam domus Israhel est, cum armatorum agminibus irruens, persecutionis tempore conturbavit... ."

[287] The whole of this key passage (*lemma: Descendi ad hortum nostrum, ut viderem poma convallis, ut inspicerem si floruisset vinea et germinassent mala punica. nescivit anima mea. conturbavit me propter quadrigas Aminadab*), IX, 431-38; CCL 19, p. 229, is: "Reddit videlicet rationem descensus sui in hoc loco Sermo Dei Patris unitus isti unicae et electae animae ex milibus. Qui unum iam effectus cum anima, quidquid hominis assumpti est totum sibi deputat factum, salva impassibili maiestate. *Descendit ergo ad hortum suum* exinaniendo se potentia deitatis per quam cum Patre unum est, ut capere eum possit humanitatis fragilitas, per quam cum homine unum est, inter utrumque mediator effectus."

[288] As does the Targum, probably composed shortly afterwards. Nicholas of Lyra would bring the historical referents into sharper relief.

[289] IX, 438-41; CCL 19, p. 229: "*Ad hortum*, id est gentem suam notitiam habentem, ubi patriarchae et prophetae non parum desudaverant laborando in doctrina. Ad convallem huius mundi, id est conversationem humanam post offensam Adae."

[290] IX, 515-19; CCL 19, p. 231: "*Descendit ergo ad hortum suum* et eius animae cui omne iudicium tradidit faciendum, demonstrando se Deum in carne, per quam a carneis oculis proximus videretur in terris, per quam colligeret velut manibus de convalle spinosa tribulationum ad paradisum sanctorum animas, ab inferis resurgendo." As König (1992), 198f, n. 92, shows, this replaces the Vulgate's *dedit* with *tradidit* which implies the inferiority of the one receiving.

3.11 The Cosmic Groom and nature imagery

Cant 8:14 et al...
8·14 Φύγε, ἀδελφιδέ μου, καὶ ὁμοιώθητι τῇ δορκάδι
ἢ τῷ νεβρῷ τῶν ἐλάφων ἐπὶ ὄρη ἀρωμάτων.

From the first redaction of the Christian *Physiologus* to the animal exemplars of virtues in Gregory the Great's *Moralia in Job*, the natural kingdom furnished theologians with the means to illustrate virtues by connecting them to the capacities of an animal (or plant). Animals, lacking higher souls, cannot be virtuous, but their bodily movments and instinctual powers correspond to something higher up the hierarchy.

The (fifth-century) Armenian fragments of Hippolytus with their interpolations show a development of the more authentically original text in the direction of an interpretation with not just a Hippolytan reference to the Incarnation but with a more pointed miaphysite emphasis. The comment on Cant 4:16/5:1 has (in German translation):

> Mit diesem gesalbt empfing die Jungfrau Maria, [die Gottgebärerin] in ihrem Leibe das Wort... O neue Veranstaltung (Ökonomie)! O unaussprechliche Geheimnisse.[291]

And on Cant 2:10:

> Der Freund ist die Menschheit, welche durch die Hände Gottes geschaffen wurde, und 'schön', weil sie Gottes Schemel schmückte.[292]

Or On Cant 5:1:

> Der Sohn meines Bruders komme in seinen Garten und esse die Frucht seiner Bäume. Es ist das Kommende der Gottheit zur Menschheit.[293]

Twoness in Christ can be spoken of *before* the Incarnation, as the preparation for the wedding of two into one. In the Hippolytan tradition, the cosmos is reduced to that small area of Palestine which staged the gospel events.

A tendency to treat the Groom as one whose *philanthropia* did not stop with Hades but went even further, as the *Pantokrator* of the *kosmos*, is clearly

---

[291] Bonwetsch (1903), p. 359, 9-12 ('Slavische Fragmente'). Cf. Bonwetsch, p. 359, n. 14: "Hier beginnt die mit Hippolyts Namen bezeichnete, nur armenisch vorhandene Erklärung des Hohelieds in der Kön. Bibliothek in Berlin, No. 89 der armenischen Hss [Karamianz S.72] (B) Bl. 155r."
[292] Ibid., p. 365, 9-11.
[293] Ibid., p. 374, 23-25.

seen in the later *addendum* to Philo of Carpasia's comment on Cant 7:5.[294] An assurance that Christ was the universal Lord developed just after the Council of Chalcedon in tandem with a growth in awareness of the theological significance of the Apocalypse of John. As there are certain points of contact (e.g. Rev 3:20; 12:1ff; 21:1-4), it is not surprising that Apponius and others developed their understanding of the Song in the light of end-times prophecy. The Song is thus about God's economy, even if the essence of Christ cannot quite be pinned down. In the East the very admission of the Apocalypse into the canon followed the progress of the Song in being taken more seriously. The type of exegesis which (e.g.) Psellus supplies is thus in keeping with this view of the horizon of time and eternity.

Nilus insisted on the oneness of Christ's person in a way that is consonant with what is found in his letters of an anti-Antiochene slant,[295] among which one states that Christ's mother was θεοτόκος,[296] and Lk 2:52 is explained in an apparently qualifed Ancyrene manner.[297] That is, the full measure of divine grace and wisdom indwelling were externalised, poured out in his ministry and he stresses the Groom-Christ's nature as "the true Solomon", the one not consigned to Hades but rather the triumphant Λόγος ἔνσαρκος. Yet there is a belief that, if not sinful, the humanity itself is very much "the man from the earth". This means Nilus envisaged the Incarnation as the Word's stamping an image on the man, allowing all other souls to become

---

[294] PG 40, 128D: Παρατρέχων γὰρ ἐξ οὐρανοῦ ἐπὶ γῆς, καὶ ἕως εἰς τὰ τοῦ ᾅδου (καὶ κατώτερον ᾅδου βυθὸν κατελθών om), ἵνα ἐκεῖθεν ἀνασπάσῃ τὸν τεθνεῶτα. This is found in Philo's Latin (C.6) but not in the *original* Greek as reported in Cosmas Indicopleustes citation; cf. Puech (1930), III, 668f. Wolska-Conus (1968), p. 296, n. 57, suggests it is a second edition of Philo — one which has reference to *below* Hades. However, Philo does not use *Word* but Son, Christ and Lord. In the first sentence of: Παραλαβοῦσα οὖν αὐτὸν ἡ σάρξ ἣν ἀνείληφε καὶ ὁ (τέλειος - PG 40, 129A) ἄνθρωπος ὃν ἐφόρεσεν. Οὗτος ὡραιώθη τῇ τῆς θεότητος ὡραιότητι συμμορφωθείς, καὶ ἱδρύνθη (ἠδύνθη) ἐν τῇ τῶν οὐρανῶν βασιλείᾳ ἐν δεξιᾷ τοῦ Θεοῦ, the αὐτὸν must mean the chamber of death (*contra* Giacomelli *ad. loc.*) which the humanity "made beautiful" by assuming flesh* and bearing the complete man enters and empties. (*nb, not vice-versa, that *caro Verbum factum est* —which Philo's mentor Epiphanius had directly warned against in *Panarion* 77, 29).

[295] Cf. Bardenhewer (1923), 168, citing the *Letter to Gainas: Ep.* 2, 292: οὐκ ἦν ἕτερος... καὶ ἕτερος, ...ἀλλ' ὁ αὐτός.

[296] *Ep.* 2, 180.

[297] That is if it is assumed that Marcellus and Antiochenes belong to the same theological tradition. See Hübner (1989): Marcellus's Jesus as the visible representation of invisible God who redeemed Christ's sinful flesh (as with Diodore): "Damit wird Christus faktisch zum ersten erlösten Menschen" (142).

3. The Groom

'Κυριακός', i.e., like the Lord who is the Word. This emphasis squares with Guérard's comment on Nilus' Christology as a whole: "Sa christologie, inspirée de celle d'Athanase, place au centre de la révélation la réalité de la mort du Verbe-Fils de Dieu et son triomphe, comme κυριακὸς ἄνθρωπος, par la résurrection."[298] Especially significant is the point that this "kinsman" is seen as the one who is everywhere — as in Nilus' parting shot on Cant 8:14 (cited above): "He is in three divisions, earthly, subterranean, heavenly realm, in the manner of a hind or fawn." In other words Christ is in all situations for the purpose of allowing *theoria*. It is a moot point whether the Word and the soul are considered to have gone to the world of the dead, and the world beyond the terrestrial one; thus the Word and soul could stay together in indissoluble union, and spread their sphere of influence further;[299] it is as Word Incarnate that he is everywhere. However the κυριακὸς ἄνθρωπος does play a part, guaranteeing intimate union by his having consubstantiality with all believing souls.

In Nilus, the Groom is clearly the divine Word who is described in a prophetic future tense as about to do great things in human form. He:

> ...condescending through human passion, will be graspable by her, and being found outside his own order, yet remaining what he was, with confidence will prepare her to enjoy words which are authentic and move pleasure within... . She will lead him into her mother's house and into the bedroom of the one who conceived her, the human wisdom. For being human he needed to share all things with her and to exchange the things of grace for those of nature. For the Lord's coming into her mother's house means the assumption of human passions without sin; through much condescension he made himself to appropriate these authentically, not an appearance of a body, nor did he take a form for himself of man-like deceit, but was truly made flesh and bore a man of our stuff.[300]

---

[298] Guérard (1982), 350. Cf. Ringshausen (1967), p. 21, referring to PG 79, 836A (*Peristeria*): "...der Terminus ὁ κυριακὸς ἄνθρωπος für Christus ist auch bei anderen (z.B. Athanasius, Epiphanius, Cassianus) belegt." R. Hanig (1993) has shown how the motif is prominent in the 'Athanasian' Psalm Catena.

[299] On the unity of the Word and Soul for the 'Alexandrians', cf. Torrance (1988), p. 209.

[300] Lucà, p. 391, ll 6-24: Τὴν ἔνσαρκον αὐτοῦ παρουσίαν ἐπιθυμεῖν ἡ νύμφη ἔοικεν, ἐν ᾗ συγκαταβαίνων διὰ τὸ ἀνθρωποπαθές, εὔληπτος αὐτῇ ἔσται, καὶ τῆς οἰκείας καταστάσεως ἔξω εὑρεθείς, μένων ὃ ἦν, μετὰ παρρησίας αὐτὴν παρασκευάσει γνησίων καὶ ἡδονὴν ἔνθεον κινούντων ἀπολαῦσαι λόγων......Εἰσάξει δὲ αὐτὸν καὶ εἰς οἶκον μητρὸς αὐτῆς καὶ εἰς ταμιεῖον τῆς συλλαβούσης αὐτήν, τῆς ἀνθρωπίνης σοφίας · ἔδει γὰρ αὐτὸν [τὸν] ἄνθρωπον γενόμενον, πάντων αὐτῇ κοινωνῆσαι καὶ ἀντιδοῦναι τὰ τῆς χάριτος καὶ λαβεῖν τὰ τῆς φύσεως. Τὸ γὰρ εἰς οἶκον εἰσελθεῖν τῆς μητρὸς ταύτης τὸν Κύριον, τὴν τῶν ἀνθρωπίνων παθῶν χωρὶς ἁμαρτίας ἀνάληψιν δηλοῖ · οἷς ἑαυτὸν διὰ πολλὴν συγκατάβασιν γνησίως ᾠκείωσεν, οὐ φάσμα σώματος, οὐδὲ ἀνδροείκελον περιμορφώσας ἀπάτην ἑαυτῷ, ἀλλὰ σαρκωθεὶς ἀληθῶς καὶ ἄνθρωπον φορέσας τοῦ ἡμετέρου φυράματος.

It is left to the mature soul to be the spectator who can "see the mystery of the assumption (ἀναλήψεως)",[301] and more, follow it from Christ's birth (the first "be like") through to his descent to Hades (the second) and reascent to heaven (the third) — envisaged as stag-like in his ability to cross the levels of reality.

The launch of a trajectory of reading the Song cosmologically was thus underway, although it seems to have failed in the East with the general retreat from speculation. In the West Christology never shook off its subordination to soteriology and thus any Christological impress through the Song was made in the formation of Ecclesiology.

3.12 Conclusion

After looking at the images which speak of the Groom in his essence, his presence, his relationships, his actions, his power, his scope, it would appear that, at the heart of all such depictions, the Word is presented as none other than the Incarnate, descending and ascending One. The Groom is clearly the Word of God. Yet this is the Word who is for (*pro*) creation both in the action of creating and in his readiness to redeem it. In his being he is externally focussed: one senses an understanding of the Word-Groom which is built on, not only Psalm 44 (LXX): 2-9, but also Psalm 18 (LXX): 5-6, and also many parts of the Song of Songs. The Song ascribed to the Groom (one whose home was in wild and remote regions) features associated with life in an area of humanly cultivated agriculture, and so the commentaries usually made reference to his incarnate state or form.

So the Groom may have picked up a soul and a body which also belong to the Bride, as the next chapter will demonstrate. (For is not the sharing of one's whole self at the heart of the concept of marriage?) However, it is the inner essence, the personality of the Groom, the Word, who initiates and

---

[301] Ibid., p. 402, 319-21: (τοῦ νυμφίου...) βουλομένου ἐκ τῆς φωνῆς γνῶναι τὸ φρόνημα τῆς ψυχῆς, εἰ δύναται καὶ τὸ τῆς ἀναλήψεως εἰδέναι μυστήριον, προμαθοῦσα γραφικαῖς αὐτοῦ. The word ἀνάληψις can mean, according to Gregory of Nyssa, Chrysostom and Theodoret, both the assumption of flesh in the Incarnation and the resurrection-ascension of Christ's humanity into heaven.

employs his soul to build up his body by means of that soul's perfection. The NT version of the marriage metaphor thus shapes much of the hermeneutic used on the Song. Early Christian writers, viewing the bible as a unity, were not slow to make such connections.

Chapter 4

The Bride

In the patristic reception of the Song the difficulty of interpretation is compounded because as well as images of the Bride, pictured as a mare (1:9) then a flower (2:2) then a dove (6:9), overlapping with each other, the referents also melt into each other. Thus, the Bride is the Church, the perfect soul, (occasionally) Mary, the soul of Christ and the cosmic soul. I shall focus on those places in the commentators where the Bride came to be seen as more than merely soul or Church, i.e., as that one human being tightly bound to Christ and the Word, according to the impress of each author's Christology.

The Bride is often understood by the Fathers as Christ's humanity in the sense either that she as the Church is the body of Christ, or that she is identified with the prepared humanity which the Word assumed. This latter model suggests a Christology of the 'two before, one after' variety yet does not necessitate the belief that the flesh was somehow 'pre-existent' (which would be Apollinarian). In fact, interpreters of the Song were mostly keen to avoid any suggestion of two agents in Christ during his lifetime on earth. The Bride thus seems to be passive, receiving the assumption she has waited for and not giving back to the Groom any energies of her own.[1] Thus, nard, oils, and coronation can all be explained as what he, the Word, has already given to her, the humanity prepared as a Bride. This tendency is confirmed most markedly where the Syriac tradition left its inspiring mark in the employment of the imagery of cloak-wearing, viz., in Gregory and Theodoret.[2] Christ is seen as divine *tout court* only when his person, the Word, is absent and the Bride-soul is looking for him. Where and when he is present (such as in Cant 5:10ff) the appearance of him as the incarnate Christ is a model for her behaviour: she is called not just to become like him but to become one with him in his person.[3]

---

[1] Cf. Nemesius, *De Natura Hominis*; Morani (ed.) (1987), p. 43, that the union of Word and body is only κατὰ τὰς ἑκατέρου δυνάμεις.

[2] Cf. Ephraim's *De Fide*.

[3] An alternative possibility which connects the bride with Christ's humanity is where the Church is viewed as a gathering of souls around the eucharistic body:— as the body we identify with Christ's pains as if our own body. This sensibility features more starkly in Western medieval writers on the Song.

4. The Bride

In Late Antiquity, just as angels appearing in dreams served to initiate a conversation with the soul's higher self,[4] so the Song gave rise to interpretations where the Incarnation became a paradigm to suggest the eternal, 'philosophical' truth that the human soul is being wooed and instructed by a more 'active and intellectual' soul. Yet there is the more common, less speculative tradition, represented by apparently divergent writers — Augustine, Gregory of Nyssa, Theodoret — in which the humanity of Christ merely functions as the location of the meeting of Word and faithful Christian soul. With such representatives this approach to the Song was bound to win the day.

4.1 The Essence of the Human Christ

Cant 1:3 and 1:14-15a

1·3 καὶ ὀσμὴ μύρων σου ὑπὲρ πάντα τὰ ἀρώματα,
μύρον ἐκκενωθὲν ὄνομά σου.
διὰ τοῦτο νεάνιδες ἠγάπησάν σε
1·14 βότρυς τῆς κύπρου ἀδελφιδός μου ἐμοὶ
ἐν ἀμπελῶσιν Εγγαδδι.
1·15 Ἰδοὺ εἶ καλή, ἡ πλησίον μου

A most striking and explicit case of the deliberate confusion of Church, soul and Christ's soul comes in the Procopian fragments of Origen (although he will go on to call the Bride simply the Church [on Cant 1:4] or the soul [on Cant 5:6] as well.) When commenting on Cant 1:3f, in programmatic fashion, Origen explains that the Bride is either the soul or the Church or the *hegemonikon* of Christ.[5] This *hegemonikon* is equated with the mind of Christ in which believing souls share; for instance, on Cant 6:11 ("There I will give you my breasts"), where "breasts" is glossed as "*hegemonikon*".[6]

In the case of Origen as translated by Rufinus, it has to be said (with Harl and against Grillmeier and Crouzel) that the text gives little weight to Christ's salvific humanity, even though it is viewed as a receptacle for grace and a focus of devotion. The Incarnation is understood not so much as the taking of

---

[4] I follow the argument of Cox Miller (1994), e.g. p. 65. She fails however to attend to the Cappadocian suspicion of *phantasia*, even if the Gregorys did value some dreams for giving a true reflection of our selves (unlike Evagrius): see Ch 9.

[5] PG 17, 253C: Εἰσήγαγέ με ὁ βασιλεὺς εἰς τὸ ταμιεῖον αὐτοῦ. Ἤγουν ἀδύνατον [ἄδυτον] τὴν ἀξιέραστον λέγει ψυχὴν ἢ Ἐκκλησίαν ἢ τὸ ἡγεμονικὸν τοῦ Χριστου. εἰς ὁ Παῦλος εἰσελθὼν ἔφη· Ἡμεῖς δὲ νοῦν Χριστοῦ ἔχομεν, ἵνα ἴδωμεν τὰ ὑπὸ Θεοῦ χαρισθέντα ἡμῖν.

[6] PG 17, 280B: ἐκεῖ δέ, φησί, δώσω σοι τοὺς μαστούς μου, τουτέστι τὸ ἡγεμονικόν·

an individual humanity, as the assumption of a special purpose-built form. The notion of the body of Christ as an *organon* would carry on through the Cappadocians to be refuted firmly by Cyril of Alexandria.[7] It is seen as functional in its promoting of a composition of the virtues:

> But all these [four elements of his body—again understood non-corporeally as mortality-immortality, purity, teaching, spiritual fervour][8] are held together by the pure 'oil', through which it is shown either that it was because of mercy alone that 'he who was in the form of God took the form of a slave', or that those elements which were taken in Christ from a material substance were reduced by the Holy Spirit to one, and into one form which became the 'person' of the mediator.[9]

Again, the teaching is that she is the *persona*, the outward presentation of one who is almost a visual aid to go along with the Word's teaching. Those who receive are those who belong to the Church which is quite distinct from the person of Christ. He protects it by being external to it. The humanity is revelatory, if not salvific. Here we see justification for Grillmeier's contested opinion that some 'Alexandrians' viewed Christ's 'person' as his humanity.

Although this "oil" is defined as "the unction of the Holy Spirit" with which Christ was anointed, this phrase is not understood as meaning that the unction is the Holy Spirit himself, but rather that the Spirit provides it. The chief created *epinoia* is Mercy. For Rufinus-Origen (and Cyril) the smallness of the drop is no hindrance to the gathering up of Jacob or even all the nations, which after all are just a drop themselves; the myrrh comes out from the teachings of the Word of God.[10] Here in this passage the effects of Christ's Incarnation are understood as making wisdom available to all souls. The Bride-Church is the gatherer while Christ the Word is the teacher.

The idea of the Bride's essence being located in a pre-existent heavenly wisdom whom the Word has 'already' taken in and made a part of himself appears in Rufinus-Origen's Commentary on Cant 1:3. The use of the

---

[7] Where Cyril speaks of an *organon* it is not of the humanity, but of the outward flesh moved by the Word into miraculous works as distinct from the soul which suffers; see *De Incarnatione*; SC 97, p. 232.

[8] Baehrens, p. 99, 5-7: "videt enim quod istae quattuor species *unguenti* illius formam tenebant incarnationis Verbi Dei, quod ex quattuor elementis compaginatum corpus assumpsit."

[9] Baehrens, p. 99, 23 - p. 100, 8: "Sed haec omnia *oleo* puro colliguntur, per quod ostenditur vel misericordiae solius causa fuisse, quod is, *qui erat in forma Dei, formam servi susceperit*, vel ea, quae ex materiali substantia in Christo fuerant assumpta, per Spiritum sanctum redacta in unum fuisse atque in unam speciem, quae est persona *mediatoris* effecta." Cf. Cant 1:3.

[10] Baehrens, p. 170, 6-9: "A *vestimentis* ergo Verbi Dei, quae est doctrina sapientiae, *myrrha* procedit, mortis dumtaxat indicium pro humano genere susceptae. *Gutta*, ut supra diximus, *exinanita divinitatis forma, servilis formae* suscepta dignatio."

commonplace liaison (cf. Hippolytus) of Cant 1:3 with Phil 2:5ff is limited in the Commentary. Phil 2:6-7 is cited and followed with the curt explanation that he, the *Unigenitus* Son, certainly emptied himself out of the "fullness" (πλήρωμα /*plenitudo*) which is understood less as a place in which he was residing (in the Valentinian sense), and more in the Pauline usage, in which it resides in him.[11] Here the emptying has nothing to do with any *kenosis* of the Word which takes him down from heaven to earth, but of the Son as already man who gives out his power on the way to the Cross. The thrust is that no-one could have received him in that fullness of deity except that Bride alone; this lone Bride is mature enough to relate to the Word directly; thus the Incarnation means accommodation. So the soul who is the Bride needs no outpouring — she received the spiritual divinity unmediated but the Word's created *epinoiai* provide distribution of his presence to many others.

Baehrens' note to this section refers to Origen's *Homilia in Gen. 14:1*, where, in a 'pre-existent' setting, the Word is called "Groom" and Wisdom is called "Bride"; and our passage too speaks of the Word of God embracing and being joined to various virtues which seem to come from the first-created intellectual universe. Mercy here, as "Wisdom" there, may be like one supreme *epinoia* of Christ in the sense of holding all his virtues together so that the Logos could descend 'onto' the virtues.

Christ here in fact is called the *substantia*, the final form of the virtues.[12] M. Borret appears to wish to read the text as if already demythologized, observing: "Des vertus identifiées à la personne du Christ, ou au Verbe, Origène parle comme d' êtres animés."[13] He draws on several passages from the commentary to show that virtues are seen as a package given by the Father which the Word shares out, through prayer, as his *epinoiai*. It would appear that this passage, however, is the only place in the Commentary where this theme has a part in Christology. However, both the translation: "nous avons coutume de comprendre le Christ comme la personification des vertus elles-mêmes"[14] or the translation: "le Christ est en personne toutes les vertus,

---

[11] Baehrens, p. 112, 28 - p. 113, 8: "Nec mireris sane, si dicimus virtutes esse, quae *diligunt* Christum, cum in aliis ipsarum virtutum substantiam Christum soleamus accipere. Quod et frequenter invenies in scripturis divinis pro locis et opportunitatibus aptari; invenimus namque ipsum et *iustitiam* dici et *pacem* et *veritatem*. Et rursus scriptum est in psalmis: '*iustitiae et pax osculatae sunt*' et '*veritas de terra orta est, et iustitia de caelo prospexit*' [Ps 84(85):11-12]. Quae utique omnia et ipse esse et rursum ipsum dicuntur amplecti. Sed et *sponsus* idem dicitur, idem etiam sponsa nominatur, ut in propheta scriptum est: '*sicut sponso imposuit mihi mitram, et sicut sponsam ornavit me ornamento* ' [Is 61:10]."

[12] Cf. *CCels* III, 81, 10f; SC 136, p. 182: ἐν Χριστῷ, τουτέστι τῷ λόγῳ καὶ τῃ σωφίᾳ καὶ πάσῃ ἀρετῇ, τέλος μακάριον τοῖς ἀμέμπτως καὶ καθαρῶς βιώσασι... .

[13] In SC 376, p. 768, in his "note complémentaire", 14.

[14] SC 375, p. 257 (Baehrens, p. 112): "...cum in aliis ipsarum virtutum substantiam Christum soleamus accipere."

et en retour elles l'embrassent"[15] are questionable. Both seem to want to stress the personal and relational side of Christ communicating with virtuous people more than the texts allow. It would be better to understand the use of *substantiam* as indicating one who functions as the fount of virtues because that bride-like soul is the passive receptacle wherein the Universal Logos resided. In the last sentence which contains the Isaian citation (61:10), the non-divine part of Christ is presented as transformed by the Logos-Groom's attentions.[16] Christ is both Bride and Groom *pro nobis* as *epinoiai* of the Word (who is the essence, the person of Christ).

Nilus of Ancyra warns early on that Scripture taken according to appearances is not only neutral but a dangerous trap. This corresponds to the Christological truth that the body of Christ is a cloak for his divinity.[17] This rational and collective humanity as purified in Gethsemane is what follows from the resurrection, even as in the meantime, the particular soul of Jesus functions to reproduce the divine 'flavour'. Thus, on Cant 1:3b, the role of Jesus' soul in being shed abroad is to make known that its essence (previously unknowable while in Jesus' body) is divine by association with the Word.[18] On the following verse Nilus stresses how the soul must start with Christ as revealed.[19] Reflection on creation or even Scripture is a second-best. Nilus provides a Christological corrective to Evagrian mysticism which does more than merely simplify it (*pace* Guérard). It is a case of *theologia* coming before *theoria* and *praktike*. Rather than describing a ladder of *logos-logoi-logikoi*, Nilus describes a condescension of the Logos God who is transcendent.

The Word's uniqueness, as being in the breast of the Father like one "grape", is contrasted with his Incarnation in which he came to hang like one among (many) "grapes" — with reference to Cant 1:14 which speaks either of the Bride or of the Groom according to two interpretations: the latter, shorter

---

[15] SC 375, p. 257 (Baehrens, p. 113): "Quae utique omnia et ipse esse et rursum ipsum dicuntur amplecti."

[16] Ibid.: "Sed et *sponsus* idem dicitur, idem etiam *sponsa* nominatur, ut in propheta scriptum est: '*Sicut sponso imposuit mihi mitram, et sicut sponsam ornavit me ornamento*'." Cf. the "de-mythologised" account of *De Princ* IV,4 rendered in *C Cels* III, 41.

[17] SC 403, p. 218, 83f: Οἶνον τὸ ἐκ τῆς πλευρᾶς ἀποστάξαν αἷμα, στολὴν δὲ καὶ περιβολὴν τὸ σῶμα τὸ δεσποτικὸν λέγων.

[18] Ibid., p. 138, 1-5: Ὥσπερ τὸ συνεχόμενον μύρον πρότερον ἀγνοούμενον τοῖς πολλοῖς διὰ τὸ συνέχεσθαι, μετὰ τὸ κενωθῆναι μάρτυρος οὐ προσδέεται ἑτέρου πρὸς τὸ γνωσθῆναι ὅπερ ἐστίν · αὐτὴ γὰρ ἡ τῆς ψυχῆς ποιότης ἐγκρινομένη ταῖς αἰσθήσεσιν ἑρμηνεύει τῇ κενώσει τὴν ἑαυτῆς φύσιν... .

[19] Ibid., p. 148, 13-15: Ἴσως δὲ ταμεῖον καὶ τὸ σῶμα λέγει τὸ κυριακόν, εἰς ὃ εἰσῆκται ἡ μακαρία ψυχὴ συνοικήσασα τῷ θεῷ λόγῳ καὶ συμβασιλεύουσα νῦν αὐτῷ.

alternative does *not* refer to 'her' as "the humanity".[20] Yet the blurring of identities which Guérard suggests, Nilus provides on Cant 1:15: "He calls her kin on account of the Incarnation when he assumed her body".[21] Likewise, the metaphor of 'the temple' is used to suggest that he came to earth in her body because it was already dedicated to God.[22] In Nilus' understanding, behind the form of the κυριακὸς ἄνθρωπος there was a Word-Groom who will always be enfleshed on account of the tight association with the assumed humanity which he perfected through the Incarnation, stamping it/her with his (the Word's) lordliness and making it a template for all brides to fit.

4.2 The Bride as a prepared Church-humanity

Cant 1:5-7.
1·5Μέλαινά εἰμι καὶ καλή, θυγατέρες Ιερουσαλημ,
 ὡς σκηνώματα Κηδαρ, ὡς δέρρεις Σαλωμων.
1·6 μὴ βλέψητέ με, ὅτι ἐγώ εἰμι μεμελανωμένη,
 ὅτι παρέβλεψέν με ὁ ἥλιος·
 υἱοὶ μητρός μου ἐμαχέσαντο ἐν ἐμοί,
 ἔθεντό με φυλάκισσαν ἐν ἀμπελῶσιν·
 ἀμπελῶνα ἐμὸν οὐκ ἐφύλαξα.
1·7 Ἀπάγγειλόν μοι, ὃν ἠγάπησεν ἡ ψυχή μου,
 ποῦ ποιμαίνεις, ποῦ κοιτάζεις ἐν μεσημβρίᾳ,
 μήποτε γένωμαι ὡς περιβαλλομένη ἐπ' ἀγέλαις ἑταίρων σου.

The significant passage in Dionysius of Alexandria, in which no mention is made of pre-existent souls — as consistent with his moderated Origenian position observed in Chapter One — interestingly interchanges the soul of Christ with the humanity of Christ. For the Bride of the Song is both of these.[23] Although she was not white from the beginning, the cloak Christ rose

---

[20] SC 403, p. 218: Εἰ δὲ καὶ κατὰ τὴν ἄλλην ἐκδοχὴν βότρυς κύπρου ἐστίν, ἐπισκεπτέον πῶς τῆς κύπρου βότρυς ὤν, οὐκ ἐν ἀμπελῶσι Κύπρου, ἀλλ' ἐν ἀμπελῶσι Γαδδεὶ λέγεται εἶναι. Τάχα οὖν ὅτε μὲν ἦν ἐν τοῖς κόλποις τοῦ πατρὸς πρὸ τῆς ἐνανθρωπήσεως, βότρυς ἦν ὁ τῆς Κύπρου, θεὸς λόγος ὤν, ὅτε δὲ τῷ κόσμῳ ἐπεδήμησε καὶ τὴν ἡμετέραν ἀνέλαβε σάρκα, ἐν ἀμπελῶσι γέγονε τῆς Γαδδεί... It seems over-bold of Guérard (p. 219) to translate with "elle" as if she is talking about herself as the humanity he becomes, when the subject of the preceding comments has been "il": "alors qu'elle est une grappe de Chypre, elle dit qu'elle est une grappe de Chypre."

[21] Ibid, p. 222: Πλησίον δὲ αὐτὴν λέγει διὰ τὴν ἐνανθρώπησιν, ἐπειδὴ τὸ ἐκείνης ἀνέλαβε σῶμα.

[22] MS Ogden, 312, 3-4: ἐπειδὴ γὰρ τὸ σῶμα ἑαυτῆς οὐ τῇ πορνείᾳ ἀλλὰ τῷ κυρίῳ, διὰ τοῦτο καὶ ὁ κύριος ἐνανθρωπήσας τῷ ἐκείνης γεγένηται σώματι.

[23] Feltoe (1904), p. 228f: Τὴν γὰρ τοιαύτην ψυχὴν ἀνισταμένην καὶ ὑπὸ τοῦ Σωτῆρος ἀναλαμβανομένην, φωτοειδῆ προσιοῦσαν ὁρῶντες, ἐροῦσιν οἱ ἅγιοι

in was a white one (like Solomon's tents). Although there is a notable silence about pre-existence, the soul having the properties of a cloak[24] is said to have become outstandingly white. 'She' as soul is the human race who, although unworthy to be assumed, was even escorted up to heaven, and is the acceptable cloak of righteousness that the Word dressed humanity in. The passage has the look of Origen (the application of Ps. 44:8 to the soul of Christ) as corrected by Methodius (the Song's imagery referred to the humanity which covered the Word-Groom in his earthly sojourn).

At the end of the fourth century the notion of the Bride as being somehow a "humanity prepared for me", which was more than just "a body prepared for me" (Heb 10:5[25]), was popular. Augustine spoke for the consensus when he affirmed that Christ came "in the likeness of human flesh".[26] The widespread view of its *natural* sinlessness at all times encouraged Epiphanius and Philo of Carpasia to superimpose the picture of the *prepared* Bride on the theology of the Incarnation. This is especially apparent in their treatment of Cant 6:8f (see below, 4.8).

ἄγγελοι· Τίς αὕτη ἡ ἀναβαίνουσα λελεγκανθισμένη, καὶ ἐπιστηριζομένη ἐπὶ τὸν ἀδελφιδὸν αὐτῆς; οὐ γὰρ ἦν ἐξ ἀρχῆς λευκὴ ἡ λέγουσα· Μέλαινά εἰμι καὶ καλή, θυγατέρες Ἰερουσαλήμ, ὡς σκηνώματα Κηδάρ, ὡς δέρρεις Σολομών. Μὴ βλέψητέ με, ὅτι ἐγώ εἰμι μεμελανωμένη. ἔστω γὰρ ἐντεῦθεν ἤδη καλή, κἂν ἔτι μέλαινα ᾖ· ἀνάγκη γὰρ εἶναι τοιαύτην ὡς τὰ σκηνώματα Κηδάρ, ἐν αὐτοῖς γε οὖσαν. συσκοτασμὸς γὰρ ἡ Κηδὰρ ἑρμηνεύεται. οἱ δὲ ἐν τῷ κόσμῳ τούτῳ καὶ ἐν τῷ σκήνει μένοντες ἐν ὑποζόφῳ διατρίβουσιν, ὥσπερ ἐν σπηλαίῳ τινί, ἐν ᾧ καὶ βραδύνων τις ὀδύρεται λέγων· Οἴμοι ὅτι ἡ παροικία μου ἐμακρύνθη, κατεσκήνωσα μετὰ τῶν σκηνωμάτων Κηδάρ. (Ps 119:5 LXX) Δέρρεις δὲ Σολομὼν ὁ δερμάτινος ἔοικεν εἶναι χιτὼν ἐπιρραφεὶς καὶ ἐπιταθεὶς τῷ προτέρῳ καὶ καθαρῷ σώματι, ὃν ὁ εἰρηνικὸς καὶ εἰρηνοποιὸς κύριος ἡμῶν τὸν ἄνθρωπον ἐνέδυσεν· τοῦτο γὰρ Σολομὼν ἑρμηνεύεται· ὃν διὰ μὲν τῆς παρακοῆς ἐνδυσάμενος ἄνθρωπος ἐξεβλήθη τοῦ παραδείσου. εἰ δὲ εἰσιέναι μέλλοι πάλιν, ἀποδύεται, ἀμείψας τὸ τῆς δικαιοσύνης ἔνδυμα, ὅπερ ἐνδυσάμενος τούτου γυμνὸς εὑρίσκεται.

[24] Later, in (e.g.) Theodoret the Word himself becomes "the cloak". Bienert's (1978) case that Dionysius was uninterested in 'Origen' (3-27) is overstated.

[25] This in turn cites Ps 39:7LXX (although Hebrews 10:5 substitutes σῶμα for ὠτία). Ambrose, *In Ps 39*, 26 (CSEL 64, 229) reports that the Apollinarians made much of "*ecce corpus, dixit praeparasti mihi, non etiam animam*". Hilary (*tr. in ps liii, 13*) prefers to take the word "preparation" as referring to getting Christ's body ready for sacrifice during his lifetime: "*perficis autem mihi corpus; deo patri legis sacrificia respuenti hostiam placentem suscepti corporis offerendo.*") It would appear that the Apollinarian hijacking of the verse rendered it unusable by the fathers for Christological purposes.

[26] See Weinandy (1993) who shows that belief in a direct assumption of fallen human flesh was restricted to a few, including Ambrosiaster. It is possible that Apponius was familiar with this issue and solved it by the soul of Christ acting as intermediary.

4. The Bride

Augustine, however, viewed the body of Christ, the Church, as the *product* of the Incarnation and in no way its presupposition.[27] As P. Simon has observed,[28] the influence of Origen on Augustine's exegesis of the Song was minimal. Thus the Bride is identified with the 'City of God'[29] which is an eschatological, not a protological or pre-Christian, phenomenon. Augustine inherited from Tyconius and then from his contemporary Donatist opponents the North African reference of key verses in the Song to matters ecclesiological[30] — an approach which avoids the dangers of Origenistic speculation. The more mature Augustine had learned to understand the 'pursuit and waiting' themes of the Song as voicing the longing of the Church as she experienced 'everyday' suffering in the vicissitudes of life.

For Augustine, the body of Christ as the universal and visible catholic Church remains black and white (on Cant 1:7 following Tyconius's second rule). Yet it is noteworthy that Augustine did not follow Tyconius into linking the notion of 'totus Christus' with the imagery of the Song, so as to identify the Bride and Christ's humanity,[31] for how could the Word have assumed "black and white" flesh? An example of his combination of the Song and simple ecclesiology in the context of an apologetic corrective exegesis of the Donatists on this passage is in Sermon 46, 35-38. Here, after establishing that *in meridie* is part of the Bride's question, he takes a more positive line as to what is going on in Cant 1:6. For the sense of "Where in the south do you graze your flock...?" is as follows:

> The church speaks and asks where the church is, and He replies, as they think, "in the south". But if she is in the south only, as they say in Africa, how does she ask where she herself is? But in fact the part of the transmarine church is asking about

---

[27] For Augustine, the Song belongs to that unreality here below; perforce it speaks in shadows and cannot tell us anything that we could understand without the more powerful witness of the New Testament.

[28] Simon (1960), p. 24.

[29] See CSEL 40, 2, p. 109.

[30] Sermo 138,9: PL 38, 768: "Sponsae verba prave usurpata a Donatistis. Haec verba quae commemoravimus de sanctis Canticis canticorum, de sponsi et sponsae epithalamio quodam: spirituales enim nuptiae sunt, in quibus nobis magna castitate vivendum est; quia Ecclesiae concessit Christus in spiritu, quod mater ejus habuit{habet} in corpore, ut et mater et virgo sit...et poposcerimus ut ostendant ipsi de Scripturis aliquod testimonium, ubi Deus praedixit in Africa futuram Ecclesiam, quasi perditis caeteris gentibus;...si ergo quae interrogat, Ecclesia est, et Dominus ubi pascit respondet, in Africa, quia in Africa erat Ecclesia: quae interrogat, non erat in Africa." Of course Tyconius had already stated in his *Liber Regularum* that God's people were in the south and his enemies in the north: see Babcock (1989), p. 120.

[31] See Babcock (1989), p. 8 & p. 10: "Nec illud erit absurdum quod ex uno totum corpus volumus intelligi, ut filium hominis Ecclesiam; quoniam Ecclesia, id est filii Dei redacti in unum corpus, dicti sunt filius Dei, dicti unus homo, dicti etiam Deus... . Et Dominus totum populum sponsam dicit et sororem... ."

the south, lest here she go astray. Christ speaks to each member of his church just as to his church. And what does he say ? "Unless you know yourself, O beautiful among women, go out." To go out is to be one of the heretics.[32]

On such enigmatic verses, Augustine is prepared to say: "let *meridies* be Africa." The point is that she is asking where in Africa heretics can be avoided. Furthermore each individual is addressed: if religion is not personal, heresy (and then judgement) effectively follows. The content of her self-understanding is that she is pure, whitened, one, redeemed; but the nuance of *nisi cognoveris te in speculo scripturae divinae* is that one must appropriate this 'new' (not a paradiasical or 'pre-existent') reality. H. Simke comments: "So vielfältig soll die Selbsterkenntnis der *ecclesia sponsa* sein."[33] Yet it is a question not so much of 'know yourself', but rather of 'know (doctrine) for yourself', so that Simke's approximation of Augustine to Origen in following the 'Socratic' translation of the LXX of Cant 1:7 is overdone.

Regarding Cant 1:5-7, Gregory of Elvira took the opposite view to Augustine, one commonly associated with Ambrosiaster, that the flesh Christ assumed was in need of purification. Although he quotes Eph 5:22 which talks of the Church as his body, Gregory of Elvira comments, at I, 7, that the Church "as the Apostle has defined it, is the flesh of Christ".[34] Schulz-Flügel thinks the Ephesian reference to be from Eph 1:22f,[35] while Collantes Lozano[36] observes there is a 'flesh of flesh' relationship — the Church is to Christ as Sarah was to Abraham; also "la túnica de José es representativa de la Iglesia, pero es al mismo tiempo la carne física del Salvador, que se revistio en la encarnación." Now the preference for *caro* over *corpus* may be no more than a sign that these two words were interchangeable for Gregory (as the equivalent Greek terms were for Apollinarius), or that what he felt Paul was indicating would be more clearly communicated by the use of the

---

[32] CCL 41, 564, 990 - 565, 997: "Ecclesia loquitur, et interrogat ubi sit ecclesia; et respondet ille, sicut putant: *In meridie.* Si *in* solo *meridie* est, ut dicunt in Africa, quomodo ipsa interrogat ubi ipsa sit? At vero portio ecclesiae transmarinae bene interrogat de meridie, ne hic erret. — Alloquitur unumquodque membrum ecclesiae suae Christus, tamquam suam ecclesiam. Et quid dicit? *Nisi cognoveris temetipsam, o pulchra inter mulieres,* exi. Exire, haereticorum est."

[33] Simke (1962), p. 266.

[34] CCL 69, p. 172: "Ecclesia etenim ut apostolus definiuit caro Christi est, qui ait: et ipse est caput corporis ecclesiae; cui tunc osculum ad osculum fida caritate impressum est, quando duo in una carne coniuncti sunt, i.e. veritas et pax mutuis inter se{sibi invicem mutuis} complexibus adhaeserunt, dicente David{sicut David dicit}: *veritas et pax complexae sunt se* (Ps 84:11). Veritas inquit de terra orta est, id est caro Christi {qui} de matre virgine nata est, cuius origo terrena est. *Pax de caelo prospexit* (Ps 84:12) i.e. verbum dei, qui dixit *ego sum pax* (Lk 24:36)... ."

[35] Schulz-Flügel (1994), p. 92.

[36] Collantes Lozano (1954), p. 59f; cf. *Tractatus Origenis* V, 47; VI, 56; XIX, 195.

term 'flesh'. Indeed, perhaps it had lost the pejorative associations of the Pauline usage. In Paul, whereas σῶμα denotes something positive or at least neutral, σάρξ stands for something negative or, at best, 'easily led'. Yet this is the point: it is a wicked flesh, a sinful corporeality that the Son of God actually wore (*contra* the view of the Laodicean and his kin).

At the end of Book One the metaphor of sexual congress becomes explicit in an otherwise curious reference to Solomon and his tents or skins. Gregory observes:

> He was a lover of women and could not tear himself away from their flesh (presumably the connotation of "skins"), since it had not yet been assumed and because the Lord in his very self took the *generalem summam* of the human body, putting on the flesh of the sinner-man which is the Church, and becoming sin for us.[37]

Schulz-Flügel takes the preference for *caro* to be an anti-Arian measure, but it seems more likely that Eph 5:30f is being read through the lens of Rom 8:3, with Gregory's concern to be Christological as much as ecclesiological and to underline the sinfulness of the body asssumed.[38]

Now the precise meaning of the phrase *generalem summam humani corporis* is unclear. That this is an outcrop of the doctrine of *Anakephalaiosis* seems unlikely: Gregory does not treat 'Christ's headship' in Irenaean terms. In fact he states merely that the patriarchs and apostles are like eyes in the Head of the ecclesiastical body.[39] Two pages later he adds that Christ as 'nerve-centre' is the Head, but treats the idea peremptorily in five lines.[40] What does seem clear is an understanding of a heavenly Son who, by a marriage to sinfulness in the human race is enabled to enter the world to absorb and cleanse it. The flesh was not specially prepared unless the idea of preparation can be stretched to include arranging that the assumed flesh be the vilest possible.

It has been remarked that for Gregory, the salvific effects of the Incarnation left a lot of room for synergism as 'Like' calls to 'like', summoning 'her' to perfect salvation. Collantes Lozano maintains that, for Gregory, while at the creation Christ overrode human wills, by the time of the Incarnation, this is no longer the case: "No así la divinización que se le dara por la conformación libre de suas acciones con las de Cristo. No es solo el hombre caído por el pecado original y levantado por la redención el que tiene

---

[37] *In Cant* I, 224-231; CCL 69, pp. 178-79: "..quod amator fuerit mulierum; ideo ab earum carne revelli non poterat, quoniam necdum a Christo fuisset assumpta et quia generalem summam humani corporis dominus in semet ipso suscepit, unde et apostolus: peccatum inquit pro nobis factus est, id est carnem hominis peccatoris induendo, quam carnem ecclesiam esse apostolus definuit cuius nos membra sumus."

[38] Schulz-Flügel (1994), pp. 49-51.

[39] At II, 226-7; CCL 69 p. 188.

[40] II, 274-75; CCL 69, p. 190.

que conformarse con Cristo. Es simplemente el hombre."[41] What distinguishes Gregory from Augustine hinges on the latter's reluctance to see Christ's humanity as sinful. *Like* Augustine, Gregory believed that a radical work of grace was needed on sin, but this has already been accomplished. So Gregory distanced himself from Origen's positive view of the "skins of Solomon" but comes close at III, 10-11 (on the assumed flesh as supplying the *omega* to the Word's *alpha*)[42] to Irenaeus on Christ as the last man (*novissimum hominem*), created after Adam to remedy sin.[43] For Gregory, Christ's humanity was the universal of all human souls which were impure by their own exercise of choice. This, inspired by Cant 1:5-7 and found in Gregory's comments on it, was also present in Marius Victorinus: the Incarnation was a monergistic work of the Logos come to clean up the universals of soul and body by making them his own.[44] Gregory for all his Platonic influences was not an *Ur-Pelagian* optimist. The Incarnation involved radical, completed action on human flesh.

It is interesting that Gregory makes a case that, according to the flesh, the genealogies show that Gentile people had a pledge of their salvation in his flesh, because although from the seed of David, that stock was partly Gentile, on account of Ruth.[45] It is for this reason that the Church can call Christ "brother" as she does in the Song of Songs, e.g., at Cant 1:16. The Son of God takes the human flesh of man, which is that of the sinful Church. However, in these last few lines of the Commentary, Gregory presents an alternative, namely that the Church's mother cannot be earthly since she

---

[41] Collantes Lozano (1954), p. 33f.

[42] Gianotti (1984), pp. 430ff.

[43] CCL 69, p. 194f; *Adv Haer* I, 14, 6 (SC 263, p. 224):"...novissimum hominem in regenerationem primi hominis apparuisse... ." Cf. A. Orbe (1976), II, p. 415 (comparing *In Cant* 27-29 with *Adv Haer* III, 2, 3. 7 & V, 2).

[44] Cf. *Adv Arium*, III, 3; SC 68, p. 446: "...cum carnem sumpsit, universalem λόγον carnis sumpsit...Item et universalem λόγον animae. nam et animam habuisse manifestum, cum idem salvator dixit (Mt 26:39)... . Item universalis animae λόγος et ex hoc ostenditur, quod et irascitur, cum maledicit et arbori fici...Haec et alia multa sunt quibus ostenditur animae λόγος universalis. Adsumptus ergo homo totus et adsumptus et liberatus est. In isto enim omnia universalia fuerunt, universalis caro, anima universalis, et haec in crucem sublata atque purgata sunt per salutarem deum λόγον, universalium omnium universalem — per ipsum enim omnia facta sunt."

[45] *In Cant* V, 78-93, CCL 69, pp. 209-10: "Et si ecclesia mater est omnium, requirendum nobis est, quae sit mater ecclesiae, in cuius domum et in cuius secretum introducturam se eum dicebat. Iam ostendi superius, quid sit ecclesia, i.e. corpus Christi ex convenientibus membris. Mater ergo ecclesiae est sancta caelestis Ierusalem, de qua apostolus dicebat Paulus: *illa* inquit *quae sursum est caelestis Ierusalem.* (Gal 4:26) Quae est mater ecclesiae, i.e. nostra qui sumus ecclesia, misit nobis Christum quem in baptismo induimus, sicut apostolus ait: quicumque in Christo baptizati estis, Christum induistis. Itaque qui habet in se Christum, deus in secretum cordis eius ingreditur...nec quisquam in illam domum caelestis Ierusalem ingredi potest, nisi in se Christum habuerit et eum inseparabili caritate tenuerit."

herself is mother of all things (created, regardless of election or race), and must be a heavenly "mother Jerusalem above" into whose house her daughter, the Church, will lead the Beloved (cf. Cant 3:4).[46] Not only is the identification of the mother different, but also the Church is now designated *corpus Christi* and no longer *caro Christi*. [47] This means that the term *corpus* is appropriate when speaking of the age after the resurrection – to denote that between Christ's conception and resurrection she, the Church, provided his humanity. Thus it is sinful and unbelieving flesh that he, the Son of God assumes, but in this process he cleans it up by his intercourse which alone is pure.[48]

As is noted in the *Sources Chrétiennes* edition of Origen as translated by Rufinus, the amount of comment shared between historical, ecclesiological and 'Word-Soul' interpretations is in the proportions 3:50:1. So the Latin Origenian intepretation of the Song is primarily 'ecclesiological' and presupposes the Incarnation, to which the interpretation on occasions pays special attention. 'The dusky maiden' of Cant 1:5 becomes the occasion for discussing the Church. Moses marrying an Ethiopian is a type of the Word (the spiritual law) becoming betrothed to the Church of the *Gentiles*.[49] Like the Queen of the South she comes to hear the wisdom concerning the immortality of the soul and the future judgement from the true Solomon, our Lord and Saviour, Jesus Christ. However, the Church who comes to Christ is also seen as part of the construction of the Incarnation. Once arrived in Jerusalem, (according to a clever piece of word-arrangement):

> 'She saw', now, 'the house which *she* (Brésard: 'il') had built' (3Reg 10:4) — no doubt, the mysteries of his Incarnation — for the Church from the nations (the signification of the *regina Saba*) sees the 'house' which she, as Wisdom built for herself (Prov 9:1).[50]

Wisdom, a pre-existent cosmic hypostasis is here the Bride, even if the bodily dwelling is humble and earthly. The allusion is to the soul of Christ's playing a bridal role, which includes preparing a place for the Word's dwelling.

---

[46] Ibid., 105-8, at CCL 69, p. 210.

[47] Cf. the *Vetus Latina* of Col 1:15; n.b., Col 1:24 *Vetus Latina* has variant "corpore meo".

[48] *In Cant* I, 235-39; CCL 69, p. 179: "ideo et *tabernaculum Cedar* i.e. vitium gentilitatis *pellem Salomonis* i.e. veteris hominis conversationem ex consortio eiusdem carnis esse dicebat, offuscatam propter transgressionem Adae et peccata parentum, sed decoram nimis propter conversationem Christi, quam habet in fide et sanctitate."

[49] Baehrens, p. 118f.

[50] Baehrens p. 120, 6-8: "*Vidit* autem *et domum quam aedificavit*, sine dubio incarnationis eius mysteria; ipsa est enim *domus* quam *sibi aedificavit sapientia.*"

4.3 The identity of the purified Bride ascending

Cant 3:6 (and its doublet, 8:5)
3·6 Τίς αὕτη ἡ ἀναβαίνουσα ἀπὸ τῆς ἐρήμου
ὡς στελέχη καπνοῦ τεθυμιαμένη
σμύρναν καὶ λίβανον ἀπὸ πάντων κονιορτῶν μυρεψοῦ;

Origen is happy to embrace polysemy in the references of the Song's verses. So when commenting on Cant. 3:6, Origen writes: 'How exceedingly beautiful is the soul, ascending in life and *logos*, fleeing the sins which are among the many, which is what it is to ascend from the desert.'[51] It seems more likely that Origen here means both the soul in every believer/human being, rather than any paradigmatic soul of Jesus. However, that is because, as the Rufinus-translated commentary makes clear, his intention is usually pastoral and not philosophical.

This tendency to side-line Christological interpretations in favour of an interest in a grace-driven, 'passive' spirituality left its mark on Jerome's own writings. Simon concludes that only once did Jerome interpret the Song 'Christologically', and then only when Cant 8:5 was interpreted in an auxiliary fashion during an exposition of Is 63:3, concerning "redness" and "whiteness". "Eine eigentümliche christologische Verwendung findet HL 8:5 in der polemischen Schrift *Contra Johannem Hierosolymitanum*, cap 34",[52] although he may simply have been reproducing Epiphanius' thought.[53] Further, the point of the comment is to reinforce the Hieronymian commonplace, that Christ's bodily resurrection reminds us that purity of the whole body is required.

The identity of the female figure in the Song is given by Cyril of Alexandria when he describes the female figure with the dove-like voice as "the soul, the Bride of the Word, that is the Church of Christ".[54] The overall meaning is clear: the Bride of Christ hears and believes through a filling with

---

[51] PG 17, 269CD: Καλὴ λίαν ἡ ἀναβαίνουσα βίῳ καὶ λόγῳ ψυχή, φυγοῦσα τὰ παρὰ τοῖς πολλοῖς ἁμαρτήματα, ἅπερ [ὥσπερ Delarue] ἐξ ἐρήμου λέγεται ἀναβαίνειν.

[52] Simon (1951), 169.

[53] PL 23, 386B: "Ideoque rubra et fulgida sunt vestimenta eius quia speciosus est forma prae filiis hominum (Ps. 44)...et propter gloriam triumphantis in stolam candidam commutata sunt; et tunc vere de Christi carne completum est: *Quae est ista quae ascendit dealabata, innitens super fratruelem suum* ? Et quid in eodem libro secundo: *Fratruelis meus rubicundus et candidus* (Cant 5:10). Hunc imitantur, qui vestimenta sua non coinquinaverunt cum mulieribus; virgines enim permanserunt qui se castraverunt propter regna caelorum."

[54] On Cant 2:14: PG 69, 1284C: Ταῦτα πρὸς τὴν τῶν δραματικῶς ἐπαγομένων σαφηνίαν, μέχρι τοῦ Ἡ φωνή σου ἡδεῖα, καὶ ἡ ὄψις σου ὡραία. Καὶ δῆλον ὡς ἡ νύμφη τοῦ Λόγου ψυχὴ, ἤγουν Ἐκκλησία Χριστοῦ... .

divine grace before she sees and understands and the reference is more to the Church as Christ's soul after Easter, rather than to any identification with his inner life at the time of the Incarnation. As in the case of the same phrase in the Origen-Procopius fragments, it is less obvious whether Cyril meant the phrase ἡ νύμφη τοῦ Λόγου ψυχή to be understood as "the soul, the Bride of the Word" or as "the Bride, the soul of [as in 'belonging to'] the Word." To translate "the Bride-soul of the Word" preserves the ambiguity of reference to both pre-Easter and post-Easter unions. Cyril on Cant 3:6 gives some clarification when he states that this "ecclesiastical soul" took part in the Incarnation:

> 'Myrrh' when she was buried through the frankincense. But 'frankincense' when, rising with him, she shared in his divinity. Now that the 'ecclesiastical soul'[55] is burnt off (sent heavenwards[56]) is not only signified by these but also by the variegated visions of knowledge.[57]

Again, the humanity of the Church is that which is 'perfumed' by the action of the divinity in the resurrection, so that once more Cyril seems to imply that the Church provides the soul which is redeemed within Christ during Easter, and in whose ascent to heaven, attached to the divine being, believers can participate here and now.

It is as if, for Cyril, the Word-flesh arrangement in Christ left room for a soul which could be taken on but would never properly be 'his own' in the sense that it was not an essential part of who he was. Thus "the soul of the Word" can mean the Church as soul which the Word came to possess like a wife, rather than indicate the 'Origenist' notion that a heavenly soul was joined to God the Word 'pre-existently', hence eternally. It would perhaps be not too bold to adduce the parallel in 'Neo-Chalcedonian' Christology

---

[55] There is another trace of Origen perhaps mediated through Jerome (it is there in Jerome's translation of Origen) in the use of the phrase *anima ecclesiastica*: Baehrens, p. 37: "Et tu ecclesiastica anima [only D,F mss] ad filias Ierusalem converte sermonem"; p. 41: "tu sponsa, tu ecclesiastica anima, omnibus animabus, quae non sunt ecclesiasticae. igitur si ecclesiastica anima es, omnibus animabus es melior". That Jerome's exegesis was valued by Cyril, see F. Abel (1941). Also PL 25, 1382D, *In Sophoniam*: "Omnis quippe Ecclesiastica anima, quae in specula constituta est, et contemplatur pacem, laetatur et gaudet iniquitatis a se esse sublatas, et [a] redemptas ab eo qui pretioso sanguine omnes redemit." Jerome goes on to contrast this soul with the 'Judaica(m) anima(m)' (1383A).

[56] Cf. the thesis of Münch-Labacher (1996), that Christ's self-offering on the Cross according to the Neoplatonic scheme of procession and return was the beginning of his and humanity's return 'up' to God in heaven.

[57] PG 69, 1285D: Σμύρνα μὲν, ὅτε συντέθαπται διὰ τοῦ λιβάνου· λίβανος δὲ, ὅτε συναναστὰς αὐτῷ κεκοινώνηκε τῆς θεότητος αὐτοῦ. Καὶ οὐ μόνοις τούτοις ἡ ἐκκλησιαστικὴ τεθυμίασται ψυχή, ἀλλὰ καὶ ποικίλοις γνώσεως θεωρήμασιν.

according to which Christ *had* a human nature for soteriological reasons while *being* divine as to his *hypostasis*.

Cyril implies that he is thinking of a salvation-historical account of the soul — the soul personified in the Song is not that of a monk or an individual believer, but rather represents a trans-historical corporate personality. This seems highlighted by the third alternative explanation of Cant 3:6 which he offers: "Someone might say that it is also the holy and ecclesiastical soul, the child once deserted of God, who comes up from the desert from the synagogue of the Gentiles, leaving teachings and words and deeds — the 'deserts' [i.e., things devoid] of God, she comes up to the things of God."[58] In other words, the rescue which the Incarnation brought is not for a closed community but potentially for all souls — represented by the universal soul.

4.4 The "bed" image

Cant 3:7,9 (with reference to Cant 1:16)
3·7 ἰδοὺ ἡ κλίνη τοῦ Σαλωμων,
  ἑξήκοντα δυνατοὶ κύκλῳ αὐτῆς
  ἀπὸ δυνατῶν Ισραηλ,
3·9 φορεῖον ἐποίησεν ἑαυτῷ ὁ βασιλεὺς Σαλωμων
  ἀπὸ ξύλων τοῦ Λιβάνου,
1·16 Ἰδοὺ εἶ καλός, ὁ ἀδελφιδός μου, καί γε ὡραῖος·
  πρὸς κλίνη ἡμῶν σύσκιος.

Here the imagery suggests that the Groom provides the shape or form for the Bride-Church's body to the point where there is overlap and identification between the two referents. Hence in Philo of Carpasia's treatment of Cant 3:7-8, the Latin version is evidently more appreciative of the mystical experience enjoyed by people of the Old Covenant. While the Greek text admits that "the sixty mighty men" are prophets, apostle-like in their testimony to Christ,[59] the Latin maintains that they are those who from the origin of the world contemplated God. It is the Latin text which is much

---

[58] Re Cant 3:6: PG 69, 1288A: Λέγοι δ' ἄν τις καὶ ὡς ἡ ἁγία καὶ ἐκκλησιαστικὴ ψυχή, τὸ τέκνον ποτὲ ἔρημον Θεοῦ, ἀπὸ συναγωγῆς ἐθνῶν ἀναβαίνει ἀπὸ τῆς ἐρήμου· καταλιποῦσα μὲν δόγματα καὶ λόγους καὶ πράξεις, τὰ ἔρημα Θεοῦ, ἀναβαίνουσα ἐπὶ τὰ τοῦ Θεοῦ.

[59] PG 40, 80 - 81A: Ἑξήκοντα δυνατοὺς κύκλῳ αὐτῆς οἶμαι λέγειν ἀπο δυνατῶν Ἰσραηλ, τοὺς ἀποστόλους, τοὺς ἀπὸ τῶν προφητῶν ὁρμωμένους, καὶ τὰς περὶ Χριστοῦ μαρτυρίας ἐκ τῶν προφητῶν συνιστῶντας. "Sexaginta potentes circa eam arbitror dicere de potentibus Israhel eos qui ab origine mundi deum speculati sunt, expositiones audiendo virtutum et in hunc solummodo contemplantes: Israhel enim est *videns deum*..." (Philo of Carpasia (Ceresa-Gastaldo) (1979), p. 112).

fuller, and whereas the Greek says little more than what is contained in the above footnote, the Latin proceeds to list names and details. These men teach the Church their virtue. There then follows a list of Old Testament worthies from Abel onwards, each with a moral lesson attached. Whereas the bed (κλίνη) of Solomon is the historical tomb of Jesus — with Jesus, as the chief wise man resting in it, the litter (φορεῖον) of Solomon in Cant 3:9 is understood as the Church. Philo's interest is more in this spiritual meaning of the historical (κλίνη) as the humanity (by metonymy) which the Word lay on. Corresponding to this, his humanity, which was raised like a litter, is the place of meeting with God in the present age. The Greek and the Latin concur in viewing this as pointing to the Church as the vehicle for Christ in the world which the spiritual Solomon, as the identity of Wisdom, has built for himself (Prov 9:1): "...the holy Church herself called together in the flesh of the Only-Begotten becomes his litter."[60]

Philo comes close to Epiphanius' idea that the Word took flesh which was located in the pure apostolic Church as the offspring of the synagogue.[61] The implication is that the Church is defined in terms of Jesus' own human nature rather than vice-versa — and it looks forward to the post-resurrection age. This is a change from Epiphanius for whom the receptive faith of OT and NT saints was constitutive of the nature of that collective humanity. For the Incarnation is the foundation of the mystery; on this Welserheimb comments: "In diesem Fleisch Christi wächst die zum Genuß des Liebesmahls zusammengerufene Gemeinde der Heiligen zu einem Ganzen zusammen, nämlich zur Sänfte des Einziggeborenen, da die Kirche in der Gemeinschaft des Fleisches zum Körper Christi wird, daher auch Sänfte des göttlichen Wortes ist wie dieser."[62] Welserheimb's idea that the betrothal on the Cross will lead to the Church's consummation with the Only-Begotten/Word overlooks Philo's emphasis that this wedding-feast is already in one sense (Christological and sacramental) a present reality. So Philo makes it clear by his Betrothal (Cross) — Feast (Church-Sacrament) — Consummation (Final Resurrection) schema that the position of the Church in its enjoyment of the nuptial blessings is more like that of wedding guests admiring the bond between Word and flesh in Christ, in which the union is fully realised, and in

---

[60] PG 40, 81D-84A: Κλίνην μοι νόει, τὸ μνῆμα τοῦ Ἰησοῦ, τοῦ εἰρηνεύσαντος τὰ πάντα διὰ τοῦ ἰδίου πάθους καὶ τῆς ἀναστάσεως. Philo (Ceresa-Gastaldo) (1979), p. 116, 65: "sepulchrum Iesu qui intelligibilis Solomon est." Cf. Rufinus-Origen on Cant 1:5 (see above s. 4. 2).

[61] PG 40, 84BC: οὕτως ὁμοίως ἐν τῇ σαρκὶ τοῦ Μονογενοῦς ἡ συγκαλουμένη αὐτὴ ἁγία Ἐκκλησία, καὶ αὐτὴ αὐτοῦ γίνεται φορεῖον. Φορεῖον οὖν οὐ μόνον ἡ σάρξ Ἰησοῦ, ἀλλὰ καὶ αὐτὴ ἡ Ἐκκλησία. Philo (Ceresa-Gastaldo) (1979), p. 118: "sic in unigeniti carne ascita ei ecclesia dignitate eius induitur... . Gestatorium autem non solum est caro Iesu, sed etiam ipsa indubitanter ecclesia quae est corpus eius... .

[62] Welserheimb (1948), p. 439.

which they will not directly share until the Resurrection of all flesh. For the time being, the Church is fully united to the Word only in an ideal sense. One might say this is an *ideal* ecclesiological Christology, with Christ's humanity providing the ideal.

In a similar vein there is an isolated fragment on Cant 3:9 where Procopius records:

> *Theophilus*: The one from the nations was the Lord according to the flesh, although his descent from Judah is preserved.[63] Who then is the wood of Lebanon? Ruth the Moabitess; for she bore Jobed from whom came Jesse. Therefore the carriage is the body [of the Lord].... In dual terms [64] it states "he made it" so as to say: (1) the whole [such] litter is love, just as the Scripture: "Love is the greatest of these". (2) "Litter" the God-bearing souls. "From the woods of Lebanon" For we were once the wood of the opposition.

R.M. Grant's translation of the extra lines given by Meursius' *catena* is as follows:

> "He made a litter": 'he made' has a double reference; as it were, the whole litter is love, in accordance with "the greatest of these is love" (1 Cor 13:13). The "litter" is God-bearing souls.... "From the wood of Lebanon": for we were once wood (matter) belonging to the Adversary.[65]

This illuminates the connection in Theophilus' mind between love and the Incarnation as God's rescue from the enemy. The chief idea of the fragment taken as a whole is that redeemed souls in the Old Testament provided the spiritual material, which God then used to form Christ's body. Christ's body is understood as an artefact made out of opposing humanity, but cut a special way — the carriage form is that of the best of the loving souls, known as "love" — Christ himself. The soul as form to the body's matter was, of course, not uncommon ever since Aristotle's *De Anima* 414a, where he writes that the soul is the ἐντελέχεια of the body. However, less usual is the picture of female souls (by inclusion from Ruth to Mary), increasingly perfect in their

---

[63] Following the translation of R.M. Grant (1963), p. 191.

[64] Cf. for "ἀπὸ κοινοῦ", Liddell and Scott, 969, VI,4.

[65] The whole text (PG 87,2, 1629B): Φορεῖον ἐποίησεν ἑαυτῷ ὁ βασιλεὺς Σαλωμών, ἀπὸ ξύλων τοῦ Λιβάνου (Cant 3,9)...Θεοφίλου.-[Ἐξ ἐθνῶν τὸ κατὰ σάρκα ὁ Κύριος, σωζομένου καὶ τοῦ ἐξ Ἰούδα. Τίς οὖν ἐστι τὸ Meursius] Ξύλον τοῦ Λιβάνου, [; Meursius] Ῥοὺθ ἡ Μωαβίτις. [Αὕτη γὰρ τέτοκε τὸν Ἰωβήδ Meursius] ἐξ οὗ Ἰεσσαι · φορεῖον τοίνυν ἐστὶ τὸ σῶμα τὸ Κυριακόν [om. Meursius]. The text continues in Meursius (PG 6, 1604) as follows: Φορεῖον ἐποίησεν. Ἀπὸ κοινοῦ τὸ ἐποίησεν ὡσανεὶ ἔλεγεν · ὅλον [ὅσον Meursius] δὲ τὸ φορεῖον ἡ ἀγάπη ἐστιν, κατὰ τό, Μείζων δὲ τουτῶν ἡ ἀγαπη [I Cor, 13, 13] Φορεῖον τὰς θεοφόρους ψυχάς. Ἀπὸ ξύλων τοῦ Λιβάνου. Ποτὲ γὰρ ξύλον τοῦ ἀντικειμένου ἦμεν.

4. The Bride

exercising a free-will response, who somehow provide the matter for Christ's humanity, with the Word himself providing the form.

4.5 The Bride as walled garden and spring

Cant 4:12
4·12 Κῆπος κεκλεισμένος ἀδελφή μου νύμφη,
κῆπος κεκλεισμένος, πηγὴ ἐσφραγισμένη·

Already in Jerome's *Adversus Jovinianum*, Cant 4:12 is used to back up the idea that אלמה in Is 7:14 meant "secret virgin".[66] The way Jerome writes is suggestive of a type of 'water through a pipe' Christology, leaning towards docetism. The image itself would become more popular once associated with Mary as the new Eve in Paradise. By the time of Hesychius of Jerusalem in his sole citation from the Song (c. 435),[67] the ideal Church personified is also the *fons et origo* of the Saviour Bridegroom's flesh. Hesychius, coming after the clarification of Mary as *Christotokos* in the 430s, builds his interpretation on a sounder Christological basis than did Jerome.

In Augustine the Church is the paradise which is purified by the heretics' fall out from it.[68] 'She' is also a lot more reliable than the mind and souls of individual human beings which have always been prone to let Satan's lies

---

[66] Jerome, PL 23, 265D: "Hortus conclusus, soror mea sponsa: hortus conclusus, fons signatus. Quod clausum est, atque signatum, similitudinem habet Matris Domini, matris et virginis... . Quid est igitur quod significat *alma*? Absconditum virginem, id est, non solum virginem, sed cum ἐπιστάσει virginem... ."

[67] Aubineau (1978), I, p. 162: ὁ ἐκ σοῦ νυμφίος, προεῖπεν ἐν τοῖς Ἄσμασι *κῆπον κελεισμένον*, ἐπειδὴ σοῦ μὲν δρεπάνη φθορᾶς ἢ τρύγητος οὐχ ἥψατο, ἄνθος δὲ τὸ ἐκ τῆς ῥάβδου τοῦ Ἰεσσαὶ καθαρῶς τῷ γένει τῶν ἀνθρώπων καὶ καθαρῶς παρίστησιν, ὑπὸ μόνου γεωργηθέν σοι τοῦ καθαροῦ καὶ ἀκηράτου Πνεύματος· *Πηγὴν ἐσφραγισμένην*, ὅτι ποταμὸς ζωῆς ἐκ σοῦ προελθὼν τὴν οἰκουμένην ἐπλήρωσεν, ἀλλὰ κλάδος γαμικὸς τὴν σὴν πηγὴν οὐκ ἤντλησε. Intro (xliv): "Hésychius présente ordinairement Marie comme la mère d'un petit enfant qui est Dieu; mais avec plus de précision il use, sept fois, du mot technique, 'mère de Dieu', particulièrement dans l'homélie V, prononcée peu de temps après le concile d'Ephèse."

[68] *De Gen Contra Manich*. 2,14; PL 34, 207: "Posuit enim Deus hominem in paradiso, ut operaretur et custodiret: quia sic de Ecclesia dicitur in Canticis canticorum, *Hortus conclusus, fons signatus* (Cant. IV,12); quo utique non admittitur perversitatis ille persuasor. Sed tamen per mulierem decipit: non enim etiam ratio nostra deduci ad consensionem peccati potest, nisi cum delectatio mota fuerit in illa parte animi, quae debet obtemperare rationi tanquam rectori viro." Cf. *De Gen ad litt*. 11, 25 (PL 34, 442): "Paradisus enim dicta est Ecclesia, sicut legitur in Cantico canticorum, *Hortus conclusus, fons signatus, puteus aquae vitae, paradisus cum fructu pomorum* (Cant 4:12,13). Inde ceciderunt vel aperta et corporali separatione omnes haeretici; vel occulta et spirituali, quamvis in ea corporaliter esse videantur, omnes conversi ad vomitum suum... ."

into them; for she is sealed and pure. It is clear that, whatever the influence of Ambrose's preaching from the Song on the younger Augustine, the later Augustine (as argued by Courcelle[69]) had transformed this theme beyond recognition by applying to the catholic Church what Ambrose had said about the soul. That this is an eschatological hope seems clear in the *De Civitate Dei* XVII, 20 where "holy minds" long to participate in the end-time marriage. What qualifies for participation is knowledge of the doctrine rather than participation through practice. This point that all right-believing Christians are involved (and are not mere spectators of holier souls who contemplate the Logos) is well-made by Simon, but he seems not to grasp fully that this is reserved for the *eschaton*: the Song, for Augustine, is a futuristic prophecy. In a passage from *Enarr. in Ps 66:4*, the Bride is a 'collective' figure and there is clear indication that Augustine overlaid the image with that from Rev 21:1-4 where the figures of "Bride" and "the city" are identified. The point is that while the city has been descending from earth to heaven since the start of time (presumably with Abel) — and in that sense Augustinian eschatology is 'realised' — the 'making public' of God's betrothal will only take place at the day of Resurrection.[70] There was, in such a grace-dominated schema, no room for a Bride-humanity to make a contribution. Augustine, unlike Hesychius does not associate the Bride with the humanity Mary provided.

4.6 The Bride as the imitator of the Groom

Cant 5:2 and 5:12, 14

5·2 Ἐγὼ καθεύδω, καὶ ἡ καρδία μου ἀγρυπνεῖ.
φωνὴ ἀδελφιδοῦ μου, κρούει ἐπὶ τὴν θύραν
" "Ἄνοιξόν μοι, ἀδελφή μου, ἡ πλησίον μου,
περιστερά μου, τελεία μου,
ὅτι ἡ κεφαλή μου ἐπλήσθη δρόσου
καὶ οἱ βόστρυχοί μου ψεκάδων νυκτός."
5·12 ὀφθαλμοὶ αὐτοῦ ὡς περιστεραὶ ἐπὶ πληρώματα ὑδάτων
λελουσμέναι ἐν γάλακτι
καθήμεναι ἐπὶ πληρώματα ὑδάτων.
5·14 χεῖρες αὐτοῦ τορευταὶ χρυσαῖ πεπληρωμέναι θαρσις,
κοιλία αὐτοῦ πυξίον ἐλεφάντινον ἐπὶ λίθου σαπφείρου,

In Homily XI, commenting on Cant 5:2, Gregory of Nyssa makes it clear that "perfect one" is a title which does not describe the Bride so much as declares

---

[69] Courcelle (1968), pp. 120-22.
[70] See *De Civ. Dei* XX,17; on Abel, see ibid., XV,1.

that which she is commanded to be. As hearers reflect on that and three other heuristic metaphors "sister, companion and dove" they are helped to experience the reality of what is signified (i.e., spiritual perfection).[71]

More a potential, ideal state than a realised one, her perfection is the mirror image of the Groom's qualities. In Homily XIII (on Cant 5:12) there is a good example of the operation of the principle of *akolouthia* — namely that Gregory exegetes a passage in the light of what is ahead in the text (namely Cant 6:8f) as well as what is behind— quite unlike Augustine's approach.[72] The problem is that Gregory can also vary the reference of the "perfect dove" image so that, although, in the passage from Homily XI just referred to and in Homily XV on Cant 6:8f, the dove image applies to the Bride, yet in Homily XIII the dove is seen to refer to the Word-Groom as the one who *has* the eyes. The text is : "Therefore for the purification of the eyes the washing with milk is judged sound by the perfect soul."[73] (As he explains, water symbolises false images of God on account of its reflection of idolatrous "fantasies".) The eyes are part of the Church only as she embodies the form of Christ which she sees. But who is this perfect soul who is qualified to make this judgement ? It cannot be Paul, for he is mentioned in a part of the larger metaphor as being like (a few?) hairs on the head of this Groom's body.[74] Each believing soul is called to imitate Christ's actions and his present Church, to discern the humanity which is perfect.

J. Gaith[75] speaks of Gregory as having a 'synthetic' Christ; the germ of the image in humankind is all but obscured; within Christ's person the human

---

[71] GNO VI, 325, 4-11: χρή σε ἀδελφήν μου γενέσθαι ἐν τῷ τὰ θελήματά μου τῇ ψυχῇ παραδέξασθαι. ...χρὴ δὲ σε καὶ προσεγγίσαι τῇ ἀληθείᾳ καὶ πλησίον ἀκριβῶς γενέσθαι, ὥστε μηδενὶ μέσῳ διατεχίζεσθαι καὶ ἐν τῇ φύσει τῆς περιστερᾶς ἔχειν τὸ τέλειον, τοῦτο δέ ἐστι τὸ ἀνελλιπῆ τε καὶ πεπληρωμένην εἶναι πάσης ἀκακίας καὶ καθαρότητος.

[72] See Daniélou (1970), 39, citing Marrou (1949), 429.

[73] GNO VI, 393, 1-5:˙Ὀφθαλμοὶ αὐτοῦ ὡς περιστεραὶ ἐπὶ πληρώματα ὑδάτων, λελουμέναι ἐν γάλακτι, καθήμεναι ἐπὶ πληρώματα ὑδάτων. Also, GNO VI, 397, 1-3: διὰ τοῦτο πρὸς τὴν καθαρότητα τῶν ὀμμάτων ὑπὸ τῆς τελείας ψυχῆς τὸ τοῦ γάλακτος λουτρὸν ἀσφαλὲς ἐκρίθη. The milk allows insight into what is false. GNO VI, 396, 9-12: ἀληθὴς γὰρ ἡ τοῦ γάλακτός ἐστι παρατήρησις ὅτι μόνον τῶν ὑγρῶν τοῦτο τοιαύτην ἔχει τὴν ἰδιότητα τὸ μὴ ἐμφαίνεσθαι αὐτῷ εἴδωλόν τινος καὶ ὁμοίωμα.

[74] At GNO VI, 392, 14ff, on Cant 5:11: ...καὶ διὰ τοῦτο βόστρυχος τῆς θείας κεφαλῆς χρηματίσας ὅτι Τὸ πρότερον ὢν βλάσφημος καὶ διώκτης καὶ ὑβριστής (1 Tim 1:13), ἕως ἦν κόραξ, πρὸς τὴν χάριν ταύτην μετεσκευάσθη βόστρυχος γενόμενος τῇ οὐρανίᾳ δρόσῳ διάβροχος... .

[75] Gaith (1953): "Dans le Christ, la divinité créatrice de l'humain sauve celui-ci en l'assumant de façon transcendente" (143). "Mais ce que le Christ restaure, ce sont surtout les énergies de l'esprit" (154). Gregory would have spoken more of the common energies of the Trinity actively at work—a concern he shared with Apollinarius and the Messalians; cf. *Orat Catech.* (GNO III, IV, 66): ὁ προσεγγισμὸς τῆς θείας δυνάμεως πυρὸς δίκην

person is transformed by divinity's requisitioning humanity in order to expel its demon (like Messalianism but unlike it in referring the decisive operation to the Incarnation itself). The humanity of Christ effects no change on human nature as a whole, but rather issues a "ray of sanctity" through the transfigured humanity which attracts other humans to follow, and the emerging restored image is not forced by God:

> All this, which gives us a description of the beauty, is not a demonstration of the invisible and incomprehensible things of the divinity but of the things manifested in the economy, when he was seen on earth and moved among men,[76] having put on human nature, through which, according to the Apostle's word, even the unseen thoughts were made apparent to those made by him, through the preparation of the 'ecclesiastical' world. For the creation of that world is the preparation of the Church. [77]

While the Groom is, as seen in the previous chapter, the Word, through his assumed humanity with whom only was there a nuptial intimacy amounting to a mixing,[78] he came to take on into himself early Christians, to whom are added the succeeding generations of believers as the Word's body. As already seen (above, s. 3. 9) the post-resurrection monism is preceded by a duality, although hardly a mutuality between God and humans. In other words, the observing believing soul sees herself in his humanity.

4.7 The Bride's chosenness as new Jerusalem

Cant 6:4
6·4 Καλὴ εἶ, ἡ πλησίον μου, ὡς εὐδοκία,
ὡραία ὡς Ιερουσαλημ, θάμβος ὡς τεταγμέναι.

ἀφανισμὸν τοῦ παρὰ φύσιν κατεργασάμενος εὐεργετεῖ τῇ καθάρσει τὴν φύσιν, κἂν ἐπίπονος ἡ διάκρισις ἦ.

[76] Cf. Baruch 3:38.

[77] GNO VI, 384, 13-21: ταῦτα γὰρ πάντα, δι'ὧν ἡ τοῦ κάλλους γέγονεν ὑπογραφή, οὐ τῶν ἀοράτων τε καὶ ἀκαταλήπτων τῆς θεότητός ἐστιν ἐνδεικτικὰ ἀλλὰ τῶν κατ' οἰκονομίαν φανερωθέντων, ὅτε ἐπὶ τῆς γῆς ὤφθη καὶ τοῖς ἀνθρώποις συνανεστράφη τὴν ἀνθρωπίνην ἐνδυσάμενος φύσιν, δι'ὧν κατὰ τὸν ἀποστολικὸν λόγον καὶ τὰ ἀόρατα αὐτοῦ τοῖς ποιήμασι νοούμενα καθορᾶται διὰ τῆς τοῦ ἐκκλησιαστικοῦ κόσμου κατασκευῆς φανερούμενα. κόσμου γὰρ κτίσις ἐστὶν ἡ τῆς ἐκκλησίας κατασκευή, ἐν ᾗ κατὰ τὴν τοῦ προφήτου φωνὴν καὶ οὐρανὸς κτίζεται καινός... καὶ γῆ καινὴ κατασκευάζεται (Cf. also, GNO VI, 390, 21 - 391, 5).

[78] On Gregory's view that union with God was only conceivable as through Christ's perfect humanity, see Stewart (1991), 185.

4. The Bride

Clearly the demands that God be recognised as the active partner in salvation had to be weighed against the observation that the process required perfect cooperation in obedient suffering and active seeking of the Father's will and communion with him. The crux of Cant 6:4ff is set in a context of a charged, clearly epiphanic experience. Her look makes him troubled, his soul ready to fly. In a way akin to Gregory in the above section, Christ's humanity is presented by Theodoret as that which believers will one day fully share in the resurrection.[79] The desired effect of the Song, as distinct from the preparatory workings of Proverbs and Ecclesiastes, is that the 'person reading' should fly away to desire the Groom.[80] Theodoret would appear deliberately vague as to whether τὸ τέλειον means the destination of a perfect state or Christ the Groom himself; the semantically close connection (it is much more than a double entendre) is inspired by Eph 4:13/Col 1:28. Yet the overall thrust is of a voyage to travel to the perfect humanity of Christ, who is kin and "beloved" to the soul who is "according to the image".[81] The Neoplatonic overtones of the soul's taking flight are equally present.[82] When they become as one in catholic harmony then they will come to consummation 'in Him': the Groom-Word's earthly humanity has the function of being the locus of the address by the Word (crudely put, his mouthpiece) and the Groom's glorified humanity that of being the soul-Church's locus of consummation with the Word.[83] There is (according to a Logos-anthropos model) a deliberate avoidance of any notion of 'physical redemption'; for in the present age there is even distance between one humanity (his glorified as the one nuptial resting-place for the Word) and another (the believer's). His humanity does not include her but is a tangible cover or 'place' so that the soul might position itself for ultimate union with the Word. It is the Word who, at the *eschaton*, will do for

---

[79] PG 81, 48B: καὶ ἐντεῦθεν λοιπὸν ἀναπτῆναι, καὶ τὸν νυμφίον ποθῆσαι, τὸν τὰ αἰώνια ἐπαγγειλάμενον ἀγαθά. Διὰ τοῦτο καὶ τρίτον τέτακται τὸ βιβλίον τοῦτο ἵνα ὁδῷ τις βαδίζων ἐπὶ τὸ τέλειον ἔλθοι.

[80] Cf. PG 81, 103C (re Cant 2:10) and, especially, 112BC (re Cant 2:16):˙Επεὶ δὲ ὡς μία εἰσὶ τῷ νύμφιῳ...τετελειωμέναι ψυχαὶ, ἑνικῶς πρὸς αὐτὸν ἀποκρινόμεναί φασιν Ἀδελφιδοῦς μου ἐμοὶ, κἀγὼ αὐτῷ · ἤγουν, Ὁ ἀγαπητός μου ἐμοὶ κατ' εἰκόνα... .

[81] Also at PG 81, 103C on Cant 2:17. Smolak (1984), 240, notes that a six-year spell in the monastery overlaid Theodoret's secular education and that this explains the 'two sides' to him. But these two aspects dovetail quite well. Thus the very concept of the spiritual Word-soul union seems a hybrid of philosophico-theological and spiritual reflection.

[82] Ibid.

[83] PG 81, 143A: Ὁ δὲ νυμφίος, καὶ Θεός ἐστι προαιώνιος, καὶ ἄνθρωπος ἐπ' ἐσχάτων ἡμερῶν ἐκ τῆς ἁγίας Παρθένου γεννηθείς· καὶ μένων ὃ ἦν, προσέλαβε τὸ ἡμέτερον, καὶ τὴν πάλαι γεγυμνωμένην ἠμφίασε νύμφην. Διὸ φησι πρὸς αὐτήν Ὀσμὴ ἱματίων σου, (ὡς) ὀσμὴ τοῦ λιβάνου· τὸν γὰρ Χριστὸν ἐνδέδυται, ὅς ἐστι Θεὸς καὶ ἄνθρωπος· θεολογίας δὲ σύμβολον ὁ λίβανος, ἐπειδὴ κατὰ τὸν παλαιὸν νόμον Θεῷ προσεφερέρετο.

each soul what he had already done for the humanity of Christ, namely infuse 'her' with himself from the outside through his human "cloak".

4. 8 The Bride as the perfect human one

Cant 6:8-10.

6·8 Ἑξήκοντά εἰσιν βασίλισσαι, καὶ ὀγδοήκοντα παλλακαί,
καὶ νεάνιδες ὧν οὐκ ἔστιν ἀριθμός.
6·9 μία ἐστὶν περιστερά μου, τελεία μου,
μία ἐστὶν τῇ μητρὶ αὐτῆς,
ἐκλεκτή ἐστιν τῇ τεκούσῃ αὐτῆς.
εἴδοσαν αὐτὴν θυγατέρες καὶ μακαριοῦσιν αὐτήν,
βασίλισσαι καὶ παλλακαὶ καὶ αἰνέσουσιν αὐτήν.
6·10 Τίς αὕτη ἡ ἐκκύπτουσα ὡσεὶ ὄρθρος,
καλὴ ὡς σελήνη, ἐκλεκτὴ ὡς ὁ ἥλιος,
θάμβος ὡς τεταγμέναι;

For Origen, the consummation of the union of the Word and the νοῦς of Christ has already taken place in the earthly life of Jesus. In the brief comment on Cant 6:8ff, Origen speaks of this noetic soul before going on to apply the epithet "perfect dove" to the *Word*. 'She' is a receptacle for all who want to be joined mystically to the Word.[84] So, in the comment on the line, "What do you see in the Shulamite?"[85] Origen writes: "the Bride is the soul of the Word or the Church of Christ". The first phrase could also be translated: "the Bride of the Word, the soul", yet the context is of one who made peace (Christ), as one who now provides the foundation for the moral sense ('repentance', as suggested by Symmachus.) Origen goes on to say that, according to Symmachus' translation (not Σουλαβίτις but ἐσκυλευμένη), with its allusion to 'Israel in exile', she is the one who has been "spoiled" by her captor and that she must return to her original noble state. The Church of Christ as the Bride has some affinity or continuity with the soul of the Word: both Church and soul are "peacemakers", carrying out his unifying work in (a) the heavenlies, (b) this earthly realm.[86] The soul who made peace by 'her'

---

[84] PG 17, 277D: λογικὸν ζῷον ἡ νύμφη· ἐὰν νοήσῃ ψυχὴ καὶ λάβῃ ὁ νυμφίος τὴν νυμφὴν ἀλλ᾽ ἐπεί ἐστιν ὁ λόγος οὗτος, οὐ μιᾷ ψυχῇ κοινωνῶν, ἀλλὰ πλείοσι καὶ διαφόροις... .

[85] Cant 7:1: Τί ὄψεσθε ἐν τῇ Σουλαμίτιδι;

[86] Crouzel (1981); (1984b). Cf. Le Boulluec (1987); also Meloni (1975), 175.

sacrifice on the Cross is the original and saving Bride of the Word in the heavens.[87]

Origen seems alone in making the Word appear as *primus inter pares* in the scene observed in Cant 6:8f. Starting with Methodius, the perfect one of this passage is, for most commentators, about the Bride, a creature. With one eye on Origen, he insists that, according to these verses the "flesh" (that is body and soul) which the Word assumed was a special one. He was uncomfortable with any idea that this "flesh" was in any sense 'pre-existent'. So, on Μία ἐστὶ περιστερά μου, τελεία μου, as E. Prinzivalli[88] notes, Methodius, in the early part of *Symposium* VII, presents the four groups in Cant 6:8f as the four stages of humankind: the antediluvian souls, the postdiluvian legalists inseminated with the Word of life, the perfect soul, and the young women who represent a thing not yet come to maturity, the future glory of the spiritual *ogdoad*.

Methodius then returns to deal with the Logos-perfect soul union[89] and seems to differ self-consciously from Origen, his controversial predecessor. Although there is a similar blending of the royal marriage theme from Psalm 44, the Bride is simply the Church. The Church is dove-like because such creatures are not satisfied with the ways of life and company of men. Then suddenly Methodius presents an alternative: it could be said that the Bride is the untainted body of the Lord, for the sake of which, leaving the Father he came down here and cleaved to and indwelled her, having become man to her.[90] The French translation reads: "... c'est la chair sans tache du Seigneur, qu'il est descendu chercher ici bas, s' éloignant d'auprès de son Père, pour faire se fondre en elle dans une étreinte fulgurante en se faisant homme."[91] Now the apparatus provided by Bonwetsch attests that in the Photius manuscript the last two words of the above sentence are αὐτῇ ἐνανθρωπίσας. This helps to clarify the notion that the marriage and the Incarnation take place at the same moment rather than to take too strongly the nuance supplied by εἰς — that the Word became man in order to be married to the flesh (at some later point). There are two points of internal evidence

---

[87] PG 17, 280CD: Ἀκύλας καὶ ἡ πέμπτη ἔκδοσις, τὸ Σουλαβίτις ἐξέδωκαν, εἰρηνεύουσα γὰρ ἐστὶ δὲ ἡ νύμφη τοῦ λόγου ψυχὴ, ἡ τοῦ Χριστοῦ Ἐκκλησία, διὰ τὸν ποιήσαντα τὸ ἕν, καὶ τὸ μεσότοιχον τοῦ φραγμοῦ λύσαντα· ἐὰν δὲ ἡ Σουλαμίτις, ἢ ἐσκυλευμένη, κατὰ Σύμμαχον, λέγοι ἂν πρὸς αὐτὴν ὁ νυμφίος, Ὦ ἐσκυλευμένη καὶ ὑπὸ τῷ αἰχμαλωτίσαντι σε γεγενημένη, *ἐπίστρεφε* εἰς τὴν προτέραν εὐγένειαν. Crouzel (1981), (1984b), has rightly emphasised the role of Christ's *epinoiai* in the effecting of salvation.

[88] Prinzivalli (1985), 55ff.

[89] VII, 8; Bonwetsch, 78.

[90] Ibid., 17-20: Δυνήσεται δέ τις καὶ ἑτέρως τὴν νύμφην φάναι τὴν σάρκα τὴν ἀμόλυντον εἶναι τοῦ κυρίου, ἧς χάριν καταλείψας τὸν πατέρα κατῆλθεν ἐνταῦθα καὶ προσεκολλήθη καὶ ἐγκατέσκηψεν ἐνανθρωπήσας εἰς αὐτήν.

[91] SC 95, 199.

which suggest that the variant should be taken seriously. First, the verb in question is used with the dative in the above passage.[92] Second, in the First Discourse (Marcella) the term ὁ λόγος ἐνανθρωπήσας is understood as naming the one who is the prototypical virgin who must be imitated. In other words becoming man and assuming flesh are the same thing.[93] Taking τῆς ἐκκλησίας as dependent on the three titles of Christ at the start of the sentence, Musurillo translates: "...the Word Incarnate became the Archvirgin as well as Archshepherd and Archprophet of His Church."[94]

The French translation by Debidour is close. According to Methodius, the divinity of Christ was joined/married to "flesh" which was "untainted" or "special humanity"; thus he was a kind of first-born man of men, yet also the last, most perfect human.[95] This must mean that the Bride is more than a mere soul and, since embodied, is in no sense 'pre-existent' part of a world of forms; yet there remains in Methodius a Platonic understanding of assuming a collective humanity which is a special and idealised one. Thus I feel E. Prinzivalli overstates her case: "Dopo l'ampio spazio dato da Origene al concetto di anima di Cristo e alla sua essenziale funzione di mediazione fra la divinità e la carne, l'uso del termine *sàrks* non ha certo il valore generico, metonimico, con il quale lo intendevano per es."[96] Moreover, Riedel's claim — that Methodius stands at the head of a tradition of interpretation which flows through Didymus, Nilus, Cyril and Ps-Athanasius and which is alternative to Origen — is similarly only 'half-right'.[97] Methodius, like Origen, believed in a universal which the Word assumed, even if that universal only came to existence by the time of the Incarnation, having been somehow 'prepared'. This would indeed be influential, but as a corrective, rather than an alternative, to Origen.

For Epiphanius, it is the apostolic truth which has existed in believers as early as the first chapters of Genesis and which, thus prepared, was betrothed to the incarnate Christ when he came. The Bride of Cant 6:8f is a canon for 'the true Church'. Epiphanius realised the limitations, even the deceitfulness

---

[92] Bonwetsch, 30, 21: τῷ πρωτοπλάστῳ καὶ πρώτῳ καὶ πρωτογόνῳ τῶν ἀνθρώπων κερασθεῖσαν ἐνηθρωπηκέναι.

[93] Bonwetsch, 13,17; SC 95, p. 64, 5-9: "Ὅτι δὲ καὶ ἀρχιπάρθενος, ὃν τρόπον καὶ ἀρχιποιμὴν καὶ ἀρχιπροφήτης, γέγονεν ὁ λόγος ἐνανθρωπήσας τῆς ἐκκλησίας,... .

[94] Musurillo in his translation of Methodius (1958), 47.

[95] *Symposium* I, IV (SC 95, p. 62, 10-12): Τὸ δὲ παλαιὸν οὐδέπω τέλειος ὁ ἄνθρωπος ἦν, καὶ διὰ τοῦτο τὸ τέλειον οὐδέπω χωρῆσαι τὴν παρθενίαν ἴσχυεν.

[96] Prinzivalli (1985), 62.

[97] Riedel (1898), 103: "...von der herkömmlichen origenistischen gänzlich abweichende Auffassung der HL... ." and n1: "Methodius hat...aber doch die anderen Deutungen bevorzugt."

4. The Bride

of a concept of the Church herself as being an immaculate and faithful Bride. Accordingly he pays respect to the former Jews who confessed true religion, the generations of those who came before the advent of the Lord, whatever their spiritual merit. But it is their issue, the embodiment of truth revealed at the time of Christ, who is our mother and who was Christ's consort during his earthly ministry. *She* is given the honour of being the object of the panegyric in Cant 6:9. Christ is usually understood by Epiphanius as the divine agent who used, rather than joined with, a humanity.[98] It was crucial that Christ was perfect God and perfect (i.e. sinless) man, rather than an amalgam of the two. Praise is given to the non-interfering, morally inoculated, passive, thus bridal human representative who, as carrier of truth through right belief, was made ready for the divinity to join with in the Incarnation.

The association of Mary with the Church through the common lien of Christ's humanity is seen only sparingly in the West. Pacianus of Barcelona combatted the heretics, notably the 'Novatianists' by holding that an essential and defining feature of the Church was her indivisibility[99] and her maternal nature which gathers in the young women.[100]

The East would receive a different inheritance.[101] For Apollinarius on Cant 6:8 in the context of a discussion of Ps 44:8: "The clothes of Christ are the things which fittingly speak of him as God" (viz, miracles).... . The soul who truly was the yoke-partner to the true king, namely the Church, queenly on account of the Bride's having golden clothes, having put on Christ."[102] Then, slightly further on: "It is not offensive if he is both the Groom and the clothing according to the one or other form and name, since he is found in the gospels to be 'shepherd' and 'lamb' and countless other (titles)."[103] She, the Church becomes fit to reign with the Word by putting on his humanity which

---

[98] Cf. *Panarion* 77, 17,3, (GCS 37, p. 430) contra the Apollinarians ("Dimoerites").

[99] *Ep.* III, 25, 130, in Fernandez (ed.) (1958): "Mater haec adulescentularum, *quarum non est numerus*. Calcule denique, si potes, catholicos greges, et duc in digitos nostrae plebis examina...Dic, dic an istae adulescentulae ex vestra (viz., Simpronian) plebe generentur, an tu solus hoc parias. Nostra est ista regina, *electa matri suae atque perfecta*. Nihil quippe electum nisi melius et maius ex alio; nihil perfectum potest esse nisi plenum."

[100] As for Augustine, Mary could only be a type of the single, maternal Church and not a present, transcendent idealisation of it. See (e.g.) *De Sancta Virginitate* 2; PL 40, 397: "Maria corporaliter caput huius corporis peperit: Ecclesia spiritualiter membra illius capitis parit."

[101] Using Cant 6:8ff to paint a cosmic hierarchy would be employed by Psellus (1992), 65f, — with baroque effect.

[102] Mühlenberg I, 339: Χριστοῦ οὖν ἱμάτια τὰ εὐλόγως περὶ αὐτοῦ θεολογούμενά ἐστιν... Ἡ τῷ Χριστῷ τῷ ἀληθινῷ βασιλεῖ ἀληθῶς σύζυγος γενομένη ψυχή, ἤτοι ἐκκλησία, βασίλισσα διὰ τὸ εἶναι νύμφη...ἱμάτια διάχρυσα ἔχει, Χριστὸν ἐνδυσαμένη.

[103] Ibid., 340, 2-3: οὐ προσκοπτέον δὲ εἰ αὐτὸς καὶ νυμφίος καὶ ἔνδυμα ἐστιν κατὰ γὰρ ἄλλην καὶ ἄλλην σχέσιν καὶ ἐπίνοιαν ταῦτα ὑπάρχει, ὥσπερ καὶ ποιμὴν καὶ ἀμνὸς καὶ ἄλλα μυρία εὑρίσκεται ἐν τοῖς Εὐαγγελίοις.

is well-divinised by association with divinity. Apollinarius continues on Cant 6:9 where the prevalent idea is that the Church even now is above all other creatures in the hierarchy.[104] Apollinarius thought the divinity and humanity of Christ were locked together so as to be the same thing. Thus the humanity is provided by the Church yet is gradually joined to the Word in order to fill up the fulness of Christ's humanity; which is not so far from the thrust of Gregory of Nyssa's Canticles-exegesis.[105]

Meanwhile for Didymus the beauty of the one "fair as the moon" in Cant 6:10 is held to consist in perfection, analogous to the moon having grown to its full strength.[106] Here the perfect soul is the Church, the archetype who also appears in Rev 21:2. That she is already connected to the Groom by the *Menschwerdung* is clear from a later piece of exegesis. While he comes close to them by being made man, they become like him by their obedience, thus sonship.[107] He does not so much share anyone's humanity but those being perfected themselves share his; the assumption is that his is no common humanity; which is the meaning of κυριακός ἄνθρωπος in Didymus' thinking.[108] A similar interpretation obtains in the (Procopian) *catena*

---

[104] Ibid., 341, 25ff: δηλοῦται δὲ ἐκ τῶν λέξεων τούτων ὡς ἄρα αἱ Χριστῷ προσερχόμεναι ψυχαὶ αἱ μὲν οὔπω καιρὸν ἔχουσαι γάμου νεάνιδές εἰσιν, αἱ δὲ συνελθοῦσαι αὐτῷ ἤδη ἀνακραθέντι αὐταῖς αἱ μὲν εὐγένιδες καὶ ὑπεραναβεβηκυῖαι τὸν ἐν ἓξ ἡμέραις γενόμενον κόσμον. Ἑξηκοντά εἰσί βασίλισσαι...ἡ δὲ πάσας ὑπερέχουσα κατὰ τὸ πνεῦμα πεποιωμένη ὥστ᾽ εἶναι περιστερὰ τελεία τοῦ λόγου ἡ ἔνδοξος ἐκκλησία ἐστὶν ἡ μὴ ἔχουσα σπίλον ἢ ῥυτίδα. Cf. Apollinarius in Procopius (PG 87, 1721B): κοσμικὴ δὲ ἡ τοῦ προτέρου λαοῦ κλῆσις, καὶ τῇ ἐξάδι σύστοιχος τῇ κοσμογόνῳ.

[105] A comparison with how Apollinarius explains Ps 44 is instructive: the anointing is like filling an already full vessel so that it spills for the benefit of others: see Grünbeck (1994), 218-21: "Die Diskussion bei Apollinaris [on 44:8] setzt aber ein *Logos*-Mensch-Modell voraus. Zunächst ist sie in ihrer Ablehnung des Verdienstgedankens sicher antiorigenistisch...für Apollinaris die Unterscheidung zwischen Christus und den Christen ein zentrales Anliegen zu sein scheint. Die Christologie Diodors von Tarsus ist sehr viel differenzierter"(221). To agree with Mühlenberg (1985) that Apollinarius was opposing Origenist word-man with a Word-(Super)Man schema ignores (a) Origenism was not so 'Pelagian' as Grünbeck describes; (b) the likelihood he is opposing Photinians, as Hübner (1989) has argued.

[106] Gronewald II, p. 282, 13f: οὕτω γοῦν ἐκκύπτει ὡσεὶ ὄρθρος ἡ νύμφη τοῦ λόγου, ἡ τελεία ψυχή, ἡ ἐκκλησία ἡ νυμφοστοληθεῖσα αὐτῷ.

[107] Gronewald IV, p. 48, 9-11: ἐν τῷ ᾄσματι γοῦν τῶν ᾀσμάτων ὁ Ἰησοῦς πρὸς τοὺς ἑταίρους ἑαυτοῦ ἔλεγεν · φάγετε, πίετε, μεθύσθητε, ἀδελφοί. τοῖς ἀδελφοῖς ἑαυτοῦ ὁ θεὸς λόγος λέγει ταῦτα· ἐνανθρωπήσας γὰρ ἔσχεν ἀδελφοὺς τοὺς κατ᾽ αὐτὸν πολιτευομένους, τοὺς τὰ μαθήματα αὐτοῦ δεχομένους καὶ υἱοποιουμένους.

[108] Cf. Simonetti (1984), 143, n. 45.

fragments on the Psalms where Didymus comments on eight verses from the Song.[109]

Unlike Evagrius Ponticus, who seems to have elevated the soul of Christ to a state where it is the redeeming element in the Incarnation, and where it, rather than the Logos, joins to the man, Gregory of Nyssa wants to say that the ψυχή in Christ must be seen as having soteriological significance by its unassuming modesty which leaves other human souls and wills free to imitate or not to imitate and so participate in salvation.[110] M.N. Esper[111] is right to point to the thinking of the Song in Gregory's own terms as "about the admixture of the human soul to the divinity", and "the prepared... partnering, through which the soul, cleaving to the Lord, becomes one spirit."[112] But Esper is on less sure ground when he claims that, for Gregory the promise of the soul's becoming "one spirit" is realised in a sort of meeting of νοῦς with Νοῦς. He is too much influenced by Mühlenberg's doubtful thesis that God's Infinity (for Gregory) means that only the intellect (once separated from human senses) could partner him.[113] The difference that the Incarnation makes to Gregory's philosophy is that, during the engagement period of the 'the fitted partnering', there takes place something more than a mere reassuring "sense of his presence" (Canévet-Daniélou), namely an awareness in ordinary, earthly but believing souls that their lives and the creation around them are being transformed by his *earthly* presence.[114]

L.F. Mateo-Seco maintains that Gregory on the Song has little to say about Christology. F. Viret's recent introduction to Gregory on Ecclesiastes has confirmed this opinion: of the Solomonic works it is the latter book which speaks prophetically of Christ's *descensus*, leaving the soul's *ascensus* for *after* the Incarnation.[115] Yet this means that the Commentary on the Song says comparatively little about the Incarnation because it merely presupposes it. For example, the passage about the winter being past and the "now" being summer hinges on the understanding that the Incarnation, which was the spring-time, the μεθόριος, is growing increasingly fuller, due to the spreading of the Word's ἐπίνοιαι. The commentary itself is suffused with a sense of the presence of the theme of the Incarnation. Furthermore the ascent of the humanity very much starts simultaneously with the descent of the

---

[109] Mühlenberg (1975).

[110] Jaeger (1954), 79, n.1; Gregory's last works were anthropological rather than theological.

[111] Esper (1979), 45-48.

[112] The two texts are: τὸ δὲ νοούμενον τῆς ἀνθρωπίνης ψυχῆς ἡ πρὸς τὸ θεῖόν ἐστιν ἀνάκρασις. (GNO VI, 22, 19 - 23, 1); ...τῆς ἀκηράτου συζυγίας ἁρμοζομένης, δι'ἧς ἡ κολλωμένη τῷ κυρίῳ ψυχὴ ἓν πνεῦμα γίνεται (GNO VI, 24, 20 - 25, 1).

[113] Mühlenberg (1966), especially 185-205.

[114] Cf. *Contra Eunomium* III/2, 121-22; GNO I, p. 92.

[115] See Viret (ed.) (1996), p. 83.

Groom in embodied form. Gregory seems to see his addressees as being touched by the timelessly incarnate One.

The ideal response by the soul is spelled out at the end of the final Homily, on "She is one to her mother" (Cant 6:9b): "So when the one begotten from the Spirit is spirit, the child is the dove and the mother of the child must be (πάντως) dove."[116] Here, if nowhere else, the perfect one as "dove" is not the Logos, but is distinctively 'female' and not only of a dove-temperament/virtue but of a spirit nature.[117] She is heading towards the perfect husband (as in Eph 4:13 ἄνδρα not ἄνθρωπον τέλειον),[118] because she is chosen 'to' ('in the eyes of', *not* 'by', as Gregory is hardly predestinarian) her mother, the Holy Spirit.

The above passage shows us how much the bride-souls choose, with the freedom the Spirit gives, their salvation. Writing about "die physischen Erlösungslehre", R. Hübner that this doctrine "ihr Fundament in der Gleichsetzung von Menschheit Christi und Kirche hat."[119] But Hübner's point is that Gregory developed his *non-universalist* "physische Erlösungslehre" as the assumption of the *Church* not so much from a belief that the Word assumed universal humanity and repaired its fragmentation than from a wish (shared with Marcellus) to define Christ's humanity (which is the object of subordination at the end of the kingdom, with reference to the exegesis of 1 Cor 15:28) as the Church.[120] Gregory believed not in a *physischen Heilsautomatismus*, but held that one starts with the whole of humanity which is given the *potential* for salvation as a power coming out into the world in *Church* history for a finite number of those who do choose to fill the space marked out by Christ's own soul. The identification of soul and Church by Gregory is parallelled by a passage in *De Instituto*

---

[116] GNO VI, 468, 9-12: τῷ γὰρ τέκνῳ πάντως ἡ τοῦ γεγεννηκότος ἐπιθεωρεῖται φύσις. ἐπεὶ οὖν τὸ γεγεννημένον ἐκ τοῦ πνεύματος πνεῦμά ἐστι, περιστερὰ δὲ τὸ τέκνον· περιστερὰ πάντως καὶ ἡ τοῦ τέκνου μήτηρ ἐστίν,... .

[117] In a review of Langerbeck's edition of the Homilies on the Song, referring to the latter's comment that the linking of "mother" with the idea of "cause" was a case of Gnosticism seeping in, H. Dörries (1963), 576 retorts: " Wenn bei Gregor ἡ τῶν ὄντων αἰτία als 'Mutter' bezeichnet wird...so wird man dabei schwerlich an die von Origenes erwähnte aus dem Syrischen abgeleitete Vorstellung des Hebräerevangeliums vom Hl Geist als Mutter zu denken haben."

[118] GNO VI, 467, 17-468, 1: ὁ τοίνυν ἐκ μὲν νηπίου πρὸς ἄνδρα τέλειον ἀναδραμὼν διὰ τῆς αὐξήσεως καὶ φθάσας εἰς τὸ μέτρον τῆς νοητῆς ἡλικίας, ἐκ δὲ τῆς δούλης τε καὶ τῆς παλλακίδος τὴν τῆς βασιλείας ἀξίαν μεταλαβών, δεκτικὸς δὲ τῆς τοῦ πνεύματος δόξης γενόμενος δι᾿ ἀπαθείας καὶ καθαρότητος, οὗτός ἐστιν ἡ τελεία περιστερά...

[119] Hübner, (1971), 229. There is no "physical" redemption of *all humanity* at the moment of Incarnation; merely the introduction of a vivifying force, a leaven, *contra* Harnack.

[120] Ibid., 214.

Christiano.[121] It is not an archetype which was assumed, but rather the collected and distilled essence of 'the whole Church', which, as F. Dünzl explains:"die alle menschlichen *Individuen* umfaßt"(*my emphasis*). Hübner is right to suggest the tag of *physische Erlösungslehre* be dropped since it is only in the resurrection (of Christ, then of believers) that the body is mixed through with divinity. Until then the soul has to choose to discipline its warring members.

Unfortunately, Seibt claims, Hübner's idea is too simplistic and has been given wider currency by Grillmeier's acceptance of it — with his characteristic clarity.[122] Even Seibt however admits that Marcellus played a role in "der allgemeinen Ekklesiologisierung der Christologie".[123] There is a continuum between the incarnate form and the ecclesial form. "Markell bettet diese inkarnationische Hoheits-Christologie immer in die *Ekklesiologie* ein. Entweder sogar so, daß er die Inkarnationsgebundenheit christologischer Titel *aus der Wirklichkeit der Kirche ableitet* (Jesus, 'Großer Priester', 'der als Sohn Gottes Vorherbestimmte', der von Gott geliebte Mensch, Jesus als 'Grund') oder aber die christologische Anthropologie *auf die Kirche überträgt*."[124] Gregory shared the concern to make sure that the assumed 'man' was no universal or pre-existent reality but was the totality of those on their way to be saved — the finite number of souls both at the present time and ultimately.[125]

What all this means for the interpretation of the Song is that Gregory, inspired by the figure of the Groom (Cant 5:10-16), then the Bride (Cant 6:8), took the one who reveals glory to be both the Word and the ideal form of the Church which incorporates his raised humanity. As F. Dünzl suggests,[126] while the whole thrust of the Homilies on the Song is sufficient evidence that Gregory saw religion very much in individual terms, it was predicated on the potential human condition or φύσις, an "überindividuelle"[127] abstraction from the mass of the eschatologically finite number of human beings.[128] As

---

[121] GNO VIII/1, 61, 14-19: "Ἵνα παραστήσω αὐτὸς ἑαυτῷ τὴν ἐκκλησίαν ἔνδοξον (Eph 5:27) ...καινὴν κτίσιν ἐκάλεσε τὴν ἐν καθαρᾷ καὶ ἀμώμῳ ψυχῇ καὶ πάσης ἀπηλλαγμένῃ κακίας καὶ πονηρίας καὶ αἰσχύνης ἐνοίκησιν τοῦ ἁγίου πνεύματος.

[122] Seibt (1994), 173, referring to Grillmeier (1979), 434 "...formuliert Grillmeier, daß der Logos als Dynamis in Gott bleibend— 'nur' als Energeia (ἐνεργείᾳ μονῃ) zur Vereinigung mit der Menschheit abgesondert wird (χωρίζειν)."

[123] Seibt (1994), 518.

[124] Ibid., 517.

[125] Hübner (1974).

[126] Dünzl (1994), 180f.

[127] Ibid., 175. Cf. GNO VI, 468, 18f: φύσις δὲ πᾶσίν ἐστι πρὸς τὸ μακάριόν τε καὶ ἐπαινούμενον τῇ ἐπιθυμίᾳ συντείνεσθαι.

[128] Dünzl (ibid., 171-73) comes close to identifying this with Heideggerian "Being" after the manner of Karl Rahner.

souls (like queens) draw near to the ecclesiastical cosmos, the beautiful order within which the ideal Church takes her place, they feel more aware of the Word's presence to them and can respond directly to him. Gregory's Christology is not, as perhaps Hübner assumed, so much shaped by the Church, but Christology with its implications for creation sets the Church in the context of a new order.

Bearing in mind that for Cyril συνάφεια denoted a much looser connection than did ἕνωσις,[129] the soul is the Bride to the Word by that mystical union (συνάφεια), as she had been his sister by the common property of ἀπάθεια. This is clear from his comments on Cant 6:8f:

> They (the angels), calling her sister through the kinship of *apatheia*; but Bride on account of the 'mystical union', say: 'Since your eye is one in looking towards the One, and the soul is one on account of being divided for various dispositions, and the setting of your neck has perfection, lifting the divine yoke on herself (for this is "by the ornament of the neck", thus the yoke of the Lord), for this reason we confess that you have heartened us with wonders — i.e., you have made for us a soul and a mind for the apprehension of the light through itself. For in you we apprehend the sun of righteousness, as in a mirror'.[130]

The idea here is of the soul who is no ordinary soul, but is the perfect one which individual belivers come to participate in, a soul which the Church seems to borrow in order to receive divine revelation and salvation. It was this soul which allowed God to descend to Hades. "Through the (symbol of) myrrh and aloes it was announced to the saints who had gone before that the Christ was buried. For having come down to Hades he led them out. On the Cross he received death on behalf of men. But his heart lies awake, wherefore as God he spoiled Hades."[131]

A still closer identification between Church and Christ's humanity in the person of the Bride is found in Apponius. According to his exposition, the

---

[129] Cf. Lampe (1961), 1309.

[130] PG 69, 1288D-1289A: ἀδελφὴν μὲν αὐτὴν καλοῦντες, διὰ τῆς ἀπαθείας συγγένειαν· νύμφην δὲ, διὰ τὴν πρὸς τὸν Λόγον συνάφειαν. Ἐπεὶ οὖν, φησὶν, ὁ ὀφθαλμός σου εἰς ἓν τῷ πρὸς τὸ ἓν βλέπειν, καὶ ψυχὴ μία διὰ τὸ μὴ πρὸς διαφόρους διαθέσεις μερίζεσθαι, καὶ ἡ θέσις τοῦ τραχήλου σου τὸ τέλειον ἔχει, τὸν θεῖον ζυγὸν ἐφ' ἑαυτῆς ἀραμένη (τοῦτο γὰρ τὸ ἐνθέματι τραχήλου σου, εἶτ' οὖν ὁ τοῦ Κυρίου ζυγὸς), τούτου χάριν ὁμολογοῦμεν ὅτι τοῖς θαύμασιν ἡμᾶς ἐκαρδίωσας· ὅπερ ἐστὶ ψυχήν τινα καὶ διάνοιαν πρὸς τὴν τοῦ φωτὸς κατανόησιν δι' ἑαυτῆς ἡμῖν ἐνεποίησας. Καὶ γὰρ ἐν σοὶ τὸν τῆς δικαιοσύνης ἥλιον, ὡς ἐν κατόπτρῳ, κατανοοῦμεν.

[131] PG 69, 1289B: Διὰ δὲ τῆς σμύρνης καὶ τῆς ἀλόης, ὅτι ἐνταφιασθεὶς ὁ Χριστὸς ἐκοινώνησε τοῖς προλαβοῦσιν ἁγίοις· κατελθὼν γὰρ εἰς ᾅδου τούτους ἀνήγαγεν... . Ἐν τῷ σταυρῷ, φησὶ, τὸν ὑπὲρ ἀνθρώπων ἀναδεχόμενος θάνατον· ἀγρυπνεῖ δὲ ἡ καρδία, καθ' ὃ ὡς Θεὸς τὸν ᾅδην ἐσκύλευσεν. Cf. Origen, *schol in Cant.* 6.7 (PG 17, 277C).

soul of Christ goes on working in history and providence so that world-history itself becomes salvation-history. But he has really introduced 'eschatology' into the Origenian schema, and the beginnings of connections between the imagery of the Song and that of the Apocalypse can be detected in his commentary.[132] Since the biblical text moves from prophecy to a glimpse of fulfilment, from the Old to the New Testament, the interpretation likewise charts a salvation-historical spiritual voyage of a people, the Roman and hence the universal human race, from searching at the start of the Christian era to finding and being found; in the last book there is a corresponding futuristic element — the enabling of God and flesh to co-exist in an everlasting union.

The union is made possible by the oneness of Christ whose soul can make room for worthy souls. However, the soul as that which bridged (not enveloped) both divinity and humanity is not 'the person', but in the best analysis is a metaphysical 'fiction' working behind the scenes, known by its effects. Apponius, while indebted to Origen, does not try to relate the soul of Christ (or something resembling it) to the person-natures schema, as did Leontius of Byzantium.[133] In Apponius, the soul fulfills the mediating role by being his vehicle for the raid on hell and also, with the body returned, by allowing human weakness to contravene nature and enter heaven.

The Spirit plays the role of facilitating the bond between Word and soul and also of revealing to the outside world the inner truth. This can be seen in the passage's continuation (to paraphrase): Now that the devil is removed, the nature of flesh is the dwelling of divinity; the Word actually dwelt in our nature and also taking this soul from the stuff of our souls united 'her' to himself through the co-tenancy of the Holy Spirit.[134] This may well be the acme of the expression of Apponian Christology of the mediating soul of Christ; it is also Apponius at his most elliptical. For instance, the subject is again far from clear, but appears to be the 'Word-became-flesh', "the one who by joining himself to the flesh as the Word made flesh dwelled among us, which (flesh) he drew from our nature from the virgin Mary"; in other words, there is no synthesis of Word and soul. The *contubernium* means the Spirit's co-dwelling in the womb of the Virgin, and is related to the preparatory work done to purify the flesh so it can receive the Word. What

---

[132] To be continued in, e.g., the work of Beatus of Liebana (late C8).

[133] Cf. Grillmeier (1989), 190-241.

[134] IX, 275-87; CCL 19, p. 224: "... per quam et in qua, contra rerum naturam, caelos mirabiliter ingressa est humana fragilitas; per quam, expulso diabolo, aula deitatis effecta est carnis natura. Is enim qui Verbum caro factum adunando se carni habitavit in nobis, quam de nostra natura traxit ex Virginis visceribus — secundum evangelistae sententiam dicentis: *Et Verbum caro factum est, et habitavit in nobis* (Jn 1:14)—, et hanc *unicam* animam de nostra materia animarum sibi indissolubiliter univit, id est per contubernium Spiritus sancti, qui corporaliter super eam semper mansurus in Iordane descendit."

the Spirit did at baptism was to confirm this visibly (*corporaliter*). H. König's confidence[135] that there is an 'Augustinian' theme of the revelation of the Trinity in Christ's baptism in Apponius' treatment ("daß er die in der Taufe offenbarte Gottheit Christi als die Gottheit der Trinität betrachtet"), stretches the evidence which speaks more of the outward declaration at the baptism of the mysterious truth that the human soul is united with God. However, there is at least a hint that the descent of the dove is equivalent to the seal of the Spirit, that with the baptism what was initiated by the Spirit is announced publicly by the Spirit,[136] who then led that soul to the perfection of the Father through her death and resurrection. It is in this sense that her epithet "dove" is brought in from Cant 6:9: it relates to the moral purity of the Holy Spirit with whom she associates and can thus be sanctified, while "perfect" relates to the eschatological authority of God the Father which she obtains.

There is a place in Apponius for the Holy Spirit not only as the cause of the Soul-Logos union but also as the *product* of the union. However, in the latter case, the identification is hardly even implicit. He does not think the Spirit 'proceeds economically' from the chosen soul:[137] there is only an inchoate understanding of some connection between *spiritus* and *caritas* which are available to humans. The key verse (Rom 5:5) where God is said to have poured his love into "our hearts" by means of the Spirit, is more crucial for Augustine than for Apponius.[138] And yet it would seem that the collective humanity of the Incarnate Saviour is the point for the distribution of divine love, as it was for Origen. 'She' holds other souls together as the place of salvation, where the Word of God meets them through the Spirit's production of souls who, in terms reminiscent of 'Syriac' theology, is called *genetrix*.[139]

Apponius comes closest to Augustinian Christology when he observes that the divine nature existed within Christ on account of the pure soul's acting as a buffer. For this the Spirit chose her alone, completely sinless to outshine all.[140] It is clear that Apponius thinks that 'she' was the crucial component in the Redeemer's mission. The human soul of Christ is not a 'common human

---

[135] König (1992), 182, n. 55.

[136] Following the insight of Stubenrauch (1991), 82.

[137] See Stubenrauch (1991), 79-88, esp. 87: "Er verstand die Einwohnung des Heiligen Geistes in die Seele Jesu als die theologische Ermöglichung ihrer innigsten Einheit mit dem Wort Gottes und damit der menschlichen sarx."

[138] *Pace* Stubenrauch (1991), 88.

[139] IX, 298-312; CCL 19, p. 225.

[140] IX, 288-95; CCL 19, p. 225: "*Columba*, virtutibus Spiritus sancti cum operatione in omnibus coaequata; *perfecta* autem, Dei Patris omnipotentiam in omnibus obtinendo. Quae sola et *unica*, Dei Verbo, ut ductilis materia igni, adhaerendo, unum redemptorem, solum iudicem, unicum Filium Patris saeculis condonatum ostendit. Quam praevidens Spiritus sanctus in medio animarum sanctarum *unam* solam sine peccati initio vel fine omnibus praefulgere... ."

soul'. If anything she is the beneficiary and benefactor as were 'the martyrs', just as the North Italian Chromatius made clear when he asserted that the humanity of the martyrs were the clothes assumed by the Groom.[141] The passage which follows 'she' is a unique human soul on account of the fact that sin was excluded in the soul's refusal to give room in her will to it:

> 'She is unique to her mother', the synagogue, the Hebrew people who, according to the flesh, bore him whose soul never gave sin the execution of her will; she alone, though she had all human properties, is proven to be alone in not having this. Elect to her *genetrix*, that is, no doubt, to the power of the Almighty who generates all souls [in the womb], who filled the blessed Virgin Mary with 'her' shadow at his conception.[142]

However, there is also, quite distinctly, her *genetrix*, who is the power of the Most High who "generates" all souls — identified with the Holy Spirit.[143] The complete identification with ordinary humans in her origins is underlined by the statement that this soul was generated (*generari*) like all other souls by the Spirit: Apponius is no traducianist. Yet, turning to his other front, against "Fotinus", Apponius asserts that it was not a matter of some representative human soul being assumed by divinity but rather the special soul of Jesus whom the Spirit saw from before as worthy of being descended upon, due to her union with the Word.[144] Here Apponius is not only concerned with the question of the humanity of Christ as the revealer in human mode of the Divine Redeemer[145], but also with the essential uniqueness of that soul as somehow symbolic of the essential Oneness of God.

Apponius feels he needs to make sure that there is no confusion here. So, 'she' is unique to her mother in that she had a non-human mode of procreation. That 'she' is chosen to "her" *genetrix* does not mean she was the Spirit's only one, or the only one created by the Spirit — Apponius insists on

---

[141] SC 154; Sermon 15, s. 4: "Denique, una tunica corporis Christi totum mundum vestivit. Et quamvis exuerit se Dominus tunicam carnis in passione, non tamn nudus erat, quia habebat indumenta virtutum." There is here, more than in Apponius, a typically Western emphasis on salvific death.

[142] IX, 298-306; CCL 19, p. 225: "Manifestissime scilicet *unica est matri suae* synagogae, plebi hebraeae, quae eum genuit secundum carnem cuius anima numquam dedit voluntatis suae dexteram peccato: quae sola, cum omnia hominis habeat, hoc solum non habuisse probatur. *Electa est genetrici suae,* illi proculdubio virtuti Altissimi quae omnes animas generat...quae beatam Virginem Mariam in eius conceptu sua obumbratione implevit... ."

[143] König (1992), 184, n. 54.

[144] *Expositio* IX, 310f; CCL 19, p. 225: "Quae virtus, dum iussione sua omnem multitudinem generet animarum, ut unus in trina potentia Deus agnosceretur, unam elegit per quam mundi ostenderet salvatorem: non sicut Fotinus blasphemando multos asserit salvatores... ."

[145] As König thinks (*Ibid.*, 184, n. 54).

'creationism', the Spirit's quickening for all souls. Rather, she is the Spirit's *choice* for the redemption of the man to be made who is to be depraved by the devil, i.e., of all humans born. She will do this by mediating between the strength of divinity and the weakness of flesh.[146] She is not special by nature and then chosen, but is necessarily different because of the function she was made to perform. Thus the election took place *ante saecula in praescientiam*. The preposition *in* with accusative may be merely a late Latinism; the point is that *contra* Photinian adoptionism, it did not happen in time, nor yet was her being 'pre-existent' (contra Apollinarianism). Stubenrauch avers that Apponius understood a pre-existent Jesus in (the form of) the Holy Spirit[147] and that Christ and the Spirit were, for him, indistinguishable in the heavenly realm.[148] However Stubenrauch over-stretches the evidence by his suggestion that the Spirit, in heaven, was somehow pregnant with the soul of Christ.[149] He may well be right to claim that some sort of spiritual-conceptual pre-existence is at least implicit in Apponius (which is as much as Grillmeier had allowed).[150] However this soul is no eternal agent, providing the one person who holds together the two natures;[151] *personam* merely means 'the outward expression'. As a formative 'idea' perhaps, she is said to be "sent" into the body, already formed, to mediate between the two spheres represented by her

---

[146] IX, 319f; CCL 19, p. 226: "*Unica est* ergo *matri suae*, genti hebraeae, quae sola de homine quidem nata, sed non humano ordine procreata...". IX, 320-27; CCL 19, p. 226: "*electa est genetrici suae,* supradictae virtuti, ante saecula in praescientiam, ad redemptionem creandi hominis, per liberam voluntatem a diabolo depravandi. Nam, ut doceret omnes animas hominum non a corporibus sed ab eius potentia generari, non dixit: Unica est genetrici suae – sicut de synagoga dixerat*: Unica est matri suae* –, sed ostendit inter multitudinem animarum unam esse *electam,* mediatricem inter robur divinitatis et carnis fragilitatem."

[147] Stubenrauch (1991), 102: "Mit der etwas einfältigen, aber sinnenfälligen Allegorisierung des Lammbildes zum Symbol des geistgesalbten Christus und der Verwendung dieses Bildes im soteriologischen Kontext der von jenem gewährten Sündenvergebung gelingt es ihm, die Existenz Jesu in besonderer Weise als eine Proexistenz im Heiligen Geist zu begreifen."

[148] Ibid., 185, n. 60.

[149] Cf. Origen/Rufinus, *De Principiis* II, 2,2 (Koetschau, p. 30): "In hac ipsa ergo sapientiae subsistentia quia omnis virtus ac deformatio futurae inerat creaturae, vel eorum quae principaliter exsistunt vel eorum quae accidunt consequenter, virtute praescientiae praeformata atque disposita."

[150] For Grillmeier (1979), 569, it was merely a case of: "Spielen mit der Idee der Präexistenz der Seele."

[151] IX, 326ff; CCL 19, p. 226: "Quae in se verum Deum veramque carnem adunatam, unam personam ostendit. Quae missa in corpus, cum corpore egressa, intactum uterum Virginis derelinquens, nec ante se nec post se habendo consortem nascendi, unica effecta, est Virgini matri, quae mammas lactigeras porrigendo iure dicitur mater, et *virtuti Altissimi* (Lk 1: 35), quae se per Esaiam prophetam genetrix docuit animarum, iusta ratione tam gloriosa anima eius electa probatur."

4. The Bride

two types of 'mother figure' — Spirit and flesh. For that reason alone it is unlikely, *pace* König, that Apponius confuses *anima* with *sarx/caro*; rather the soul belongs to the middle order in the realms of being.

According to König, the *anima mediatrix* idea goes back to Origen.[152] She then confuses matters by referring to the *Menschgewordenen* as "the Soul of God" as in *De Principiis* II, 8, 5 as lying behind Apponius' usage. König argues that the Word made flesh is the Saviour, while the soul is the one who reveals who the Saviour is, and is thus to be equated with Christ's humanity. Yet at IX, 431-38[153] it is clear that it is only by uniting to the soul that the Word can become joined with the humanity and is thus a mediator *for* humanity. Neither in Origen nor Apponius does 'the soul' stand for the *Menschgewordenen* but is indeed conceived of as a (vital) part (*Bestandteil*) in him, his 'outwardness'. In the later writer the soteriological impact is described by extending the metaphor — the soul is like a coal which, lit by contact with fire, spreads the fire by coming into contact with dead coals. Stubenrauch, has helpfully shown how the saving effects of Christ and the Spirit are identified,[154] but the theme of the interchangeability of Word and Spirit is not really *à propos*; it is more in the light of Origen's *communicatio idiomatum* that the use of the coal metaphor should be applied. It is Christ, Word and soul locked together, who provides the blaze for other souls.[155]

Apponius moves on from metaphor towards a level closer to literal realism: the soul is said to bring to (spiritual) life all souls who believe in her and to beautify them (morally) as she is fair. She outshines all glorious ones, whether souls or stars in heavenly creation.[156] The impressionism of his description avoids a conceptually satisfying Origenist account of heaven, but at no time is his picture prey to the charge of a pre-existent scenario. Heaven and earth simply co-exist. To confirm this, Cant 6:10 is explained as the view of both which is the privilege of the celestial residents. A poetical doublet operates, in which the sense (but not the tenses) is chiastic.[157] What belongs to prescience is her election by the Spirit which is put into effect at the baptism in the Jordan. Access to the Word was built on the mediation of the perfect soul, an elect human being who was foreknown from all time. In

---

[152] König (1992), 186f, n. 64. *De Principiis* II, 8,4: "Unde videtur quasi medium quiddam esse anima inter carnem infirmam et spiritum promptum."

[153] CCL 19, p. 229.

[154] Stubenrauch (1991), 103-107.

[155] Cf. II, 25; CCL 19, p. 394f with XII, 17-18; CCL 19, p. 275.

[156] IX, 341ff; CCL 19, p. 226: "In quarum [viz. animarum] tamen medio, unica splendore ut luna, perfecta in caelo inter stellas, super omnes micare probatur in pulchritudinem sempiternam; et electa ut sol in maiestate paterna inter omnes virtutes caelestium potestatum... ."

[157] IX, 348ff; CCL 19, p. 226: "Viderunt eam scilicet quaecumque sunt virtutes, caelestis Hierusalem cives, ...claritati paternae unitam, nascentem in terris, pannis obvolutam, maiestatis gloria coruscantem... ."

down-to-earth terms, the human soul may well be understood in its effects, as the ordering authority of Christ within the Church.[158]

4.9 Conclusion

The need for Christ to be a perfect man, in the sense of completeness, was strong in the Marcellan-Antiochene tradition. Such a view seemed absurd to their opponents for whom perfection was moral, so that the Church as identified with the humanity of Christ and a Bride who seeks to be saved after 'marriage', would have seemed unhelpful. Yet the Antiochenes, for their part, made nothing of the Song in their Christology. The human form of Christ was to be reverenced like a saint, but not worshipped in the passionate way reserved for the deity which was invisible and to be sought mystically.

However for those more sympathetic to Platonism, the already and eternally pure sphere of the soul meant the Word-soul-Church nexus was central to a now renewed cosmology. The soul was often viewed in passive, 'feminine' terms by later Platonists.[159] For many commentators on the Song, it was the soul as an ideal of humanity, not humanity as such, with whom the Word as Groom was joined. The idea of a simple ether-like substance which alone was simple had already found an echo and some approval in the Pseudo-Clementine *Recognitiones*.[160]

Whether through influences Gnostic, philosophical or Origenian, the soul seems to have been elevated in the fourth century to a sort of δεύτερος λόγος, one which, to employ terminology at least as old as Philo, was προφορικός.[161] Thus, in Didymus, there is a tendency to view the soul as a

---

[158] IX, 515-19; CCL 19, p. 231: "Descendit ergo ad hortum suum et eius animae cui omne iudicium tradidit faciendum, demonstrando se Deum in carne, per quam a carneis oculis proximus videretur in terris, per quam colligeret velut manibus de convalle spinosa tribulationum ad paradisum sanctorum animas, ab inferis resurgendo." As König (1992), 198f, n. 92, shows, this replaces the Vulgate's *dedit* with *tradidit* which implies the inferiority of the one receiving.

[159] As a contemporary pagan parallels, Proclus, *In Tim*. II 260, 26 (Kroll, p. 29), mentions that the life-giving force of Psyche was symbolized in the Chaldean doctrine by her temples, hands and loins; also wreath and forehead. Like a girdle the cosmic soul constricts the universe; she comes from the *Intellect* of the Father and is represented by Hecate who mediates between intelligible and sensible worlds.

[160] *Recog* I, 28; Rehm-Paschke, p. 24: "...hominem fecit, propter quem cuncta praeparaverat, cuius interna species est antiquior et ob cuius causam omni aquae sunt, facta sunt." *Recog* VIII, 15, (p. 226): "Aristoteles etiam quintum introducit elementum, quod acatonomaston, id est inconpellabile nominavit, sine dubio illum indicans, qui in unum quattuor elementa coniungens mundum fecerit."

[161] Evidence in Photius *Bibliotheca*, cod 109; Henry, p. 80: "Λόγους τε τοῦ πατρὸς δύο τερατολογῶν ἀπελέγχεται, ὧν τὸν ἥττονα τοῖς ἀνθρώποις ἐπιφανῆναι,

4. The Bride

uniting principle, formally, if not materially.[162] Yet there is no real confusion with the Word himself — Didymus, like Origen was no Apollinarian that νοῦς should mean Logos and vice-versa.[163] If there was any blurring it was between νοῦς and πνεῦμα, especially in Alexandrian circles;[164] this allowed Apponius to speak of a soul who in a feminine, maternal way was able to envelope the human world through belonging to the Word.

However, among Syrian philosophers (e.g., Iamblichus[165]) and Syrian-influenced Christians (e.g., Gregory of Nyssa) πνεῦμα had a primary reference to the divine nature, so that a distinction between it and the human rational faculty was preserved. For Gregory, the Bride was absolutely ψυχή, in the sense of her being passive, earthly and contemplative, (while the Groom, divine but receiving humanity as his body, was active, not confined to earth and redemptive); yet Gregory's Platonism meant this soul was pure enough and sufficiently akin to the Word that, given her purification by the association with him, an intimate oneness of souls (as soul) and God was assured as an eschatological hope. This feature means that, in Gregory's perpetuation of the Origenian tradition, it is harder to speak of a very close union between soul and Logos.

The soul, then, can be viewed as that which, or better she who, by receptivity to the above and solidarity with the earthly, allowed the potentially blissful but actually agonic union in Christ to take place. The soul is an entity which mirrors the Logos in its ability to perform a unifying role,

---

μᾶλλον δὲ οὐδε ἐκεῖνον «Λέγεται μὲν καὶ ὁ Υἱὸς λόγος, ὁμωνύμως τῷ πατρικῷ λόγῳ, ἀλλ' οὗ νυν οὗτός ἐστιν ὁ σάρξ γενόμενος· οὐδὲ μὴν ὁ πατρῷος λόγος, ἀλλὰ δύναμίς τις τοῦ Θεοῦ οἷον ἀπόρροια τοῦ λόγου αὐτοῦ, νοῦς γενόμενος τὰς τῶν ἀνθρώπων καρδίας διαπεφοίτηκε." Cf. Frede (1987), 1074, who finds in Numenius the idea of two souls, one of which is not an irrational soul as much as "the wisdom of flesh and matter"— as in Origen *De princ* III,4,2, Koetschau 266, 17f. But it is doubtful that Numenius (fr 52,128) and Origen are discussing the same thing.

[162] The form, εἶδος, which guarantees the continuity between the mortal body and the body of the resurrection must be understood philosophically, as Crouzel has convincingly shown, as the particularizing form and therefore as the principle of substantial continuity. The soul carries this seminal reason (cf. Augustine also Stoic), which is the form of the body of each human.

[163] Origen and Apollinarius shared a tripartite anthropology: cf. *C Cels* II, 16 using Ps 15:6 to speak of the soul which separated, in order to redeem in Hades; however this was only as co-worker with the Word, not, as with Apollinarius, *as* the Word. What Richard (1945) says about *nous* as *hypostasis* in Apollinarius shows the similarities to Origen, despite Muhlenberg's protests.

[164] Didymus *In Zach*, IV, 237; SC 85, p. 924: ὁμολογοῦμεν τὸν Θεὸν Λόγον ἐπιδεδημηκέναι, τὸν ἐκ ψυχῆς καὶ σώματος καὶ πνεύματος τέλειον ἄνθρωπον ἀνειληφότα.

[165] Even in pagan circles, by the end of the fourth century theurgy in Iamblichus involved an uplift which the mind could not achieve by itself; it needed a higher agent for illumination and salvation.

to be realised eschatologically. This is not monopsychism but a truth realised in this life in the unity of love between those who cleave to the Logos.

Chapter 5

Conclusion

5.1 Factors militating against a Christology inspired by the Song's imagery

5.1.1 The limits of imagic theology
Those who saw God coming close to humanity in the Song thought that the inspired Scriptural text was transparent to divine revelation in a way analogous to the humanity in the Incarnation. Something similar could be claimed for the ascendant 'Neo-Chalcedonian' consensus, namely the iconodule belief that the human form could well represent the hidden divine.[1] Contrary to this however, and perhaps more persuasive at the time leading up to Chalcedon, was the notion that God continued to be revealed in his sacraments and Church, the latter perhaps the finest piece of redemptive recreation out of negativity. In the context of iconology Thümmel observes: "Eine Grundstimmung jener Zeit, die im Neuplatonismus ihren philosophischen Ausdruck gelden hätte...die göttliche Herrlichkeit sei nicht darstellbar. Das Göttliche ist das Geistige, das sich allen Sinnlichen entzieht".[2]

As A. Cameron has observed, the dual preoccupation of matters bodily and matters Christological should not be waved away as pure coincidence. She locates the real movement as from conceptual Christology to image, but implies that prior to this comes the anthropological development of the worth of the corporeal.[3] However, it can be contended that, in the crucial era of the fixing of doctrine up to 451 (and arguably during Justinian's era too), the opposite movement took place, at least officially, with the Song never serving or inspiring Christology, but occasionally pressed into service of pre-formulated doctrine. Nevertheless, the process for which Cameron promotes a case can perhaps be seen as having operated in a less obvious way. An interest in *eros* as the cosmological driving force was crucial in the collective imagination; the same applied to the Word, sustainer of universe by his power

---

[1] See Cameron (1994), esp., 222ff. For the early stages of iconographic controversy, cf. Thümmel (1994), Schönborn (1976).

[2] Thümmel (1994), 201.

[3] Cameron (1994), 226-30.

and action in the world — already seen in the simile of the Groom of Ps 18:6 LXX,[4] who comes close enough to be attractive, his descent to humiliation a further quality in his winsomeness. The stag in Christian art and poetry recalled the serpent/dragon's removal; the dove pointed to the simplicity, both moral and metaphysical and as πυροειδής περιστερός[5] was seen to have elemental powers.

Such trancendentals in Christian aesthetics as focussed more on actions in the heavenly realm according to a realism[6] — that there is something just behind the veil of visibility to be removed totally at death since glimpses of it have already come through it — than on metaphysical equations.

The popular triumph of folk religion, poetry and art over arid negative theology which served only to throw people back to experience and the natural world to find God at second hand, might suggest that the Song would have been a welcome source for early Byzantine theology. However, at an official level, the theology of revelation of God's very self as Logos became shrouded in 'negative theology'. So the imagic theology would have been unwelcome in expressing Christology. Yet icons involved the viewer, the reader; less defining than alluding and stirring the imagination, allowing space for mystery, encouraging personal engagement, worship and understanding too deep for words. The danger of reading icons wrongly meant any guiding text could not also be as impressionistic as the Song and its commentaries. The transfer of this spectacular theology into iconology demoted it from the realm of doctrinal Christology.

The Syriac tradition of poetry of love for God, from the *Odes of Solomon* to Ephraim, in which the writer invites the reader to step into the frame and become the passive bride observing, was also responsible for a refusal to objectify the Song's contents for the purpose of Christological dogma — most clearly in the case of Gregory of Nyssa. But the elevation of the ordinary soul that the 'Hellenistic' concept of *eros* allows, and which Gregory describes, would not have appealed to most in that tradition that they might have drawn on the Song *even* for their spirituality.

---

[4] καὶ αὐτὸς ὡς νυμφίος ἐκπορεόμενος ἐκ παστοῦ αὐτοῦ, ἀγαλλιάσεται ὡς γίγας δραμεῖν ὁδὸν αὐτοῦ.

[5] Picture Christology was of interest to the school of Gaza, if Procopius' works of *ekphrasis* on pictorial art and Hesychius of Jerusalem are anything to go by. See Friedländer (1939), 90-95. I would argue that the Christian *Physiologus* finds its inspiration in Origen's exegesis rather than vice-versa.

[6] Cf. Soskice (1985), 120. It seems the sense of a term cannot tell us everything about a thing (even a non-supernatural one) to which it refers; metaphor in theology is like a model in science which is *more than* an epistemic help, but follows traces and hints. God comes to us as cause in experience or imagined re-enactment while only "God" (the thought of him) comes to us by Anselm's conceptualising.

5. Conclusion

The fortunes of metaphor underwent a rise and fall during the period between the councils at Constantinople and Chalcedon. E. Grünbeck concludes her work by asserting that as a reaction to Eunomian scholasticism it came to be believed, particularly by Gregory of Nyssa, that biblical metaphor could be explained by metaphor yet still manage to express something about God. What ended this appreciation of theology by pictures was, in part, Cyril of Alexandria's literalistic method.[7] A preference for dialectic, and a conomitant focussing on the titles of Christ, took over.

5.1.2 "No" to mutuality in Christ

John McGuckin, in a defence of Cyrillian 'orthodoxy', has recently opposed Grillmeier's bias towards the attractive idea of the centre of Christ's being as psychological. He writes: "Neither the soul of Christ, nor the human *nous* were, for Cyril, the ultimate locus of personhood. For him this was to be strictly reserved for the hypostasis of the Logos."[8] The idea is that it is the Image of God only who is Person.[9] Cyril certainly had no place for a pre-existent entity other than the Word as 'the inner Christ'. The crucial idea was, as Abramowski has averred,[10] a Neo-Platonic standard: "the appropriate perfection of each object is union with its cause"; thus for Iamblichus it was possible and desirable to advance from the base that as human one is ὁμοιούσιος θεῷ towards a συναφή then a κοινώνια then ultimately a ἕνωσις with God. For Cyril this had already happened in Christ — unlike the Antiochenes (who inherited an emphasis on the distinctiveness of any ὑπόστασις from Trinitarian theology and for whom an ἀσύγχυτος ἕνωσις might have been a good compromise), ἕνωσις then described something a lot more intimate than did συναφή. We could compare the idea in Proclus of the soul's ascent to the intellect, in which the one who, as the One-multiple of *Parm.*144, E5, is not *primus inter pares* but is of a not dissimilar nature,[11] through a hierarchy, including a casting off of a tunic;[12] the One itself is no 'entity' but rather the principle of unity.[13]

Cyril even saw Christ's anointing with grace (really in the conception; symbolically in the Jordan-baptism) as done to the *Logos* for the sake of

---

[7] Grünbeck (1994), 413: "Die Einzelargumentation Cyrills von Alexandrien basieren auf der sprachlogischen Struktur. Die Metaphorik verliert an Gewicht."

[8] McGuckin (1994), 206 [with reference to Abramowski (1981)].

[9] Ct. Balthasar (1978) for whom, for soteriological reasons, one has to speak of "Personen in Christus" (see esp. 196ff).

[10] Abramowski (1981b).

[11] Proclus (1968-81); see I, 3 (p. 13).

[12] Ibid., (p. 16).

[13] Ibid., IV, 10 p. 32.

believers' nature[14] and thus there was no room in Christology for the mutuality which was at the heart of the Song's theme. Likewise in the post-Chalcedonian world it was spelled out by Diadochus of Photike that in terms of soteriology or 'action' within the one *eidos* there were two factors, but that the second (*passivum humanum*) was merely a recipient of the first (*activum divinum*).[15]

Yet even Cyril's opponents would agree that the humanity in Christ deserved no independent status. With particular reference to Nestorius, McGuckin writes: "Nestorius' thought on this point is comparable to Origen's notion of the soul of Jesus adhering in love so closely to the Logos that they become 'as it were' one... . The Cappadocians mediate Origen's influence on Christology to Nestorius."[16] Yet Theodoret, as a reader of Origen and a user of the concept of Divine Persona-human persona *schesis* coined by Gregory Nazianzen,[17] does not seem to have made himself vulnerable to the taint of 'two sons'. Nestorianism was a temptation Theodoret could resist. Likewise, the Chalcedonianism of Leo's 35th Epistle reveals how the notion of a pre-existent soul of Christ who, prior to embodiment, was united with the Logos, was identified with Eutychianism, not with a 'two sons' heresy.[18] Theodoret was enough of a Platonist to highlight unity at the expense of duality. He betrays some familiarity with matters numerological and philosophically monistic in his comments on Cant 8:8ff; the notion of the "supercelestial place" (ὑπερουράνιος) is another feature he shares.

As an Antiochene, Theodoret refused in his Psalm Commentary to allow that Scripture (or Ps 44 LXX at least) could be speaking simultaneously of the divinity and the humanity of Christ, or even of them in tandem. There were some images that seemed appropriate when speaking of *God* in symbolic

---

[14] Cf. ibid., 364-89. C. Markschies in a recent review (1996) wonders how much a verse like Ps. 44:2 was crucial in leading the fathers to their doctrine, and how much the latter controlled the exegesis of the former. While Origen and Arius were hesitant in using Ps 44:2 Christologically, since that would mean saying that the Son was an ἐρυγή of the Father, the Antiochenes saw Christ as a "word" from the Father's mouth. Of course, Cyril's position was that the Father did speak out the word but the latter in his constant return is equal and there is mutual influemce; the use of νοῦς as a philosophical equivalent for Father shows how Cyril employed his Platonism to good effect: see *Dialogue sur le Trinité*, II, 450; Durand (ed.), (1976), p. 322.

[15] See Grillmeier (1987), 233f. Cf. Beyschlag's controversial attack (1991) on the Grillmeier-De Halleux consensus that Chalcedon was really Cyrillian (127ff). "Das ist es, was Cyrill sagen will, wenn er das gott/menschliche Einssein Christi nicht nur als ἕνωσις κατὰ φύσιν, sondern zugleich und mit Vorliebe als ἕνωσις καθ' ὑπόστασιν, d.h. als 'individuierte Natur'... bzw. als 'eine Art personaler Einheit'...verständlich zu machen sucht (70-71)."

[16] Ibid., 163, n. 69.

[17] McGuckin (1994), 151.

[18] See Leo the Great (1932), VI, 16.

5. Conclusion

terms; for instance both Theodore and Diodore valued Ps 44 alone among the Psalms as directly pointing to Christ with the Church as his queenly bride. Because it speaks of preparation, and points through and beyond to the end-time consummation via the Incarnation, and not of an ongoing relationship, Psalm 44 was acceptable as a prophecy in a way the Song could not be. For Theodore, however, the dualism, to be anathematised in 553,[19] is to the fore: in Ps 44 the flesh which cloaked his divinity during the Incarnation is *not* the bride but the king's apparel. He will only 'wear' the bride-Church in the age to come. Grünbeck rightly remarks that in Theodoret's *Canticles* Commentary: "Es geht um die Gottheit und Schönheit des Bräutigams. Insofern als er erst noch erwartet und ersehnt wird, ist der Mensch gemeint; aber es besteht kein Zweifel, daß der Handelnde Gott ist."[20] Christ's outward beauty is his human virtue as a radiation from his fullness of divinity. The dismissal of neo-Arianism meant also that the Holy Spirit who inspired Scripture is co-equal with Father and Son and thus transcendent, and not one who holds a *Zwischenstellung* between God and Humankind. There was no *tertium comparationis*. For those of the school of Diodore, any idea that the coming of Christ had realised or 'consummated' the divine-human union was dangerously close to divinisation teaching and the *physichen Erlösungslehre*. In Antiochene circles it was unthinkable that humanity, even in its most perfect form, should be united to God in a way analogous to sexual congress, even within the special case of Jesus Christ.[21] Even on Psalm 44 Theodore manages to speak of the union of regeneration, of she as "queen" and of Christ as head of the body rather than of Bride and Groom.[22] Such avoidance of intimacy explains his reluctance to contemplate a spiritual message behind the text of the Song. Theodoret would correct his own low estimation of Christ's humanity by seeing it as one transfigured during the Incarnation in his (later) commentary on the Psalm.[23] For, as Grünbeck points out, in his

---

[19] *ACO*, 71: "...ut inseparabilem ad divinam naturam habens coniunctionem, relatione dei et intellectu omni ei creatura venerationem adtribuente. et neque duos dicimus filios neque duos dominos, quoniam unus filius secundum substantiam deus verbum, unigenitus filius patris...et dominus secundum substantiam deus verbum... ."

[20] Ibid., 362.

[21] See Abramowski (1981b).

[22] Devreesse, p. 288. Whereas G. Koch (1974), 241, contends that for Diodore (*In Rom* 5,13-14 and 7,1-3 Staab p. 83; 86), "So ist auch der Christus Haupt der Kirche, *insofern er als ihr Bräutigam bezeichnet wird...* . Ihr inneres Wesen wird begriffen aus ihrer Verbindung mit Christus" (my italics). Each soul's freedom to make a decision about Christ after baptism meant, for Diodore, that the Church was only "physically" or ontologically joined to the Word when each member so chose.

[23] See also the argument in *Eranistes*, Dial. III; (Ettlinger, ed.), pp. 193ff: it is not the soul which has immortality but the transformed whole human nature; even though it remains distinct and in some sense apart from the Word in heaven ('theologically' they are not united as closely as in the one person 'economically'; cf. p. 228).

commentary on Psalm 44, Theodoret is much more ready to underline the oneness of the Light with the enlightened humanity. In his earlier Commentary on the Song,[24] which shows the influence of the Antiochene view of the Incarnation as a 'cloaking', the humanity of Christ is too much associated with those sinners he came to save.

None of the writers examined executed a wholly Christological interpretation in the sense of relating all or many verses of the Song to the Incarnation, not even those, like Cyril and Theodoret who stood guard at the parting of the ways. In the commentaries, matters of spirituality preoccupied them, with the fact of the Incarnation as a background. Even for Apponius it is just one thing among others, much more to the fore in his Ninth Homily than elsewhere. The driving force is the inspiration spirituality gets from soteriology. Apponius hardly gives us Christology in terms of the relationship of agents (as modern people would understand it). The Bride-Soul is, as for Rufinus, a functionary which enables a union of two different substances.[25] Sex and marriage as metaphors to help sublimate, edify, and, most of all, encourage, was only for those who were spiritually minded; public Christological truth itself could not be metaphorical. Similarly, the soul-body metaphor became perceived as more a help than a hindrance in the era leading up to Chalcedon, partly because it meant people read the metaphor backwards as confirming that every soul had divine status.[26]

The mutual correspondance of Christology and biblical interpretation can be seen from the Song's treatment in the aftermath of our chosen period: Armenians and Jacobite Syrians, happier to countenance the metaphor of full, nuptial union, were keener on the Song's use as canonical than were Chalecedonian Syrians and Georgians,[27] while the Ethiopian Church, (as Euringer and Grillmeier have observed), actually made theological use of its imagery: "(i)nspiriert von der Bibel, und hier besonders durch das Hohelied, das alexandrinisch-allegorisch interpretiert wurde, zeigt die äthiopische Kirche eine große Vorliebe für Symbole und Bilder, deren Zahl kaum zu fassen ist."[28] S. Euringer had established that the Ethiopian Church did not

---

[24] Thus, Grünbeck (1994), 352-54.

[25] *In Symbolum Apostolorum* 11; CCL 20, 148f: "Anima ergo media, et in secreta rationabilis spiritus arce Verbum Dei capiente... . Et ideo nihil ibi turpe putandum est, ubi sanctificatio Spiritus inerat, et anima, quae erat Dei capax, particeps fiebat etiam carnis." It seems the soul was more naturally with God, having a special place for him, than with the flesh to which it needed miraculous binding. Souls may not be considered pre-existent, but they are other-worldly.

[26] Especially among the "Chalcedonians"; see Gahbauer (1984), 316-25; Liébaert (1975), 151ff.

[27] Tarchnishvili (1955), 327; cf. the full commentary on the Song by Armenian Gregory of Narek; see Thomson (1983).

[28] Grillmeier (1990), 372.

5. Conclusion

follow Syriac/Nestorian 'literal' exegesis.[29] A good example is the translation of Cant 1:5 as "the Sun [of righteousness] did not look on me." Euringer makes it clear that the tradition goes back to Origen in Procopius (PG 87, 1556), possibly through Philo of Carpasia (PG 40, 45f).[30] An even better case was the Ethiopic for ἀδελφιδοῦς μου which "wäre eine Umschreibung für: Gottesmensch."[31]

Yet such examples are of modest significance. The theme of two-way relationality in the Song, which occasionally inspired 'alternative' Christological interpretations, was left out by so many who did comment on it simply because the text itself presented the Bride and Groom not in relation to each other but as individual figures in the descriptive verses, while passages which described activity were taken to be about moral-spiritual behaviour in the absence of the Groom. As Meloni has observed,[32] when the Groom was invisible to the Bride his perfume went with him, leaving behind a bride who reproduces his aesthetic quality with ethical activity.

5.2 The abiding message: Love and loves

There is indeed a bond of love in Christ which included the dialectic of *agape* (condescending, or, in terms of the Song's imagery, descending to the garden and house) and *eros* (ascending like the deer on the mountains). A. Ceresa-Gastaldo notes that Jerome, in translating Origen's Homily on Cant 1:3, had preferred *effusum* (with reference to Mt 26:6's woman pouring ointment), while Rufinus renders *exanitum* which (with its allusion to Phil 2:7) is more theologically self-conscious.[33] Yet Origen meant *agape* in the Incarnation to be the overflow of fullness of the human Christ, a pouring out which is not the Word's *kenosis*. Although in the state of perfection where humans will be like God there will be an end of obstacles to transcend and choices between what are only possibilities, for the time being *eros* is required for the process of filling-up which is the presupposition of kenotic *agape*.[34] For Origen, only the

---

[29] Euringer (1936-37).
[30] Euringer (1937), 27.
[31] Ibid., 30.
[32] Meloni (1989), 46f.
[33] As in LXX: μύρον ἐκκενωθὲν ὄνομά σου. Likewise on Cant 1:5 he is keen to emphasise the translation *fusca* rather than mere *nigra* as Jerome (Baehrens, p. 37) who was probably following Symmachus ("*nigra*...in aliis exemplaribus": Baehrens, p. 113), in order to avoid the pejorative moral connotation of 'blackness'.
[34] Siclari (1985), 275: "la libertà si perfeziona nel dilatarsi dell'*eros* celeste, reso possibile dalla presenza e dalla venuta del Verbo. Già in Origene si profila dunque l'idea, sviluppata poi da Gregorio di Nissa e da Massimo il Confessore, che la libertà dalla scelta è la pienezza della libertà, e che essa si attua nella perfetta unione d'amore dove l'assoluta donazione di Dio provoca, senza però determinarlo, l'assoluto desiderio della creatura... ." As in

perfect actually love as *agape*; the *simpliciores* have *eros* to motivate them. But the whole vision inspired by the Song, especially Cant 6:8, is of a dialectic of *agape* and *eros*, according to the rhythm of the Incarnation in which humanity is divinised through its descent.

The idea of the Church as that which was assumed by the Word really operates to mean an ideal Church within a Church. Yet for most patristic interpreters, the concrete example of the realisation of the possibility of pure but passionate love was seen only in the martyrs' experience. Even then, Augustine and Epiphanius shared a reluctance to speak of any part of the Church as involved in the salvific process: the Church is like a bride preparing herself to be taken. According to P. Meloni, while the Song and Psalm 44 are the Bible's only *epithalamia*, the former is also a prophecy:

> È il canto di una coppia terrestre e di tutte le coppie del mondo, che manifestano l'aspirazione di tutta l'umanità con parole che hanno il sapore di una profezia. Profezia è la promessa di Dio che sarà mantenuta quando gli uomini potranno gustare la perfezione dell'amore. Il *Cantico* è la profezia dell'avvento dello Sposo divino nella carne umana. Il *Cantico* è profezia del sacramento nuziale cristiano (Ef 5,32).[35]

Meloni in the same passage goes on to suggest that in this schema the Word makes the human Christ, prepared from a waiting people, from Bride into Groom so that the present *Ecclesia triumphans* is somehow a divinised humanity in heaven and joined with the Word "come sposo di tutta l'umanità nella prospettiva futura." However, the fathers never went as far as that monism: love requires the maintenance of difference and even (the possibility of) distance.

The motif of 'call and response', which one recent theory has seen as central to any concept of 'the person',[36] is also prominent in the Song. Traditional soteriology too reckons that believers must be left free to play their responsive part and it is partly on these grounds that the consensus was that Jesus Christ was one *hypostasis*. At the level of ontology this is reinforced by the argument that since Christ, by his divine hypostasis *is* a person, Christ did not need to *have* a human person, merely a human nature or essence which he saves: each is called to existentialise their essence.[37]

Neoplatonic thinking the fall of souls was a personal matter, and thus their redemption "si fonda sulla volontà salvifica divina ed è richiesto, in ultima analisi, dalla natura stessa dell'amore... ." (276)

[35] Meloni (1989), 52.

[36] McFadyen (1990), Chs 4&5, who claims that a good relationship does not require its participants to be "equals" in it.

[37] Cf. John of Damascus *De fide orthodoxa* III, col 1024A; *De recta sententia*; PG 74, 1464BC.

5. Conclusion

God loves as a father of all: generally, the OT Wisdom books are as much about revelation to those outside the religious tradition as instruction for those within it. However, in Christ, the Son is an 'erotic' lover in that he does value human persons, although he may well not *need* them. It is more than an 'unconditional' love in the negative sense of that term. He values the visible and invisible good that human beings produce — hence their individuality is preserved. He does not simply say: "you are my child so I defend you as one of my own creations, nor because you have returned to me", but, taking the initiative, returns any responses with interest — in the Spirit who assures believers that they are loved. The Father's love for the Son is eternal; but souls have to seek it, or rather be available and 'in position' for it. Overall: if the Song showed these early Christians anything, it was that love was at the heart of the Incarnation, and that this had unique, transforming effects. As has been repeatedly demonstrated, divine-human love, as a religious theme of soaring transcendence in embodied state, of expectation and frustration, was transposed on the key of the Incarnation so as to become its dominant cadence.[38]

This work has claimed *not* that the Song was seen as depicting or symbolising a relationship between God the Word and the man in Christ but rather that these two are both described by the terms Bridegroom and Bride. *He* is the Word who does all, even to the point of writing the Scripture itself — a point made obvious in the Ps-Athansasian fragment[39], but with which all the authors examined would have concurred. *She* is the humanity who receives and gathers all, who, at least eschatologically, will be the one, assuming into herself as Christ's exalted humanity all souls who are drawn into her by his energies. The pouring together of images led to a blurring of referents — God, Word, Christ: Soul, Humanity, Christ. It meant a confusion of theology; ecclesiology and spirituality and Christology. After this period around 400 CE, when it seemed they might helpfully intermingle, they would once again pursue separate, if parallel, lines.

---

[38] See, e.g., Vacek (1994), esp. 321-26; Pelikan (1985), 122-32.
[39] See the beginning of Ch. 3.

Bibliography of Primary Works: Texts And Translations

Acta Conciliorum Oeconomicorum, E. Schwarz (ed.), Argentorati-Lipsiae-Berolini, 1914: IV/1, J. Straub (ed.), Berlin, 1971.

Ambrose, *De Isaac* , C. Schenkl (ed.), CSEL 32/1, Prague-Vienna-Leipzig, 1896, 639-700.

Apologia David Altera, C.Schenkl (ed.), CSEL 32/2, Prague-Vienna-Leipzig, 1897, 357-408.

De Spiritu Sancto, O. Faller, M. Petschenig (eds.), CSEL 79, Vienna-Leipzig, 1964.

In Ps 118, M. Petschenig (ed.), CSEL 62, Vienna, 1913.

De Obitu Valentiniani, In: *Le Orazioni Funebri*, G Banterle (ed.), (Sancti Ambrosii Episcopi Mediolanensis Opera Omnia 18), Rome, 1985.

Guglielmo di Saint-Thierry: Commento Ambrosiano al Cantico dei Cantici, G.Banterle (ed.), (Sancti Ambrosii Episcopi Mediolanensis Opera Omnia 27), Rome, 1993 (=PL 15, 1851-1962).

De fide ad Gratianum, O. Faller (ed.), CSEL 78, Leipzig 1962.

Ambrosiaster, *Quaestiones de Veteri et Novo Testamentis*, = *Pseudo-Augustini, Quaestiones Veteris et Novi Testamenti* CSEL 127, ed. A. Souter, Vienna-Leipzig, 1908.

Apollinarius *in Canticum* (from: *Procopius Gazaei In Cantica Canticorum*). PG 87, 1545-1780.

In: Mühlenberg, E. (ed.) *Psalmenkommentare aus der Katenenüberlieferung: Apollinaris von Laodicea zu Ps 1 bis 150; Didymus der Blinde zu Ps 1 bis 150*. (3 vols), Berlin, 1975, 1977, 1978.

Apponius, *In Canticum Canticorum Expositio*, B. Vregille and L. Neyrand (eds.), CCL 19, Turnhout, 1986.

Commentaire sur le Cantique des Cantiques, B. Vregille and L. Neyrand (eds., trs.), SC 420, Paris, 1997.

Apostolic Fathers,The, I/2 J.B. Lightfoot (ed.), London, 1890.

Apuleius: *Apuleius: The Golden Ass*, P. Walsh (ed.), Oxford, 1994.

Athanasius, *Fragmenta in Cantica Canticorum*. PG 27, 1349-61.

Epîtres à Serapion sur la divinité du St. Esprit, J. Lebon (ed.), SC 15, Paris, 1947.

Augustine, *De Genesi Contra Manicheos.*, PL 34, 173-220.

Enchiridion, E. Evans (ed.), CCL 46, Turnhout, 1969.

De sancta virginitate, PL 40, 395-428.

Sermo 138, PL 38, 763-769.

Sermones de Vetero Testamento, C. Lambot (ed.), CCL 41, Turnhout, 1961.

Enarrationes in Psalmos I-L , D.E. Dekkers, I. Fraipont (eds.), CCL 38, Turnhout, 1956.

De Doctrina Christiana, *CCL* 32, J. Martin (ed.), Turnhout, 1962, 1-167.

De Trinitate, W.J. Mountain (ed.), *CCL* 50, Turnhout, 1968.

De Civitate Dei, B. Dombart-A. Kalb (eds.), 1981 (=CSEL 40).

Basil of Caesarea, Letter *CCCLXIV*; see Loeb Classics Basil IV: R.J. Deferrari (ed.), London-Cambridge, MA, 1961, 361-366.

Bernard of Clairvaux, *On the Song of Songs*, K. McDonnell, I. Edmonds (transls.), Kalamazoo, 1980-81. (Based on J. Leclercq, H.M. Rochais, C.H. Talbot (eds.), *Sancti Bernardi Opera* (Rome: Editiones Cistercienses), 1957-77.

Chromatius: *Chromace d'Aquilée: Sermons*, J. Lemarié (ed.), *SC* 154 & 163, 1969; 1971.

Chromatii Opera, R Étaix - J. Lemarié (eds.), *CCL* 9a, Turnhout, 1974.

Clement of Alexandria, *Clement d'Alexandrie: Stromateis*, A. Le Boulluec, P. Voullet, Paris, 1985.

Cosmas Indicopleustès, *Topographie chrétienne*, Vol. I, W. Wolska-Conus (ed.), SC 141, 1968.

Cyril of Alexandria, *Sancti Patris Nostri Cyrilli Archiepiscopi Alexandrini* Vols VI & VII, P.E. Pusey (ed.), Oxford, 1875-77.

Select Letters, L.R. Wickham (ed.), Oxford, 1983.

Dialogues sur le Trinité, G.M.de Durand (ed.), *SC* 231, 237, Paris, 1976, 1977.

Scholia in Canticum Canticorum, PG 69, 1277-1294 (A. Mai, 1864).

Didymus: *Didymus der Blinde, Psalmenkommentar*, M. Gronewald(ed.), Bonn, I (1969), II (1968), III (1969), IV (1969).

Psalmenkommentare aus der Katenenüberlieferung: Apollinaris von Laodicea zu Ps 1 bis 150; Didymus der Blinde zu Ps 1 bis 150 (3 vols), E. Mühlenberg (ed.), Berlin, 1975, 1977, 1978.

Diodore of Tarsus, *Commentarii in Psalmos I-L*, J.-M. Olivier (ed.), *CCG* 6, Turnhout, 1980.

In: K. Staab, *Pauluskommentare aus der griechischen Kirche, (Neutestamentliche Abhandlungen XV)*, Münster, 1933.

Dionysius of Alexandria: *The Letters and other Remains of Dionysius of Alexandria*, C.L. Feltoe, (ed.), Cambridge, 1904.

Epiphanius,*Werke* I, *GCS* 25, K. Holl (ed.), Leipzig, 1915.

Werke II, *GCS* 31 (2 Aufl.), K. Holl/J. Dummer (eds.), Leipzig, 1980,

Werke III, *GCS* 37, (2 Aufl.), K. Holl/J Dummer (eds.), Leipzig, 1985.

Panarion of Epiphanius of Salamis Bk I, F.Williams (tr.), Leiden-New York-Köln, 1987.

Panarion of Epiphanius of Salamis Bks II & III, F.Williams (tr.), Leiden-New York-Köln, 1994.

Ephraim: *Das Heilige Ephraem des Syrers Hymnen De Fide*, E. Beck (ed.), Louvain, 1955.

Evagrius: *Evagrius Ponticus Les six centuries de Kephalaia gnostica*, A. Guillaumont (ed.), *PO* 28,1, Turnhout, 1958.

Gregory of Elvira: *Gregorii Iliberritani Episcopi, Tractatus Origenis; In Canticum Canticorum Libri Quinque, CCL* 69, Turnhout, 1967, 1-146; 169-215.

Gregorius Eliberritanus: Epithalamium sive Explanatio in Cantico Canticorum, E. Schulz-Flügel (ed.), Freiburg-Wien, 1994.

Gregory of Nazianzus: *Grégoire de Nazianze, Discours 38-41*, C. Moreschini, P. Gallay, (eds.), *SC* 358, 1990.

Faith Gives Fulness to Reasoning. The Five Theological Orations of Gregory of Nazianzen, F.W. Norris (transl.) (*SVigChr* 13), Leiden, 1990.

Grégoire le Grand: Commentaire sur le Cantique, R. Bélanger (ed.), *SC* 314, 1984.

Gregorii Nysseni Opera I, II: Contra Eunomium, W. Jaeger (ed.), Leiden, 1960.

   III/1: Antirheticus adversus Apollinarem, F. Mueller (ed.), Leiden, 1958.

   III/4: Oratio catechetica, E. Mühlenberg (ed.), Leiden, 1996.

   VI: In Canticum Canticorum, W. Jaeger (ed.), Leiden , 1986.

   VIII/2: EpIII , G. Pasquali (ed.), Leiden, 1959.

   IX: De deitate adversus Evagrius (vulgo: In suam ordinationem oratio), E. Gebhardt (ed.), Leiden, 1967, 331-440.

Gregorio di Nissa, *La vita di Mosè*, M. Simonetti (tr.), Milan, 1984.

Gregorio: Omelie sul Cantico dei Cantici., C. Moreschini (tr.), Rome, 1988.

Gregory of Nyssa: Commentary on the Song of Songs, C. McCambley (ed.), Brookline, MA, 1987.

Gregory of Nyssa's Treatise on the Inscription of the Psalms: Introduction, Translation and Notes, R. Heine (ed.), Oxford, 1995.

Grégoire de Nysse: Sur l'Ecclésiaste, F. Viret (ed.), *SC* 416, 1996.

Hesychius of Jerusalem: *Les Homélies Festales d'Hésychius de Jerusalem* Vols I &II, M. Aubineau (ed.), (*Subsidia hagiographica* 59), Brussels, 1978.

Hippolytus, ΕΙΣ ΤΟ ΑΣΜΑ in: G.N. Bonwetsch, H. Achelis (eds.) GCS *Hippolytus Werke I*, Leipzig, 1897, 344-374..

   In: M. Richard "Une paraphrase grecque résumée du Commentaire d'Hippolyte sur le Cantique des Cantiques." *Le Muséon* 77 (1964):   137-54.

Traités d'Hippolyte sur David et Goliath, sur le Cantique des cantiques et sur l'Antéchrist: version géorgienne, G. Garitte (ed.), *CSCO* 263 (*Scriptores Iberici* 15), Louvain, 1965.

Hippolyte contre les hérésies, P. Nautin (ed.), Paris, 1949.

Iamblichus: *The Theology of Arithmetic: attributed to Iamblichus*, R. Waterfield (ed.), Grand Rapids, 1988.

Irenaeus, *Contre Les Héresies I;* A. Rousseau, L. Doutreleau (eds.), *SC* 264, Paris, 1979.

Itala, A. Jülicher (ed.), 2. Auflage, Berlin, 1972.

Jerome, *Adversus Jovinianum*, PL 23, 211-38.

   Epistulae CSEL 54, I. Hilberg (ed.), Vienna-Leipzig, 1910.

John Chrysostom: Jean Chrysostome, *Huit Catechéses Baptismales*, A.Wenger (ed.), *SC* 50, Paris, 1970.

Leo the Great: *Tomus Leonis ad Flavianum* C. Silva-Tarouca (ed.) Textus und Documenta 9, Rome, 1932.

Macarius: Makarius/Symeon: *Reden und Briefe. Die Sammlung I des Vaticanus Graecus 694 (B)*, H. Berthold (ed.), *GCS*, Berlin, 1973.

   Die 50 geistlichen Homilien des Makarius, Berlin, 1962.

   Pseudo-Macarius: *The fifty spiritual homilies and the Great Letter*, G.A. Maloney (tr.), New York, 1992.

Ps-Macaire: Oeuvres Spirituelles (Collection 3), V. Desprez (ed.), *SC* 275, 1980.

Mansi, G.D. *Sacrorum conciliorum nova et amplissima collectio*, 31 vols, Florence, 1758-98.

Marius Victorinus, *Adversus Arium*:, PL 8, 993-1310.

Marius Victorinus: Traités Théologiques sur la Trinité , I& II, P. Henry-P. Hadot (eds.), SC 68, 69, Paris, 1960.

Melito of Sardis: *On Pascha and Fragments* , S.G. Hall (ed.), Oxford 1979.

Methodius, *Werke*, G.N. Bonwetsch, Leipzig, 1917.

The Symposium, H. Musurillo (tr.), Westminster, MY, London, 1958.

Le Banquet, SC 95 H. Musurillo-V.H. Debidour (eds.), Paris, 1963.

Nemesius, *De natura hominis*, M. Morani (ed.), Leipzig, 1987.

Nilus of Ancyra: *Nil d'Ancyre. Commentaire sur le Cantique des Cantiques*, M.-G. Guérard (ed.), SC 403, Paris 1994.

In: S. Lucà "La fine inedita del commento di Nilo d'Ancira al Cantico dei Cantici." Aug 22 (1982): 365-403.

Nilus: MS Ogden 36: University College, London.

Origen, *Contra Celsum*, H. Chadwick (tr.), Cambridge, 1953.

Origen, *Philocalia* J.A. Robinson (ed.), Cambridge, 1893.

Origène: Philocalie 1-20, M. Harl-A. Le Boulluec (eds.), Paris, 1983.

Origen In Canticum Canticorum, W. Baehrens (ed.) *Origenes Werke VIII*, GCS 33, Leipzig, 1925, pp 61-241.

Origène: Commentaire sur le Cantique des Cantiques. 2 Tomes, L. Bresard-H. Crouzel-M. Borret (eds.), SC 375, 376, (1991).

Origen: Contra Celsum, P. Koetschau (ed.) *Origenes Werke I-II* . Leipzig, 1899.

Origen De Principiis, P. Koetschau (ed.) *Origenes Werke IV*, Leipzig 1913.

Origenes: *De Principiis. Vier Bücher von den Prinzipien*. H. Görgemanns, H. Karpp (eds.), Darmstadt, 1976.

Origenis Scholia in Cantica Canticorum, PG 17, 253-65; also PG13, 197-216.

Origène: Lettre à Africanus. N.R.M. de Lange (ed.), Paris. 1983.

Pacian of Barcelona, *San Pacianus : Obras*, L.R. Fernandez (ed.), Barcelona, 1958.

Pacien de Barcelone. Écrits, C. Granado (ed.), SC 410, Paris, 1995.

Philastrius, *Diversarum Hereseon Liber*, CSEL 38.

Philo of Carpasia, *Enarratio in Canticum Canticorum*. PG 40: 27-162.

Filone di Carpasia: commento al "Cantico dei Cantici" nell'antica versione Latina d'Epifanio Scolastico, A. Ceresa-Gastaldo (ed.), Torino, 1979.

Photius, *Bibliotheca* Vol 2, R. Henry (ed.), Paris, 1960.

Physiologus. *Physiologus. Naturkunde in Frühchristlicher Deutung*; aus dem Griechischen übersetzt und herausgegeben von Ursula Treu, Hanau, 1981.

Proclus, *Theologie Platonicienne* I-IV. H.D. Saffrey and L.G.Westerink (eds.) Paris. 1968-81.

In Platonis Timaeum commentaria, E. Diehl (ed.), Leipzig, 1903.

Psellus, *Pselli Poemata* , L.G. Westerink (ed.), Stuttgart-Leipzig, 1992.

Ps-Athanasius, *Synopsis Sacrae Scripturae*, PG 28, 349-357.

Ps-Clement: Die Pseudoklementinen, II, *Recognitiones*, B. Rehm, F. Paschke (eds.), *GCS* 51, Berlin, 1965.

Ps-Dionysius, *Corpus Dionysiacum* II, G. Heil and A.M. Ritter (eds.), *PTS* 36, Berlin-New York, 1991.
Rufinus, *Opera*, M. Simonetti (ed.), *CCL* 20, Turnhout, 1961.
Sevère d'Antioche, *Orationes ad Nephalium*, J. Lebon (ed.), CSCO 119,120, Louvain, 1949.
Tertullian: *Opera*, E. Dekkers et al.(ed.), *CCL* 2 (1954).
Theodore of Mopsuestia, *On the Epistles of Paul*, I-II, Cambridge, H.B. Swete (ed.),1880-82.
  Théodore de Mopsueste: Fragments syriaques du Commentaire des Psaumes, L. van Rompay (ed.), CSCO 435 (S. Syr. 189), Louvain, 1982.
  Theodore: Le Commentaire de Théodore de Mopsueste sur les Psaumes (I-LXXX): R. Devreesse, (ed.), *Studi e Testi* 93, Vatican City, 1939.
Theodoret of Cyrus, *Eranistes*, G.H. Ettlinger (ed.), Oxford, 1975.
  Théodoret de Cyr: Correspondance, Y. Azéma (ed.), SC 111, Paris, 1965.
  Théodoret de Cyr: Thérapeutique des Maladies Helléniques, SC 57, P. Canivet (ed.), Paris, 1958.
  Theodoreti Cyrensis Episcopi, *Opera omnia*. PG 81, 27-214.
Vetus Latina 25, II, H.-J. Frede (ed.), Freiburg, 1983-91.
Vetus Latina: Canticum Canticorum., E. Schulz-Flügel (ed.), Freiburg, 1992.
Victorinus of Petovium: *Sur l'Apocalypse: suivi du fragment chronologique et de la construction du monde*, M. Dulaey (ed.), SC 423, Paris, 1997
Zeno Veronensis, *Tractatus*, *CCL* 22, B. Löfstedt (ed.), Turnhout, 1971.

Bibliography of Secondary Works

Abbreviations used are in accordance with the 'Abkürzungsverzeichnis' of the Theologische Realenzyklopädie.

Abel, D. C. 1981, "The Doctrine of Synergism in Gregory of Nyssa's *De Instituto Christiano*", *Thom* 45: 430-48.
Abel, F.M. 1941, "Parallélisme exégétique entre S. Jerôme et S. Cyrille d'Alexandrie, *Vivre et Penser* 1: 94-119; 2: 212-30.
Abramowski, L. 1981a, "Ein Gnostischer Logostheologe: Umfang und Redaktor des Gnostischen Sonderguts in Hippolyts 'Widerlegung aller Häresien'", in *idem, Drei christologische Untersuchungen (BZNW* 45), Berlin-New York, 18-62.
___ 1981b, "ΣΥΝΑΦΕΙΑ und ΑΣΥΓΥΤΟΣ ΕΝΩΣΙΣals Bezeichnung für trinitarische und christologische Einheit", in *Drei christologische Untersuchungen (BZNW* 45), Berlin-New York, 63-109.
Akers, R. L. 1985, The perfected soul as an exegetical goal in Origen's writings on the Song of Songs, (PhD. diss. Evanston, IL: North-Western University, 1984) [*UMI Microfilm Dissertation Abstract* 45,7 2142 A.]
Alcain, J. A. 1976, *Cautiverio y redención del hombre en Origenes*, Bilbao.
Alès, A. d' "Origénisme", *DAFC* III: 1228-58.
Alexander, P. D. 1976, "Gregory of Nyssa and the Simile of the Banquet of Life", *VigChr* 30: 55-62.
Alexandre, M. 1971, "La théorie de l'exégèse dans le *De Hominis Opificio* et l'*In Hexaemeron*", in M. Harl (ed.), *Écriture et Culture Philosophique dans la Pensée de Grégoire de Nysse*, Leiden, 87-110.
___ 1981, "Lire en grec la recit de la création: Interprétation de la Genèse dans la littérature judeo-hellenistique", *M'yn, Sources* 2 , 95-118.
___ 1981, "Prologue et eschatologie chez Grégoire de Nysse", in U. Bianchi, H. Crouzel (eds.), *Arche e Telos: L' antropologia di Origene e di Gregorio de Nissa. Analisi storico-religioso (Colloquio Milano 1979)*, Milan, 122-59.
___ 1988, *Le Commencement du Livre: Genèse I-V*, Paris.
Altaner, B. 1960, *Patrology* (translated H. Graef), Freiburg-Edinburgh-London.
Altermath, F. 1977, *Du corps psychique au corps spirituel (BGBE* 18), Tübingen.
Aly, W. 1957, "Prokopius", *PRE* 23: 259-72.
Alzati, C. 1993, *Ambrosiana ecclesia: studi su la chiesa milanese e l'ecumene christiana tra tarda antichita e medioevo*, Milano.
Amann, E. 1946, "Theodore de Mopsueste", *DTC* 15: 235-79.
Andresen, C. 1961, "Zur Entstehung und Geschichte des trinitarischen Personbegriffes", *ZNW* 52: 1-39.

Angstenberger, P. 1997, *Der reiche und der arme Christus: die Rezeptionsgeschichte von 2 Kor 8,9 zwischen dem zweiten und dem sechsten Jahrhundert*, Bonn.
Apostolopoulos, Ch. 1986, *Phaedo Christianus. Studien zur Verbindung und Abwägung des Verhältnisses zwischen dem platonischen 'Phaidon' und dem Dialog Gregors von Nyssa 'Über die Seele und die Auferstehung'*, (Europäische Höchschulschriften Reihe XX, Bd./Vol. 188.) Frankfurt - Bern - New York.
Arens, H. 1982, *Die christologische Sprache Leos des Großen*, Freiburg-Basel-Vienna.
Armstrong, A. H. 1954, "Plotinian Nous in Patristic Theology", *VigChr* 8: 23-26.
___ 1962, "Theory of the non-existence of matter in Plotinus and the Cappadocians", *StPatr* 5 *(TU* 80): 427-29.
___ 1967, "Plotinus" in *idem* (ed.) *The Cambridge History of Later Greek and Early Medieval Philosophy*, Cambridge, 195-263.
___ 1980, "The Self-Definition of Christianity in Relation to later Platonism", in E. P. Sanders (ed.), *Jewish and Christian Self-definition*, London, Vol. 1, 74-99
Babcock, W. (ed.) 1989, *Tyconius: The Book of Rules*, Atlanta.
Bailleux, E. 1970, "Le personalisme trinitaire des Pères grecs", *MSR* 27: 3-25.
Baillie, D.W. 1955, *God was in Christ*, London.
Baker, A. 1966, "Pseudo-Macarius and Gregory of Nyssa", *VigChr* 20: 227-34.
Balás, D. 1966a, "Christian transformation of Greek Philosophy illustrated by Gregory of Nyssa's use of the notion of Participation", *PACPA* 40: 152-57.
___ 1966b, Μετουσία θεοῦ. *Man's Participation in God's Perfections according to St. Gregory of Nyssa*, Rome.
___ 1979, *"Plenitudo Humanitatis.* The Unity of Human Nature in the Theology of Gregory of Nyssa", in D.F. Winslow (ed.), *Disciplina Nostra (In mem. R. F. Evans)*, Philadelphia.
___ 1985, "Gregor von Nyssa", *TRE* 14: 177-81.
Balthasar, H.-U. von 1939, "Die Hiera von Evagrius Pontikus", *ZKTh* 63: 86-106; 181-206.
___ 1954, *Der versiegelte Quell: Auslegung des Hohen Liedes* (2. Aufl.), Einsiedeln.
___ 1960, *Sponsa Verbi. Skizzen zur Theologie*, I. Einsiedeln. .
___ 1961, *Kosmische Liturgie: Das Weltbild Maximus des Bekenners* (2. Aufl.), Einsiedeln.
___ 1975, "The Christian and Chastity" in *Elucidations* (ET, J. Riches), London.
___ 1978, *Theodramatik, II: Die Personen des Spiels/2:Die Personen in Christus*, Einsiedeln.
___ 1988, *Présence et Pensée: Essai sur la Philosophie Religieuse de Grégoire de Nysse*, Paris.
Barbara, M.-A. 1992, "Per una riedizione di Origene sul Cantico", in *Letture cristiane dei Libri Sapienzali: Studia Ephemeridis "Augustinianum"* 37: 349-66.
___ 1993, "Progetto di edizione critica dei frammenti di Origene sul Cantico. Spoglio delle catene e stato delle ricerche", *ASEs* 10: 439-50.
Bardenhewer, O. 1923, *Geschichte der altkirchlichen Literatur* Bd III, Freiburg.
Bardy, G. 1923, *Recherches sur l'histoire du texte et des versions latines de 'De Principiis' d' Origène*, Paris.
___ 1936, "Faux et fraudes littéraires dans l'antiquité chrétienne", *RHE* 32: 5-23; 275-302.
___ 1946, "Théodoret", *DTC* 15: 299-325.
Barthélemy, D. 1965, "L'Ancien Testament a mûri à Alexandrie", *ThZ* 21: 358-370.

Baus, K. 1954, "Das Nachwirken des Origenes", *RQ* 49: 26-29.
Bavel, T. van 1954, *Recherches sur la Christologie de Saint Augustin*, Fribourg.
Beck, E. 1981, *Ephräms Trinitätslehre im Bild von Sonne/Feuer, Licht und Wärme.* CSCO 425, Subsidia 62, Louvain.
Beck, H.-G. 1977, *Kirche und Theologische Literatur im Byzantinischen Reich* (2e Aufl.) München.
Beierwaltes, W. 1985, *Denken des Einen*, Frankfurt.
Benoit, P. 1963, "L'inspiration de la Septante d'après les Pères", in idem, *L'Homme devant Dieu*, Paris, Vol. 1, 169-87.
Beyschlag, K. 1982, *Grundriß der Dogmengeschichte I: Gott und Welt*, Darmstadt.
___ 1991, *Grundriß der Dogmengeschichte II: Gott und Mensch/1: Das christologische Dogma*, Darmstadt.
Bienert, W.A. 1972, *"Allegoria'"und "Anagoge" bei Didymos dem Blinden von Alexandria*, Berlin.
___ 1978, *Dionysius von Alexandrien: Zur Frage des Origenismus im dritten Jahrhundert*, Berlin.
Bjerre-Aspergen, K. 1977, *Bräutigam, Sonne und Mütter: Studien zu einigen Gottesmetaphern bei Gregor von Nyssa*, (Diss.) Lund.
Blum, G.G. 1969, *Rabbula von Edessa; der Christ, der Bischof, der Theologe*, CSCO 300 (*Subsidia* 34), Louvain.
Boer, S. de. 1968, *De Anthropologie van Gregor van Nyssa*, Assen.
Bogaert, P.M. 1988, "Revue: Apponius, *In Canticum Canticorum Expositio*, B. Vregille and L. Neyrand (eds.), *CCL* 19, Turnhout, 1986," *RBen* 98: 238-39.
Bonwetsch, G.N. 1903, *Die Theologie des Methodius von Olympos*, Berlin.
Borgomeo, P. 1972, *L'Église de ce temps dans la prédication de Saint Augustin*, Paris.
Bouchet, J. R. 1967, "A propos d'une image Christologique de Grégoire de Nysse", *RThom* 67: 564-80.
___ 1968a, "La vision de l'économie du salut selon saint Grégoire de Nysse", *RSPhTh* 52: 613-44.
___ 1968b, "Le vocabulaire de l'union du rapport des natures chez Grégoire de Nysse", *RThom* 68: 533-82.
Bouhot, J.-P. "Revue: Apponius, *In Canticum Canticorum Expositio*, B. Vregille and L. Neyrand (eds.), CCL 19, Turnhout, 1986", REAug 33 (1987): 186-87.
Bou Mansour, T. 1988, *La pensée symbolique de Saint Ephrem le Syrien*, Kaslik.
Breen, A. 1987, "The evidence of antique Irish exegesis in Pseudo-Cyprian, De Duodecim Abusivis Saeculi", in *The Proceedings of the Royal Irish Academy* 87, C.4, 83-85.
Brock, S. 1980, "Bibelübersetzungen I: Die Übersetzungen ins Syrische. 4.1. Altes Testament", *TRE* 6: 181-89.
___ 1982, "Some Clothing Metaphors", in M. Schmidt (ed.), *Typus, Symbol, Allegorie*, Regensburg, 11-40.
___ 1989, *Spirituality in the Syriac Tradition*, Kottayam.
Brouwer, A. de 1959, "Note critique sur un passage du Commentaire d'Origène sur le Cantique", *RBen* 59: 202-203.

Brox, N. 1980, "Spiritualität und Orthodoxie. Zum Konflikt des Origenes mit der Geschichte des Dogmas", in E. Dassmann und K.S. Frank (eds.), *Pietas. FS B. Kötting (JAC,* Ergänzungsband 8), Münster, 139-54.
___ 1987, "Häresie", *RAC* 13 : 248-97.
Bruns, P. 1990, "Arius Hellenizans?: Ephräm der Syrer und die neoniceanischen Kontroversen seiner Zeit", *ZKTh* 101 :21-57.
Bultmann, R. 1994, *Die Exegese von Theodore von Mopsuestia,* Bonn-Stuttgart, u.a.
Bunge, J.G. 1983, "Evagre le Pontique et les deux Macaire" *Irén.* 56: 215-26 & 323-60.
___ 1986, "Origenismus—Gnostizismus: Zum geistesgeschichtlichen Standort des Evagrios Pontikos", *VigChr* 40:24-54.
___ 1990, "Palladiana I: Introduction aux fragments coptes de l'Histoire Lausiac", *StMon* 32:79-129.
Buonaiuti, E. 1921, "The Ethics and Eschatology of Methodius of Olympus", *HTR* 14: 255-66.
Burton-Christie, D. 1991, *The Word in the Desert,* Cambridge.
Cahill, J.B. 1981, "The Date and Setting of Gregory of Nyssa's Commentary on the Song of Songs", *JThS* 32: 447-60.
Callahan, J. F. 1958, "Greek Philosophy and the Cappadocian Cosmology", *DOP* 12: 29-57.
___ 1960, "Gregory of Nyssa and the Psychological View of Time", in *Atti del XII Congresso Internationale di Filosofia, Venezia, 12-18 sept.,* 1958, 59-66. Florence.
Cambe, M. 1962, "L'influence du Cantique sur le N.T." *Rev Thom.* 2: 5-26.
Camelot, P.-T. 1950, "La théologie de l'image de Dieu", *RSPhTh* 40: 443-71.
Cameron, Alan 1976, "The authenticity of the letters of St Nilus of Ancyra", *Greek, Roman and Byzantine Studies* 17: 181-96.
Cameron, Averil 1994, *Christianity and the Rhetoric of Empire,* Berkeley-Oxford.
Canévet, M. 1971, "Exégèse et théologie dans les traités spirituels de Grégoire de Nysse", in M. Harl (ed.), *Écriture et Culture Philosophique dans la Pensée de Grégoire de Nysse,* Leiden.
___ 1972, "La perception de la présence de Dieu: A propos d'une expression de la XIe homélie sur le Cantique des cantiques", in *Epektasis: Mélanges offerts au Cardinal Daniélou,* Paris, 445-54.
___ 1983, *Grégoire de Nysse et l'hérmeneutique biblique: études des rapports entre le langage et la connaissance de Dieu,* Paris.
Canivet, P. 1961, "Théodoret et le Messalianisme", *RMab* 51: 26-34.
Cantalmessa, R. 1980, "Cristo 'Imagine di dio': Le traduzioni patristiche su Col. 1:15", *RSLR* 16: 181-212; 345-80.
Cavalcanti, E. 1976, "Teologia trinitaria e teologia della storia in alcuni testi di Gregorio di Nissa", *Aug* 16: 117-24.
Cavallera, F. 1905, *Le schisme d'Antioche,* Paris.
___ 1920, "La lettre sur l'évêque Bonose est-elle de saint Sirice ou de saint Ambroise?", *BLE* 21: 141-47.
Cavarnes, J. P. 1955, "St. Gregory of Nyssa on the Nature of the Soul", *GOTR* 1: 133-41.
___ 1956, *St. Gregory of Nyssa on the Origin and Destiny of the Soul,* Belmont (MA).

Ceresa-Gastaldo, A. 1974, "L'Esegesi Biblica Nel Commento al Cantico dei Cantici di Filone di Carpasia", in *Forma Futuri: Studi in onore del Cardinale M. Pellegrino*, Turin.

___ 1979, "La dimensione dell'amore nell'interpretazione origeniana del 'Cantico dei Cantici'", in R. Cantalmessa and L.F. Pizzolato (eds.), *Paradoxos Politeia: Studi patristici in onore di Giuseppe Lazzati*, Milan, 187-94.

___ 1980, "L'esegesi origeniana del 'Cantico dei Cantici'", in H. Crouzel and A. Quacquarelli (eds.), *Origeniana Secunda*, Rome, 245-52.

___ 1989, "Nuove richerche sulla storia del testo, le antiche versioni e l'intepretazione del Cantici dei Cantici", *ASEs* 6: 31-38.

Chadwick, H. 1948, "Origen, Celsus and Resurrection", *HTR* 41: 83-102.

___ 1951, "Eucharist and Christology in the Nestorian Controversy", *JThS* 2: 145-64.

___ 1987, "Philoponus the Christian Theologian" in R. Sorabji (ed.), *Philoponus and the rejection of Aristotelian Science*, London, 41-56.

Chappuzeau, G. 1976 "Die Auslegung des Hohenliedes durch Hippolyt von Rom", *JAC* 19: 45-81.

Chesnut, R.C. 1976, *Three Monophysite Christologies: Severus of Antioch, Philoxenus of Mabbug and Jacob of Sarug*, Oxford.

Chifar, N. 1993, *Das VII. ökumenische Konzil von Nikaia: Das letzte Konzil der ungeteilten Kirche*, Erlangen.

Clark, E.A. 1990, "New Perspectives on the Origenist Controversy: human embodiment and ascetic strategies", *ChH* 59: 145-162.

___ 1991, "From Origenism to Pelagianism: elusive issues in an ancient debate," *Princeton Seminary Bulletin*, 282-303.

___ 1992, *The Origenist Controversy*, Princeton.

Cohen, M.S. 1985, *The Shi'ur Qomah: Texts and Recensions*, Tübingen.

Collantes Lozano, J. 1954, *San Gregorio de Elvira: Estudio sobre su Ecclesiologia*, Granada.

Conca, F. 1982, "Osservazioni sullo stile di Nilo Ancirano" in *XVI. Internationaler Byzantinisten Kongreß: Akten*, Vienna, II/3, 219-25.

Courcelle, P. 1948, *Les lettres grecques en Occident de Macrobe à Cassiodore*, Paris.

___ 1967, "Grégoire de Nysse lecteur de Porphyre", *REG* 80:402-406.

___ 1968, *Recherches sur les Confessions de S. Augustin*, Paris (2ed).

Courth, F. 1988, *Trinität: in der Schrift und Patristik (Handbuch der Dogmengeschichte II/1a)*, Rome-Freiburg-Vienna.

Cox Miller, P. 1994, *Dreams in Late Antiquity: studies in the imagination of a culture*, Princeton.

Crociani, L. 1990, *Apponii, In Canticum Canticorum Explanationes Libri VI. Tradizione del testo, fonti, liturgia, teologia* (Estratto della Dissertazione), Rome.

Crouzel, H. 1957, "Grégoire de Nysse, est-il fondateur de la théologie mystique? Une controverse récente", *RAM* 33: 189-202.

___ 1975, "Comparaisons précises entre les fragments du Peri Archôn selon la Philocalie et la traduction de Rufin", in H. Crouzel, G. Lomiento, J. Rius-Camps, (eds.), *Origeniana: Premier Colloque international des études origéniennes*, Bari, 112-21.

___ 1981, "Le Christ Sauveur selon Origène", *StMiss* 30: 63-84.

___ 1984a, "Le Coeur selon Origène", *BLE* 85: 5-16; 99-110.
___ 1984b, "La christologie d'Origène: selon son Commentaire sur le Cantique des Cantiques", in L. Lies (ed.), *Praesentia Christi: FS J Betz*, Düsseldorf, 421-33.
___ 1989, *Origen*, Edinburgh.
Curti, C. 1992, "Victorinus of Petovium", *EEC* II, 867.
Daniélou, J. 1940, "L'apocatastase chez s. Grégoire de Nysse", *RSR* 30: 328-47.
___ 1948, *Origène*, Paris.
___ 1953, "Mystique de la ténèbre chez Grégoire de Nysse", *DSp* 2, 1872-85.
___ 1960, "Grégoire de Nysse et le Messalianisme", *RSR* 48: 119-34.
___ 1961, "La notion de confins (methorios) chez Grégoire de Nysse", *RSR* 49: 161-87.
___ 1964, "Joh. 7,38 et Ézech. 47,1-11", *StEv* 2 (=*TU* 87), 158-63.
___ 1966a, "L' 'Adversus Arium et Sabellium' de Grégoire de Nysse et l'origenisme cappadocien", *RSR* 54: 61-66.
___ 1966b, *Études d'exégèse judéo-chrétienne: les Testimonia*, Paris.
___ 1966c, "La Chronologie des oeuvres de Grégoire de Nysse", *StPatr* 7 *(TU* 92): 159-69.
___ 1970, *L'Etre et Le Temps chez Grégoire de Nysse*, Leiden
___ 1971, "Orientations Actuelles", in M. Harl (ed.), *Écriture et Culture Philosophique dans la Pensée de Grégoire de Nysse*, Leiden, 3-17.
___ 1977, *Origins of Latin Christianity*, London-Philadelphia.
Dassmann, E. 1978, "Ambrosius von Mailand", *TRE* 2: 362-68.
David, E.A. 1968, *Das Bild vom neuen Menschen*, Salzburg-München.
De Aldama, J.A. 1963, "La carta ambrosiana 'De Bonoso'", *Mar* 25: 1-22.
De Lange, N.R.M. 1976, *Origen and the Jews*, Cambridge.
De Lubac, H. 1959, *Exégèse Médiévale, 1. Les quatre sens de l'écriture*, Paris.
Dechow, J.F. 1987, "Origen's 'heresy': from Eustathius to Epiphanius", in L. Lies (ed.), *Origeniana Quarta*, Innsbruck, 405-409.
___ 1990, *Dogma and Mysticism in Early Christianity*, Macon (Ga).
Denzinger, H. 1991, *Enchiridion symbolorum definitionum et declarationum de rebus fidei et morum* (37. Aufl.: P. Hünermann, Hrsg.), Freiburg-Basel-Rome-Vienna.
Desjardins, R. 1966, "Le Christ 'sponsus' et l'église 'sponsa' chez S. Augustin", *BLE* 67: 241-56.
Devreesse, R. 1928, "Chaines Exégètiques", *DBS* I: 1084ff.
___ 1949, *Les Homélies Catéchétiques de Théodore de Mopsueste*, Vatican City.
Diego Sanchez, M. 1991, *El Commentario al Ecclesiates de Didimo Alessandrino: Exegesis y espiritualidad*, Rome.
Diekamp, F. 1899, *Die origenistischen Streitigkeiten im VIten Jahrhundert und das Vte allgemeine Concil*, Münster.
Doignon, J. 1990, "Hilaire de Poitiers face à la mystique de la purification par l'amour", *REAug* 36: 217-24.
Dölger, F.J. 1950, "Christus als himmlischer Eros und Seelenbräutigam bei Origenes", *AuC* 1: 273-75.
Domagalski, B. 1994, "Hirsch", *RAC* 15: 551-577.
Dominguez del Val, U. 1989, *Gregorio de Elvira: Obras Completas*, Madrid.

Dorival, G. 1984, "Des commentaires de l'Ecriture aux chaînes", in C. Mondésert (ed.), *Le monde grec ancien et la Bible*, Paris, 361-86.

___ 1987, "Origène et la résurrection de la chair", in L Lies (ed.), *Origeniana Quarta*, Innsbruck-Vienna, 291-321.

Dörrie, H. 1974, "Zur Methodik antiker Exegese", *ZNTW* 65:121-38.

Dörries, H. 1963, "Griechentum und Christentum bei Gregor von Nyssa. Zu H. Langerbecks Edition des Hohelied-Kommentars in der Leidener Gregor- Ausgabe", *ThLZ* 88: 569-82.

___ 1966, *Gregor von Nyssa's Lehre vom Heiligen Geist*, Leiden.

___ 1966, "Urteil und Verurteilung - Kirche und Messalianer", in idem, *Wort und Stunde* I, Göttingen, 334-51.

Drijvers, H. 1980, *Cults and Beliefs at Edessa*, Leiden.

___ 1984, *East of Antioch: Studies in early Syriac Christianity*, London.

Drioton, E. 1915-17, "La Discussion d'une moine anthropomorphite Audien avec le patriarche Théopile d'Alexandrie en l'année 399", *ROC*, 2e ser, 10: 92-100, 113-128.

Drobner, H. 1982, "Die Beredsamkeit Gregors von Nyssa im Urteil der Neuzeit", *StPatr 17/3*: 1084-94.

___ 1986, *Person-Exegese und Christologie bei Augustinus. Zur Herkunft der Formel Una Persona*, Leiden.

Dummer, J. 1987, "Zur Epiphanius-Ausgabe der 'Griechischen Christlichen Schriftsteller'", in idem (ed.), *Texte und Textkritik: eine Aufsatzsammlung*, Berlin, 119-26.

Dünzl, F. 1990, "Gregor von Nyssa's Homilien zum Canticum auf dem Hintergrund seiner Vita Moysis", *VigChr* 44: 371-381.

___ 1993, *Braut und Bräutigam*, (*BGBE* 32), Tübingen.

___ 1994, "Formen der Kirchenväter-Rezeption am Beispiel der sogenannten physischen Erlösungslehre des Gregor von Nyssa", *ThPh* 69 :161-81.

Dupuis, J. 1967, *L'Esprit de l'homme: étude sur l'anthropologie religieuse d'Origène*, Paris.

Durand, G.M. 1985, "Etudes sur Marc le Moine II" *BLE* 86, 5-23.

Duval, Y.-M. 1973a, *Le Livre de Jonas dans la littérature chrétienne grecque et latine*, Paris.

___ 1973b, "Les relations doctrinales entre Milan et Aquilée durant la seconde moitié du IVe siècle. Chromace d'Aquilée et Ambroise de Milan", *AAAd* 4, 171-234.

Eberhard, B. 1859, *Die Beteiligung des Epiphanius an dem Streit über Origenes*, Trier.

Escribano-Alberca, I. 1968, "Von der Gnosis zur Mystik. Der Übergang vom 3. zum 4. Jh. im alexandrinischen Raum", *MThZ* 19: 286-94.

___ 1972, "Zum zyklischen Zeitbegriff der alexandrinischen und kappadokischen Theologie", *StPatr*11 (*TU*108): 42-51.

___ 1974, *Glaube und Gotteserkenntnis in der Schrift und Patristik*, (Handbuch der Dogmengeschichte IV/7d) Freiburg-Basel-Vienna.

Esper, M. N. 1979, *Allegorie und Analogie bei Gregor von Nyssa*, Bonn.

Euringer, S. 1936/1937, "'Schöpferische Exegese' im Äthiopischen Hohenliede", *Bib* 17: 327-44 & 477-500; 20: 27-37.

Eynde, C. van den 1939, *La version syriaque du Commentaire de Grégoire de Nysse sur le Cantique des Cantiques. Ses origines, ses témoins, son influence*, Louvain.

Falk, M. 1982, *Love Lyrics from the Bible*, Sheffield.

Farges, J. 1929, *Les idées morales et religieuses de Méthode d'Olympe*, Paris.
Faulhaber, M. 1902, *Hohelied-Proverbien-und Prediger-Catenen*, Vienna.
Feuillet, A. 1984, "La femme vêtue de soleil (*Apoc.*12) et la glorification de l'Epouse du Ct. des Ct. (6,10). Réflexions sur le progrès dans l'interprétation de l'Apocalypse et du Ct. des Ct.", *Nova et Vetera*, 1: 36-67.
Flint, V.J. 1974, "The Commentaries of Honorius Augustodunensis on the Song of Songs", *RBen* 84: 196-211.
Folliet, G. 1957, "Des moines euchites à Carthage", *StPatr* 2 (*TU* 64) : 386-99.
Fraenkel, P. 1963, "Histoire saint et héresie chez S. Epiphane de Salamine", *RThPh* 12: 175-91.
Frank, K.S. 1975, *Frühes Mönchtum im Abendland*, Zürich-München, Bd. I.
___ 1985a, "Geordnete Liebe: Cant 2,4b in der patristischen Auslegung", *WiWei* 49, 15-30.
___ 1985b, "Apponius, In Canticum Canticorum Explanatio", *VigChr* 39: 370-83.
Frede, H.-J. 1991, *Vetus Latina: Kirchenschriftsteller*, I/2, Freiburg.
Frede, M. 1987, "Numenius", *ANRW* 36.2:1034-75.
Frickel, J. 1989, "Ippolito di Roma Scrittore e Martire", in *Nuove Ricerche su Ippolito* (*Studia Ephemeridis 'Augustinianum'* 30), Rome, 23-41.
Friedländer, P. 1939, *Spätantiker Gemäldezyklus in Gaza: Der Prokopios von Gaza ΕΚΦΡΑΣΙΣ ΕΙΚΟΝΟΣ*, Vatican City.
Gahbauer, F.R. 1984, *Das anthropologische Modell: Ein Beitrag zur Christologie der frühen Kirche bis Chalkedon*, Würzburg.
Gaith, J. 1953, *La conception de la liberté chez Grégoire de Nysse*, Paris.
Gallus, T. 1956, "Ad Epiphanii interpretationem mariologicam in Gen 3,15", *VD* 34: 272-79.
Galtier, P. 1940/41, "Unité ontologique et unité psychologique dans le Christ", *BLE* 41/42: 161-75; 216-32.
___ 1952, "Saint Cyrille et Apollinaire", *Gr.* 37: 351-98.
Gargano, I. G. 1970/71, "Introduzione all' esegesi biblica di Gregorio Nisseno", *VM* 24: 131-58; 25: 211-31.
___ 1981, *La teoria di Gregorio di Nissa sul Cantico dei Cantici. Indagine su alcune indicazioni di metodo esegetico*, (*OCA* 216) Rome.
Garso an, N. 1971, "Byzantine Heresy. A reinterpretation", *DOP* 25: 85-113.
Geerlings, W.A. 1981, "Hiob und Paulus" *JbAC* 24 : 56-66.
Gesché, A. 1959, "L' âme humaine de Jésus dans la christologie du IVe siècle", *RHE* 54: 385-425.
___ 1962, *La Christologie du 'Commentaire' sur les Psaumes découvert à Toura*, Gembloux.
Gianotti, D. 1984, "Gregorio di Elvira interprete del Cantico", *Aug* 24: 421-40.
Gill, E. 1921, *'Songs without clothes'*, *being a dissertation on the Song of Solomon and suchlike songs*, Ditchling, 1921.
Gorday, P. 1983, *Principles Of Patristic Exegesis: Romans 9-11 in Origen, John Chrysostom, and Augustine*, New York and Toronto.
___ 1990, "The Economic Interpretation of Paul in Origen and Gregory of Nyssa", in W. S. Babcock (ed.), *Paul and the Legacies of Paul*, Dallas, 141-63.

Gouillard, J. 1976, "L'Hérésie dans l'empire byzantin des origines au XIIe siècle", in idem *Travaux et mémoires* I, Paris. (= *La Vie religieuse à Byzance*, London, 1981), 299-324.

Gould, G., 1992, "The Image of God and the Anthropomorphite controversy in fourth century monasticism", in *Origeniana Quinta*, 549-57.

Grant, R.M. 1963, "The Fragments of the Greek Apologists and Irenaeus", in J.N. Birdsall, R.W. Thomson (eds.), *Biblical and Patristic Studies in memory of R.P. Casey*, Freiburg, 179-218.

Greer, R. 1983, "The Analogy of Grace in Theodore of Mopsuestia's Christology", *JThS* 34: 82-98.

Gribomont, J. 1962, "Le 'De instituto christiano' et le messalianisme de Grégoire de Nysse", *StPatr* 5 (*TU* 80): 312-22.

___ 1972, "Le Dossier des origines du Messalianisme", in *Epektasis: Mélanges offerts au Cardinal Daniélou*, Paris, 611-25.

___ 1984, "Jerome et Origène avant la querelle origeniste", *Aug* 24: 471-94.

___ 1987, "La terminologie exégetique de S Jerôme", in idem (ed.), *La terminologia esegetica nell'antichita* (*QVetChr*, 20), Bari.

Grillmeier, A. 1975, *Christ in Christian Tradition*, I [ET of German 2nd(1974) edn.] London-Oxford.

___ 1977, Ὁ Κυριακὸς Ἄνθρωπος. Eine Studie zu einer christologischen Bezeichnung der Väterzeit", *Tr* 33: 1-63.

___ 1979, *Jesus der Christus im Glauben der Kirche* I, Freiburg (3 Aufl.).

___ 1980, "Marco Eremita e l'origenismo", *Christianesimo nella storia* 1: 9-58.

___ 1987, *Christ in Christian Tradition* II/1 (ET), London-Oxford.

___ 1989, *Jesus der Christus im Glauben der Kirche* II/2, Freiburg-Basel-Vienna.

___ 1990, *Jesus der Christus im Glauben der Kirche* II/4, Freiburg-Basel-Vienna.

___ 1995, *Christ in Christian Tradition* II/2 (ET), London.

Grünbeck, E. 1994, *Christologische Schriftargumentation und Bildersprache*, (*SupplVigChr* 26), Leiden.

Guérard, M.-G. 1982, "Nil d'Ancyre", *DSp* 11: 345-54.

Guillaumont, A. 1961, "Evagrius et les anathématismes antiorigenistes de 553", *StPatr* 3 (*TU* 78): 219-26.

___ 1962, *Les 'Kephalaia Gnostica' d'Évagre le Pontique et l'histoire de l'Origénisme chez les Grecs et chez les Syriens*, Paris.

___ 1980, "Messalianisme", *DSp* 10: 1074-83.

Guinot, J.-N. 1984, "Théodoret a-t-il lu les homélies d'Origène sur l'Ancien Testament?", *VigChr* 21: 285-312.

___ 1984, "L'importance de la dette de Théodoret de Cyr à l'égard de l'exégèse de Théodore de Mopsueste", *Orph* 5: 68-109.

___ 1985, "La christologie de Théodoret de Cyr dans son commentaire sur le Cantique", *VigChr* 39: 256-72.

___ 1988, "L'exégèse du bouc émissaire chez Cyril d'Alexandrie et Théodoret de Cyr", *Aug* 28: 603-30.

___ 1989, "Présence d'Apollinaire dans l'oeuvre exégétique de Théodoret", *StPatr* 19:166-72.
___ 1992, "Le Commentaire de Théodoret de Cyr sur Le Cantique est-il un Opus Mysticum?", in *Letture cristiane dei Libri Sapienziali (Studia Ephemeridis "Augustinianum"* 37):437-59.
___ 1995, *L'exégèse de Théodoret de Cyr (Theologie historique* 100), Paris.
Hadot, I. 1987, "Introductions aux Commentaires Exégétiques", in M. Tardieu (ed.), *Les règles de l'interprétation,* Paris, 99-102.
Hadot, P. 1987, "Théologie, Exégèse, Révélation, écriture, dans la philosophie grecque", in M. Tardieu (ed.), *Les règles de l'interprétation,* Paris, 13-34.
Halleux, A. de 1976, "La définition christologique à Chalcédoine", *RTL* 7: 3-23; 155-70.
___ 1989, "'Manifesté par le Fils': aux origines d'une formule pneumatologique", *RTL* 20, 3-31.
___ 1994, "À propos d'une lecture cyrillienne de la définition christologique de Chalcédoine", *RThL* 25: 445-71.
Hamblenne, P. 1990, "Peut-on dater Apponius?", *RThAM* 57: 5-33.
Hammond Bammel, C. 1977, "The last ten years of Rufinus' life and the date of his move south for Aquileia", *JThS* 28: 372-429.
___ 1985, *Der Römerbrieftext des Rufin und seine Origenes-Übersetzung,* Freiburg (Schweiz).
___ 1996, *Origeniana et Rufiniana (VetusLatina: Aus der Geschichte der lateinischen Bibel* 29), Freiburg.
Hampson, D. 1990, *Theology and Feminism,* Oxford.
Hanig, R. 1993, "Christus als 'wahrer Salomo' in der frühen Kirche", *ZNW* 84: 111-34.
Harl, M. 1958, *Origène et la fonction révélatrice du Verbe incarné,* Paris.
___ 1967, "A propos d'un passage du 'Contra Eunomium' de Grégoire de Nysse. ἄπορροια et les titres du Christ en théologie trinitaire", *RSR* 55: 217-26.
___ 1971, "Y-a-t-il une influence du 'grec biblique' sur la langue spirituelle des chrétiens ?", in A. Benoit et P. Prigent (eds.), *La Bible et Les Pères,* Paris, 243-62.
___ 1972a, Introduction to *La Chaîne Palestinienne sur le Psaume 118,* SC 189, Paris, 1972.
___ 1972b, "Origène et la sémantique du langage biblique", *VigChr* 26: 161-187.
___ 1974, "Cadeaux de fiançailles et contrat de mariage pour l'épouse du Cantique des cantiques selon quelques commentateurs grecs", in *Mélanges d'histoire des religions offerts à H.-Ch. Puech,* Paris, 243-62.
___ 1975, "La Bouche et le Coeur de l'apôtre", in *Forma Futuri: Studi in Onore del Cardinale Michele Pellegrino,* Turin, 17-42.
___ 1987a, "Les trois livres de Salomon et les trois parties de la Philosophie dans les Prologues des Commentaires sur le Cantique des Cantiques", in J. Dummer (ed.) *Texte und Textkritik: eine Aufsatzsammlung,* Berlin, 249-69.
___ 1987b, "La Préexistence des âmes dans l'oeuvre d'Origène", in L. Lies (ed.) *Origeniana Quarta,* Innsbruck, 237-52.
Harnack, A. 1908, "Vicarii Christi vel Dei bei Aponius", *FS Delbrück,* Berlin, 37-46.

Hausherr, I. 1966, "Les Orientaux, connaissent-ils les 'nuits' de saint Jean de la Croix?" in idem, *Hésychasme et Prière* (*OCA* 176), Rome, 87-128.

Haykin, M.A. 1994, *The Exegesis of 1 and 2 Corinthians in the Pneumatomachian Controversies of the Fourth Century*, Leiden.

Heimann, P. 1988, *Erwähltes Schicksal: Präexistenz der Seele und christlicher Glaube im Denkmodell des Orignenes*, Tübingen.

Heine, R. 1984, "Gregory of Nyssa's Apology for Allegory", *VigChr* 38: 360-70.

___ 1986, "Can the Catena Fragments of Origen's Commentary on John be trusted?", *VigChr* 40: 118-34.

Heither, Th. 1990, *'Translatio Religionis': Die Paulusdeutung des Origenes*, Köln-Vienna.

Hengel, M. 1994, "Die Septuaginta als 'christliche Schriftensammlung', ihre Vorgeschichte und das Problem ihres Kanons", in M. Hengel and A.M. Schwemer (eds.), *Die Septuaginta zwischen Judentum und Christentum*, 182-284.

Hennings, R. 1992, "Rabbinisches und Antijüdisches bei Hieronymus Ep 121, 10", in J. van Oort and U. Wickert (eds.), *Christliche Exegese zwischen Nicaea und Chalcedon*, Kampen, 49-71.

Hermann, W. 1958, "Ambrosius von Mailand als Trinitätstheologe", *ZKG* 69: 197-218.

___ 1978, "Ambrosius von Mailand", *TRE* 2

Heussi, K. 1920, *Untersuchungen zu Nilus dem Asketen*, *TU* 42, Leipzig.

Hoffman, M. 1966, *Der Dialog bei den christlichen Schrifstellern der ersten vier Jahrhunderte*, *TU* 96, Berlin.

Holl, K. 1904, *Amphilochus von Ikonium in seinem Verhältnis zu den großen Kappadoziern*, Tübingen.

___ 1928, "Die Zeitfolge des ersten origenistischen Streites", in ibid. *Gesammelte Aufsätze zur Kirchengeschichte II: Der Osten*, Tübingen, 310-50.

Hörmann, J. 1919, "Anakephalaiosis", *BKV* 38:185-263.

Horn, G. 1925, "L'Amour divin. Note sur le mot 'Eros' dans saint Grégoire de Nysse", *RAM* 6: 378-89.

___ 1927, "Le miroir, la nuée, deux manières de voir d'après saint Grégoire de Nysse", *RAM* 8: 113-31.

Hübner, R.M. 1971, "Gregor von Nyssa und Markell von Ankyra", in M. Harl (ed.), *Écriture et culture philosophique dans la pensée de Grégoire de Nysse*, Leiden.

___ 1974, *Die Einheit des Leibes Christi bei Gregor von Nyssa. Untersuchungen zum Ursprung der 'physischen' Erlösungslehre*, Leiden.

___ 1987, "Ps-Athanasius Contra Sabellianos: eine Schrift des Basilius oder des Apolinarius?", *VigChr* 41: 386-95.

___ 1989, *Die Schrift des Apollinarius von Laodicea gegen Photin (Ps-Athanasius Contra Sabellianos) und Basilius von Caesarea*, Berlin.

Ihnken, T. 1986, "Zum 13. Kapitel des Großen Briefes des Makarios/Symeon", *ZKG* 97: 79-84.

Irmscher, J. 1992, "Procopius of Gaza", in A. Di Berardino (ed.), A. Walford (tr.), *Encyclopedia of the Early Church*, New York.

Ivánka, E. van 1951, "Zur geistesgeschichtlichen Einordnung des Origenismus", *ByZ* 44: 291-303.
___ 1959, "Dunkelheit, mystische", *RAC* 4: 350-58.
___ 1960, "Der geistige Ort um περὶ ἀρχῶν zwischen dem Neuplatonismus, der Gnosis und der christlichen Rechtgläubigkeit", *Schol* 35: 481-502.
___ 1972, "Hellenisches im Hesychiasmus. Das Antinomische der Energienlehre", in *Epektasis: Mélanges offerts au Cardinal Daniélou*, Paris, 491-500.
___ 1990, *Plato Christianus* (2. Aufl.), Einsiedeln .
Jacob, C. 1990, '*Arkandisziplin*', *Allegorese, Mystagogie. Ein neuer Zugang zur Theologie des Ambrosius von Mailand*, (Theophaneia, 32), Frankfurt.
___ 1992, "Zum Hohenlied bei Ambrosius von Mailand: Exegese und literarische Ästhetik", *Letture cristiane dei Libri Sapienzali (Studia Ephemeridis "Augustinianum"* 37), 367-75.
Jaeger, W. 1954, *Two rediscovered works of Ancient Christian Literature: Gregory of Nyssa and Macarius*, Leiden.
___ 1960, "Die asketisch-mystische Theologie des Gregors von Nyssa", in idem (ed.), *Humanistische Reden und Vorträge,* Berlin, 266-86.
___ 1966, *Gregor von Nyssa's Lehre vom Heilige Geist. Aus dem Nachlaß* (Hermann Dörries, ed.), Leiden.
Jaspert, B. 1974, "Stellvertreter Christi bei Aponius, einem unbekannten 'Magister' und Benedikt von Nursia. Ein Beitrag zum altkirchlichen Amtsverständnis", *ZThK* 71: 261-324.
Jouassard , G. 1957, "'Impassibilité' du Logos et 'Impassibilité' de l' âme humaine chez saint Cyrille d'Alexandrie", *RSR* 45: 209-54.
Jülicher, A. 1928, "Bemerkungen: Die Zeitfolge des ersten origenistischen Streits", in K. Holl (ed.), *Gesammelte Aufsätze zur Kirchengeschichte* I, Tübingen, 310-50.
Kaestli, J-D. 1984, "Le récit de IV Esdras 14 et sa valeur pour l'histoire du canon de l'Ancien Testament", in J.-D. Kaestli, O. Wermelinger (eds.), *Le Canon de l'Ancien Testament,* Geneva, 71-97.
Kampling, R. 1983, *Das Blut Christi und die Juden,* Münster.
Kannengiesser, C. 1967, "L'infinité divine chez Grégoire de Nysse", *RSR* 55: 55-65.
___ 1971, "Logique et idées matrices dans le recours biblique selon Grégoire de Nysse", in M. Harl (ed.), *Grégoire de Nysse et la Philosophie*, 85-103.
Kelly, J.N.D. 1972, *Early Christian Creeds* (3 edn.), Harlow.
___ 1975, *Jerome*, London.
Kemmer, A. 1956, "Gregor von Nyssa und Ps.-Makarius. Der Messalianismus im Lichte östlicher Herzenmystik", in *Antonius Magnus Eremita, 356-1956* (StAns 38), Rome, 268-82.
___ 1962, "Messalianismus bei Gregor von Nyssa und Ps-Macarius", *RBen* 72: 278-306.
Kenney, E.J. 1990, *Psyche et Cupido*, Cambridge.
Kerrigan, A. 1952, *St Cyril of Alexandria: Interpreter of the Old Testament*, Rome.
Kimmelman, R. 1980 "Rabbi Yohanan and Origen on the Song of Songs: A third-century Jewish-Christian disputation." *HTR* 73: 567-95.

Kirchmeyer, J. 1966, "Un commentaire de Maxime le Confesseur sur le Cantique?" *StPatr* 8 (*TU* 93): 406-14.

Kittay, E.F. 1987, *Metaphor*. Oxford.

Klock, C. 1987, *Untersuchungen zu Stil und Rhythmus bei Gregor von Nyssa. Ein Beitrag zum Rhetorikverständnis der griechischen Väter* (*BKP* 173), Frankfurt.

Klostermann, E. 1895, *Analecta zur Septuaginta, Hexapla und Patristik*, Leipzig.

Koch, G. 1974, *Strukturen und Geschichte des Heils in der Theologie des Theodoret von Kyros*, Frankfurt.

Koch, H. 1932a, *Pronoia und Paideusis: Studien über Origenes und sein Verhältnis zum Platonismus*, Berlin-Leipzig.

___ 1932b, "Gregors von Elviras Schrifttum und Quellen", *ZKG* 51: 238-72.

Koen, L. 1991, *The Saving Passion*, Uppsala.

König, H. 1991, "'Vestigia antiquorum magistrorum sequi.' Wie liest Apponius Origenes?", *ThQ* 170: 129-36.

___ 1992, *Apponius, die Auslegung zum Lied der Lieder*, Freiburg.

Kopecek, T.A. 1979, *History of Neo-Arianism*, Cambridge, MA.

Kramer, G.H. 1983, *Ambrosius van Milaan; en de geschiedenis*, Amsterdam.

Laistner, L.M.W. 1953/54, "Some early medieval commentaries on the Old Testament", *HTR* 46/47: 27-46.

Lampe, G.W.H 1961, *A Patristic Greek Lexicon*, Oxford.

___ 1977, *God as Spirit*, Oxford.

Langerbeck, H. 1957, "Zur Interpretation Gregors von Nyssa", *ThLZ* 82:81-90.

Lawless, G. 1991, "Augustine and Human Embodiment", *RechAug* 25: 167-86.

Layton, B. 1978, "The Soul as a Dirty Garment", *Le Muséon* 91:155-89.

La Bonnadière, A.-M. 1955, "Le Cantique dans l'oeuvre de saint Augustin", *REAug* 1: 225-237.

Le Boulluec, A. 1985-86, "La question du docétisme aux II et III siècles et son incidence sur les débats christologiques ultérieurs", *EPH: Ve section - Sciences Réligieuses* 94: 471-75.

___ 1985, *La notion d'hérésie dans la littérature grecque IIe-IIIe siècles*, Paris.

___ 1987, "Controverses au sujet de la doctrine d'Origène sur l' âme du Christ", in L. Lies (ed.), *Origeniana Quarta*, Innsbruck-Vienna, 223-37.

Leanza, S. 1990, *Gregorio di Nissa, Omelie sull'Ecclesiaste. Traduzione, introduzione e note*, Rome.

Lebon, J. 1951, "La Christologie du monophysisme Syrien", in A. Grillmeier, H. Bacht (eds.), *Das Konzil von Chalkedon: Geschichte und Gegenwart*, Würzburg, I, 425-580.

Lejay, R. 1908, "L'héritage de Grégoire d'Elvire", *RBen* 25: 435-57.

Lenz, J. 1925, *Jesus Christus nach der Lehre des hl. Gregor von Nyssa: Eine dogmatische Studie*, Trier.

Lerch, D. 1957, "Zur Geschichte der Auslegung des Hohenliedes", *ZThK* 54: 257-77.

Léthel, F-M. 1979, *Théologie de l'Agonie du Christ*, Paris.

Lewy, H. 1929, *'Sobria ebrietas'* : *Untersuchungen zur Geschichte der antiken Mystik* (*BZNW* 9), Giessen.

Leys, R. 1948, "Die Theologie der Christusmystik Gregor von Nyssa." *ZKTh* 70: 49-93, 129-68, 315-40.

___ 1951, *L'image de Dieu chez St Grégoire de Nysse: Esquisse d'une doctrine*, Brussels-Paris.

___ 1957, "La théologie spirituelle de s. Grégoire de Nysse", *StPatr* 2 (*TU* 64): 495-511.

Liébaert, J. 1965, *Christologie (Handbuch der Dogmengeschichte III/1a)*, Freiburg-Basel-Vienna.

Lietzmann, H. 1904, *Apollinaris von Laodicea und seine Schule*, Tübingen.

Lorenz, R. 1978, *Arius Judaizans? Untersuchungen zur dogmengeschichtlichen Einordnung des Arius*, Göttingen.

___ 1983, "Die Christusseele im Arianischen Streit. Nebst einigen Bemerkungen zur Quellenkritik des Arius und zur Glaubwürdigkeit des Athanasius", *ZKG* 94: 1-51.

Lossky, V. 1957, "Le problème de la 'vision face à face' et la tradition patristique de Byzance", *StPatr* 2 (*TU* 64): 512-37.

Lot-Bordone, M. "La doctrine de la 'déification' dans l'église grecque jusqu'au XIe siècle", *RHR* 53: 5-43; 525-74; 54: 8-55.

___ 1939, "L'anthropologie théocentrique de l'Orient Chrétien comme base de son expérience spirituelle", *Irén* 16: 6-21 1932/1933,

___ 1970 *La déification de l'homme selon la doctrine des Pères grecs*, Paris.

Louth, A. 1981, *The Origins of the Christian Mystical Traditon: From Plato to Denys*. Oxford.

___ 1982, "Messalianism and Pelagianism", *StPatr* 17/1: 127-135.

___ 1983, *Discerning the Mystery: An Essay on the Nature of Theology*, Oxford.

___ 1993, "Eros and Mysticism. Early Christian Interpretation of the Song of Songs", in J. Ryce-Menuhin (ed.), *Jung and the Monotheisms*, London, 241-54.

Lucà, S. 1981, "Il commentario al Cantico dei Cantici di Nilo di Ancira", in *Atti del IV Congresso nazionale di studi bizantini*, 111-26.

Maccarone, M. 1952, "Vicarius Christi. Storia del titolo papale", *Lat.* 18: 41-45.

McFadyen, A. 1990, *The Call to Personhood: A Christian theory of the individual in social relationships*, Cambridge.

McGinn, B. 1991, *The Foundations of Mysticism: Origins to the Fifth Century*, London.

___ 1994, *The Growth of Mysticism: from Gregory the Great to the Twelfth Century*. London.

McGuckin, J. 1986, *The transfiguration of Christ in Scripture and Tradition*, Lewiston.

___ 1990, "Did Augustine's Christology depend on Theodore of Mopsuestia?", *HeyJ* 31:39-52.

___ 1994, *St. Cyril of Alexandria: The Christological Controversy. Its History, Theology, and Texts*, Leiden.

MacLeod, C.W. 1971, "Allegory and Mysticism in Origen and Gregory of Nyssa", *JThS* 22: 362-79.

McLynn, N.B. 1994, *Ambrose of Milan: Church and Court in a Christian Capital*, Berkeley-Los Angeles-London.

McMullen R., 1984, *Christianising the Roman Empire (AD 100-400)*, New Haven.

McNamara, K.M. 1955, "Theodoret of Cyros and the Unity of the Person in Christ", *IThQ* 22: 313-28.
McNeill, B. 1977, "Avircius and the Song of Songs", *VigChr* 31: 21-33.
Manns, F. 1990, "Une tradition juive dans les Commentaires du Cantique des Cantiques d'Origéne", *Antonianum* 65, 3-22.
Marcovich, M. 1986, "Introduction" to *Hippolytus: Refutatio Omnium Haeresium*, (*PTS* 25), Berlin-New York.
Markschies, C. 1992, *Valentinus Gnosticus? Untersuchungen zur valentinianischen Gnosis mit einem Kommentar zu den Fragmenten Valentins* (*WUNT* 65), Tübingen.
___ 1993, "'Die wunderliche Lehre von den zwei Logoi.' Clemens Alexandrinus, Fragment 23 – Zeugnis eines *Arius ante Arium* oder des arianischen Streites selbst?", in H.C. Brennecke, E.L. Grasmück, C. Markschies (eds.), *Logos: FS Luise Abramowski*, (*BZNW* 67), Berlin, 193-219.
___ 1994, "Die platonische Metapher vom 'inneren Menschen'", *ZKG* 105: 1-17.
___ 1995, *Ambrosius von Mailand und die Trinitätstheologie: kirchen- und theologiegeschichtliche Studien zu Antiarianismus und Neunizänismus bei Ambrosius und im lateinischen Westen*, Tübingen.
Marrou, H-I. 1949, *Augustin et la fin de la culture antique*, Paris.
Marti, H. 1974, *Übersetzer der Augustin-Zeit*, München.
Martin, J. 1907-8, "St. Epiphane", *Annales de philosophie chrétienne* 155: 113-150, 606-618; 156 (1908-9): 32-49.
Mateo-Seco, L.F. 1971, "Kenosis, Exaltaciòn de Cristo y Apocatastasis en la exegesis a Filipenses 2,5-11 de S. Gregorio de Nisa", *ScrTh* 3: 301-42.
___ 1990, "La cristologia del In Canticum Canticorum", in H.R. Drobner, Ch. Klock (eds.), *Studien zu Gregor von Nyssa und der christlichen Spätantike*, Leiden, 173-90.
May, G. 1966, "Gregor von Nyssa in der Kirchenpolitik seiner Zeit", *JÖBG* 15: 105-32.
___ 1971, "Die Chronologie des Lebens und der Werke des Gregor von Nyssa", in M. Harl (ed.), *Ecriture et culture philosophique dans la pensée de Grégoire de Nysse*, Leiden, 51-67.
Meloni, P. 1975, *Il Profumo dell' immortalità* (*Verba Seniorum* N.S. 7), Rome.
___ 1977, "Ippolito e il Cantico dei Cantici", in *Richerche su Ippolito* (*Studia Ephemeridis "Augustinianum,"* 13), Rome, 97-120.
___ 1984, "L'amore nel Cantico dei Cantici commentato dei Padri della chiesa", *PSV* 10: 242-52.
___ 1989, "Amore e immortalità nel 'Cantico dei Cantici' alla luce dell' interetazione patristica", in *Realtà e allegoria nell' interpretazionedel Cantico dei Cantici*, Genova, 45-62.
Meo, M.S. 1963, "La verginità di Maria nella lettera di papa Siricio al vescovo Anisio di Tessalonica", *Mar.* 25: 447-69.
Meredith, A. 1974, "Proverbes VIII, 22 chez Origène, Athanase, Basile et Grégoire de Nysse", in C. Kannengiesser (ed.), *Politique et Théologie chez Athanase d'Alexandrie*, Paris, 349-57.
___ 1982, "Gregory of Nyssa and Plotinus", *StPatr* 17/ 3, 1120-1125.

___ 1988, "The Divine Simplicity: Contra Eunomium I, 223-41", in L.F. Mateo-Seco and J.L. Bastero (eds.), *El 'Contra Eunomium I' en la produccion literaria de Gregorio de Nisa* (*Coloquio Internacional sobre Gregorio de Nisa*), Pamplona, 339-352.

Meyendorff, J. 1970, "Messalianism or Anti-Messalianism? A Fresh Look at the 'Macarian' Problem", in *Kyriakon. FS J. Quaesten* II, Münster, 585-90.

Meyer, H.B. 1988, "Rezension: *Apponii in Canticum Canticorum Expositionem ediderunt B Vregille et L Neyrand, CCL 19*", *ZKTh* 110: 250.

Micaelli, C. 1986, "L'Anima di Cristo nella Teologia Occidentale tra il quarto e il sesto secolo: tracce della presenza di Origene", *Aug* 26: 261-72.

Molina, M.A. 1983, "La remoción del velo o el acceso a la libertad,"*Estud Bibl* 41: 285-324.

Mommsen, T.E. 1955, "Apponius and Orosius on the significance of the epiphany", in *Late Classical and Medieval Studies in Honor of AM Friend*, Princeton, 96-111.

Monaci, Castagno, A. 1980, "L'idea della preesistenza delle anime e l'esegesi di Rm 9: 9-21", in H. Crouzel and A. Quacquarelli (eds.), *Origeniana Secunda*, Rome, 69-78.

Montalverne, J. 1948, *Theodoreti Cyrensis doctrina antiquior de verbo 'inhumanato', a. circiter 423-35*, Rome.

Mopsik, C. 1984, "La datation du *Chi'ur Qomah* d'après un texte néo-testamentaire", RSR 68: 129-146.

Moutsoulas, E. 1966, "Der Begriff 'Häresie' bei Epiphanius von Salamis", *StPatr* 7(*TU* 92): 362-71.

Mühlenberg, E. 1966, *Die Unendlichkeit Gottes bei Gregor von Nyssa,* Göttingen.

___ 1969, *Apollinaris von Laodicaea*, Göttingen.

___ 1985, "Apollinaris von Laodicea und die origenistische Tradition", *ZNTW* 76: 270-83.

Mulard, A. 1949, "Le libre arbitre et la grâce chez Saint Jean Chrysostome", *L'Année Théologique* 10: 151-79.

Münch-Labacher, G. 1996, *Naturhaftes und geschichtliches Denken bei Cyrill von Alexandrien: Die verschiedenen Betrachtungsweisen der Heilsverwirklichung in seinem Johannes-Kommentar*, Bonn.

Munro, J.F. 1995, *Spikenard and Saffron: a study in the poetic language of the Song of Songs*, Sheffield.

Murphy, F.X. 1945, *Rufinus of Aquileia*, Washington (DC).

Musurillo, H. 1980, "Méthode d'Olympe", *DSp* 10, 1109-1117.

Nautin, P. 1949, "Deux interpolations orthodoxes dans une lettre d' Arius", *AB* 67: 131-41.

___ 1977, *Origène: sa vie et son oeuvre*, Paris.

___ 1992, "Hippolytus", *EEC* I, 383-85.

Neuschäfer, B. 1987, *Origenes als Philologe*, Basel.

Norris, R.A. 1967, *God and World in Early Christian Theology*, London.

Nygren, A. 1953, *Agape and Eros* (ET), London.

O' Cleirigh, P. M. 1980, "The Meaning of Dogma in Origen", in E.P. Sanders (ed.), *Jewish and Christian Self-definition*, Vol. 1, London, 201-216.

Olivar, A. 1956, "Los Saltos del Verbo: Una Interpretación Patrística de Cant 2,8", *Analecta Sacra Tarragonensia* 29: 3-15.

Orbe, A. 1976, *Cristología Gnóstica: Introducción a la soteriología de los siglos II y III*, Madrid.
Osborne, C. 1992, "Neoplatonism and the Love of God in Origen", in R. Daly (ed.), *Origeniana Quinta*, Louvain, 270-83.
___ 1994, *Eros Unveiled: Plato and the God of Love*, Oxford.
Oxford Latin Dictionary (*OLD*), 1968, A. Souter et al. (eds.), Oxford.
Pace, N. 1990, *Richerche sulla tradizione di Rufino del 'De principiis' di Origene*, Florence.
Paredi, A. 1985, *Sant' Ambrogio*, Milano.
Parmentier, M. 1976/77/78, *St Gregory's Doctrine of the Holy Spirit*. (Diss. Oxford, 1973), published in: *EkklPh* 58: 41-100, 387-444; 59: 323-429; 60: 697-730.
___ 1985, "Evagrius of Pontus' 'Letter to Melania'", *Bijdr* 46: 2-38.
Patterson, L.G. 1966, "The Creation of the World and Methodius", *StPatr* 9 (*TU* 117), 240-50.
___ 1992, "Methodius on Origen in the De Creatis", in R. Daly (ed.), *Origeniana Quinta*, Louvain, 497-508.
Paveerd, F. van der 1978, "Confession and Penance in the *De Lepra* of Methodius of Olympus", *OrChrP* 44 : 309-41.
Pelikan, J. 1974, *The Spirit of Eastern Christendom (600-1700)* (= Vol. 3 of *The Christian Tradition*), Chicago.
___ 1981, "The spiritual sense of Scripture: the exegetical basis for St. Basil's doctrine of the Holy Spirit", in P.J. Fedwick (ed.), *Basil of Caesarea: Christian, Humanist, Ascetic* (2 vols.), Toronto, I, 337-66.
___ 1985, *Jesus through the Centuries*, New Haven, CN.
Pelletier, A-M. 1989, *Lectures du Cantique des Cantiques: de l'enigme du sens aux figures du lecteur*, Rome.
Penna, A. 1950, *Principi e carattere dell' esegesi di S Gerolamo*, Rome.
Pépin, J. 1987, *La tradition de l'Allégorie de Philon d'Alexandrie à Dante*, Paris.
Peretto, E. 1989, "Mariologia patristica" in Quacquarelli, A. (ed.), *Complementi Interdisciplinari di Patrologia*, Roma, 697-756.
Petré, H. 1948, *'Caritas'. Etudes sur le vocabulaire latin de la charité chrétienne*, Louvain.
Petterson, A. 1986, "Did Athanasius deny Christ's fear ?", *SJT* 39: 327-40.
Pietras, H. 1988, *L'Amore in Origene* (Studia Ephemeridis Augustinianum 28), Rome.
Pietrella, E. 1986, "L'Antiorigenismo di Gregorio di Nissa", *Aug* 26: 143-76.
Piret, P. 1983, *Le Christ et la Trinité selon Maxime le Confesseur*, Paris.
Pizzolato, L. 1978, *La dottrina esegetica di sant'Ambrogio*, Milan.
Places, E. des 1970, "Diadoque de Photice et le Messalianisme", *Kyriakon FS J. Quaesten* II, Münster, 591-95.
Pourkier, A. 1992, *L'hérésiologie d'Epiphane de Salamine*, Paris.
Prinzivalli, E. 1985, *L'Esegesi biblica di Metodio d'Olimpo* (Studia Ephemeridis Augustinianum 21), Rome.
___ 1992, "Philo of Carpasia", *EEC* (= ET of *DPAC*), 683.
Quacquarelli, A. 1985, "Le nozze eterne nella concezione e nell'iconografia cristiana antica", *Vet Chr* 22, 5-34

Quispel, G. 1964, "The Syrian Thomas and the Syrian Macarius", *VigChr* 18: 226-35.
___ 1974, "L conception de l'homme dans la gnose valentinienne", in idem., *Gnostic Studies*, I. Istanbul, 37-57.
Rahner, H. 1964, *Symbole der Kirche. Die Ekklesiologie der Väter*, Salzburg.
Rahner, K. 1972, *Theological Investigations 9* (ET), New York.
Raven, C.E. 1923, *Apollinarianism*, Cambridge.
Refoulé, F. 1961, "La christologie d'Evagre et l'origénisme." *OCP* 27: 221-66.
___ 1963, "Evagre, fut-il Origéniste?", *RSPhTh* 47: 398-402.
Renan, E. 1860, *Le Cantique des Cantiques traduit de l'hébreu*, Paris.
Richard, M. 1935, "L'activité littéraire de Théodoret avant le concile d'Éphèse." *RSPhTh* 24: 82-106.
___ 1936, "Notes sur l'évolution doctrinale de Théodoret de Cyr", *RSPhTh* 25: 459-81.
___ 1938, "Les Fragments exégétiques de Théophile d'Alexandrie et de Théophile d'Antioche", *RevBib* 47: 387-97.
___ 1945, "L'introduction du mot 'hypostase' dans la théologie de l'incarnation", *MSR* 2: 5-32; 243-70.
___ 1949, "Mélanges", *MSR* 6: 129.
___ 1969, "Hippolyte", *DSp* 7, 536.
___ 1976, "Une paraphrase grecque du Commentaire d'Hippolyte sur le Cantique des Cantiques", in idem*Opera Minora* I, Louvain.
___ 1977a, "Saint Athanase et la psychologie du Christ selon les Ariens", in idem, *Opera Minora* II, Louvain.
___ 1977b, "Un écrit de Théodoret sur l'unité du Christ après l'incarnation", in idem, *Opera Minora* II, Louvain.
Ricoeur, P. 1971
___ 1978, *The Rule of Metaphor: multi-disciplinary studies of the creation of meaning in language*, London.
Riedel, W. 1898, *Die Auslegung des Hohenliedes in der jüdischen Gemeinde und der griechischen Kirche*, Leipzig.
Riedinger, R. 1975, " 'Seid klug wie die Schlange, einfältig wie die Taube.' Der Umkreis des Physiologos'", *Βυζαντινά* 7: 15-32.
___ 1978, "Akoimeten", *TRE* 2: 148-52
Riedlinger, H. 1958, *Die Makellosigkeit der Kirche in den lateinischen Hoheliedkommentaren des Mittelalters*, Münster.
Riedmatten, H. de 1951, "Sur les notions christologiques opposées à Apollinaire", *RThom* 51: 553-72.
___ 1952, *Les Actes du procès de Paul de Samosate. Étude sur la christologie du IIIe et IVe siècles*, Freiburg.
Riggi, C. 1972, "Comprensione umana nella Bibbia secondo Epifanio", in *Studi classici in onore di Quintino Cataudella*, Catania, Vol. II, 607-35.
___ 1979, "Formule di Fede in Sant'Epifanio di Salamina", *Sal* 41: 309-21.
___ 1981, "Questioni cristologiche in Epifanio di Salamina", *Bessarione* 2: 63-70.
___ 1982, "La catéchèse adaptée aux temps chez Epiphane", *StPatr* 17/1: 160-68.

___ 1984, "La dialoge des Marcelliens dans le Panarion", *StPatr* 15: 368-73.

___ 1985, "Il termine 'Hairesis' nell'Accezione di Epifanio di Salamino", in idem *Epistrophe*, Rome 583-607.

Ringshausen, H. 1967, *Zur Verfasserschaft und Chronologie der dem Nilus Ancyranus zugeschriebenen Werke*, Frankfurt am Main (Diss.).

Rist, J. 1975, "The Greek and Latin Texts of the discussion of Free Will in De Principiis Book III", in H. Crouzel, G. Lomiento, J. Rius-Camps (eds.), *Origeniana: premier colloque international des études origeniennes*, Bari, 97-109.

Ritter, A.M. 1965, *Das Konzil von Konstantinopel und sein Symbol. Studien zur Geschichte und Theologie des zweiten Ökumenischen Konzils*, Göttingen.

Rius-Camps, J. 1987, "Subordinacianismo en Origenes?", in L. Lies (ed.), *Origeniana Quarta*, Innsbruck-Vienna, 154-86.

Robert, A. and Tournay, R. with Feuillet, A. 1963, *Le Cantique des Cantiques*, Rome.

Rondeau, M.-J. 1969, "Le Commentaire des Psaumes de Diodore de Tarse et l'exégèse antique du Psaume 109/110", *RHR* 176: 5-33;153-88 & 177: 5-33.

___ 1985, *Les Commentaires Patristiques du Psautier (IIIe-Ve siècles)*, Rome.

Roques, M. 1996, "L'authenticité de l'*Apologia David Altera*: historique et progrès d'une controverse", *Aug* 36: 53-92; 423-58.

Rorem, P. 1993, *Pseudo-Dionysius: a commentary on the texts and an introduction to their influence*, New York-Oxford.

Rosenbaum, H-U. 1980, "Der Hoheliedkommentar des Nilus von Ancyra: MS Ogden 30 und die Katenenüberlieferung", *ZKG* 29:187-206.

Rowland, C. 1982, *The Open Heaven*, London.

Rowley, H.H. 1965, "The Interpretation of the Song of Songs", in idem,*The Servant of the Lord and other Essays on the Old Testament*, Oxford, 197-245.

Ruh, K. 1990, *Geschichte der abendländischen Mystik I. Die Grundlegung durch die Kirchenväter und die Mönchstheologie des 12. Jahrhunderts*, München.

Sagi-Bunic, T. 1965, *"Deus Perfectus et Homo Perfectus" a Concilio Ephesino (a.431) ad Chalcedonense (a.451)*, Rome.

Sagot, S. 1981a, "Une récente édition du 'Commentaire sur le Cantique des Cantiques' de Philon de Carpasia", *VigChr* 35: 358-76.

___ 1981b, *Le Cantique dans le 'De Isaac et anima' d'Ambroise de Milan: Étude textuelle et recherches sur les anciennes versions latines*, (Recherches augustinienners XVI), Paris.

Schäublin, C. 1974, *Untersuchungen zu Methode und Herkunft der Antiochenischen Exegese*, Köln-Bonn.

Schibli, H.S. 1987, "Apponius on the Origin of the Soul", *StPatr* 23: 178-85.

___ 1990, *Pherekydes of Syros*, Oxford.

___ 1992, "Origen, Didymus and the Vehicle of the Soul", in R.J. Daly (ed.), *Origeniana Quinta*, 381-91.

Schlam, C.C. 1992, *The Golden Ass of Apuleius*, London.

Schlieben, R. 1979, *Cassiodors Psalmenexegese: eine Analyse ihrer Methoden als Beitrag zur Untersuchung der Geschichte der Bibelauslegung der Kirchenväter und der*

Verbindung christlicher Theologie mit antiker Schulwissenschaft (Göttinger akademische Beiträge, 110), Göttingen.

Schneemelcher, W. 1962, "Bild", *RAC* 5: 909-27

Schönborn, C. 1976, *L'Icône du Christ*, Fribourg.

___ 1984, "'Gott will für ewig Mensch bleiben.' Anmerkungen zur Auslegungsgeschichte des Glaubensartikels 'Sedet ad dexteram Patris'", *IKaZ* 13: 1-13.

Schultz, B. 1986-1987, "Das Filioque bei Epiphanius von Cypern (im Panarion)", *Ostkirkliche Studien* 35: 105-34; 36: 381-300.

Schulze, U. 1983, "Die 4. geistliche Homilie des Makarios/Symeon. Gedanken zur Textüberlieferung", in W. Strothmann (ed.), *Makarios-Symposium über das Böse* (*Göttinger Orientforschungen*, I, *Syriaca*, 24), Wiesbaden, 85-98.

Schulz-Flügel, E. 1992, "Bericht" in *36. Arbeitsbericht der Stiftung, Vetus Latina*, Beuron, 19-22.

Schwager, R. 1982, "Der wunderbare Tausch: Zur 'physischen' Erlösungslehre Gregors von Nyssa", *ZKTh*: 104: 1-24.

Schwartz, E. 1924, "Der sg. 'Sermo maior de fide' des Athanasius", *SAM* 6, München.

Scipioni, L.I. 1974, *Nestorio e il concilio di Efeso. Storia dogma critica,* Milan.

Scopello, M. 1985, *L'Exégèse de l'Ame*, Leiden.

Seibt, K. 1994, *Die Theologie des Markell von Ankyra*, Berlin-New York.

Sfameni Gasparro, G. 1987, "Il Problema delle Citazioni del Peri Archon nella lettera a Mena di Giustiniano", in L. Lies (ed.), *Origeniana Quarta*, Innsbruck-Vienna 54-75.

Sherwood, P. 1969, "The Refutation of Origenism", *StAns* 36: 72-102.

Siclari, A. 1985, "L'unità dell'amore nel 'Commento al Cantico dei Cantici' di Origene", in *Spienxza Antica: Studi in onore di Domenico Pesce*, Milano, 269-96.

Sieben, H.J. 1979, *Die Konzilsidee der alten Kirche*, Paderborn.

Siegmund, A. 1949, *Die Überlieferung der griechischen christlichen Literatur in der lateinischen Kirche bis 12 Jh.*, München.

Simke, H. 1962, "Cant 1,7f in altchristlicher Auslegung", *ThZ* 18 : 256-67.

Simon, P. 1951, *Sponsa Cantici. Die Deutung der Braut des Hohenliedes in der vornizänischen griechischen Theologie und in der lateinischen Theologie des 3. und 4. Jahrhunderts* (Diss.), Bonn.

___ 1960, "Die Kirche als Braut des Hohenliedes nach dem hl. Augustinus", in *Die Kirche und ihre Ämter und Stände. FS J. Frings*, Köln, 24-41.

Simonetti, M. 1974, "Ancora sulla paternità della ps.athanasiano 'Sermo maior de fide'", *VetChr* 11: 332-43.

___ 1975a, *Studii sull' Arianesimo*, Rome.

___ 1975b, *La crisi ariana nel IV secolo*, Rome.

___ 1981, "Teodereto e Origene sul Cantico dei Cantici", in *Letterature comparate: probleme e metodo. Studi in onore di E. Paratore*, Bologna, 919-30.

___ 1982, "Alcune osservazioni sul monofisismo di Cirillo di Alessandria", *Aug* 22: 493-511.

___ 1984, "Didymiana", *VetChr* 21: 129-55.

___ 1985, *Lettera e/o allegoria. Un contributo alla storia dell'esegesi patristica*, Rome.

___ 1986, "Eusebio e Origene. Per una storia dell' Origenismo", *Aug* 26: 323-34.

___ 1989, "Aggiornamento su Ippolito", in idem (ed.), *Nuove Ricerche su Ippolito*, Rome, 75-130.
___ 1996, "Una Nuova Proposta su Ippolito", *Aug* 36: 13-46.
Smolak, K. 1984, "Theodoret", in M. Greschat (ed.), *Gestalten der Kirchengeschichte* Bd. 2.2 (*Alte Kirche*), 239-50.
Soskice, J.M. 1985, *Metaphor and Religious Language*, Oxford.
Spoerl, K.M. 1993, "The Schism at Antioch since Cavallera", in M.R. Barnes, D.H. Williams (eds.), *Arianism after Arius: Essays on the Developments of the Fourth-Century Conflicts*, Edinburgh, 101-126.
Staats, R. 1979, "Die Basilianische Verherrlichung des Heiligen Geistes auf dem Konzil zu Konstantinopel 381", *KuD* 25: 232-53.
___ 1982, "Beobachtungen zur Definition und zur Chronologie des Messalianismus", *JbÖB* 32: 235-44.
___ 1994, "Messalianer", *TRE* 22: 607-19.
Stead, G.C. 1976, "Ontology and Terminology in Gregory of Nyssa", in H. Dörrie et al. (eds.), *Gregor von Nyssa und die Philosophie*, Leiden.
___ 1990, "Why not three Gods? The Logic of Gregory of Nyssa'a Trinitarian Doctrine", in H.R. Drobner, Ch. Klock (eds), *Studien zu Gregor von Nyssa und der christlichen Spätantike*, Leiden, 149-63.
___ 1994, *Philosophy in Christian Antiquity*, Cambridge.
Stewart, C. 1991, *Working the Earth of the Heart*, Oxford.
Stickelberger, H. 1982, "Freisetzende Einheit: über ein christologisches Grundaxiom bei Maximus und Karl Rahner", in F. Heinzer and C. von Schönborn (eds.), *Maximus Confessor: Actes du Symposium sur Maxime le Confesseur*, Fribourg (Suisse).
Stockmeier, P. 1982, "Das Konzil von Chalkedon. Probleme der Forschung", *FZPhTh* 29: 140-56.
Strousma, G. 1984, "'König und Schwein'. Zur Struktur des manichäischen Dualismus", in J. Taubes (ed.), *Gnosis und Theologie*, München, 141-53.
Stubenrauch, B. 1991, *Der Heilige Geist bei Apponius: Zum theologischen Gehalt einer spätantiken Hoheliedauslegung*, Rome-Freiburg-Vienna.
___ 1992, "Apponius und sein Kommentar zum Hohenlied: Anmerkungen zu Entwicklung und Stand der Forschung", *Aug* 32: 161-76.
Studer, B. 1966, "Zur Frage des westlichen Origenismus", *StPatr* 9 (*TU* 94): 270-87.
___ 1968, "A propos des traductions d'Origène par Jérôme et Rufin", *VetChr* 5: 137-155.
___ 1972, "Zur Frage der dogmatischen Terminologie in der lateinischen Uebersetzung von Origenes' De Principiis", in *Epektasis. FS Daniélou*, Paris, 403-414.
___ 1985a, *Gott und unsere Erlösung im Glauben der Alten Kirche*, Düsseldorf.
___ 1985b, "*Una persona in Christo*. Ein augustinisches Thema bei Leo dem Großen", *Aug* 25: 453-87.
___ 1986, "Zur Hochzeitsfeier der Christen in den westlichen Kirchen", *StAns* 93: 51-85.
___ 1987, Rezension: *Apponii in Canticum Canticorum Expositionem ediderunt B Vregille et L Neyrand, CCL 19, Aug* 27: 635-39.

___ 1988, "Der geschichtliche Hintergrund des Ersten Buches 'Contra Eunomium' Gregors von Nyssa", in *El 'Contra Eunomium' en la Produccion Literaria de Gregorio de Nisa (VI Colloquio Internacional sobre Gregorio de Nisa)*, Pamplona, 139-71.
___ 1989, *La riflessione teologica nella chiesa imperiale (sec. IV e V)*, Rome.
___ 1994, *Storia della Teologia*, Roma.
Tajo, M. 1961, "Un confronto tra S. Ambrogio e S. Agostino a proposito dell' esegesi del Cantico dei Cantici", *REAug* 7: 127-51.
Tarchnishvili, M. 1955, *Geschichte der kirchlichen georgischen Literatur (Studi e Testi 185)*, Rome.
Thiel, M. 1969, *Grundlagen und Gestalt der Hebräischkenntnisse des frühen Mittelalters (StMed 10/3)*, Spoleto.
Thomson, R.W. 1983, "Gregory of Narek's *Commentary on the Song of Songs*", *JThS* 34: 453-96.
Thümmel, H.-G. 1994, *Die Frühgeschichte der Ostkirchlichen Bilderlehre zur Zeit vor dem Bilderstreit, (TU 139)*, Berlin.
Timiadis, F.M.L. 1985, "God's Immutability and Communicability", in T.F. Torrance (ed.) *Theological Dialogue Between Orthodox and Reformed Churches*, Edinburgh, 23-49.
Torjesen, Karen J. 1986, *Hermeneutical Procedure and Theological Method in Origen's Exegesis (PTS 28)*, Berlin.
Torrance, I. 1988, *Christology After Chalcedon*, Norwich.
Trigg, J.W. 1983, *Origen: The Bible and Philosophy in the third-century Church*, Atlanta.
Truzzi, C. 1985, *Zeno, Gaudenzio, e Cromazio*, Brescia.
Tsirplanis, C.N. 1982, "The Concept of Universal Salvation in St. Gregory of Nyssa", *StPatr* 17/3: 1131-1144.
Turner, D. 1995, *The darkness of God: negativity in Christian mysticism*, Cambridge.
Underhill, E. 1930, *Mysticism*, London.
Urbach, E. U. 1971, "The Homiletical Interpretations of the Sages and the Expositions of Origen on Canticles, and the Jewish-Christian disputation", *Scripta Hierosolymita* 22: 247-75.
Vaccari, A. 1952-58, *Scritti di erudizione e di filologia*, Rome.
___ 1961, "Notulae Patristicae. 1. Apponii in Canticum Canticorum", *Gr.* 42: 725-28.
Vacek, E.C. 1994, *Love, Human and Divine: the heart of Christian Ethics*, Washington, D.C.
Van Parys, M. 1971, "Exégèse Et Théologie Dans Les Livres Contre Eunome", in M. Harl (ed.), *Écriture et Culture Philosophique dans la Pensée de Grégoire de Nysse*, Leiden.
Viciano, A. 1989, "Theodoret von Kyros und der Manichäismus in seinem Kommentar zu den Paulusbriefen", in *Akten des zweiten Internationalen Kongresses zum Manichäismus*, Bonn.
___ 1990a, "Christologische Deutung von Röm 8,19-22 bei Gregor von Nyssa und Theodoret von Kyros", in Ch. Klock, H. Drobner (eds.), *Studien zur Gregor von Nyssa*, Leiden.
___ 1990b, *Cristo el Autor de nuestra Salvacion; estudio sobre el commentario de Teodoreto de Ciro a las Epistolas Paulinas*, Pamplona.

___ 1992, " Ο ΣΚΟΠΟΣ ΤΗΣ ΑΛΗΘΕΙΑΣ: Théodoret de Cyr et ses principes herméneutiques dans le prologue du Commentaire du Cantique des Cantiques", in *Letture cristiane dei Libri Sapienziali* (*Studia Ephemeridis Augustinianum*) 37: 419-35.

Vickers, 1988, *In defence of rhetoric*, Oxford.

Villain, M. 1937, "Rufin d'Aquilée. La querelle autour Origène", *RSR* 37: 5-37; 165-95.

Vogt, H.-J. 1974, *Das Kirchenverständnis des Origenes* (*Bonner Beiträge zur Kirchengeschichte*, 4), Köln.

___ 1987, "Warum wurde Origenes zum Häretiker erklärt?", in L. Lies (ed.), *Origeniana Quarta*, Innsbruck-Vienna, 78-111.

___ 1990, "Beobachtungen zum Johannes-Kommentar des Origenes", *ThQ* 170, 191-208.

Voisenet, J. 1994, *Bestiaire Chrétien: L'imagerie animals des auteurs du Haut Moyen Âge (Ve-XIe s.)*, Toulouse, 1994.

Völker, W. 1930, *Das Volkommenheitsideal des Origenes*, Tübingen.

___ 1955a, *Gregor von Nyssa als Mystiker*, Wiesbaden.

___ 1955b, "Zur Gotteslehre Gregors von Nyssa", *VigChr* 9: 103-128.

Vosté, J.M. 1929, "L'oeuvre exégétique de Théodore de Mopsueste au IIe concile de Constantinople", *RBen* 38: 382-95; 542-54.

Wallace-Hadrill, D.S. 1982, *Christian Antioch*, Cambridge.

Warnach, P.V. 1951, "Das Mönchtum als 'Pneumatische Philosophie' in den Nilusbriefen", in A. Meyer et al. (eds.), *Vom Christlichen Mysterium*, Düsseldorf, 131-51.

Weinandy, T. 1993, *In the likeness of human flesh*, Edinburgh.

Welserheimb, L. 1948, "Das Kirchenbild der griechischen Väterkommentare", *ZKTh* 70: 393-449.

Wermelinger, O. 1975, *Rom und Pelagius*, Stuttgart.

Wickham, L.R. 1981a, "Symbols of the Incarnation in Cyril Of Alexandria", in M. Schmidt (ed.), *Typus, Symbol, Allegorie*, Regensburg, 41-53.

___ 1981b, "Chalkedon", *TRE* 7: 668-75.

___ 1981c, "Soul and Body: Christ's Omnipresence. (*De tridui spatio* 290,18-294,13)", in A. Spira, C. Klock (eds.), *The Easter Sermons of Gregory of Nyssa*, Cambridge (MA), 1981, 279-92.

___ 1984, "Cyril of Alexandria and the Apple of Discord", *StPatr* 15: 379-92.

Wilken, R. L. 1971, "Liturgy, Bible and Theology in the Easter Homilies of Gregory of Nyssa", in M. Harl (ed.), *Écriture et Culture Philosophique dans la Pensée de Grégoire de Nysse*, Leiden, 127-43.

Williams, R.D. 1985, "Origen on the Soul of Jesus", in R. Hanson, H. Crouzel (eds.), *Origeniana Tertia*, Rome, 131-37.

___ 1987a, *Arius: Heresy and Tradition*, London.

___ 1987b, "The Son's Knowledge of the Father in Origen", in L. Lies (ed.), *Origeniana Quarta*, Innsbruck, 146-50.

___ 1987c, "Jesus Christus II: Alte Kirche", *TRE* 16:726-45.

___ 1990, *The Wound of Knowledge*, (2nd edn.), London.

___ 1992, "Methodius von Olympos", *TRE* 22: 680-84.

___ 1993, "Macrina's Deathbed Revisited: Gregory of Nyssa on Mind and Passion", in L.R. Wickham, C.P. Bammel (eds.),*Christian Faith and Greek Philosophy in Late Antiquity: FS G.C. Stead*, Leiden, 227-46.

___ 1995, "Origenes/Origenismus", *TRE* 25: 397-420.

Wilmart, A. 1911, "L'ancienne version latine du Cantique I- III,4", *RBen* 28: 11-36.

Winkelmann, F. 1970, "Einige Bemerkungen zu den Aussagen des Rufinus von Aquileia", in *Kyriakon. FS J Quaesten* II, 532-47.

Winkler, G. 1983, "Ein bedeutsamer Zusammenhang zwischen der Erkenntnis und Ruhe in Mt 11, 27-29 und dem Ruhen des Geistes auf Jesus am Jordan. Eine Analyse zur Geist-Christologie in syrischen und armenischen Quellen", *Muséon* 96: 267-326.

Winling, R. 1988, "La résurrection du Christ dans les traités Pseudo-athanasiens *Contra Apollinarium*", *RSR* 62: 22-41; 101-110.

___ 1990, "Mort et résurrection du Christ dans les traités Contra Eunomium de Grégoire de Nysse", *RSR* 64: 127-40; 251-69.

Winston, D. 1986, "Creation ex nihilo revisited", *JJS* 37: 88-91.

Winterbottom, M. 1988, "Review: *Apponii in Canticum Canticorum Expositionem ediderunt B. Vregille et L. Neyrand, CCL 19*", *JThS* 39: 273-76.

Witek, F. 1986, "Apponius", *RAC Suppl* 4: 506-14.

Witte, J. 1904, *Der Kommentar des Aponius zum Hohenlied* (Diss.), Erlangen.

Wolfson, H. A. 1947, *Philo,* Cambridge, MA.

Yannaras, Ch. 1982, *Person und Eros. Eine Gegenüberstellung der Ontologie der griechischen Kirchenväter und der Existenzphilosophie des Westens*, Göttingen.

Young, F.M. 1982, "Did Epiphanius know what he meant by 'heresy'?" *StPatr* 17: 199-205.

___ 1983, *From Nicea to Chalcedon*, London.

___ 1989a, "Exegetical Method and Scriptural Proof", *StPatr* 19: 297-303.

___ 1989b, "The rhetorical schools and their influence on patristic exegesis", in R.D. Williams (ed.), *The Making of Orthodoxy: Essays in honour of Henry Chadwick*, Cambridge, 182-99.

___ 1990, "Alexandrian Interpretation", in R.J. Coggins, J.L. Houlden (eds.), *Dictionary of Biblical Interpretation,* London, 10-12.

___ 1992, "Nemesius von Emesa", *TRE* 22: 256-59.

Zahn, Th. 1890, *Geschichte des Neutestamentlichen Kanons* 2,1, Erlangen-Leipzig.

___ 1923, "Herkunft und Lehrrichtung des Bibeluebersetzers Symmachus", *NKZ* 34: 197-209.

Zani, A. 1984, *La cristologia di Ippolito*, Brescia.

Zeiller, J. 1918, *Les origines chrétiennes dans les provinces danubiennes de l'Empire Romain*, Paris.

Zincone, S. 1985, "Il tema dell' uomo/donna immagine di Dio nei Commenti paolini e a Genesi di area antiochena (Diodoro, Crisostomo, Teodoro, Teodoreto)", *ASEs* 3: 103-13.

___ 1988, *Studi sulla visione dell'uomo in ambito antiocheno (Diodoro, Crisostomo, Teodoro, Teodoreto),* Rome.

Zizioulas, J. D. 1985, *Being As Communion*, Crestwood, NY.

Scripture Index

Genesis
2:6	91
3:2	118

Numbers
19:15	58

1 Samuel
28	6

1 Kings
10:41	32

Esther
16:13	45

Psalms
15:6	159
17	68
18 (19): 6	161
28:9	76
39	68
39 (40):7	126
44 (45)	137, 146, 154, 155, 163
44 (45):1	19
44 (45): 2	162
44 (45):4	101
44 (45):8	61, 85, 101, 106, 109, 145, 146
47:3	19
65:9	7
84 (85):11-12	123, 128
85 (86):6	79
90 (91):1	70
104 (105):15	100
118	17
118 (119):57	65
119 (120):5	126
122 (123):7	79

Proverbs
5:19	80
9:1	62, 131, 135

Isaiah
7:14	137
40:15	81
61:10	124
63:3	101, 132

Jeremiah
2:19	7

Baruch
3:10-12	7
3:38	140

Ezekiel
47	3

Daniel
2:34	81

Habakkuk
2:19	57
3:3	19

Song of Songs (Cant.)

1:1	52	5:4	85-89
1:2	18, 51, 52	5:5	85-89
1:3	18, 53-56, 59, 121, 122, 124, 165	5:6	85, 106, 121
		5:9	18, 94
1:4	53, 62, 106, 121	5:10	93, 139, 149
1:5	125, 128, 130, 131, 165	5:10-16	3, 93-101, 120, 149
1:6	33, 125, 127	5:11	93, 139
1:7	18, 63, 64, 125	5:12	93, 138, 139
1:10	73	5:14	93, 99, 138
1:11	63, 65	5:17/6:1	84
1:12	1, 57, 58.	6:3	18
1:13	57, 59	6:4	140
1:14	1, 57, 121	6:8	30, 106, 107, 110, 127, 139, 142, 143, 145, 149, 166
1:15	121, 125		
1:16	69, 130, 134	6:9	18, 25, 37, 100, 105, 111, 120, 142, 145-148, 152
2:1	48		
2:2	37, 120	6:10	105, 113, 142, 144, 155
2:3	69	6:11	121
2:4	106	6:12	4
2:5	28	7:1	81, 106, 142
2:6	63, 73	7:4	37
2:8	76, 77	7:5	116
2:9	79	8:1	52
2:10	18, 79, 115	8:2	97
2:14	52, 62, 103, 132	8:5	4, 18, 132
2:15	31	8:8	163
2:16	64, 64, 141	8:9	55, 163
2:17	18, 141	8:14	115, 117
3:1	91		
3:3	63, 64, 67	Matthew	
3:4	63, 67	6:28	37
3:6	4, 18, 30, 62, 132, 133, 134	19:5-6	109
3:7	104, 134	26:6	165
3:9	63, 134-136	26:39	130
3:10	75		
3:11	82	Luke	
4:2	61	1:35	71
4:12	3, 137	2:52	116
4:15	3	24:36	128
4:16/5:1	18, 19, 20, 83, 84, 115		
5:2	3, 25, 85, 89, 90, 92, 138	John	
5:3	18, 85, 87, 91	1:14	113, 151

7:38	3
14:9	80
20:19	83
20:22	19

Acts
3:21	19

Romans
5:5	152
6:5	102
8:3	129

1 Corinthians
11:1-4	2
13:13	136
15:28	148
15:53	19

Galatians
4:26	130

Ephesians
1:22	3, 128
4:13	141, 148
5:22	128
5:27	149
5:30	129
5:32	166

Philippians
2:5-9	33, 108, 122
2:6	33, 56, 123
2:7	69, 122, 165

Colossians
1:15	131
1:20	63
1:24	131
1:28	141
3:4	73

1 Timothy
1:13	139

Hebrews
10:5	126

2 John
1	3

Revelation
3:16	3
3:20	116
12	3
12:1	116
21:1-4	116, 138
21:2	146

Odes of Solomon
8:6	74

Name Index

Abramowski, L. 161
Akiva, R. 3
Albianos 38
Aly, W. 17
Alypius 47
Ambrose 22, 23, 29, 41, 42, 44, 48, 49,
    50, 53-58, 63, 65, 66, 77, 78, 79, 99,
    100, 137, 138
Ambrosiaster 60, 128
Amphilochus 25
Aphrahat 3
Apollinarius 20, 21, 38, 84, 129, 145, 146
Apponius 4, 13, 41-50, 60, 61, 66, 99,
    110-114, 116, 151-155, 158, 164
Aquila 4
Arens, H. 46
Aristotle 2, 7, 85, 136
Arius 42
Armstrong, A.H. 102
Athanasius 7, 18, 21, 40
Augustine 9, 11, 29, 33, 34, 46, 47, 70,
    73, 100, 111, 121, 126, 127, 128, 130,
    137, 138, 139, 152, 166
Baehrens, W. 16, 31, 123
Balthasar, H. Urs von 86, 87, 88
Bammel, C. 34
Barbara, M.A. 17
Bardy, G. 35
Basil of Caesarea 25
Bauer, W. 55
Baus, K. 63
Beck, H.-G. 17
Bienert, W. 7, 18

Bjerre-Aspergen, K. 95, 96
Bogaert, P.-M. 41
Bonosus 42, 43
Bonwetsch, N. 143
Borgomeo, P. 73
Borret, M. 123
Bouhot, J.-P. 42
Cahill, J.B. 24
Cambe, M 3
Cameron, Averil 159
Canévet, M. 88, 89, 147
Cassian 70
Cassiodorus 21, 44, 45
Ceresa-Gastaldo, A. 21, 165
Chadwick, H. 108
Chappuzeau, G. 76
Chromatius 10, 48, 153
Chrysostom 27, 35-40, 43, 48
Clark, E. 32
Collantes Lozano, J. 128, 129
Courcelle, P. 138
Crociani, L. 43, 44
Crouzel, H. 68-72, 108, 121
Cyprian, 3
Cyril of Alexandria 6, 39, 40, 43, 73-76,
    98, 99, 122, 132, 133, 134, 144, 150,
    161, 162
Damasus 23
Daniel 41
Daniélou, J. 3, 24, 28, 88, 90, 147
Dassmann, E. 23, 66
Debidour, V.H. 144
Dechow, J. 21, 27

Index

Desjardins, R. 73
Diadochus 162
Didymus 6, 7, 20, 21, 84, 85, 94, 95, 103, 144, 146, 147, 157
Diodore 6, 7, 26, 27, 35, 102, 163
Dionysius of Alexandria 18, 125
Dionysius (Pseudo-) 1, 2, 8
Drijvers, H. 55
Dummer, J. 29
Dünzl, F. 25, 95, 96, 149
Eliezer, R. 3
Ephraim 3, 160
Epiphanius of Salamis 7, 9, 21, 27-30, 40, 44, 103, 126, 130, 135, 144, 145, 166
Epiphanius Scholasticus 21, 44
Esper, M.N. 16, 147
Eunomius 10, 86
Euringer, S. 165
Eusebius of Caesarea 30, 55
Eustathius 5
Eustochium 22, 81
Evagrius 7, 8, 32, 33, 37, 38, 39, 103, 147
Falk, Marcia 3
Feltoe 18
Field, F. 4
Flavian 27
Frank, K.S. 44
Frede, H.-J, 41
Gaith, J. 28, 139
Galtier, P. 75
Garnier, M. 35
Geerlings, W. 48
Gennadius 43
Georgios Monachos 36
Gesché, A. 20, 94
Gill, Eric 1
Granado, C. 22
Grant, R.M. 30, 136
Gratian 99
Gregory of Elvira 23, 44, 49, 64, 128

Gregory of Nazianzus 67, 162
Gregory of Nyssa 10, 16, 17, 24, 25, 30, 39, 55, 85, 94, 103, 121, 138, 146, 147, 158, 160, 161
Gregory the Great 44, 115
Gribomont, J. 37, 44
Grillmeier, A. 35, 45, 72, 109, 121, 122, 149, 154, 161
Grünbeck, E. 161, 164
Guérard, M.-G. 37, 38, 39, 102, 103, 104,, 116, 124
Guinot, J.-N. 35, 67, 100, 101
Harl, M. 17, 72, 121
Heine, R. 17, 26
Heither, T. 34
Helladius 28
Herder, J.G. 1
Hesychius of Jerusalem 40, 137, 138
Heussi, K. 36, 37
Hilary 43, 47, 49, 112
Hippolytus 3, 4, 12, 15, 50, 53, 54, 55, 76, 77, 78, 109, 110, 115, 122
Holl, K. 29
Hübner, R. 148, 149, 150
Iamblichus 158
Innocent I 42
Irenaeus 3, 49. 100, 130
Irmscher, J. 17
Isidore of Pelusium 36
Ivánka, E. von 107
Jaspert, B. 44
Jerome 7, 15, 16, 21, 22, 24, 27, 31, 41, 44, 45, 47, 49, 50, 58, 81, 103, 132, 137, 165
Johanan, R. 4
John of the Cross 87
Jouassard, G. 75
Jovinian 22, 43, 147
Julian (the Apostate) 10
Justinian 10, 43, 109, 159
Klostermann, E. 40
König, H. 44-47, 112, 113, 152, 155

Kramer, G.H. 100
Lampe, G. 55
Langerbeck, H. 24
Le Boulluec, A. 20, 68
Leo I 45, 46, 162
Leontius (monk) 38
Leontius of Byzantium 151
Leys, R. 87
Luca, S. 37
Macarius 28
MacLeod, C.W. 86
Mai 39, 75
Marcellus 7, 19, 20, 60, 84, 103, 148, 149
Marius Victorinus 60, 130
Mark the Hermit 36, 105
Mateo-Seco, L.F. 147
Maximus 17
May, G. 24
McGuckin, J. 161, 162
Melania 32
Meletius 27
Melito 4
Meloni, P. 53-56, 77, 109, 110, 166, 167
Methodius 12, 15, 18, 105, 126, 143, 144
Montanus 42
Mühlenberg, E. 147
Musurillo, H. 144
Nautin, P. 17
Nemesius 68, 86
Nestorius 42, 162
Neyrand, L. 44, 45
Nicephorus 36
Nilus 36-39, 50, 58, 102-105, 116, 117, 124, 125, 144
Noetus 77
Olympias 8, 24, 25
Origen 3, 4, 6, 7, 9, 12, 15-18, 21, 22, 24, 25, 27, 30-34, 39, 44, 48, 49, 50, 56, 58, 59, 60-63, 66, 67, 68, 71, 72, 72, 78-81, 94, 96, 97, 99, 101, 103, 105-110, 122, 123, 124, 126-129, 131, 133,
134, 143, 144, 145, 152, 153, 159, 163, 166
Osborne, C. 108
Pacianus 22, 146
Palladius 36
Paul of Pannonia 43
Pelagius 42, 44, 45
Pelagius II 35
Pelletier, A.-M. 43
Pépin, J. 8
Philastrius 30
Philo of Alexandria 9, 156
Philo of Carpasia 21, 30, 41, 50, 62, 82, 116, 127, 135, 166
Photius 18, 144
Photinus 42, 43, 60, 61, 85, 112
Pietras, H. 108
Plotinus 89, 102, 108
Prinzivalli, E. 21, 144, 145
Procilla 18
Proclus 162
Proclus of Constantinople 36
Procopius of Gaza 16, 17, 20, 50, 56, 134, 137, 166
Prosper of Aquitaine 45
Psellus 116
Pseudo-Athanasius 40, 50, 98, 145
Pseudo-Pelagius 45
Renan, E. 1
Richard 15, 19, 30, 31, 35
Ricoeur, P. 2
Riedel, W. 145
Ringshausen, H. 36, 37, 39
Rist, J. 33
Robert, A. 66
Rondeau, M.-J. 21, 85
Rufinus 7, 15, 24, 31, 32, 34, 44, 48, 50, 56, 58, 60, 63, 68-71, 73, 79, 80, 107, 122, 123, 132, 133, 165, 166
Schäublin, C. 5, 6, 35
Schlieben, R. 45
Schulz-Flügel, E. 24, 65, 129

Seibt, K. 150
Severus 74, 75
Sieben, H. 6
Simke, H. 129
Simon, P. 133, 139
Simonetti, M. 23, 43, 64
Simpronianus 22
Staats, R. 29
Stubenrauch, B. 61, 155, 156
Studer, B. 32, 44, 45
Symmachus 80, 143
Tertullian 3
Theodore of Mopsuestia 5, 6, 26, 27, 34, 103, 164
Theodoret 6, 7, 16, 35, 36, 50, 52, 53, 59, 60, 67, 69, 100-103, 121, 122, 142, 163, 164, 165
Theodosius I 10, 24
Theodosius II 45

Theophilus 30, 31, 68, 137
Theodotus 74
Theopropus 21
Thümmel, H.G. 159
Trigg, J. 17
Truzzi, C. 48
Tyconius 11, 128
Valentinian 99, 100
Victorinus of Petovium 49
Viret, F. 148
Vogt, H.-J. 73
Vregille, B. 41, 44, 45
Welserheimb, L. 82, 136
Wenger, A. 43
William of St. Thierry 23
Williams, R. 108
Witte, J. 42
Zeiller, J. 43
Zeno of Verona 10

Subject Index

Allegory 3, 5, 7, 8, 9, 10, 26, 27, 49, 89, 165
Angels 60, 92, 104, 120, 150
Apollinarianism 15, 20, 21, 30, 38, 75, 83, 84, 90, 91, 101, 114, 120, 129, 154, 157
Arianism 10, 23, 32, 43, 63, 67, 78, 103, 112, 128, 163
Asceticism 8, 36, 38, 51 104
Baptism 4, 29, 43, 49, 61, 63, 67, 152, 156
Beauty 51, 58, 69, 72, 91, 96, 97, 102, 128, 132, 140, 146, 150, 155, 163
Bride 1, 11, 12, 18, 19, 49, 51, 59, 62, 63, 66, 82, 83, 88, 97, 100, 102, 106, 110, 124-158
(Bride-)groom 4, 5, 12, 18, 34, 48, 50, 51-119, 123-126, 134-141, 146, 148, 153, 156, 158, 160, 163
Catena 16, 17, 18, 20, 22, 31, 36, 39, 40 136, 147
Chalcedon 12, 45, 46, 47, 116, 161, 164
– Chalcedonian 45, 46, 72, 161, 162
– Neo-Chalcedonian 133, 159
Christ
– body of 1, 19, 31, 54, 58, 62, 64, 69, 70, 74, 75, 83, 92, 94-99, 102, 117, 120-125
– cross of 19, 20, 62, 63, 82, 84, 87, 106, 112, 118, 123, 125, 143, 150
– death of 19, 54, 63, 98, 101, 102
– divinity of 54-65, 67, 71-74, 83, 87, 90, 94, 99-102, 105-112, 118, 119, 130, 133, 140, 145, 146, 166, 167
– double consubstantiality 46, 71, 116

 duality in 91, 115, 150, 156, 163
– figure of 1, 2
– humanity of 11, 12, 19, 46-62, 65-72, 74, 76, 77, 81, 83, 90, 94-105, 111, 112, 114, 116, 117, 120, 121-126, 139-148, 153-158, 163
 kenosis 56, 64, 81, 123, 166
– mind of (*nous, hegemonikon*) 29, 56, 62, 70, 84, 88, 121, 161
– resurrection of 17, 28, 38, 56, 67, 76 83, 89, 104, 124, 125, 126, 130, 131, 133, 139, 146, 145, 149, 152
– sinlessness 47, 65, 126, 138, 145
– (perfect) soul of 21, 28, 33, 43, 45-48, 57-62, 66-73, 76, 77, 94, 99, 106-113, 115, 117, 120, 121, 126, 140, 143, 145, 147, 151-156
– type of flesh assumed 19, 43, 47, 48, 49, 51, 65, 80, 84, 93, 95, 111, 114, 120, 125-131, 135, 137, 143, 144, 152, 163
– unity of 4, 22, 46, 56, 61, 76, 97, 98, 105, 109, 152, 153, 155, 162, 163
Christianisation 9, 159
Christology, 10-13, 20, 21, 45, 49-52, 55, 57, 67, 68, 71, 73, 78, 79, 94, 95, 98, 102, 104, 108, 112, 116, 118, 120, 128-131, 141-145, 159-164
Church 1, 2, 5, 10, 22, 39, 45, 46, 49, 51, 52, 57-63, 68-73, 76-79, 86, 92, 96, 97, 99, 110, 120, 123-140, 142, 145-149, 150-152, 156, 159, 166
– ecclesiology 10, 34, 45, 51, 97, 118, 127-136, 149

Clothing   67, 101, 102, 145
- cloak   59, 67, 84, 110, 120, 124, 126, 142, 164
Commentary writing   12, 34-39
Consummation   51, 52, 56, 60, 86, 92, 135, 141, 142, 163
Death   63, 98, 108, 114, 143, 150, 160
Donatism   9, 34, 73, 127
Economy   55, 64, 71, 74, 76, 92, 95, 97, 110, 116, 140,
Election   72, 153, 153, 156
Energies   28, 48, 65, 84-88, 120, 167
Epinoiai   7, 88, 122-124
Eschatology   95, 100, 114, 127, 138, 151, 158, 167
Fragrance   19, 53-57, 81, 98, 106, 110
Gnosticism   4, 11, 62, 148
Grace   45, 47, 54, 57, 60, 73, 78, 85, 114, 116, 117, 121, 130, 132, 162
Heresy   10, 24, 29, 32, 43, 62, 128, 162
Hexapla   4, 17, 22, 41, 106
History (of salvation)   51, 53, 77, 84, 105, 110, 111, 114, 148, 151
Image of God   19, 32, 70, 71, 72, 84, 109, 116, 139, 141, 142, 160
Imagery   1, 2, 12, 15, 22, 37, 55, 63, 67, 69, 78, 85, 92, 100, 104, 109, 115, 118, 120, 126, 128, 134, 137, 139, 151, 159-165
Interpretation of the bible
—   'Alexandrian'   5-7, 12, 122, 158
—   'Antiochene'   5, 6, 25, 35, 40, 52, 59, 67, 100, 101, 163, 164
Israel   3, 34, 52, 113, 142
Kyriakos anthropos   59, 103, 104, 116, 117, 125, 146
Love
- divine and human   1-6, 11, 52, 56, 68, 70, 73, 78, 92, 100, 107, 109, 136, 152, 160, 162, 165-167
Martyr(dom)   45, 54, 63, 153, 166
Messalianism   9, 27, 28, 29, 140
Metaphor   2, 3, 5, 28, 59, 65, 73, 74, 75, 80, 90, 97, 118, 125, 129, 139, 155, 161, 164
Millenarianism   49
Monasticism   7, 8, 9, 25, 35-38, 44, 45, 85
Mysticism
- Christian   6, 8, 25, 43, 56, 63, 86, 96, 102, 124, 134, 152, 156
- Jewish   3
Nations   46, 52, 58, 94, 122, 131, 126, 136
(Neo)platonism   2, 5, 55, 58, 63, 67, 73, 79, 85, 88, 90, 95, 100, 105, 107, 130, 141, 144, 156, 158
Origenism   7, 9, 21, 27, 30, 32, 33, 36, 48, 49, 61, 65, 68, 72, 101, 127, 133, 155
Orthodoxy   26, 29, 38, 64, 105, 161
Pelagianism, semi-Pelagianism   9, 45, 70
Power   29, 48, 54-58, 60-61, 71, 75, 79, 81, 91, 101, 104, 112-115, 118, 123, 148, 153, 160
Pre-existence   6, 56, 72, 85, 94, 109, 120, 122, 123, 125, 126, 128, 131, 133, 143, 147, 154, 155, 161
Revelation   3, 57, 62, 76, 87, 92, 96, 97, 111, 150, 152, 159, 160, 167
Rome   15, 45, 100
Satan   34, 62, 68, 69, 83, 101, 137, 151
Scholia   16, 18, 20, 50
Scripture
- canon   4, 5, 13, 40, 116, 144, 164
- *Itala*   41
- Vulgate   22, 41, 65, 114, 154
- literal sense of   4, 6, 7, 10, 26, 164
- allegorical sense of   3, 5, 7, 8, 9, 26, 37, 49, 89, 164
'Sense of his presence'   85-89, 95
Sin(fulness)   116, 129-131
- (original) sin   46, 47, 79, 83, 130, 153
skopos   6, 13
Son (of God)   2, 6, 7, 11, 23, 24, 29, 40,

43, 46, 54, 55, 60, 64, 68-71, 73, 77, 78, 81, 84, 107, 108, 112, 113, 123, 129, 130, 131, 167
(Human) Soul (s)   1, 11, 20, 28, 29, 32, 52, 55-65, 67-76, 78-81, 84-112, 116-121, 125, 130, 134-144, 164, 167
Spirit (Holy)   6, 8, 19, 28, 32, 48, 51, 53-58, 59-61, 73-80, 111, 112, 117, 122, 148, 152-155, 163, 167
Synagogue   58, 82, 134, 135, 153
– 'one spirit'   108, 147
synapheia   52
Theology
– negative   2, 85-93, 160
– trinitarian   6, 11, 32, 33, 46-49, 55, 64, 77, 79, 87, 92, 104, 109, 111, 113, 152

theoria   7, 26, 92, 111, 117, 124
Virgin Mary   43, 47, 62, 81, 84, 97, 98, 104, 120, 137, 138, 145, 151, 153
Virginity   23, 59, 105, 137, 144
Virtue   51, 53, 56, 59, 62, 71, 85, 86, 97, 99, 100, 103, 110, 112, 115, 122, 123, 124, 135, 148, 163
Wisdom   40, 58, 70, 82, 97, 116, 117, 122, 123, 135
Word (of God)   1, 6, 11, 12, 13, 19, 20, 23, 45, 47, 51-64, 67-70, 72- 85, 87, 89, 93-114, 116, 117, 118, 120, 122-127, 130-136, 140-153, 155-158, 160, 161, 166, 167

www.ingramcontent.com/pod-product-compliance
Lightning Source LLC
Chambersburg PA
CBHW051801230426
43670CB00012B/2379